THE COMPLETE WORKS
OF THOMAS SHADWELL

THE COMPLETE WORKS OF THOMAS SHADWELL EDITED BY MONTAGUE SUMMERS ❧ VOLUME II

BENJAMIN BLOM, PUBLISHERS

First published London, 1927
Reissued 1968,
by Benjamin Blom, Inc. Bx 10452

Library of Congress Catalog Card No. 68 - 20247

Printed in U.S.A. by
NOBLE OFFSET PRINTERS, INC.
NEW YORK 3, N. Y.

Contents

THE
MISER,
A
COMEDY.

ACTED

By His Majesties Servants

AT THE

Theater Royal.

Written by *THOMAS SHADWELL*.

LONDON,
Printed for *Thomas Collins* and *John Ford*,
at The Middle Temple-gate in Fleet-
street, 1672.

Source.

L'AVARE of Molière, the play upon which Shadwell as he frankly acknowledges—and indeed he could do no less—has founded his comedy, was produced on 9 September, 1668, with the author as Harpagon; La Grange Cléante; Du Croisy Valère; Mademoiselle Molière Élise; Mademoiselle de Brie Mariane; and Madeleine Béjart Frosine. *L'Avare* itself is taken from the *Aulularia,* a piece in which the "Plautina elegantia," as our Holy Father S. Jerome loved to phrase it, shows in witty and vivid colouring. It is true that one must not compare the Euclio of the Roman poet with Molière's Harpagon, so complete and complex a psychological study. Life was simpler in the days of Plautus. I do not know that I can wholly subscribe to Émile Faguet's "La pièce de Plante n'est guère qu'une jolie pièce anecdotique; celle de Molière une grande comédie de caractère." His verdict concerning Molière is incontestably true; but I rate the *Aulularia* something higher than the French critic, who is, I conceive, looking *apud Plautum* for sentiment and character which would have been improper, nay impossible, in a Roman comedy. Whilst allowing every jot of the supreme greatness of Molière I can yet love the charm and sunny humour of the Latin poet.

The incidents conveyed across the Channel from Molière Shadwell has set in a most realistic background of London life in the heyday of King Charles. Faguet, speaking of Harpagon's children, Cléante and Élise, says that the dramatist shows his miser "puni par ce que son vice a fait de son fils et de sa fille l'un débauché, joueur et un peu escroc, l'autre un peu dévergondée, tous deux irrespecteux et complètement exempts de piété filiale." What would be his opinion of Theodore and Theodora! And yet if I mistake not the young people of to-day think Cléante and Élise a very old-fashioned Victorian son and daughter, whilst Goldingham's two children treat their father just as the silly old put deserves, and are indeed a thoroughly up-to-date cocktail couple.

Shadwell's scenes of Restoration life, although they centre on the bagnio and the dice, are amusing, and naturally by their atmosphere they change the complexion of the principal characters.

Fielding's clever adaptation from *L'Avare, The Miser,* was produced at Drury Lane, 17 February, 1733, with Griffin as Lovegold. It is a brisk bustling comedy and held the stage until well within the nineteenth century. It owes scarcely a hint to Shadwell, although much matter has been added to the original. It is doubtful whether the appearance of Mrs.

Wisely is an improvement, but the scene of the servants which commences Act V, and the irruption of upholsterers, jewellers, mercers, tailors, and Charles Bubbleboy, are vastly amusing episodes and support the intrigue with unflagging zest. One cannot be surprised at the continued popularity of Fielding's play.

There are various translations from Plautus, such as that by Bonnell Thornton, 8vo, 1767. This writer appended a new conclusion to the *Aulularia*, the text of which has come down to us in a mutilated state ; the final scenes being lost. In the older editions these were generally given in the version of Antonius Codrus Urceus, Professor of Latin at Bologna in the fourteenth century. Lorenzo Guazzesi imitated the play in Italian, and the original was seen both at Rome and Ferrara. Giovanni Battista Gelli adapted it with great cleverness in his famous *Sporta*, certain scenes of which are within measuring distance of Molière.

There are several eighteenth century direct translations of *L'Avare*, as by Ozell, 12mo, 1732 ; by Michael de Boissy, 12mo, 1752 ; and, the first act only, by John Hughes, which appeared in the *Works* 8vo, 1735. *The Miser* has its place, of course, in the various collected editions of Molière Englished.

In 1788 was printed octavo *The Miser* " for the Use of private Theatres," (sometimes announced as *The Cut Miser*), the comedy contracted into a farce by Edward Tighe. Fielding was also curtailed by James Wild, the prompter at Covent Garden, and this three-act version appeared octavo, 1792.

A grotesque entertainment, or rather pantomime, by John Thurmond, *The Miser ; or, Wagner and Abericock*, performed at Drury Lane 1727 ; 8vo, 1727, calls for nothing more than a bare reference. The title, *The Miser*, has also been used in more recent plays such as *The Miser* by G. H. Gomm with music by W. Fullerton, produced at the Prince's 17 July, 1884 ; *The Miser* by Julian Foss, produced at the Theatre Royal, Brighton, 16 November, 1887, and at the Globe, London, 5 May, 1890 ; *The Miser* by G. W. Mitchell given at the Olympic, 9 May, 1891.

There is a *Miser's Retreat*, from the French *La Maison Rustique*, seen at Goodman's Fields in 1734 ; *The Miser of Shoreditch*, Standard, 2 November, 1854 ; *The Miser's Treasure* by J. Mortimer, Olympic, 29 April, 1878 ; *The Miser's Will* by T. Craven, produced at Hastings 3 December, 1888, and seen in London at the Surrey 4 November, 1889 ; *The Miser's Legacy*, Theatre Royal, Llanelly, 20 May, 1907.

The Miser's Daughter was performed at Drury Lane 24 February, 1835 ; and upon the great success of Ainsworth's capital romance *The Miser's Daughter*, which ran through *Ainsworth's Magazine*, vols. I and II, 1842, a dramatization of this by Edward Stirling was produced at the Adelphi on Monday, 24 October of that year. Stirling, the adapter, played Miser

Scaur, and Miss Faucit Hilda. George Cruikshank's illustrations were scrupulously followed, and it was said that the stage pictures "might be mistaken for the artist's actual designs enormously magnified, and mysteriously made to breathe."

Perhaps the finest representation of the typical miser wallowing in his gold which the stage of the last half-century has seen is that of Gaspard in Planquette's *Les Cloches de Corneville*, the English version of which was produced at the Folly 28 February, 1878. The scene of the old man, all alone in the haunted castle, plunging his hands into the coin, when the midnight bell rings and the phantoms, knightly crusaders and haughty ancestry appear with frowning faces and gestures of doom to menace the unfaithful servant, was a moment of tense dramatic power not easily forgotten and not easily surpassed.

Theatrical History.

*T*HE *Miser*, as Shadwell informs us, was " the laſt Play that was Aćted at the Kings Theater in *Covent-Garden,* before the fatal fire there." On Thursday, 25 January, 1672, the Theatre Royal ſtanding in Bridges Street and Russell Street, which we for convenience sake generally call the firſt Drury Lane, was burned to the ground by a terrible con- flagration that wrought fearful deſtrućtion in the vicinity. A news- letter, 27 January, 1671-2, has : " A fire at the King's playhouse between 7 and 8 o'clock on Thursday evening laſt, which half burned down the house and all their scenes and wardrobe ; and all the houses from the Rose Tavern in Russell Street on that side of the way of Drury Lane are burned and blown up, with many in Vinegar Yard ; 20,000*l.* damage. The fire began under the ſtairs where Orange Moll keeps her fruit. Bell the player blown up." Orange Moll was Mary Meggs, the chief vendor of fruit at the theatre. Richard Bell was a rising young aćtor of great promise. Donnes tells us that he had been bred up from a boy " under the Maſter Aćtors." He had already appeared in several rôles of considerable importance, such as Frapolo, the brigand, in a revival of Shirley's *The Siſters ;* Mr. Vincent in Wycherley's *Love in a Wood ;* Amariel the Angel in *Tyrannick Love ;* Cæsar in *Julius Cæsar ;* and also in the famous revival of *Catiline,* Friday, 18 December, 1668.

In this calamity the fanatics, of course, saw the fiery vengeance of Heaven, and a ballad " On the Burning of the Theatre Royal " has this couplet :

> He cryes juſt Judgement and wished when poor *Bell*
> Rung out his laſt, 't been the Stage's kNell.

A contemporary note upon the British Museum copy of this lampoon says that this was conſtrued as the obvious reflećtion on Nell Gwyn which was intended, and Sir Roger L'Eſtrange threatened the printer with a prosecution for making a capital N, although the verses had been duly licensed.

The King's Company, after their disaſter, were compelled to migrate to Lincoln's Inn Fields, which had juſt been vacated for a new theatre by their rivals the Duke's Company, and here they opened on Monday, 26 February, 1672, with *Wit without Money,* Mohun aćting Valentine.

The Miser, then, was produced at the Theatre Royal in January, 1672. It would, no doubt, have been very successful had it not been crushed by so overwhelming a catastrophe. Yet it remained in the repertory of the theatre, and from time to time it was received with favour by the Town.

On 5 June, 1704, it was given at Drury Lane for the benefit of Bullock, who appeared as Timothy Squeeze. However, it does not seem to have kept the stage after the reign of Queen Anne, and when Fielding's *The Miser* was produced at Drury Lane on 17 February, 1733, the audience had entirely forgotten Shadwell's comedy.

To the Right Honourable
C H A R L E S
Lord *BUCKHURST*,

Gentleman of His MAJESTIES BED-CHAMBER.

My Lord,

THE Favour which your Lordship was pleased to shew to this Play, I value more than all the loud Applauses of a *Theater* : Nor can it be less esteemed by any Man that has had the Honour of knowing your Lordships Person, or the Pleasure of reading the diversions of your pen. It seems by your obliging kindness to the Poets, and your great example in writing, as if you were design'd by Heaven, among many other great uses, for the sustaining of declining Poetry. This consideration, with the boldness which your frequent favours have given me, pull the trouble of this Dedication upon you. You see, my Lord, the danger of encouraging any of us, who are too apt without it to use the names of great men for the defence of our weaknesses and follies ; nay, some are so arrogant to believe their injurious Dedications competent returns for all the Obligations they receive from the generosity of their Patrons. But I, my Lord, have been too much obliged by you to think of making any return : all that I can do, is to beg leave to make an humble acknowledgment of all your favours ; and to take this occasion to publish my self to the World,

My Lord,

Your Lordships

Most Obliged

Humble Servant,

THOMAS SHADWELL.

READER.

THE Foundation of this Play I took from one of *Moliere*'s call'd *L'Avare* ; but that having too few Persons, and too little Action for an *English Theater*, I added to both so much, that I may call more than half of this Play my own ; And I think I may say without vanity, that *Moliere*'s part of it has not suffer'd in my hands, nor did I ever know a *French* Comedy made use of by the worst of our Poets, that was not better'd by 'em. 'Tis not barrenness of wit or invention, that makes us borrow from the *French*, but laziness ; and this was the occasion of my making use of *L'Avare*. This Play, as it was wrote in less than a moneth, and was the last Play that was Acted at the Kings Theater in *Covent-Garden*, before the fatal fire there ; the great hast I made in writing it, that made me very doubtful of the success of it, which was the reason that at first I did not own it, but conceal'd my Name. I have resolved to take my leave of long Prefaces, and will give you no farther trouble here, for fear you should find too much afterwards.

PROLOGUE.

[*The Authors Name not being then known.*]

OUR Poet never doubts the good success
    Of Farce that's in half *French*, half *English* dress :
    And this was made with little pains and wit,
As any cobling Poet e're wrote yet,
And therefore he's resolv'd not to submit.
The Fortune of his Fellows he has seen,
Who in dull Farce have so successfull been,
That could he write true wit, he is in doubt
Whether you would endure to sit it out.
But though he has no wit, he has some shame,
And ſtealing from the *French* conceals his name.
French Plays, in which true wit's as rarely found
As Mines of Silver are in *English* ground ;
A foolish Marquis, or his knavish man,
Or some poor Pudden fool's the beſt they can.——
But ſtay, I've been too bold ; methinks I see
The *English* Monsieurs rise in mutiny,
Crying confound him, does he damn *French* Plays,
The only *Pieces* that deserve the Bayes :
France that on fashions does ſtrict Laws impose
The Universal Monarchy for Cloaths,
That rules our moſt important part, our dress,
Should rule our wit, which is a thing much less.
But *Messieurs* he says, farther to provoke ye,
He would as soon be Author of *Tu Quoque*,
As any Farce that e're from *France* was sent,
And all consider'd 'tis a complement,
And yet he hopes the advantages they gain,
That he may please ye with small ſtock of brain :
For our good natur'd Nation thinks it fit,
To count *French* Toys, good Wares ; *French* nonsence, wit.

EPILOGVE.

WHen Sieges now by Poets are prepar'd,
And Love and War 'gainſt Nations is declar'd;
When *Affrica* and *Asia* are not spar'd,
By some who in Rime will all the World o'rerun,
Who in their Conqueſts will no Country shun,
Not scaping the *Mogul,* nor *Preſter John,*
No *American* Prince is in his Throne secure,
Not *Totty Potty Moy* himself is sure:
But may the fury of their Rime endure,
Nay in time each Prince in *Guinny* will be fought,
And under these Poetick Fetters brought;
And we shall see how the black Rogues lov'd and sought.
When such great things are for the Stage design'd,
We fear this trifle will no favour find.
But as a fop that's dress'd in Masquerade,
Will any place with impudence invade,
And little rambling Punks nare be so rude,
Among the beſt of Ladies to intrude:
So Poets sure, though ill, may be allow'd
Among the beſt in Masquerade to crowd.
Our Poet who wrote this *Incognito,*
Does boldly claim this priviledge as his due;
He presses in, and will not be kept out,
Though he deserves to ſtand amongſt the rout,
Those fifteen hundred Poets who have writ,
And never could have one Play acted yet.
But now he's in, pray use him civilly,
Let him, what e're he says, unqueſtion'd be,
According to the Laws of Masquerade,
Those sacred Laws by dancing Nations made,
Which the young Gallants sure will ne're invade.
If ye resolve that yee'l be angry now,
Ye vent your spleen upon an unknown Foe;
Or if he be not, yet yee'l make him so:
But if a kindness to him ye intend,
And though 't deserves it not, the Play commend:
Each Man for ought he knows is kind to's friend.

(18)

THE ACTORS' NAMES.

Goldingham	*The Miser.*
Theodore	*His Son.*
Squeeze	*A Scrivener.*
Timothy	*His Son.*
Bellamour	{ *A Gentleman in disguise, his true name* Raines, *and servant to* Gold, *but a lover of* Theodora.
Rant and *Hazzard*	{ *Two Gamesters of the Town.*
Robin	Theodore's *Servant.*
James and *William*	{ *Servants to* Goldingham.
Justice.	
Two Bullies.	
Constable and Watch.	
Three Counterfeit Baylifs.	
Fidlers.	

WOMEN.

Theodora	*Daughter to* Goldingham.
Isabella	*Sister to* Bellamour.
Cheatly	*A Procurer.*
Lettice	*Her Daughter a Wench.*
Joyce	*A Wench.*
Bridget	*The same.*

The MISER.

ACT I. SCE. I.

Enter Rant, Hazard, Theodore.

Rant. WHat a devil makes thee in so musty a humour ? Thou art as dull and dumpish as a fellow that had been drunk over night with Ale, and had done nothing but drunk Coffee, talked Politicks, and read Gazettes all this morning.

Haz. Hast lost thy money, or thy wench.

Rant. Nay faith *Hazard*, if he has lost his money, I am sure he has lost his wench, in spight of the noble vertue of constancy.

Haz. Come *Theodore*, a lucky hand or two at the Groom Porters, will get thee as good a Mistress as any about the Town.

Rant. No pox on't they are kept so high by foolish elder Brothers, that poor younger Brothers must despair of 'em.

Haz. No *Rant*, thou art mistaken, the Elder Brothers are so kind to keep 'em for the younger, that can not do't for themselves ; they are civil to the one for love, and the other for money.

Rant. I am not of your opinion, there was never so much ready money and so little love stirring, as at this time.

Haz. Faith then we (that have but shallow purses) must three or four club for one, shee'l serve us all, considering how we drink.   Come *Theodore*, be not melancholy, if thou hast lost thy Mistress, I'le club with thee for another.

Theo. So Gentlemen, this Dialogue runs off very smartly ; you had rehearsed it before, but I find you have the effects of last nights debauch upon you, and are hot headed this morning, what else should make you think me melancholy ?

Rant. Come faith, thou art.

Theo. I must confess Gentlemen I am not in so brisk a humour as to leap over Joynt-stools, or come over a stick for the King, or any of those pretty frolicks ; but I have no trouble, unless you will create me one.

(21)

Haz. I am so far from that, that I'le tell thee news that will rejoyce the heart of thee, if thou wert as dumpish as a young Spark that is newly denied to be trusted for a white Periwig.

Theo. Prethee what's that?

Rant. That which I am sure you'l bite at.

Haz. There is the most delicate, charming creature, come to lie over-against us in *Bow-street*! Oh 'tis a melting Girle, she looks as if she would dissolve like an Anchovee in Claret.

Rant. She would relish better (when a Man has the hot fit upon him) than small Beer in a Feaver.

Haz. Then small Beer a pox on't, she would be more welcome to thee than a Reprieve would, if thou art just now trolling out *Hopkins* and *Sternhold* upon a Ladder.

Theo. You are mighty witty, and full of similies; but who the Devil is this incomparable Lady?

Rant. Pox on't, thou art as testy as an old Leane Judge fasting, upon the Bench, between eleven and twelve.

Haz. I'le put him into a better Humour; with this young Lady, is Mrs. *Cheatly, party per pale* Match-maker, and Baud, got acquainted, and has promised to bring her to a Ball at the Bear at *Charing-Cross*, where you know there is a very convenient Couch.

Rant. Oh she's a delicate bit for him that can get her, she's fit for one of us honest Fellows to debauch, and for a dull rich Fellow (born to the drudgery of Plowing Land and getting Heirs) to Marry.

Theo. But (if you be not too much transported to tell me) Pray who is this young Lady?

Haz. Why, 'tis one *Isabella* that lyes over-against our Lodging at the Blew Balcone.

Theo. 'Sdeath what said he? [*Aside*]

Rant. How now, are you nettled? Gad I'le lay my life this Rogue has been before-hand with us.

Theo. No faith Gentlemen, but this Lady I have seen, and know she has some qualities very unfit for your Company.

Haz. What are those Man?

Theo. Dam'd unfashionable qualities, call'd vertue, and modesty.

Rans. Pish, but if she be not too much season'd with vertue in this warm age, she cannot keep long.

Theo. Indeed but she will, in spight of that Villanous Seducer *Cheatly*, whose Clutches scarce any young Lady can scape.

Rant. Prethee speak not against thy Mother-in-Law, thou hadst the debauching of her Daughter *Lettice*.

Theo. I the debauching of her; she was debauch'd from her Mothers Womb, she has it *ex Traduce*.

Haz. I'le hold thee ten pound *Cheatly* brings this Lady to Supper, for all her vertue and modesty.

Theo. 'Sdeath Sir, I know she cannot, shall not do't.

Rant. On my Conscience he's in downright abominable love with this Lady.

Theo. Well, because you are a couple of good honest Fellows, that is, as farr as those that use *Cater-deuce-azes*, and smooth Boxes, and Cheat at Dice, can be.

Haz. Cheat? we do play a little upon advantage I confess, (as many People of Quality and most Gentlemen that are Gamesters do.)

Theo. Indeed false Boxes, and Dice are an advantage, but to let that pass : I will prevent your Errour, with this *Isabella* I am unreasonably and desperately in Love.

Rant. But it's in an honourable way, I hope, not at all inclining to wedlock.

Theo. Yes faith, I am in Love, even to Matrimony.

Haz. Pox on thee for an unseasonable Fellow, to think of Matrimony in this age, when an honest Woman is almost asham'd to shew her Face, she finds triumphant Punk so much preferred before her.

Rant. If we, honest Fellows of the Town, go on as we begin, honest Women will come to be Ston'd in the Streets.

Haz. What, thou art turn'd a publick spirited Fellow, I warrant, and wisely considerest, that people are wanting in *England*, and that more frequent Marriage would be a means of Propagation.

Rant. And I believe thou hast subtilly found out that Whoring, and Monasteries, are as great causes of their wanting people in *Spain*, as their *West-Indian* Colonies.

Theo. None of these Politick Considerations I assure you ; and yet ever since I saw *Isabella* I care less for a Whore, than you do for an honest Woman : Yet you shall find I am not wholly unfit for your Company, I have not given over all sins at once, for if you'l go before and bespeak Dinner at *Shatolins* you shall see how I'le sowce you in *Burgundy*.

Haz. Well, wee'l go and hope, by the helpe of *Burgundy*, to recover your Senses again.

Theo. Have a care of loosing your own.

Rant. That we may have no advantage over you, wee'l each of us drink 2 or 3 Beer glasses, before you come.

Haz. Adieu.   [*Exeunt. Haz. Rant.*]

[*Enter Bellamour.*]

Theo. How now *Bellamour*, where's my Father.

Bell. Sir, he's busie upon a question in Arithmetick, to see how much 15 *l.* comes to in seven years, with use upon use.

(23)

Theo. What use, his fifty in the hundred, that he takes of Herb-women and Oyster-women? For which they Pawn their dear Rings, and Wedding Petticoats.

Bell. Sir, he's willing to make the most of his money.

Theo. Has he taken account what Dripping has been sold this week to the Kitchen-stuff Women? Has he weighed the ends of Candle, and Suet, to change for Candles of 20 in the pound?

Bell. All this Sir, and he has been higling with a Fellow, above half an hour this morning, about 5 Coney-Skins he sold him; nay, Good man, he's very careful, and all for you.

Theo. For me, 'Sdeath I expect he should live fifty years longer, unless the Parliament would bring down money to four in the hundred; and faith I thought the report of that last Sessions, would have done an honest *Filius ante Diem* some kindness, but a pox ont he's recover'd, but no more of him, prethee send in my man to me.

Bell. I will Sir.   Robin. [*Exit Theodore.*]

[*Enter Robin.*]

Robin. What say you Sir?

Bell. Go in to your Master [*Ex. Robin*]   [*Enter Theodora.*]   Here comes the Mistress of my Heart, my dearest *Theodora*, I see you now this morning, with as much Joy, as the *Persians* do the Rising *Sun*, that gives e'm all their Comfort.

Theo. For all your complements *Bellamour*, I find little prospect of comfort for either of us.

Bell. My dearest *Theodora*, I have observed much dejection in your Countenance, ever since the obliging assurances you have given me of your faith; do you repent of that engagement? then I am miserable.

Theo. No *Bellamour*, I cannot repent of any thing I do for you; you have too great a power over me, to suffer such resentments in my mind.

Bell. What then can be the reason, that in the midst of all my Joyes, I see you grieve.

Theo. The thousand difficulties we are to undergo.

Bell. Ah Madam, do but Love enough, and there are none.

Theo. There is an impossibility of getting my Fathers consent, though it would be so much to my advantage: His covetous Shagrin Humour makes him hate a Gentleman.

Bell. I have gained so much upon him, that I do not despair of it; But since I have your consent, I have too much happiness for one Man.

Theo. I must confess, my *Bellamour*, I could justifie my Love to you to all the world, but to my Father; I have to defend me your Person, and your Merit: I can never repay the obligations I have received from you, that after seven years Travel, you can be content to stay from your Countrey, your Friends, and Kindred, and conceal your self from all the world but me : But above all, to put your self for my sake, in so base a condition, as to serve my Father, which is worse than Rowing in Gallies ; this Testimony of your Love can never be forgotten.

Bell. Ah Madam ! one kind look from you will overweigh a thousand such small Services : *I* must confess, serving your Father is the severest Task I have, to minister to his wretched Avarice, and endure the curses of all whom his extortion grieves. Pardon me, dear *Theodora*, that I take this liberty before you : This is a Subject, you know I can speak little good of.

Theo. I am too sensible of it, but I am extreamly glad to see you gain so much upon him by your Artifices.

Bell. You see Madam, Love is able to turn a Man into all Shapes, nay into the worst, a Flatterer, to a Covetous Man : But by the sordid applauding of what he does, and observing all his Rules and Maximes, I have gained this point ; That he will hear or believe no man so soon as me.

Theo. But why do you not discover this to my Brother, and procure his assistance in it ?

Bell. Your Father's and Brother's tempers are so opposite, that it is impossible to accommodate my selfe to both of 'em, but do you please to manage our interests with your Brother, he Loves you extreamly, and will hear you ; I hear him coming, I'le away. [*Ex Bellamour.*]

[*Enter Theodore and Robin.*]

Theo. *Robin* go stay within till I call you.

Robin. I will Sir. [*Exit Robin.*]

Theodore. Dear *Theodora* I am glad you are here, I have a secret of the greatest concernment in the world to me, to discover to you.

Theodora. I shall be glad to hear't, and (if I can) to serve you in it ; what have you to say ?

Theodore. A thousand things, in one little word, Love.

Theodora. How Brother are you in Love, I'le tell you—

Theodore. Hold Sister, I know as well as you that I depend [*Scommatically*] upon a Father, and that the name of Son, carries an inviolable Duty along with it.

Theodora. But Brother———

Theodore. And that I ought not to engage my heart without the consent of him who gave me breath.

Theodora. Do you hear———

Theodore. And that Heaven has made our Parents disposers of our wills, and that they are in a condition to see more and be less deceived than we.

Theodora. Hold a little.

Theodore. And that we ought to trust the Eyes of their wisdom before the blindness of our own passion.

Theodora. Are you mad——

Theodore. And that the heat of our youth misleads, and betrays us often to dangerous precipices.

Theodora. Not one of these wise things would I have said to you, but tell me, are you engaged to her you Love?

Theodore. No, but resolv'd, in spight of all opposition, and I conjure you, give me no reasons.

Theodora. Why do you believe I will?

Theodore. You are no Lover, and faith I am damnably affraid of your wisdom.

Theodora. You know not my condition Brother; but pray who is it that has Charm'd you thus?

Theodore. A young Lady that Lyes near this place, of so excellent a Beauty, so delicate a creature, I cannot think of her without an extasie.

Theodora. Pray save your oratory, and in short, tell me who she is.

Theodore. Her name is *Isabella;* but that which is my extreamest trouble, I have discover'd under hand, that she is the Daughter of a sickly Widdow, and of a small Fortune: You know the abominable humour of my Father (whose damn'd covetousness, if I had not now and then a Lucky hand at play, would make me forget all use of money) so that I have scarce any possibility of giving this Lady the least proof of my affection; and if I find not some means to do it, I am lost.

Theodora. It is an inhumane thing of him to put us both to our Shifts thus, to get but ordinary Cloths.

Theodore. Prethee Sister, let's Joyn in our Complaints to him; and if he opposes us, we will quit our selves of his insupportable Tyranny, and seek our Fortunes together.

Theodora. I hear him coming, he's inraged at something, pray let us retire and consult what to say to him, here he comes, step in.

Theodore. Come on.   [*Exeunt Theodore and Theodora.*]

[Enter Goldingham and Robin.]

Gold. Out of my House you Dog, begon, make no replyes, you Rascal, that are a Sworn Thief; the Gallows groans for you.

Robin. Well, there was never any thing so wicked as this [*Aside*] damn'd old Fellow, and I think, under correction, the Devil's in him.

Gold. What's that you mutter between your Teeth Sirrah?

Robin. Why do you hunt me up and down thus?

Gold. Out you Hang-Dog, must you ask questions? Out of my Doors, or I'le knock you down.

Robin. A pox on this damn'd flea-flint, [*Aside*] Why what have I done to you ?

Gold. Dispute no more, begon.

Robin. My Master gave me order to stay here for him.

Gold. Get you gone and wait in the Street, you Rascal, must you stand here like a Sentinel, and (with your damn'd watchful Eyes) be a Spy upon my actions, to devour what I have, and to ferret up and down to see what there is to Steal.

Robin. What a Devil do you think I should steal, unless I should steal you ? [*Aside*] Besides, He's as watchful as an Owl, a man that had killed seven men, Pissing against a wall, would rest more quietly.

Gold. You Dog must I be daily in danger to be Rob'd by you ?

Robin. You are not a man to be Rob'd, all you have is under Lock and Key ; besides you profess your self to be in great want.

Gold. [*Aside*] Oh how I tremble ! Lest this Rogue should suspect I have money hidden in my Garden : If he do's I am ruin'd. Though I have but little Sirrah, I should be loth to loose it by such Rascals as you are. Besides what's Lock't up, is not there a Tin Candlestick, a pair of Brass Snuffers, a Nutmeg-Grater, Bellows, and a Darnock Carpet.

Robin. I scorne 'em all.

Gold. Come Sirrah, you are one of the Rogues that reported that I have Money hid.

Robin. How, have you money hid say you ?

Gold. No no you Dog, I don't say so, I have no money hid you Villain you. [*Aside*] 'Sdeath he distracts me.

Robin. Why what is't to me whether you have or have not.

Gold. What are you arguing ? I'le beat your foolish reasons out of your head, once more, begon.

Robin. Well, I go.

Gold. Stay, have you taken nothing with you ?

Robin. You had best search me.

Gold. Shew me your hands.

Robin. There.

Gold. The other——Both together——Stay have you put nothing here ?
[*He feels in his Coat Pockets.*]

Robin. What a Devil should I put there ?

Gold. Let me see here.   [*All this while Groping Robin.*]

Robin. Such a Man as you deserves to be Rob'd.

Gold. What say you ?

Robin. I say I think you'l grope me all over.

Gold. So I will Sirrah.

Robin. A Plague on all covetousness, and covetous men.

Gold. What's that ?

Robin. I say, a Plague upon all covetousness, and covetous men.

Gold. Of whom do you speak Sirrah?

Robin. Of covetous men.

Gold. What are those covetous men?

Robin. Rogues, Villains, Dogs, Caterpillers, Horse-Leeches, Vipers, Thieves, Robbers, Sons of Whores.

Gold. How now you Rascal.

Robin. Why do you trouble your selfe Sir, you are none of those; may not I curse covetous Rogues?

Gold. Sirrah, to whom did you speak thus? tell me.

Robin. I spoke it—I spoke it—to that Rogue *Dives* in the Picture there.

Gold. And I speak to your fools Head there, Sirrah take that, do you feele me Rogue?

Robin. Ay, pox on you, against my will.   [*Aside.*]

Gold. Again Sirrah, out of my doors, I say, you insolent Villain.

Robin. A curse on him, he has broken my bones.   [*Ex. Robin.*]

Gold. Oh the pains, the jealousies, and fears a Man must suffer that has great summes of money to guard; I cannot find one place safe enough about the house; Coffers and Trunks Thieves can never scape. Let me see this particular. *Imprimis*, a Thousand Pound, for which I have Pawnes worth two, at above fifty *per Cent*. *Item* in the City five thousand Pound, for which I have ten *per Cent*. and the best security in *England*.

[*Enter Theodore and Theodora.*]

Item, in Morgages of Land from young Gay Sparks 6000 *l*. Oh but that dear Sum of six thousand broad-pieces in my Garden, that transports me. [*He sees his Son and Daughter.*] 'Sdeath that I should read this Note loud, I have betrayed my self, they have over-heard me, and I am ruin'd; would they were both hang'd: Well, what's the matter with you, have you been long there?

Theo. No Sir, but now come.

Gold. What do ye stand listening?

Theo. Not we, I assure ye.

Gold. Come come ye did: if they over-heard me, I shall hang my self——

Theodora. Not we, I assure you Sir.

Gold. I was saying to my self, how happy should I be if I had but Six thousand Pound in the world.

Theo. You need not wish that.

Gold. 'Tis false, 'tis false, Oh would to heaven I had! Oh how happy should I be, I should never complain then, that the times are hard, not I.

Theodora. This is all but Raillerie Sir.

Theodore. You have more than five times as much.

(28)

Gold. 'Sdeath, what says he? O thou Villain, thou Viper thou, have I bred thee up to destroy me? are my Children become my greatest Enemies?

Theo. Are those your enemies that say you are rich?

Gold. Oh it is the vilest injury you can do me, such discourses as these will make my throat be cut, Thieves will believe I am all made up of Gold; your extravagant expences too, will make 'em think so.

Theo. I know none I am guilty of, unless keeping my self clean be so.

Gold. Oh your Periwigs, your Ribbands, your Laces, you are as much a Spark as any of those that go fine, keep Whores, and pay no debts, about the Town; and if the truth were known, you, and your Sister, here, must Rob me to do it.

Theo. He will have good luck that Robs you: [*Aside.*]
You know my Sister ventures some Money at Sea, (that was left her by an *Aunt*) and (for me) I am sometimes lucky at play, and I eat and drink, and keep my self handsomly drest with it.

Gold. Handsomly, foolishly; to what end are these multitudes of Ribbands, this Flaxen Mop of Whores Hair, and this *Flanders* Lace upon the Shirt; I warrant this Habit cost thirty Pound: now if you do win money, put it to other uses, (you foolish young Knave) 30 *l.* comes to six and thirty shillings a year, according to Statutable use; but thou mightest make twenty Pound a year on't if thou hadst any braines, and (with such use upon use) what would 30 *l.* come to in seven years!

Theodora. But Sir, my Brother and I came to talke with you of other business.

Gold. Well, and I have something to say to you, of other business.

Theo. 'Tis concerning Marriage, Sir.

Gold. And I intended to speak to you, concerning Marriage.

Theodora. Ah Father!

Gold. Ah Father! what's that for? what? what? you would be at it already would you? soft and fair young Gentlewoman.

Theo. No Sir, my Sister is affraid that your opinion of Marriage will not agree with ours.

Gold. Fear not, you shall have no cause of complaint, I shall do well for you both; and (first of all) have you *Theodore*, seen one *Isabella*, that lyes near this place?

Theo. O yes Sir, several times, in her Balcony.

Gold. And you?

Theodora. I have heard of her, Sir.

Gold. Well Son, and how do you find that Lady?

Theo. She's admirably handsom, I have never seen her equal.

Gold. Her face, ha?

Theo. Beyond what e're a Lover fancied of his Mistress.

Gold. Her shape, is it not well?

Theo. Not only faultless, but excellent to a miracle.

Gold. Her meen, ha——

Theo. Graceful, and admirable.

Gold. Her ayer, and her manner——

Theo. The most charming in the world; her ayer so full of modesty and wit, her carriage so allureing and gentle, I have never seen the like.

Gold. Oh ho, would not this Lady make a pleasant bed-fellow?

Theo. It were a happiness beyond all expression, such as 'twere not safe to think on't.

Gold. But there is one point to be consider'd, her Portion.

Theo. Oh Sir, that (with so fine a Lady) is not considerable, not to be mentioned.

Theodora. Besides Sir, I have heard she has a tollerable fortune.

Theo. Never think of that.

Gold. Well, I am glad we agree so well in our opinions of this Lady; for (by these charming qualities) she has so won upon me, that I am resolved forthwith to marry her.

Theo. Oh heaven!

Gold. What say you?   [*Hastily.*]

Theo. Are you resolved say you——

Gold. Yes, to marry *Isabella.*

Theo. Who you? you?

Gold. Yes I, I, I, why, what do you make of me, young Cox-comb?

Theo. 'Sdeath this has struck me to the heart.   [*Ex. Theo.*]

Gold. Who cares, go get some Aqua-Vitæ, I hope this young Prodigal Ass will hang himself at the news of a young Mother-in-Law——This Daughter, is that which I resolve for my self: now for him, I have provided a grave Matron of about 50, with a great deal of money; and you, I intend to marry to *Timothy Squeeze,* the rich Scriveners Son, a very thrifty young man.

Theodora. Heaven, what do I hear!

Gold. He's a very pretty young Man, and knowes how to make sixty *per Cent.* of his money.

Theodora. Sir, if you please, I will not marry.

Gold. Madam, if you please, you shall marry.

Theodora. Pray pardon me Sir.

Gold. Pray pardon me Madam.

Theodora. You may command me in any thing, but this.

Gold. I will command you in this, and to night too.

Theodora. To night, that shall not be.

Gold. That shall be.

Theodora. No Sir.

Gold. Yes Sir.

Theodora. I'le kill my self, before I marry him.

Gold. You shall not kill your self, and you shall marry him ; but did ever Father endure such insolence from a Daughter ?

Theodora. Was ever Daughter so severely used by a Father ?

Gold. All the world will allow of my choyce.

Theodora. No Man of sense will.

[*Enter Bellamour.*]

Gold. Here comes *Bellamour*, will you be judg'd by him.

Theodora. With all my heart.

    This is lucky enough.   [*Aside.*]

Gold. Look you *Bellamour*, my Daughter disputes with me, which do you think has reason, she or I ?

Bell. Oh Sir, you without question.

Gold. Do you know what we were talking of ?

Bell. No Sir, but you cannot be in the wrong.

Gold. Look you, you are to be Judge, I would marry her to *Timothy Squeeze*, the rich Scriveners Son this night ; and the baggage despises him.

Bell. And am I to be Judge ?

Gold. Ay of this.

Bell. Oh heaven !

Gold. What say you ?

Bell. I am of your opinion Sir, in the main, but your Daughter is not wholly in the wrong.

Gold. Why, why is Mr. *Timothy*'s Person, or Fortune, to be rejected ? where can she have a better ?

Bell. That's true Sir, but she may say, 'tis too rash to resolve to do it so suddenly ; and that she ought to have some time to accommodate her inclinations to him.

Gold. Time, come I must take occason by the fore-lock ; his Father (that is very rich, but of mean extraction) will (for the sake of good Allyance) let his Son marry her without a Portion.

Bell. Nay then, I must say no more, that is a convincing reason, she must submit to that.

Theodora. What means *Bellamour* ?   [*Aside.*]

Gold. I know not what 'tis to her, I am sure 'tis the most considerable reason in the world to me.

Bell. Without doubt Sir, no man can contradict that, but your Daughter may answer you, that Marriage is the most solemn thing in the world, and that which must make her always either happy, or miserable.

Gold. Without Portion ! mark that———

Bell. You have reason Sir, that decides all. But Sir, people will tell you, that the inclination of your Daughter, ought to be a little regarded; and that forcing affections has often ruined the best of Families.

Gold. What without Portion?

Bell. Nay, there can be no reply to that : 'tis true, there are a great many Fathers that prize the satisfaction of their Daughters, and would never Sacrifice them to interest, but would consult their affections.

Gold. But again I say, without Portion.

Bell. 'Tis true, without Portion is an answer to every thing; and who can resist such reason as yours.

Gold. [*To himself*] O heaven I hear the Dog bark, I am so afraid of this money, I must into the Garden : stay here.   [*Ex. Goldingham.*]

Theodora. Bellamour you are in the wrong, to talk thus with him.

Bell. If I should oppose him Madam, I should ruine our design, and you will do better to feign a consent to what he commands.

Theodora. But for this sudden Marriage, to night.

Bell. Wee'l find means to break it, and make him consent to it.

Theodora. What can you invent?

Bell. Feign some sickness, and desire him to delay 't for that.

Theodora. Physicians will find out that deceit.

Bell. Madam, he would scarce be at the charge of one to save his own life, much less yours.

Theodora. But he has Kindred, that will give him their advice for nothing.

Bell. Madam do you believe in Doctors? Do you think they know more than Nurs-keepers? I warrant you Madam, counterfeit what distemper you please, they'l find reasons enough to tell you from whence it comes.

[Enter Goldingham.]

Gold. Heaven be praised, all's well, there was no body.

Bell. Besides Madam, our last recourse shall be to discover our selves, and our affections, and if you can be constant, as I doubt not—— [*Goldingham is seen by them.*]   Madam (as I was saying) a Daughter ought not to dispute her Fathers will, or once think whether she likes the man or no, whom he chuses for her, especially where that invincible reason, of without Portion, offers its self.   [*Theodora flings from him hastely, and goes out.*]

Gold. Well said *Bellamour.*

Bell. Sir, I ask you pardon, that I make so bold with your Daughter.

Gold. I am orejoy'd at it, you have done exceeding well.

Bell. Sir, I will never fail to urge her with arguments, and especially, that undeniable one, of *without Portion.*

Gold. 'Tis very well.

Bell. Oh Sir, there's nothing (in this world) so precious as money, not Honour, Birth, Education, Wit, Courage, Vertue, Wisdom, Religion, Loyalty—

Gold. Oh there spoke an Oracle! dear *Bellamour,* I could hug thee for this, thou shalt follow, and advise her. But first, give me some little account of this days business; Has *Sarah* the Orange-Wench redeem'd her Thumb-Ring, that I lent her ten shillings upon last week?

Bell. No Sir.

Gold. 'Tis forfeited then, it weighs two and twenty. Has the fellow that cryes old Cloths, redeem'd the new Velvit Coat, (which I believe he stole) or the Oyster-Woman her Red Petticoat with Silver Lace on't? Or has the Cobler redeem'd his Pewter that he Pawn'd for Money to buy Soles? Or has the Country Gentlewoman (that lost her money at play) taken out her Watch, for which she is feign to make excuses to her Husband, and say 'tis a mending?

Bell. None of these.

Gold. Has the *Whetston* Whore redeem'd her Mantoplicee, and her Silk-dy'd Petticoat, with Gold and Silver Lace?

Bell. No poor soul, she has had ill trading of late.

Gold. There is a Bauds Silver Aqua-Vitæ Bottle, a Midwife's hackny Satin Mantle, with old fashion'd Gold Lace; a Herald Painter's Hears-Cloth, and Velvit Pall; besides (let me see) an Attoney's Clerk Pawn'd a Beaver of his Masters in the Country; there is too, a Porters and a Water-mans Silver Badge, the Fidler's Violin, the Hackny Trumpeter's Brass Trumpet, the Barber's inlayd Razor Case, with Silver Heads to his Instu-ments, are any of these redeem'd to day?

Bell. None of 'em Sir.

Gold. They are forfeited, to Hell with them, *ab inferis nulla redemptio,* this has been a happy week *Bellamour:* two young Sparks have forfeited Morgages this week: they are the sweetest People to deal with, they seldom fail of forfeiting them, and I never fail to take 'em, but prethee go to my Daughter, and advise her.

Bell. I will Sir,
Better then you think.   [*Aside.*]

Gold. How happy am I in this servant! well, (if this trade hold) I shall tumble in Money; and next to that.

> *The greatest pleasure I can have of life,*
> *Is in cold age, to have a warm young wife.*

ACT II. SCE. I.

Enter *Squeeze, Timothy, Roger.*

Sque. IS Mr. *Goldingham* at home?

Roger. He is in the Garden, (where he always is) I'le tell him you are here. [*Ex Roger.*]

Sque. Come *Timothy*, Cheere up, has't not thou forgot to put on thy little Cuffs, to Comb thy head, and get thy hair powder'd.

Tim. No no, I have my best Cloaths on too, just as I used to go to Church; but de' hear Sir, I shall be asham'd when *Theodora* comes, de' see, for (on my conscience and soul) I shall never learn how to Suitour a Woman.

Sque. Take my directions, and I warrant thee.

Tim. How did you go to work to Suiter my Mother?

Sque. Why, I'le tell thee, when I was a young man, (Oh the happy days we lived in then) I could woe a young Gentlewoman, with as much dexterity as the Sprucest Gallant on 'em all.

Tim. I long to hear, before Mrs. *Theodora* comes.

Sque. Why look you, suppose thou wert thy Mother, stand there, (and I'le tell you she was as fine a young Lass, as any Aldermans Daughter, (though she was but a Button-makers Daughter) and as well bred too; I am sure it cost her Father ten Shillings a month for her learning to Dance, and she play'd most violently upon the Cittern too. But stand still, thus I begun [*He Salutes, and Kisses* Timothy.] Then forsooth your Servant, said I, won't you please to sit down? here's a Chair, and please you. [*He sets a Chair for* Timothy, *and sits down by him.*]

Tim. I vow this is very well, de' conceive me?

Sque. Then thus I went on; pray give me leave to kiss your hand. [*He Kisses* Timothy's *hand.*]

Tim. O Lord Sir!

Sque. I protest and vow, I have a very great affection for you; the very thoughts of you, has often broke my sleep; and made me fetch many a sigh.

Tim. Ha, ha, ha, very well I vow.

Sque. For you are very handsom (as I am an honest man,) and I cannot but love you, an I were to be hang'd for't.

Tim. 'Tis your goodness more than my desert.

Sque. Good lack, to see the luck on't, she made that very answer, I protest.

Tim. Oh *Gemini*, why did she?

Sque. Yes; but to go on, said I, I am come to see if you can love such a one as I am, (and I was then as pretty a young Fellow as any in the City) and if you can, said I, I shall be very well content to make you my wife.

Tim. Ay but Mrs. *Theodora*, they say, is most pestilent Coy.

Sque. 'Tis no matter, be thou bold, and she'l not deny thee.

Tim. Ay and I will now you bid me, though I venture my life for't, de' understand me ?

Sque. Do, stand up to her man, and kiss her, she'l not deny thee, for thou art a very pretty Fellow, though I say't ; stand up, let me see, turn thee about, well made too, well thou takest just like me, I was just such another when I was young.

[Enter Goldingham and Bellamour.]

Gold. Mr. *Squeeze* you are welcome.

Sque. Thank you good Sir.

Gold. And you Mr. *Timothy*.

Tim. Thank you good Sir, (as my Father said before me.)

Sque. This is the young man I bring to your Daughter.

Tim. Ay Sir, I make bold to come a woing to Mrs. *Theodora*, de' conceive me, if your worship please.

Gold. With all my heart.

Bell. An excellent Choice, an accomplisht Rival have I : I should sooner be jealous of a Ballad-finger, or a Pickpocket.   *[Aside.]*

Gold. Bellamour, go call my Daughter.

Bell I will Sir, A curse on him, must she be baited by this Bandog.
                                                                    [Ex. Bell.]

Gold. While the young People are together, wee'l drink a Cup ; I would send for a Pint of white Wine, or half a Pint of Sack for you, but the Vintners do play the Rogues so, and put Horse-flesh, dead Dogs, mens bones, Molossus, Lime, Brimstone, Stumme, Allom, Sloes, and Arsnick into their Wine——but I'le send for a Cup of wholsome Ale for you.

[Enter Bellamour and Theodora.]

Sque. With all my heart.

Bell. There's the sweet youth, he has provided for you.

Tim. Now Father stand by me.

Gold. This Daughter, is the pretty young Man I told you of.

Theodora. He looks more like a Corn-Cutter than a Lover.   *[Aside.]*

Sque. Your Servant young Gentlewoman.   *[He Salutes her.]*

Tim. Your Servant forsooth, I make bold to Salute you, de' see : I vow 'tis the sweetest Kiss that ever I had in all my life ; you kiss very well Mrs. *Theodora*, pray let me have another.

Theodora. Hold Sir, not too fast.

Tim. Why look you Father, did I not tell you how 'twould be ?

Sque. You were a little too forward Son.

Gold. Come let's leave the young people, they'l do best together.

Sque. Ay I warrant you, they had rather be alone.

Gold. D'y' hear *Theodora ;* be civil to him *Bellamour !*

[*Ex. Goldingham, Squeeze,* and *Bellamour.*]

Tim. So now we are alone Mrs. *Thea,* I call you *Thea* for shortness, de' see ?

Will you please to sit down ?

I'le try now if I can out-do my Father. [*Aside.*]

Theodora. To wait upon you I will Sir.

What a ridiculous Lover have I ? [*Aside.*]

Tim. Come Mrs. *Thea,* I profess my Legs are very weary, I have been all this morning dunning for money, at this end of the Town ; and I promise you I mind my business as well as e're a young man in this City that wears a head, but (a deus take 'em) they do fob me off with Protections hereabouts.

Theodora. They do ill, to disappoint so fine a Person.

Tim. Ah forsooth, you are pleased to say so, but come (now I think on't) pray where's your Maid ?

Theodora. Why do you ask ?

Tim. If you please to send her to some Tavern, where you have Credit, I'de make bold to send for a Pint of Sack for you, (there I out-do my Father a whole half Pint.)

Theodora. Oh admirable breeding. [*Aside.*]

By no means I don't love it, I assure you.

Tim. Then I'le send for a Bottle of white Wine ; I have Sugar in my Pocket, the Rogues at Taverns make us pay three pence a Paper for it.

Theodora. A thrifty consideration, but I drink no Wine.

Tim. Nay peuh Mrs. *Thea,* you say this now to save me Charges, de' see ; but alass I care no more for Money than I do for the dirt under my foot, d' you understand me ? If I had you at the *Popes-Head,* I'de give you half a peck of Oysters, I have as good Credit there as ere an Alderman's Son of 'em all, no dispraise ; but faith I will send for White-wine now, you shall not say me nay.

Theodora. Oh intollerable ! I will have none sent for.

[*Enter James.*]

James. Sir, your Father bids me tell you he is sent for to *Chatolins,* to some young Blades, whom he is to take up money for.

Tim. 'Tis very well. Come Mrs. *Thea.* pray be not angry, but let us to our business.

Theodora. Have you any with me ?

Tim. Yes that I have, and very earnest business too, I'le tell you that.

Theodora. What is it?

Tim. Look you Mrs. *Thea, pauca verba,* the short and the long on't is, I have had a very great affection for you, any time these two months, ever since I saw you at *Covent-Garden* Church, de' conceive me?

Theodora. Oh wonderful!

Tim. As I am an honest Man, you have stuck as close to my Heart (all the time) as a Burr (de' understand me) nay I have scarce slept a quiet night, all that time, for dreaming on you.

Theodora. 'Tis impossible.

Tim. Nay feck now 'tis true, whereupon my Father seeing me in this condition, advised me to come to you for cure, de' hear me?

Theodora. Oh Sir, doubt not but you may command me.

Tim. No forsooth pardon me, I shall intreat you.

Theodora. To do what?

Tim. Feck only to love me a little, that's all.

Theodora. No more but that! how can I chuse?

Tim. Ay but will you have me for a husband, de' see? that's the business I come about: if you will, I shall for my part, be very glad to make you my Bed-Fellow, as the saying is.

Theodora. Oh Sir, you deserve one of a greater Beauty and Fortune than I am.

Tim. Pshaw what's matter for that, 'tis all one as long as my Father bid me ask you Mrs. *Thea,* de' conceive me?

Theodora. Sure this Holiday Fool, ha's never been bred to any thing but throwing at Cocks, or demolishing evil houses on Shrove-Tuesday; or may be, he has Rid on a Pageant for a *Neptune,* or a Sea-God, or perhaps waited at my Lord Mayor's Table upon a Feast-day.   [*Aside.*]

Tim. What say you to the proposition, ha?

[*Enter Robin.*]

Robin. Did you see your Brother Madam?

Theodora. He's gone out.

Tim. A deus take this Fellow for interrupting us.

Gold.
Within.} *Theodora.*

Theodora. Heark, I am call'd, farewell.   [*Ex. Theodora.*]

Tim. Nay and I leave you, the King shall know it.   [*Ex. Tim.*]

[*Enter at the other Door Mrs.* Cheatly.]

Cheat. Oh dear *Robin,* art thou here?

Robin. Mrs. *Cheatly,* what makes you here for heavens sake?

Cheat. That which makes me go every where; I love to be serviceable to the Nation, in my faculty, I bring People together, and make work for the Parsons, and the Midwives. But where's Mr. *Goldingham.*

Robin. What business can you have with him? of all mankind.

Cheat. That which I hope to get by; you know I have no Rents, Industry, and Intrigue muſt maintain me; but thou art sure not to lose by it, my dear *Robin.*

Robin. And you not to get by it here, I assure you.

Cheat. You don't know, there are some things within my power, that may touch very nearly.

Robin. Why thou may'ſt sooner hope to get by thy Trade in a Town three years besieged, and almoſt famished.

Cheat. I warrant you, I have a way of tickling of 'em as they do Trouts out of their senses, but I muſt work upon him by degrees.

Robin. Why he would not give a shilling to save thy soul, nor eighteen pence for his own; I have heard him wish that that word Give, were blotted out of the *English* Tongue: you'l put him into Fits, if you but propound it to him. 'Slife here he comes, I muſt be gone I am sure.

[*Ex. Robin.*]

[*Enter Goldingham.*]

Cheatly. Ah dear Sir, how briskly you look to day, good lack! If I had not been in your house, I proteſt I should not have known you.

Gold. I look well, alas, alas!

Cheat. I never saw any creature so chang'd in my life, sure you drink nothing but Viper Wine.

Gold. Nay you wheadle.

Cheat. Upon my life, you amaze me, you look so delicately, so fresh, and gay.

Gold. Nay but do I? hah.

Cheat. Sir, you were never so young in your life, I have seen men of five and twenty in white Periwigs, have less youth about them.

Gold. But (for all that) I am above six and fifty.

Cheat. Six and fifty! alass that's nothing, that's the season of a perfeĉt Man, you are now in the flower of your Age——it was the time when the *Patriarchs* you know began to get Children.

Gold. That's true, but if I were twenty years younger, 'twould do me no hurt.

Cheat. You jeſt Sir, you need no youth, I'le lay my life you will live till you are a hundred years old.

Gold. No no, but do you think so really?

Cheat. Moſt certainly Sir, you have all the markes of long life; let me see, hold a little: Oh what a sign of life there is upon your Forehead! I am sure you'l have four wives more.

Gold.——I care not how many wives I have, I love to bury wives much.
                                                                    [*Aside.*]
But have you such skill in these things ?

Cheat. Ay as much as e're an Almanack-maker, or Cunning-man of 'em all ; let me see your hand, Heaven ! what a Line of Life is here.

Gold. How, let me see.   [*He puts on his Spectacles.*]

Cheat. Do you not see how far that Line goes ?

Gold. Yes, but what does that import ?

Cheat. A hundred did I say ? If you don't live to Sixscore, I'le be content to be hang'd, when I am so old my self.

Gold. 'Tis impossible.

Cheat. You will live to bury all your Children, Grand-children, Great-grand-children, and Posterity, to the fifth and sixth Generation.

Gold. The more I bury, the better ; what care I for Posterity, I would be my self the last man of my family.

Cheat. Yes Sir, as you are the first.

Gold. But pray Mrs. *Cheatly*, how goes our affair ?

Cheat. If it did not go extreamly well, you would not have me in so good a humour. Well, on my conscience no woman in *England* has that faculty in Match-making, that I have : there are no two persons, so opposite, that I cannot bring together : (if I had liv'd in that time) I would have have been hang'd if I had not Married the Pope to Queen *Elizabeth*.

Gold. But I would not have had that done, that might have spoil'd the reformation : but tell me ?———

Cheat. Why Sir ? I acquainted the Mother with your proposition, and brought *Isabella* to the window, (as you appointed,) where she survey'd your person, your age, your youth, I mean your meen and all your motions.

Gold. And how lik'd she, ha ?

Cheat. She likes your person infinitely, and her Mother, and she entertained the proposal with a great deal of joy ; and *Isabella* says, you are the most Reverend charming old young Gentleman in all *Covent-Garden*.

Gold. 'Tis her goodness, but in troth that was a little too much : but have you spoke with her Mother about Portion ?

Cheat. Oh she'l be a vast Fortune, she will be worth above two thousand Pound a year to you (besides her Beauty,) which, if you would, you might make as much more of, if she would consent.

Gold. And (if I can make so much more of her) I am sure I'll make her consent, or I'll strangle her.   [*Aside.*]
But how will she be worth so much besides ?

Cheat. Why first, she has the most thrifty Stomach of any woman in *Europe ;* she loves nothing but Sallads, Milk, Cheese, Butter, and Apples, nor does she ever desire sweet meats above Almonds and Raysins, you need not keep a table furnished with varieties or delicacies for her : Wine she drinks none, this will be worth a thousand Pound a year; then she hates all finery, Lace she detests out of hatred to the *French*.

Gold. She does well, it was a Roguish invention, and he that first invented it, is damn'd.

Cheat. She hates rich Cabinets, Pictures, rich furnished Closets, and costly furniture extreamly, this (with her own thrift in Habits) will mount to above six thousand Pounds; then she has a horrible aversion for Gaming, then Playes she detests.

Gold. This is admirable, I am each minute more in love with her.

Cheat. Then she never gives a farthing to the poor, though she sees 'em starving.

Gold. How admirably shall we agree, for I hate the poor as much as she can do.

Cheat. Then she abominates Singing-Masters, *French*-Masters, Dancing-Masters, Harpsical-Masters, above measure; now to sum up all these things they will amount to 2450 *l.* a year, for her life, there's four hundred and fifty Pound above your sum.

Gold. Mrs. *Cheatly*, these things are very good, but they are not real goods, I would have something that I might give an Acquittance for, and say, *I say Received per me Humphry Goldingham*.

Cheat. Are not all these excellent qualities real Goods? and I assure you, you may receive them when you please.

Gold. These are not Goods and Chattels Mrs. *Cheatly;* I must touch something.

Cheat. Touch! why, you shall touch her, and touch her all over, and as much as you please, there's a delicate creature to touch, there's a touch for you.

Gold. Ay, but I must touch money; there's a delicate thing to touch, there's a touch for you!

Cheat. Money you shall have too, they have a good Estate in the North, which I have heard them speak of——

Gold. That must be seen: But there's one difficulty more; she is young and I fear will not be brought to love an old man.

Cheat. Cods me, I had like to have forgot that quality of hers, she has the most unconquerable aversion, in the world, for all young men; she was to have been Married t'other day, and broke off the match, because she found the man was not above fifty.

Gold. It cannot be, sure.

Cheat. Upon my word 'tis true, she says, the young men of this age are nothing but brisk, airy, conceited, gay, proud, ignorant, foolish, singing, dancing, *Baboones* in huge Periwigs, not fit for wives.

Gold. It is impossible.

Cheat. If you did but see her Seals, and the few Pictures she has, not of

Adonis, Paris, Apollo, Narcissus, or any young Figures, but of *Saturne,* King *Priam, Anchises, Nestor, Methusalem,* and some of the old *Patriarchs, John* of the times, and old *Parre.*

Gold. This is incomparable indeed, if I were a young woman I should never endure young Fellows; for my part I wonder what they can see in them, to love 'em so.

Cheat. Ay, I wonder what pleasure they can take in 'em! Oh your fine old man for my money he's the civilest, quietest Bed-fellow; worth a thousand of these young Fops, that are ever upon the spur, like a Citizen on a Journey.

Gold. 'Tis your goodness: But canst thou not bring this *Isabella* to Supper, to night to my house? I am to give Mr. *Squeeze* and his Son a Supper; who shall marry my Daughter immediately, and (if you can bring this Lady) I would kill two Birds with one stone, as that excellent thrifty Proverb says.

Cheat. Ne're doubt it Sir, I'le bring her after Dinner to see your Daughter and they may take the ayr in your Coach together, and so come back to Supper.

Gold. Prethee go about it instantly.

Cheat. But Sir————

Gold. Nay prethee Mrs. *Cheatly* go about it, make no delays, prethee go now————

Cheat. One word more.

Gold. No more for heaven sake, go now.

Cheat. I must speak to you.

Gold. By no means, go just now about it, now, go quickly. [*He thrusts her on towards the door.*]

Cheat. Well, there is nothing to be done with this old Fellow now. [*Ex. Cheatly.*]

Gold. This *Cheatly* is a rare Woman, but I was plaguily afraid she would have asked to borrow Money of me, after she had done her Story. 'Sdeath what do I hear! the Garden door opens, she's gone in there; I must watch her, and my dear dear money. [*Exit.*]

[*Enter Bellamour and Theodora, as Gold. is going out.*]

Theodora. What makes my Father in such hast? I believe he is gone into the Garden; where he goes a hundred times a day: But pray *Bellamour,* is your Man returned, you sent into the North to enquire of your Father?

Bell. Madam I expect him to night. But my dearest *Theodora,* since I have your heart, there's nothing else I have within my eye, or thought! let us not think of business, but imploy this happy minute in talking of love.

Theodora. Here's my Father, to your advice again.

(41)

[Enter Goldingham.]

Gold. So all's safe in the Garden.

Bell. Madam you must obey, and marry him to night, your Father will not delay the making of you happy.

Theodora. To night, is too sudden *Bellamour.*

Bell. 'Tis never too soon to obey your Father Madam.

Gold. Admirably well said, dear *Bellamour*, never was man so happy in a servant! Come into the next Room Daughter; I warrant you, my man and I will soon convince you.

Theodora. Let me beg you will defer it Sir.

Gold. I will have it dispatch'd to night, come along.

[Exeunt omnes.]

[Rant, Hazard, Lettice, and *Joyce* at *Chatolins.]*

Rant. That *Theodore* should be such a Villain, to disappoint us.

Hazard. I wonder he should have no more care of his own soul, than to break his word with honest Fellows.

Lettice. I believe he knows of my being here; and has not the face to see me (after some inconstancy, I have taken him in lately).

Joyce. That she should pretend to an interest in him, Mr. *Rant!* but if every body that has injoy'd her should be constant to her, (as she calls it) she would have an Army of Lovers.

Rant. God-a-mercy Mrs. *Joyce*, I'le drink thy health for that; here Boy give me a Glass. *[Boy gives a little Glass.]*
A pox on this Thimble, give me such a Glass as your *Nonconforming* Parsons drinks in, after labouring at a Conventicle; as big as King *John*'s Cup at *Lyn*, or *John Calvins* at *Geneva:* That is fit for nothing but to wear in a mans Bandstring (as your Citizens do Rings.)

Boy. Here's one will fit you Sir.

Rant. Fill it, and strike it.

Lettice. Here's thy health in a brimmer, *Hazard* have at thee.

Hazard. I'le do thee reason, dear Rogue, an 'twere a Pulpit full of *Burgundy;* I love such honest Fellows, that let drinking and wenching go hand in hand.

Rant. Faith they are such sweet sociable Sins, 'tis pitty they should ever be parted.

Hazard. Come Boy, my Glass.

Lettice. But where's the Fidlers you promised us?

Rant. Here's Captain *Theodore.*

[Enter Theodore.]

They cannot be far off.

(42)

Theodore. How now Gentlemen, what so forward already? Ladies your servant.

Rant. You see *Theodore* we are not wanting, we provide you good Company; but I am sorry you came not to Dinner.

Lettice. You see Mr. *Theodore* what I venture for your Company; to undergo the Scandal of these Gentlemen.

Theodore. No Scandal I hope Mrs. *Lettice!* for women of your Tribe (like *Fanaticks*) are above Ordinances.

Joyce, Mr. *Theodore*, you are very unkind of late, one can never see you: But you see I can venture to be ruin'd with my Alderman to see you; but not a word of this.

Theodore. Fear it not, I am as much affraid of the Scandal as you are.

Hazard. Come *Theodore*, thou wantest two or three Beer-Glasses; Is it not better to drink, and be free with these glorious Harlots, than to crouch to a foolish simpering Lady that's honest?

Rant. Thou art like a dry-foot-Dog, that (out of a whole Heard of Deer) singles out one, whose Scent he only followes, and tires himself to catch that, when he might have twenty in the mean time.

Theodore. Gentlemen! the Devil is much obliged to you, you are his great Champions; and defend Whoreing with as good arguments as any of his controversial Divines about the Town: But all this will not make me think ill of an honest woman.

Hazard. I tell you there is not a woman in the world, that's honest at all times, and upon all occasions.

Theodore. What not thy Mother, or thy Sister?

Hazard. No gad, if they were, I would disown them, they had none of my Blood in 'em.

Rant. *Theodore* let me advise thee not to speak contemptibly of Sons of Punks, for (if thou dost) Gad thou wilt raise a world of enemies.

Theodore. I'le assure you, I have a better opinion of the Sex than what ill company, and your leud lives, have given you.

Hazard. Ay pox on't, thou art not *compos mentis*, thou art in love; but here's a couple of remedies for that Disease; which (if thou dost not nip in the bud) will prove more dangerous than three Claps.

Rant. I hope it's nothing but some fumes of the Spleen, that make him base Company, (for the present:) I hope (with these Ladies assistance, and a Bottle or two of *Burgundy*) to set them right yet.

Lettice. I am Mr. *Theodore*'s humble Servant, he shall want no assistance I can give him.

Joyce. Nor will I be deficient in any thing to serve him.

Lettice. Alas, Madam, he does not ask your service, nor would it do him much good.

Joyce. Goodlack, Mrs. *Lettice*, you are so exalted by the bounty of Mr.

Squeeze the Scrivener, and twenty or thirty more, that (unknown to him) Club with him.

Lettice. Twenty or thirty, thou insolent Creature? did you learn no better Manners of your Alderman?

Rant. Hold, Ladies, here are the Fiddlers.   [*Flourish of Fiddles.* Let them reconcile your quarrel. Come in, youths.
    [*Enter Fiddlers.*]   [*Enter Mrs.* Cheatly *and Mrs.* Betty.]

Cheat. Come, Gentlemen, you shall not be merry without me, I will participate.   [*They all salute* Betty.

Hazard. Who is this thou hast brought with thee, Mrs. *Cheatly?*

Cheat. A pretty young Girle, which I am to marry to an old Prebend; but mum for that.

Rant. Boy, give me a mighty Glass of *Burgundy: Theodore,* here's thy Mistriss's Health; *Hazard,* to you; Fiddlers, play a Health. [*They Flourish.*

Theodore. You are very brisk, but I shall tame you, I warrant you.

Hazard. Come, Ladies, faith you shall not 'scape, wee'l warm ye first with Wine, and then with a Dance, Mrs. *Cheatly.*

Cheat. I'le pledge you Sir, but with allowance.   [*They Flourish.*

Hazard. With all my heart, take your liberty.

Cheat. Mrs. *Joyce,* Mr. *Theodore's* Mistriss.

Joyce. With all my Heart, Madam *Cheatly.*   [*They Flourish.* There's one in this Room, perhaps, is as nearly concerned in it, as any body.

Lettice. For all that you know, Mrs. *Joyce,* I vow, Mr. *Theodore,* her confidence makes me asham'd of her.

Theodore. Alas, poor Modesty! Fa, la, la.

Cheat. If you will have any singing, I'le sing you a little Countrey-Song shall stir up these Girles more than your Fiddles and Voyces can do.

Hazard. Prethee do, *Cheatly.*

SONG.

As I walk'd in the woods one evening of late,
A Lass was deploring her hapless estate;
She sigh'd, and she sob'd, Ah wretched, she said;
Will no Youth come succour a languishing Maid?
Shall I still sigh and cry, and look pale and wan,
And languish for ever for want of a man?

At first when I saw a young man in the place,
My colour would fade, and then flush in my face;
My breath would grow short, and I shiver'd all o're;
I thought 'twas an Ague, but Alas, it was more;
For e'er since I've sigh'd, and do what I can,
I find I must languish for want of a man.

(44)

When in bed all the night I weep on my Pillow,
To see others happy, while I wear the Willow;
I revenge my selfe on the innocent sheet,
Where in rage I have oftentimes made my Teeth meet:
But all this wont serve, let me do what I can,
I find I must languish for want of a man.

Now all my fresh colour deserted my face,
And let a pale greenness succeed in the place:
I pine and grow faint, and refuse all my meat,
And nothing but Chalk, Lime, *or* Oatmeal, *can eat:*
But in my despair I'll die if I can,
And languish no longer for want of a man.

Joyce. Really, Madam *Cheatly*, 'tis a pretty Song.
Cheat. 'Tis a little too wanton, that's the fault on't.
Rant. Nay, it cannot be too much of that; how dost like it, *Theodore?*
Theodore. Pox on't, there no Wit in't.
Rant. Don't all your greatest Wits make Songs without any Wit at all in 'em, that take extreamly?
Hazard. Come, *Theodore*, take out thy woman; wee'l bounce their Bodies in a Dance.

[*Enter Robin.*]

Cheat. Is *Robin* here? He Dances well, (with his Master's leave) he shall be my partner.
Theodore. With all my heart; but what news, *Robin?*
Robin. Mr. *Squeeze* the Scrivener, Sir, will come to you, and bring the Gentleman that will lend the money.
Theodore. Squeeze does not know me.
Robin. No, Sir, I told him it was a young Gentleman in whom he must be satisfied, when he knew his name.
Rant. Come *Theodore*, I bar all business now.
Theodore. Come, Gentlemen, I'le be as Idle for a while as the best of you, strike up. [*They Dance.*

[*After the Dance, Enter* Timothy.]

Tim. Gentlemen, by your leave; is my Father here among ye?
Rant. Pox of this Rascal, knock him on the head.
Hazard. Hold, *Rant*, who is your Father?
Tim. Mr. *Squeeze* the Scrivener, de' understand me? Lord! that Gentleman needed not have been so angry; my Father is a Livery-Man, de' see? I am no such contemptible person, I promise you.

(45)

Hazard. Be civil to him, he has the Countenance of an excellent Buble.

Rant. I warrant thee, I'll make much of him; Sir, I hope you'll forgive my ignorance of your person; had I known you, I should not have been so unmannerly.

Tim. Nay, 'las, I'll be Friends with you, for my part, with all my heart; but my Father was sent for to this house, to some Gallants that wanted money; and by the noise and Ranting you kept here, de' understand me, I thought you had been the men.

Hazard. We expect him here every minute.

Theodore. Now will you brace of Knaves, Cheat this fool.

Hazard. If he 'scapes us one way or other, I'll forswear *Cater-deus-ace*, and smooth Box, as long as I live.

Lettice. Heaven! if Mr. *Squeeze* finds me here, I shall be ruin'd for ever.

Cheat. Pray let's withdraw into another Room more private.

Theodore. Go all into another Room, and I'le come to you suddenly; I will but speak one word with my man.

Rant. Come on, Ladies: Come, Sir, we must engage you till your Father comes.

Tim. Sir, your servant, I don't care if I spend my Pint with you; and it be a Quart, I have money enough, de' see?

Hazard. And shall have little enough, de' see? before we leave you.

[*Aside.*

[*Ex.* all but *Theodore* and *Robin.*

Theodore. Come, *Robin*, is there any hopes of procuring the three hundred Pound?

Robin. Yes, Sir, you may have the money upon some few conditions; and I (feeling you could not have it upon other termes) told him you must have the money upon any condition.

Theodore. So I must, but what are they?

Robin. I'le read 'em to you, Sir, I have 'em here in writing; first, you must engage some reversion of Land for security.

Theodore. That's reasonable.

Robin. Item, Mr. *Squeeze* will have 30 *l.* for Broakerage, for he but procures it.

Theodore. Oh damn'd *Jew!*

Robin. Have patience, Sir, you shall hear more: *Item*, the Gentleman that Lends it, will not in conscience take above 6 in the hundred; but he will have a Present of 30 *l.* for a pair of Candlesticks.

Theodore. What cursed Exaction's this!

Robin. Item, he will have you take the greatest part of it in Goods.

Theodore. A Curse on him, what *Moor* or wild *Arab* is this?

Robin. Hold, Sir, *Imprimis*, a fine new Razor-Case, with Razors, and every thing suitable ; the Case in-layd with Silver, and all the Instruments with Silver Heads, very fit for your man to learn to shave by.

Theodore. Death and Hell ! what's this ?

Robin. Item A *Bolonia* Lute, a *Roman*-Arch Lute, 2 Gittars, a *Cremonia* Violin, 1 *Lyra* Viol, 1 Viol *de Gambo*, and a Trump-Marin, very fit for you, if you be a Lover of Musick ; *Item* a very neat Chess-Board, and a pair of Tables, very good to pass away the time with.

Theodore. What abominable Villains are these ?

Robin. Item 15 large Pewter Dishes, 2 Dozen of Pewter Plates, 2 Brass Pots, and a Kettle, very useful for you against you keep house. *Item* a Furnace of Brick, with the Cornues and Recipients, very fit for you if you be curious in Distilling. *Item* 1 Scrued Pistol, 3 Muskets, 1 Back, Brest, Head-piece, and Gauntlet, and 5 Swords ; these things are valued at 160 *l.*

Theodore. What Inhuman bloody Rogues are these ? I should not have above 80 *l.* of all this money : Heaven what shall I do ! money I must and will have, though by all the extremities in the world.

[*Enter* Squeeze *and* Goldingham.]

Gold. But do you think there is no danger ?

Sque. None at all, he says his Father is so well known, that no man will question him : Besides he is so pressed for money, that hee'l undergo whatever you can put upon him.

Gold. That's very well.

Sque. Besides, he'l go to the ensurance-Office, and ensure his own life and his Father's death, as you know they will ensure any thing.

Gold. That's well again.

Theodore. 'Sdeath who's here, my Father ? I am betray'd by this Rogue.

Sque. Oh Sir, your Servant, this is the young Gentleman Mr. *Goldingham* that wants the money.

Gold. Oh Heaven, my Son ! I am amaz'd.

Sque. Is it his Son ? This is lucky, above my wishes,   [*Aside.*] He will disinherit him ; and my Son will have a Portion then, a large one with his Daughter.

Theodore. You Rascal, did you betray me ? I'll cut your throat you Dog.   [*Softly.*]

Sque. I betray you ! heaven forbid it.

Gold. Oh you Villain, is it you that abandon your self to these wicked extremities ?

Theodore. Is it you Sir that are guilty of these abominable extortions ?

Gold. Is it you that would ruin your self by your debauchery ? and borrow money upon such conditions ?

Theodore. Is it you Sir that seek to enrich your self by the Ruin of people, in lending money upon such shameful conditions ?

(47)

Gold. Dare you appear before me after this?

Theodore. Dare you appear before the world after this?

Gold. Have you no shame in you, you debauched Villain! to spend thus impiously, what I have sweat for; to make away the reversion of your Estate, upon such dishonourable conditions?

Theodore. Do not you blush to dishonour your Name and Family, by the most cruel exaction, and unheard-of subtleties, that the most infamous of Usurers, nay *Jews* themselves, could ne're invent.

Gold. Are you such a borrower?

Theodore. Are you such a lender?

Gold. Come along Mr. *Squeeze*, I cannot endure the sight of this Villain any longer.   [*Ex.* Goldingham *and* Squeeze.]

Theodore. So, my affairs are in a very good posture, I am disappointed of money, and undone with my Father, if I cannot find out a way to bring my self off.

Robin. Make him believe, that it was for another you enquired for the money; and knowing that *Squeeze* dealt with your Father, (which I am sure you ne're suspected till now) that you intended it for your Father's advantage.

Theodore. Wee'l think on't, and for *Squeeze*, I hope my friends in the next Room will revenge me to the full upon his Son; I'le into 'em, and set them on.

Robin.   *Do* Sir, *and at misfortunes ne're repine,*
            While there are handsom Women, *and good* Wine.

ACT III. SCENE III.

Enter Theodore *and* Bellamour.

Theo. SIR, I have at length broke loose by force from my Company to wait on you; my Sister has told the honour you have done her, and me.

Bell. Sir, I humbly beg your pardon for not first making my address to you; My long absence had made me a stranger to all the Town, and by that means to your Character; had I known you to be a man of that honour I find you, I should not have gone so indirect a way.

Theo. Sir, I am happy that (any way) this favour can be conferred by a person of your worth upon my Sister; and so much honour on my selfe;

and therefore 'tis my interest, as well as inclination, to desire of you that all Names may be laid by between us too, but that of Brother.

Bell. It is a Name that, since you are pleased to honour me with it, shall not be forgotten, or ungratefully own'd while I live.

Theo. Dear Brother, let me embrace you.

Bell. Let this eternally bind us, my dearest Brother.

Theo. I am extreamly glad you have prevailed so upon my Fathers opinion, since it may be of great use, as well to your own affairs, as to mine.

Bell. Do not distinguish our interests, for yours is now become mine.

Theo. I am extreamly oblig'd to you for your kindness, and I have now occasion to use you in a business of my own ; I know you will excuse my freedom.

Bell. There's nothing you can ever do to me, can need an excuse ; nor is there any thing you can ask of me, which I can deny.

Theo. I doubt not but my Father has e're this told you of his anger against me.

Bell. He has, and I am very sorry for it, but I hope to serve you in this affair.

Theo. I can put you in a way to do it, as thus, I'le tell you immediately.

[Enter Cheatly.]

Cheatly. Oh Mr. *Theodore,* your friends are very angry with you for leaving of 'em ; but yon Coxcomb young *Squeeze* is as drunk as a Bully, and so sweet upon Mrs. *Joyce* (who is the only woman I have left with them) that there is no staving him off her : She perswaded him to play with *Hazard* at Backgammon, and he has already lost his *Edward* Shillings that he kept for Shovel-board, and was pulling out Broad-pieces (that have not seen the *Sun* these many years) when I came away.

Theodore. I am heartily glad on't, I am sure the Rogues have no more mercy than a Bayliff with an execution in his pocket ; but prethee what brings you hither ? Does my Father go astray towards the flesh ?

Cheatly. No no, I come to borrow Money of him upon Security ; good enough, as you shall find to your cost.   [*Aside.*]

Theodore. I'le send him to you, come my dear Brother.

Bell. I wait on you.   [*Ex. Bellamour* and *Theodore.*]

Cheatly. If I be not reveng'd of *Theodore,* for using my Daughter unkindly, I have lost my cunning ; I am sure there can be no Instrument of it so certain, as a Mother-in-Law.

[Enter Robin.]

Robin.———Dear Mrs. *Cheatly !* were not you discourag'd enough last time, but you must venture again hither ?

Cheatly. I'le never give him over till I prevail upon him.

Robin. It is impossible, you'l sooner perswade a profeſt *Jew* to Swines flesh and Images, than him to parting with money.

Cheatly. Diſtruſt not my art.

Robin. I heartily wish it might prevail, though I despaire on't, for (to say truth) Mrs. *Cheatly* I have need at present for a great deal of love, not forgetting a little Money, from you.

Cheatly. Thou shalt want neither, as long as I can help thee; here's something, come to my house at night, and thou shalt have more.

Robin. Thank you dear Miſtress, it comes seasonably————Though loving such a one as she deserves very well; yet this is the freeſt Titt that ever had inclination to mankind.   [*Aside.*]

[*Enter Goldingham.*]

Gold. S'death you Rogue, are you about my House? begon Rascal.

Robin. Call me Rascal before my Miſtress? I could find in my honour to beat him for an old *Sink-cater.*

Cheatly. Why do you use *Robin* so unkindly? he's a pretty ingenious young man.

Gold. Hang him Rascal! But prethee how goes our business on?

Cheat. As you can wish: she says, she saw you even now walk under her Window, and made me the pleasanteſt description, and is so taken with you! She says, you are of a fit Age and Beard for her, and infinitely admires the Gravity and Decency of your Habit.

Gold. Does she like me, say you?

Cheat. To admiration: Pray Sir turn you; juſt that delicate shape, that convenient height that she describ'd! Pray let me see you walk: juſt that free and janty meen, that very easie and unconſtrained motion which she describ'd.

Gold. It is ſtrange she should take so much notice of me in so short a time, hah.

Cheat. She says, you look as if you had no kind of Infirmity.

Gold. I have none very great, (thank heaven) I have only a defluction that troubles me sometimes.   [*He Coughs.*]

Cheat. Oh, you are ne're the worse for that Rheume; you have an adm ble grace, a good air and meen in Coughing; it becomes no man in *Europe* so well as you.

Gold. No, no, you jeſt, you are a wag; but will *Isabella* come to see my Daughter?

Cheat. Yes Sir, I am to go and wait on her hither immediately.

Gold. Dear Mrs. *Cheatly*, you oblige me infinitely.

Cheat. I oblige her of all things in the world.   [*He Smiles.*]
But Sir, I have an humble Petition to you.   [*He Frownes.*]

Gold. What the Devil says she?

Cheat. I am just now at the point of being cast in a Suit, for want of a little mony to Fee my Lawyers with ; you may if you please easily supply me, [*He Smiles.*] you cannot imagine what joy she had, when I told her I would wait on her to your house ; you cannot believe what pleasure she'l have to see you.

Gold. Me, alas ! alas !

Cheat. Upon my word Sir, this Suit is of that consequence to me, that I shall be ruin'd, if I lose it ; and a little assistance from you, [*He Frownes.*] will restore my Business again ; Oh ! if you could but have seen what transport she was in, when I was speaking of you, what joy shin'd [*He Smiles again.*] through her Eyes, when I repeated your excellent qualities to her : in fine, I have made her very impatient till this Marriage be concluded.

Gold. You have done me the greatest pleasure imaginable, and I owe all the kindness in the world to you.

Cheat. Sir, since it is so, I beg of you that you will afford me the small supply which I demand. [*He Frownes again.*]

Gold. Well adieu, I'le go see all things prepar'd for her reception in time.

Cheat. I assure you, you could never supply me in so great an exigence.

Gold. Well, I'le see my Coach and Horses put in order for ye to take the air.

Cheat. I should not importune you, if I had not the greatest necessity in the world.

Gold. Let me know what she and you love best, that I may bespeak it to Supper.

Cheat. I beg of you, do not refuse me ; you cannot imagine the pleasure a little sum of money would do me.

Gold. Well, I must go see that Supper be ready in good time, for fear ye should be sick, if ye eat too late.

Cheat. Pray consider my condition————

Gold. I warrant ye you shall have Supper ready early enough, I'le bespeak it instantly : Farewel. [*He rushes from her, and Exit.*]

Cheat. This is the most obdurate, inhuman old Fellow, that are yet ventur'd a foul to the Devil for money.

[*Enter* Robin.]

Robin. What, you have succeeded just as I expected.

Cheat. A curse on him, he was prepar'd and fortified against all my Attaques.

Robin. I tell you, you will sooner perswade *Quakers* to conform, and wear the *Surplice ;* or Bauds to become *Nuns ;* than him to part with any money.

Cheat. I'le bait him once with the sight of this Lady here ; and if that does not mollifie him, I can soon bring her over to another that shall bid high enough for her.

Robin. This Trafficking for Maiden-Heads is an excellent profession ; but they are very dear, for their Rarity.

Cheat. But I think I muſt wholly leave off Trading about Marriages, the Market runs higher at present t'other way.

Robin. Faith then, it's the wiseſt course.

Cheat. I'le consider on't, but come you shall usher me to the Lady I speak of.

Robin. Allons.   [*Exeunt.*]

Hazard, Rant, Timothy, Joyce,   Boy.
Tim. and *Haz.* at Tables.

Tim. On my conscience and soul you Cog, de' see ? look on the *Motto* o'th' Tables, *Play fair and swear not,* de' hear me ?   [*Drunk.*]

Haz. On my honour Sir.

Tim. A Devil take your honour for me, de' see ? that's all your word at this end of the Town ; de' conceive me ? but for all that, one can't truſt a man of ye : Here it goes *Size-Ace, Hazard* hold out.

Tim. Did ever man see the like ! on my conscience and soul you deal with the Devil, de' mark me ? Mrs. *Joyce,* let me have but one kiss, de' conceive me, and I shall win the Game fack.

Joyce. Nay fie Mr. *Timothy.*

Tim. Nay, ne're offer to resiſt, de' see ? for would I might ne're ſtir if I han't it, if I set upon't ; Come Come.   [*They ſtruggle, he kiſſes her.*]

Joyce. You are but a rude person, let me tell you that.

Tim. I told you I'de have it, I faith ; now Sir, I am for you.

Rant. Prethee *Joyce* be not so coy to this young Fool, he may be of great advantage to us all, and especially to thee.

Joyce. I hope he might use more Courtship to a person of my quality, there is some difference sure.

Rant. Prethee let there be none, I am sure you will not repent it.   Mr. *Timothy,* here's the Ladies health in a brimmer.

Tim. I'll pledge you an't were a Peck, (*six and three,*) for would I might ne're go home alive if she be not one of the Prettieſt Gentlewomen I ever saw in my life, (*Sink-Duce* ;) Come drink it off.

Rant. 'Tis off, and there's a brimmer for you.

Tim. Where are the Fiddles ? I'le vow and swear I will not drink without Fiddles.

Rant. They are drinking in the next Room, Boy, call 'em in.

Haz. *Twelve,* there's a Back-Gammon, the Gold is my own.   [*Ex. Boy.*]

Tim. A duce take't, I have loſt all, as I am an honeſt man, on my Con-

(52)

science you have made a League ; I make no more of Mr. *Selware*'s Journey-man next Door to us, I give him one in five.

Rant. If you want any money, you shall have what you will of me ; but drink the health first.

Tim. Come on, Musicianers, strike up, Hey : Here forsooth, here's your health ; and would I might ne're go out of this place, if I would not drink it sooner than my Sisters, or my Mothers, if she were alive : [*He drinks, they Flourish.*] Ha ha, this is the prettiest way of drinking I vow ; it incourages us, as Drums and Trumpets do, when we let off our Guns at a Muster. Come Hey, what care I for losses, my Father ha's money enough de' see ? Mrs. *Joyce*, with your Cozens leave, I make bold to love you with all my heart.

Joyce. I am oblig'd to you really, but I know not how to return it.

Tim. O your love ! I warrant you, you know well enough if you would ; well to morrow we show at *Hide-Park*, and (if I know your Lodging) I'le give you a Gun as I come back, and steal a Bottle of Sack, and the Tip of a Neats-Tongue, and bring you, I tell you that.

Rant. Nay prethee *Hazard* give an honest account, don't sink for shame.

Haz. Upon my honour, he lost no more, what dost take me for a Cheat ?

Tim. Come Gentlemen you don't drink, give me a Glass, here's my Mistris's health ; I make bold to call you so, de' see ?

Joyce. O your servant.

Tim. Come Gentlemen, an't I pure Company now ? strike up Musicianers, Hey ; Gad you think we Citizens are good for nothing, [*He drinks.*] de' conceive me ? But there's a knot of us, of about sixteen or eighteen, if we get together, can be as merry as the best of you ; we can I faith, and sing, *A Boat, a Boat*, or *Here's a health to his Majesty, with a fa la la la lero* ; and Roar gallantly Mrs. *Joyce*.

Joyce. Methinks you are as Pretty a Spark as any about the Town.

Tim. I think so fack, I'll scorn any of 'em should out-do me if I set upon it. Hey !   [*He Leaps and falls down.*]

Joyce. What, have you hurt your self ?

Tim. Pshaw, not at all, *fa la la lero*, come Mrs. *Joyce*,   [*He Sings.*] wee'l have a Song faik now ; Violin-men, (I dare not call 'em Fiddlers, for fear they should be angry) sing us a Catch ; Oh I have seen one of these Act the Countrey-man, and *Simkin* in the Chest rarely ; and you may talk of your Playes, but give me such Pretty harmless Drolls for my money.

Rant. Well, you are a merry man.

Tim. I'le be as merry as the best, hang losses, *Hey, hey*, strike up, *fa la la la la lero*.

Haz. Let me embrace you, dear Mr. *Timothy ;* well he's admirable Company Mrs. *Joyce*.

Tim. Oh! am I so? Sing a Catch you Rogues, or I'le break your Heads; give me a Glass; here Adversary, here's to you.

Rant. A pox on him, hee'l be too drunk.   [*They Sing.*]

A C A T C H in four Parts.

COme lay by your cares, and hang up your sorrow,
    Drink on, he's a Sot that e're thinks on to morrow;
Good store of good Claret supplies every thing,
And the man that is drunk, is as great as a King.
Let none at misfortunes, or losses repine,
But take a full Dose of the juice of the Vine;
Diseases and troubles are ne're to be found,
But in the damn'd place, where the Glass goes not round.

Tim. An admirable Song Mrs. *Joyce,* thank you honest friends: I have heard these men sing gallantly before my Lord Mayor; *Diseases and Troubles are ne're,* &c.   [*He sings out of Tune.*]

Rant. Come will you take Revenge on *Hazard,* here's twenty Pound if you will.

Tim. Hang revenge fack, he's a very honest Gentleman, besides I have in my Fob 20 *l.* in broad Gold I did not tell you of.

Rant. Is not that good news *Hazard?*

Tim. Come Mrs. *Joyce,* let's sing and be merry a bitt; *Diseases and Troubles,* &c. Hey. Mrs. *Joyce,* come to Bed: [*He falls down dead drunk.*] Come I say quickly, I am in hast, come away.

Haz. So now you have done well, this Rogue has 20 *l.* about him; and you have made him so drunk, he cannot lose it to us.

Rant. Let's carry him into another Room to sleep, and pick his Pocket; gad it's all one.

Haz. No pox, our way is a little more honourable.

Joyce. I have had excellent company of you to day Gentlemen.

Rant. I know thou hast goodness enough to pardon it; but if my design succeeds, you shall have cause to thank me; I will watch this Fellow, as *Bacon* did his Brazen Head; and (if I do not marry him to the) I'le be bound never to Cheat the Son of a Citizen again.

Joyce. Flatter not your self, 'tis impossible.

Haz. Ne're doubt him, you know not his Art; but whilest he watches him, I'le wait on you to my Lodging; whither he shall bring *Timothy* as soon as he wakes.

Joyce. Come on, your Servant, Mr. *Rant.*

                    [*Ex. Joyce* and *Hazard.*

(54)

Rant. Your Servant, sweet Mrs. *Joyce.*
Mr. *Timothy,* wake a little.

Tim. I'le not wake for my Lord Mayor, the Aldermen, and all the Common Council, de' see?

Rant. Here, Waiter, help to carry him into the next Room.   [*Exeunt.*

[*Goldingham, Theodore,* and *Theodora.*]

Gold. But it is really, as *Bellamour* tells me, that you would procure the money for another?

Theodore. Upon my word, Sir, the young Gentleman will give you a meeting to morrow morning.

Gold. 'Tis somewhat better, but why did you keep such scurvy Prodigal company.

Theodore. I did it only to draw him in, and get money of him.

Gold. That's very well. Now, Son, I have something else to say to you; the Lady which I intend for your Mother-in-Law, will be here inftantly; and I charge you betray not the dislike of any thing in your Countenance, but use her with all the refpect imaginable.

Theodore. I can't promise you to be glad of the coming of a Mother-in-Law; but I am sure I will not mislike her you have Chosen.

Gold. Nor you, Daughter?

Theodore. I have never given you occasion to sufpect so ill a thing of mee.

Theodore. 'Sdeath! what Inftrument of the Devil has he made use of, to seduce *Isabella* hither?

Gold. Leave me now, and send in all my servants.

[*Ex. Theodore* and *Theodora.*

[*Enter Oldwoman, Roger, James, Will.*]

Here, where are you all? mind all your Charges. *Oldwoman* firft, to you it belongs to make every thing clean: But do you hear? do not Rub my Moveables too hard, to wear them out; if you do, I shall ftop your Wages.

James. Hey, what's to do now?

Gold. You, *Roger,* take all the Bottles and Glasses, and rince them; and take Charge of 'em; if there be one loft or broke, I'll bate it out of your Wages, Sirrah.

James. That I am sure of.

Gold. Then do you, *William,* fill the Drink; but, never but when they are dry, and let 'em call for't twice or thrice, pretend to be a little thick of Hearing: Here are a company of Roguish Lackey's about the Town, that are always offering the Glass, and provoking people to drink, and kill themselves, I will have no such Rogues about me.

William. I warrant you, Sir, I'le look to the Drink.

Gold. Then look you have your best Cloathe's on when the people come.

Roger. I have my best, and all I have on, but they are so horribly greasie before, that they are fit for nothing but to give to a Soap-boyler, or Kitchin-stuff-Woman.

William. And mine are so full of holes behind, as if I had a Volley of Musket-Bullets in my Posteriors.

Gold. You foolish Knaves, cannot you Sirrah take your Hat, and hold it before you to hide the Grease? And do you Sirrah turn your Face always to the People, to hide those holes behind; and when you are sent for any thing, go backward, thus you Rascal. Now to you *James.*

[*Ex.* Old-woman *Roger,* and *William.*]

James. Would you speak to me as your Cook, or Coach-man? for you know I serve in both Offices.

Gold. As my Cook.

James. Good Sir hold a little.

[*He puts off his Coach-mans Cloak, and appears like a Cook.*]

Gold. What a Devil is this Ceremony for? you Rascal.

James. Good Sir have a little patience: Now speak, I am ready.

[*Enter Bellamour.*]

Gold. Oh *Bellamour* come and assist me; *James,* I am to give a Supper to night.

James. The most miraculous thing I ever heard of!

Gold. Can you make us good Cheer?

James. Yes, if you will let me have a great deal of money.

Gold. Money! you Rascal you, have ye nothing to say but money; nothing in your mouth but money, money, money?

Bell. I never heard so impertinent an answer, every fool can do that; but you must make a good entertainment with a little money.

James. Good Mr. Steward, I would you would teach me that secret.

Gold. Peace Sirrah, and tell me what we must have.

James. There's your *Fac-totum,* let him tell you.

Gold. Answer me, or I'le break your Head.

James. Hold Sir, I will, how many will there be?

Gold. Ten in all, but provide enough but for eight.

James. Why you must have, first, two great Soupes made of Veal, Ducks, Chickens, Coxcombs, Sweet-Breads, Mushromes, Palates, Forced-meat, Artichoak-bottoms.——

Gold. 'Sdeath you Rogue, you would Feast all the Town.

James. Then Fricasees, Ragousts, a huge Dish (with all sorts of Fowles) as Duck, Teal——

Gold. Hold your Tongue you Rogue, you would undo me.

(56)

James. Then Plover, Dotril——

Gold. Hold you Rogue.   [*He stops* James's *mouth with his hand.*]

James. Snipes, Ruffs, Woodcocks.

Gold. Hold you Dog, he puts me into a cold sweat.

James. Partridges, Gnats, Godwits.

Gold. Will the Rogue never have done ?

James. Pheasants, Heath-Pouts, Black-Cocks, Quails, Rails, Larks, *&c.*

Bell. What do you intend to cramm all the Town ? my Master does not invite People, to Murder 'em with eating.

James. But he would not starve 'em sure.

Bell. People should eat to live, not live to eat ; as the *Proverb* says.

Gold. O dear *Bellamour*, let me Embrace thee for that word, he was a great man that said that ; I will have that Sentence Engraven in Great Letters over my Hall Chimney.

Bell. Ne're trouble him Sir, I'le take care of the Supper.

James. Pray do Sir, with a little money, we shall see what 'twill be.

Gold. But now for my Coach.   [*He puts on his Coach-man's Cloak.*]

James. Hold good Sir, good Sir hold a little : Now Sir, what were you saying of your Coach ?

Gold. Let it be clean'd, and the Horses Harnessed.

James. Horses Sir, why they are in that poor condition, that a man must stretch devillishly to call 'em Horses ; they are but the Shadows or Ghosts of Horses.

Gold. Can they be sick and do nothing ?

James. Yes Sir, you make 'em keep such severe Lents, they eat no more than *Chamelions ;* I look every day when they should depart this life : For my part, it grieves my heart, for I have a tender love and respect for my Horses ; and indeed a Man should not be so hard hearted, or unnatural, not to pitty his Neighbour in distress.

Gold. The Journey will not be far.

James. I have not the Courage to put 'em in ; how can they draw the Coach, that cannot drag their Legs after them.

Bell. Sir, I'le engage one to drive 'em.

James. I had rather they should die under any bodies hands than mine ; but you have a mighty necessary Man here to your Superintendent.

Gold. Peace you unmannerly Rascal.

Bell. I'le about these things instantly.

Gold. Do good *Bellamour.*

James. Sir, I cannot endure these Flatterers, and Pickthanks, I speak my mind plainly ; and it made me mad to hear him say things to your Face, of you, that none of all mankind besides will say.

Gold. Why, what does the world say of me ?

James. Pardon me Sir, you'l be angry if I tell you.

Gold. On the contrary, it will please me infinitely to see that plain dealing in you, let the world say what they will.

James. Truly I must deal plainly with one I love, and (next to my Horses) you are the Person in the World, that I have the greatest respect for.

Gold. Come speak.

James. Why Sir, in plain honest sincerity of heart, I tell you in short, no man gives one good word of you ; one says you never fail to pick Quarrels with your Servants at Quarter day, that you may turn 'em away without their Wages, that you have been taken Robbing of your own Horses of their Provender : That (when you go by Water to your House at *Putney*) you take a Sculler, and make him bate half his Fair, for your helping him to Row, in short, you would Rob, Pick Pockets, Murder, betray your Countrey, and do any Villany in the world for money ; your Name is never used without Cursing, and calling you Villain, Wretch, Knave, common Barreter, Oppressor, Horse-Leech.

Gold. You are a Rogue, a Son of a Whore, a Dog, a Rascal.

[He beats him with his Cane.]

James. I was affraid this would be the end on't, a pox on plain dealing for me ; did you not command me to tell you ?

Gold. I'le teach you how to speak Rogue another time. [*Ex. Goldingham.*]

James. Well, I see it is not safe for any man to be honest in this Age.

Bell. How now Mr. *James*, your plain dealing is rewarded very ill.

James. 'Sdeath do you make sport at my beating ? Laugh at your own, when you have one.

Bell. Nay prethee be not passionate.

James. He intreats me, I'le huff a little and try [*Aside.*] if he fears me : Do you know Sir that I cannot endure to be laught at ? and that I will make you laugh in another fashion. [*He presses upon Bellamour.*]

Bell. Nay softly *James*, if you please.

James. No Sir, it does not please me. [James *presses still upon* Bellamour.]

Bell. Nay good *James*.

James. You are a very impertinent Fellow.

Bell. Have patience a little.

James. I will have none ; If I take a Cudgel, I will so Chastise you.

Bell. How Rascal a Cudgel, did you say a Cudgel ? [*James Retreats.*]

James. No no no Sir, alas I have no occasion for one, not I.

Bell. Do you think I am to be beaten Sirrah ?

James. Alas Sir not I, I have better thoughts of you.

Bell. Are you not a Son of a Whore ?

James. Yes Sir, any thing in the World, what you please, I am a Son of a Whore Sir, a Son of a damn'd Whore.

Bell. Do you know me Rascal ?

[Bellamour pursues James, who retires round about the Stage.]

(58)

James. O Lord Sir, I honour you abundantly.

Bell. Did you say you would Cudgel me?

James. I was in jesting, I did but Droll upon my honour.

Bell. And I shall beat you in jesting.

James. Hold, hold, for heaven's sake.

Bell. Remember Sirrah, against another time, you are a very scurvy Railleur. [*Ex. Bellamour.*]

James. A pox on all sincerity, and plain dealing for me, I have had a couple of good substantial beatings; but if I be not reveng'd on this domineering Fellow, I will give Dogs leave to piss upon me.

[*Enter* Isabella *and* Cheatly.]

Cheatly. Do you know whether your Master be within?

James. A pox on't, I know but too well.

Cheatly. Pray tell him, we are here. [*Ex. James.*]

Isabella. But (that I am bound to obey my Mother) you should never have made me run my selfe into the danger of seeing this old man, for (though his Daughter, whom I come to wait on, I hear is an excellent person, yet) I strangely apprehend the trouble of seeing him.

Cheatly. Consult your Interest Madam, he's very rich, and very old, and will leave you a great deal of money, that may qualifie you to marry any young Gentleman you please, hereafter.

Isabella. But I have a natural antipathy to old men, as some have to Cats.

Cheatly. This old man will not have the Impudence to trouble your Ladyship above a year, after you are Married to him.

Isabella. I shall never wait for that time, to make my self happy; one year of such punishment would out-weigh all the pleasure I could have all my life after.

Cheatly. I find the young Brisk Gentleman you spoke of yesterday is still in your head.

Isabella. He is I confess, and in my heart too, and I think nothing will e're get him out; he keeps such a stir there, he will never let me rest a minute.

Cheatly. Do you know who 'tis Madam?

Isabella. No, but I have often seen him walking by my Lodging, and perpetually looking up at the Balcony, either upon me when I was there, or watching for my coming thither; and by his look, and air, I guess all is not well with him neither; I hope he's in the same condition with my self.

[*Enter Goldingham.*]

Cheatly. Here comes the old Gentleman.

Isabella. What Spectacle's that?

Gold. God save you Lady, I am obliged to you for the honour you do my poor house, which (if you can love an old man,) know Lady I am above Six and fifty, and it shall be yours: What a devil Mrs. *Cheatly!* she answers nothing, nor shews any kind of pleasure at the sight of me.

Cheatly. O Sir! she's surprised extreamly; besides, Maids endeavour what they can to hide their affections; she is so full of joy, she cannot speak to you.

Gold. That's something indeed.

Isabella. What a prodigious, ridiculous old Fellow is this?

Gold. What says my fair one?

Cheatly. That you are a most admirable person.

Gold. Fair Lady, you do me too much honour.

Isabella. What an abominable, odious old Fellow's this!

Gold. I am infinitely obliged Madam, for your good opinion of me: Here's my Daughter Madam.

[*Enter Theodora.*]

Isabella. Madam, I have too long delay'd waiting on you, but I hope you will pardon it.

Theodora. Madam, you do what I ought to have done; 'Twas on my part, to have prevented you.

[*Enter Theodore.*]

Gold. Here's my Son comes to kiss your hand.

Isabella. Oh Mrs. *Cheatly!* what accident's this? This is the young Gentleman I spoke of.

Cheatly. This is wonderful.

Gold. I see you are a little amazed to see me have such lusty Children, but I will soon be rid of them both.

Theodore. Madam, this is an adventure which I did not expect; nor was I ever in my life so surprised, as when my Father told me his design.

Isabella. Sir, I am not less surprised than you, I assure you, I was not at all prepar'd for what I see now.

Theodore. 'Tis true, Madam, my Father cannot in the World make so fair a Choice, and I am infinitely happy to see you here; but you are the Person in the world, I would not have my Mother-in-Law; that would break my heart: Madam, I know you have apprehension enough to take what I say in the right sense, and not be offended at it.

Gold. You coxcomb, what an impertinent, silly complement is this! you must be making confessions, must you?

Isabella. Sir, we are so much upon even terms, that you are the man in the world, whom I would not have my Son-in-Law; and (if I were not brought here by an absolute power,) I should have given you no shadow of suspition.

Gold. She is in the right, your complement deserves no better return; I know you would anger her: I beg you Madam to forgive my Son's impertinence, he's a young Sot, that does not understand himself.

Isabella. What he said, was so far from offending me, that it pleased me extreamly to hear him so frankly declare his opinion, and (if he had spoke in any other manner) I should have esteemed him less.

Gold. You have a great deal of goodness to forgive his faults; in time hee'l be wiser, and change his opinion.

Theodore. Sir, I can never be capable of changing, and Madam, I beg of you to believe me.

Gold. 'Sdeath what extravagance is this?

Theodora. Brother, you will provoke him too much.   [*Softly.*]

Theodore. 'Sdeath Sir, would you have me lye?

Gold. Again, I say, change the discourse, you Sot.

Theodore. Well Sir, since you command me to speak in another fashion, give me leave Madam to put my self in my Fathers place; and now Madam, I protest to you, I never yet saw so charming a creature: This is the happiest minute of my life, indeed my life began but from the time I saw you; the Name of your husband, is an honour, which I would prefer to the Titles of all the Princes upon Earth; and there is nothing which I would not dare to do, for so glorious a conquest.

Gold. Softly, hold a little.

Theodore. 'Tis a complement I make for you to this Lady.

Gold. I have a Tongue to express my self, I need no advocate.

Isabella. I am not so dull of apprehension not to know for whom that complement was intended, and am glad to find it.   [*Aside.*]

Cheatly. Sir, if you please let us take the air, I hear your Coach at the door.

Gold. Oh, is it? but I am sorry you will make such haste, I have not time to prepare you a Collation before you go.

Theodore. Sir, I foresaw that, and provided beforehand upon your account, a great Dish of *China* Oranges, Cittrons, all sorts of Sweet-meats, Limonades, Sherbets, and all sorts of Wines.

Golding. [*Softly, but in anger.*]   Villain, who gave you commission to do this.

Theodore. Pardon me Sir, if there be not enough, I know this Lady has goodness enough to excuse it; besides, I can soon have more.

Gold. Is the Sot mad?

Theodore. Madam did you ever see a finer Stone, than that Diamond upon my Father's Finger?

Isabella. It sparkles delicately.

Theodore. With your leave Sir.
       [*He takes it off his Father's finger, and gives it* Isabella.
Madam be pleased to look on't nearer.
Gold. What means the Rascal.   [*Aside.*]
Isabella. It is a delicate clear Stone indeed.
[*She is going to give it* Goldingham, Theodore *puts himself between her and his Father.*]
Theodore. No Madam, no returning of it, it is in too fair hands already, it is a Present my Father makes to you Madam.
Gold. Who I?
Theodore. Is it not true, that you would have this Lady keep the Ring?
Gold. What do you mean you Villain, are you mad?   [*Softly.*]
Theodore. Madam, he desires you, by me, that you would please to accept of it.
Gold. The fear, she will take it, distracts me.
Isabella. Pardon me Sir, I use not to receive Presents.
Theodore. Madam, I am sure my Father will never receive it.
Gold. Oh this lying Rascal! you are mistaken.
Theodore. Look you Madam, your Refusal has made him stark distracted.
Gold. O this damn'd Villain!
Theodore. Do you not see how he frets, and fumes? for heaven's sake Madam receive it.
Isabella. Well Sir, (rather than offend your Father,) I will keep it.
Gold. 'Sdeath, I am undone, but there is no remedy. Madam, I thank you for the favour you do me. But would they were all hang'd, and I had my Ring again.   [*Aside.*]

[*Enter Will.*]

Will. Sir, there's one to speak with you.
Gold. I am engag'd, I cannot come.
Will. He has brought you Money.
Gold. Oh has he, I ask your Pardon Madam: Remember to go backward
Will.   [*Ex. Goldingham and Will.*]
Theodora. You have infinitely provoked my Father, and yet I could not but be pleased with it.
Theodore. I had a violent temptation upon me, that I could not resist Madam; will you do us the honour to take part of this Collation.
Isabella. Your humble servant Sir.
Theodora. Come Madam.   [*To Cheatly.*]
Cheatly. I attend your Ladyship.

ACT IV. SCENE I.

Enter Theodore, Theodora, Isabella, Cheatly.

Theo. MAdam, you are one of the most hard-hearted Ladies that ever triumphed over man.

Isabella. And you the most violent Lover, that ever attack'd a woman ; but this storm of love is too great to last.

Cheatly. Never blame this violence, 'tis the best quality a Lover can have, to my knowledge.   [*Softly to* Isabella.]

Theodora. Madam, my Brother has made me his confident in this affair, and I can answer for his truth ; do not think me partial, for I assure you, I will value your interest equal with his, or with my own.

Isabella. You extreamly oblige me with your kindness ; and your friendship will be able to sweeten all misfortunes that can happen to me.

Cheatly. You Lovers had need have something to sweeten, for ye are an unlucky sort of people.

Theodore. Love, when inclinations meet, is the only condition to be enjoy'd.   Love ! there is no life without it ; we do but sleep, and dream we live, when we are not in love ; and pray Madam, will you be pleased to wake out of this dream, and think a little of one that loves you so, that his life or death depends upon your breath.

Isabella. You let me take no breath, Sir.

Theodore. A good Souldier, when he has made a breach, assaults it presently ; and never gives time to repair, and fortifie.

Isabella. But extemporary love, is most commonly as Hypocritical, as extemporary prayer : But if not dissembled, 'tis seldom constant.

Theodore. Let me beg to know your resolutions, must I live or die ?

Cheatly. Come Madam, be merciful, and reprieve the Gentleman, that may be otherwise so far given over, as to hang himself for your Ladyships love.

Theodora. Let me beg you will please to encourage my Brothers affection, which I am sure is true, and honourable.

Isabella. Madam, think your self in my place, and imagine whether I have not given too much incouragement for the first time ; and whether it becomes my honour to give more.

Theodore. Pox o' this canting word Honour, it never did good yet, it is often the occasion of Killing men, and prevents the getting of 'em.
                                                                    [*Aside.*]
(*To* Isabella.) Madam, there is no honour but in love, the rest is but a

shadow of honour; which the Authors of Romances have perplext with intricacies, more than the Schoolmen have Divinity.

Isabella. You give me no time to think of love.

Theodore. I that have so little time, ought to make what use I can of this; if my Father perceives this, he will, with all the malice that can be, seek to prevent me.

Isabella. But, Sir, I have a Mother (whom yet I never disobey'd) that hath engag'd her self to your Father; and though I confess I can never think of marrying him, yet I must think of no other without her consent.

Theodore. This is you that made that engagement, I thank you, a Plague of all Matchmakers; but I must make use of her yet, & not undeceive [*Aside.*] *Isabella* in the Character of her.

Cheatly. Sir, I did not know you had a passion here, but I will make you amends: if I can marry her to *Theodore*, he's liberal, and will reward [*Aside.*] me well; but his Father is the most hidebound Fellow——he has the Villany of fifty *Jews*, and, which is more, of ten *London* Brokers, in him.

Theodore. Madam, let me have but some assurance, not to have your unkindness, and all other oppositions in the world are trifles.

Cheatly. Come Mrs. *Isabella*, hold off no longer; in short, you told me you loved this Gentleman violently, and wish't he were captivated with you; you did not wish it, that you might use him ill; therefore, since 'tis your inclination, dissemble no longer: Here's the Gentleman, take him by the hand, he is your own *ipso facto,* he's a proper Gentleman, make much of him; here he is for you, and there's the short and the long on't. Now Mr. *Theodore,* I think I have made you amends.

Theodore. Can I believe so great a happiness, I am so transported, Madam, you must expect no sense from me.

Isabella. Sir, since she has betray'd my weakness, which she for her Sex sake ought to have concealed, and I ought in modesty not to have told you, pardon my easiness, and think me not guilty of levity, if you do, you will be very unjust to censure one that esteemes you so well.

Theodore. I should as soon censure heaven for granting my prayers; I have not words enough to tell you, how welcom this minute is to me.

Theodora. Now I hope you will do me the honour to let me call you Sister.

Isabella. I shall be proud to be call'd so by you, but I cannot be so till my Mother consents.

Theodore. Shall I have your leave Madam to use all the means I can to procure her consent?

Isabella. I freely give you leave to do and say what ever you can to obtain it; but I believe you will find it hard to break off her engagement with your Father.

Cheatly. Now comes my part, to set my braines at work, I'le shew you the mastery of my Art, and make your Father break off first.

Theodore. It is impossible he should be such a wretch, as willingly to quit so great a Prize.

Cheatly. I warrant you, trust me, there is one of my acquaintance who I will perswade him is worth 500 *l*. more than this Lady; and though, Madam, he loves you very much, yet he loves a little money much more: This friend of mine is but a Taylors Daughter, but I will make her Act a Countess with some odd Title; and she can behave her selfe as proudly and stately, as the best of 'em, I will make him believe that she has a very great mind to marry him for his care and thrift, &c. This may make him release my Lady of her engagement.

Theodore. I think you have reason.

Cheatly. Reason ay, I think so; if I han't, who should have it? alas, I have done things that shall be nameless, that no woman of intrigue but my self has been capable of, though I say it; and if I do not bring this about, I will never pretend to an intrigue again.

Theodore. You will infinitely oblige me.

[*Enter* Isabella's *Foot-Boy*.]

Foot-boy. Madam, my Lady your Mother desires your company instantly.

Isabella. I wait on her. Madam, if possible I will wait on you at Supper.

Theodora. I hope your affairs will permit you to do us that honour.

Theodore. Let me have the honour to wait upon you to your Mother; and be pleas'd to make me so happy, as to assist me in perswading her to break off the Engagement with my Father.

Isabella. A man of your deserts needs no advocate with me, I am sure. Madam, your humble Servant: Your Servant Mrs. *Cheatly*.

[*Exeunt* Theodore, Isabella, *and Foot-boy*.]

Cheatly. Now Madam I have something to impart to your Ladyship's Privacy.

Theodora. To me, what is it?

Cheatly. Your Ladyship is very young, and mighty Pritty, really I have never seen so charming an Eye, so delicate an air in any Face, so excellent, such pleasant motion, and so bewitching a way——

Theodora. Pray Madam do'nt raily me at this rate——

Cheatly. I protest Madam I speak my opinion. Now Madam there is an acquaintance of mine is extreamly taken with your Ladyship; he is one of the handsomest and most accomplish'd Sparks in Town: He has fifteen hundred Pound a year, and his love is honourable too; now if your Ladyship will be pleased to walk in *Grays-Inn* walks with me, I will design it so that you shall see him, and he shall never know on't.

Theodora. I ask your pardon, I have no thoughts of putting my self off to Sale ; but when I have, that Mart is too scandalous.

Cheatly. In the *Mulberry-Garden,* then Madam he shall never know of it ; I vow the poor Gentleman is ready to die for your Ladyship.

Theodora. You muſt excuse me.

Cheatly. In *Coven garden* Church, will you see him ? I'll order it so with him that keeps the Gallery, that you shall both set together there.

Theodora. I assure you, I carry no such thoughts about me to Church.

[*Enter Robin.*]

Robin. Mrs. *Cheatly,* your Daughter has urgent business with you, and desires you to come home immediately ; I find Mr. *Squeeze* is there privately.

Cheatly. I thank you dear *Robin.* Madam, I hope to convince you next time I see you ; in the interim I kiss your Ladyships hand.

Theodora. Your Servant.　　　　　　　　　　[*Ex.* Cheatly *and* Robin.]

(*To her self.*) This woman I fear is a little scandalously given, I will not truſt her.

[*Enter* Bellamour.]

Bell. Oh Madam, I have been seeking you at the *Park* and the *Mulberry-Garden ;* and thought it an Age till I saw yon.

Theodora. What's the matter ? you look as if you had some ill news for me.

Bell. I am sorry I muſt tell you, that which we muſt speedily provide againſt. Your Father has prepared an entertainment, and will have a *Hackney* Parson ready, that will venture all his Preferment, and go againſt the Canonical Hour, to marry you this night to that Rascal *Timothy :* and in spight of all my perswasion, your Father is resolv'd on't.

Theodora. How sudden are these resolutions ? I shall not need to counter-feit sickness, I shall have enough when I see him.

Bell. Be pleased suddenly to make use of that Artifice ; and if that prevents not, I hope you will give me leave to own my person, and my love.

Theodora. What disease muſt I make choice of now ?

Bell. Here's one comes to help you to one.

[*Enter* Timothy *very drunk.*]

Timothy sings. { *Diseases and Troubles are ne're to be found,*　*But in the damn'd place where the Glass goes not round.*

Bell. This is lucky, above my wishes ; he is very drunk, and that will certainly defeat your Fathers intention ; this night, if you dare truſt your self with him, I'le bring your Father to see him in this condition.

　　　　　　　　　　　　　　　　　　　　　　　　[*Ex.* Bellamour.]

Theodora. Pray do, it will do very well.

Tim. Oh dear Mistress, have I found you ! let me Salute you, de' see?

Theodora. Hold Sir.

Tim. Nay prethee Mrs. *Thea* don't be so coy, look what I have brought you here ; here's a Bottle of *Campaigne*, I think they call it, and almost a whole Neats-Tongue, and a power of Sweet-Meats, for you dear Mrs. *Thea*, there they are.

Theodora. This Fellow has that advantage by nature, that not drunkenness nor any condition, can make him worse. [*Aside.*]

Tim. Well Mrs. *Thea*, I have been with the finest Ladies, and the merriest Gentlemen ; we did rant, and roar, and sing, and tear, Hey, *Diseases and Troubles are*, &c. Faith I am as drunk as a Drum, or as the driven Snow, or as *David*'s Sow, as the saying is, de' see? Hey, *fa la la la,* prethee dear Mrs. *Thea* let me kiss thee now, nay prethee do, nay shaw poise on't.

Theodora. Be not so passionate good Sir. [*She thrusts him almost down.*]

Tim. Nay peuh, I can't abide this, you might have given one a fall now, would I might ne're stir ; but 'tis no matter for that, I'le drink six go-downs upon reputation in *Campaigne* to your health, de' see? I can be merry when I set on't : i'faith here's your health upon my knees, de' understand me? Oh if I had but Fiddles to play a health now.

[*He drinks upon his knees.*]

[*Enter Goldingham and Bellamour.*]

Bell. Do you see Sir how abominably drunk he is ?

Gold. He is a little in Beer, he is ; he is disguis'd, that's the truth on't.

Tim. There Mrs. *Thea* I have done it, faith you shall pledge me by word of mouth ; de' see, nay fack I am sound, you may drink after me, de' conceive me?

Bell. You see Sir he is too drunk to be married to night.

Gold. Come come, he's the fitter for't, for being drunk, if he be sober, he may repent him, and ask a Portion : stay here, I will fetch a Parson immediately. [*Ex. Goldingham.*]

Bell. This is worse and worse, Madam did you hear him?

Theodora. Yes to my grief, I must into my Chamber, and be very sick.

[*She offers to go.*]

Tim. Nay, if you stir I am a Rogue, a very Rogue, de' see? we'l be very merry, *Diseases and Troubles*, &c.

Bell. Who taught you this insolence? unhand her.

Tim. Why you saucy Fellow you, what's to do with you? Ha, you are so purdy. [*Exeunt Bellamour and Theodora.*]

[*Enter Rant, and Will, Goldingham's Man.*]

Will. Where's Mr. *Timothy Squeeze.*

Rant. 'Slife, what makes this Rascal here? if I do not carry him off, I lose the hopefullest Bubble in *Christendom.*

Tim. Where's Mrs. *Thea,* Mrs. *Thea?*

Rant. Mr. *Timothy* come along with me, Mrs. *Joyce* is impatient till she sees you.

[*Enter Bellamour.*]

Tim. I'le not stir till I see Mrs. *Thea,* where's Mrs. *Thea?* Hey, hey.

Bell. She says you are a drunken Rascal, and she will have you kick'd out.

Tim. Does she so? would I might ne're stir if I do not do her errand to her Father.

Rant. Come away and leave her: Mrs. *Joyce* is a Person of Quality, and Fortune, and will use you with more civility.

Tim. I know she's a fine Person, and I'le wait on her, but I am resolved to stay till Mr. *Goldingham* comes, that I may tell him of this Gilflirt his Daughter.

Rant. Nay then, I must to my last shift; Bayliffs come in.   [*Softly.*]

[*Enter three counterfeit Bayliffs.*]

Bayliff. I Arrest you, at the Suit of *Humphrey Nit* a Barber.

Tim. Sirrah, you lie like a Rogue, I owe him not a farthing.

Bayliff. No Sir, but you did *vi et armis* break, or cause to be broken a very large Window, where he us'd to expose his Flaxen Periwigs.

Rant. Is that all? I'le Bail him for that——

Tim. Will you? nay then I'le break 'em again, I'le break Windows with e're a Gentleman that wears a head.

Bayliff. Come come and talk of these things in another place.

Tim. Ay with all my heart, *Diseases and Troubles,* &c.   What a pox care I, come.   [*Exeunt all but Bellamour.*]

Bell. This is a lucky Fellow that came in to our rescue.

[*Enter Theodore.*]

Theodore. Dear Brother, I am glad I have found you, I have a design, and upon my Father too, in which I am confident you will join.

Bell.——You may be sure to command me in any thing.

Theodore. I know some may blame me, but love excuses all.

Bell. Love, like the Crown, takes away all Attainders.

Theodore. My design is to work so upon my Fathers covetousness, as to draw him into a Plot against the Government; and he is you know, a mighty well wisher to the damn'd good old Cause, yet.

Bell. This will be dangerous tampering with; how can you draw him into one, without being guilty your self?

Theodore. It shall be but a seeming Plot, you may be sure; I would not engage my self in a real one; 'tis only a design to invert the order of nature for a while, and keep my Father in awe.

Bell. How can you contrive it?

Theodore. I have several great Chests almoſt full of Lumber, but cover'd on the top with a great many fine Arms, here he comes, I have not time to tell you the reſt; but pray second me, in what I shall say to him.

[Enter Goldingham.]

Bell. I'le not examine your design, but serve you.

Gold. Have you the confidence to appear before me, after your giving my Ring away, and sending for those mountains of Sweet-Meats, and that Ocean of Wine and Limonades?

Theodore. I humbly beg your pardon; but I thought I had done well, since you commanded me to shew all the respect imaginable to my intended Mother-in-Law.

Gold. Respect with a pox, de' call it?

Theodore. I beseech you be not angry, I'le get your Ring again for you, and put you in a way to get forty Guinnes this night, but I muſt be very private in it.

Gold. How! can you do that? then I will forgive all your extravagance; but how is it? speak, you may truſt *Bellamour*.

Theodore. Sir, there is one that was my School-fellow, that I am very well acquainted with, that is called a *Phanatick* according to the flesh, he (after he had made me take an Oath of Secrecy, told me of a design his Brethren had, who (out of pure Zeal againſt *Surplice* and *Common Prayer Book*) were resolved upon an Insurrection, and to seize in one night upon *Whitehall* and the *Exchequer*.

Gold. What say you?

Theodore. They have accordingly provided Arms and Ammunition, which they dispose of in packs of goods, to their secret friends, and well-wishers, for which they reward them liberally.

Gold. What can this come to? [*Aside.*]

Theodore. He remembring that (when we were Boys together) I had shewn him a secret Vault in the Garden, that is known but to few, pro-pounded to me the concealing six Chests of Armour there, and promised forty Guinnes, and an Oath of Secrecy; this Sir you may chuse, whether you will accept of or no, but I thought I was obliged in Duty to tell you, knowing you take all occasions whatsoever for the getting of money.

Gold. I got a good part of my Eſtate by Rebellion (as many other Eſtates were raised) but I would be loath to lose it by Rebellion again. [*Aside.*]

Theodore. There is no danger, we will all take Oaths of Secrecy.

Bell. Ready money, Sir, is not to be despised, 'tis a precious thing.

Gold. There spoke an Angel.

Bell. Besides Sir, if the Chest should be discover'd, (which will be almost impossible) some of your Swearers in Ordinary shall testifie you took 'em in Pawn.

Gold. The money is sweet, but the attempt is [*Aside*] dangerous ; hold [to *Theodore.*] Now Sir, I am glad you have put me in a way to be revenged of you for all your Villanies ; I will immediately acquaint the King with your Treason, and you shall be hang'd.

Bell. For Heaven's sake, betray not your own Son.

Gold. My Loyalty is dearer to me than Son and Daughter, and all the Relations in the World ; I will hang him, I'le to the King immediately.

Theodore. I am at your disposal Sir, but be pleased to remember I did this for your advantage, and out of love and duty to you.

Gold. No Sir, I will hang you, never speak on't ; farewel, shall I betray my Countrey ?

Theodore. Hold Sir, for Heaven's sake conceal it, I will return the twenty Guinnes he gave in earnest ; here they are, I will go and give 'em him immediately.

Gold. Did he give you twenty Guinnes, hum ?

Theodore. Yes Sir, and promised twenty more at the delivery of the Chests.

Gold. Fourty Guinnes is a most delicious Sum, where are they ? let me see them.

Theodore. Here they are Sir, but I beseech you be not angry ; I will carry them immediately.

Gold. Hold, it may be there's no necessity of that——I would hang this Rogue ; but fourty Guinnes, dear fourty Guinnes.   [*Aside.*]

Bell. He comes on a-pace.   [*To Theodore.*]

Theodore. Sir, I will by no means offend you with the sight of 'em, I am gone.

Gold. Stay I say, and let me see them.

Theodore. I am afraid it will provoke you to talk any more of this business ; do not be offended, I will return them instantly.

Gold. 'Sdeath Sir, I will see them.   [*He lays hold on* Theodore.]

Theodore. There they are Sir.

Bell. Oh Sir, how I could hug that Gold.

Gold. Ay *Bellamour*, does it not look beautifully ? they talk of the beauty of Women ; but give me the beauty of Gold, Oh dear, dear, sweet Gold.
                                        [*Kisses the Gold.*]

Theodore. Shall I return 'em Sir ?

Gold. No Sir, you shall not : Oh dear, dear Guinnes, are we all secret ?

Bellamour.⎫
          ⎬ We are.   [*He kisses them again.*]
Theodore.⎭

Gold. Swear never to reveal this.

Bellamour. ⎫
Theodore. ⎬ We do Swear.

Gold. Well Son, your importunity at laſt has overcome me, when shall these Arms be delivered?

Theodore. This night at ten a Clock.

Gold. Do you *Bellamour* see it done, and take his Oath of Secrecy. But I had forgot, where is Mr. *Timothy?* the Parson is ready in the Parlour.

Bell. He was Arreſted here by Bayliffs, for breaking Windows when he was drunk, who have hurried him I know not whither.

Gold. 'Sdeath how unlucky is this! send immediately to all the Bayliffs hereabouts, to find him out; go *Bellamour*.

Theodore. Pox on't, I might have saved money, he would have consented to have betray'd his Countrey for half the Sum; and so will any covetous Man, that can do it safely.   *[Exeunt Theodore and Bellamour.]*

[Enter at another Door Cheatly.]

Cheatly. Sir, I am very glad I have taken you alone; I have a secret to impart to you.

Gold. 'Sdeath she's come to borrow money of me.   *[Aside.]*

Cheatly. Though it may be to no purpose, I think it my duty to acquaint you, that I have since I parted with you discovered a Countess that is not above thirty, that is extreamly in love with you for your person, besides your care and thrift, which she says to me, would be very useful to her in the management and improving of her Fortune, she has Five hundred Pounds more than *Isabella*.

Gold. What you are merry, Mrs. *Cheatly?*

Cheatly. Nay Sir, if you diſtruſt me, there's no hurt done; I did not think you would embrace the offer; but I thought my self bound to discharge my truſt, for the truth is, she engaged me (though something unwilling) to use my care in this business.

Gold. Why, sure thou art not in earneſt?

Cheatly. If ever you were (when you said your prayers) I am.

Gold. There muſt be something in this.   *[To himself.]* This is ſtrange Mrs. *Cheatly*.

Cheatly. You may chuse whether you will believe me or no, for my part I don't desire you should change; for I think if there be any difference, Mrs. *Isabella* is something more desirable.

Gold. Good faith, but if this be true, she is not more desirable, fifty Pounds is a noble Sum, and more than any womans person is worth: for my part fifty Pounds with me would turn the balance, were there ne're so much difference in their persons. But who is this?

Cheatly. You muſt not know, till you see her.

Gold. Can all this be true thou tell'st me?

Cheatly. If I make it not good, I'le forfeit my life; but I'le take my leave now, I have done my errand; but truly Sir, I think you ought not in honour to quit *Isabella*.

Gold. In good faith but I ought, I take it; Honour! quoth she; lose Five hundred Pounds in Honour! what a Pox care I for their Persons in comparison with Money?

Cheatly. I am a little in haste, but I beseech you let not Mrs. *Isabella* know of this, she will be distracted.

Gold. Hold a little, it was unlucky we did not know of this before you brought *Isabella* acquainted with my Daughter, I shall be troubled with her: but canst thou oblige me to contrive an interview between the Countess and me?

Cheatly. Ay and a Marriage too, if I would; but really I think you are too far engaged to *Isabella*.

Gold. Engag'd, I am not engag'd, I will have nothing to do with her; I will forbid her my House.

[Enter a Foot-Boy.]

Foot-Boy. Is Mrs. *Theodora* here?

Gold. What would you have with her?

Foot-Boy. Mrs. *Isabella* presents her service to her, and says she cannot possibly wait on her at Supper.

Gold. 'Tis very well, 'tis no matter whether she does or no, go get thee about thy business Lad; go go. This is very lucky: Mrs. *Cheatly* you'l Sup here. [*Ex. Foot-Boy.*]

Cheatly. Sir, I must go home first. Your Servant. This will be joyful news for the two Lovers. [*To her self.*]

[Enter William.]

Will. Sir here's a Porter come from Mr. *Squeeze*, who says he is engaged upon extraordinary business, and cannot Sup here to night.

Gold. The Devil take thee for thy news.

[Enter Roger.]

Roger. Mr. *Timothy* was at the *Rose* Sir, under an Arrest, but was Bail'd by Mr. *Rant* and Mr. *Hazard*; and is gone along with them we know not whither.

Gold. All my designs are crossed this night, here's my Supper lost, and I have not given one this dozen years before, but I'le make these Rogues fast this month for't; begon Rogues, and call my Son: Oh here he is. [*Ex. William and Roger.*]

[Enter Theodore.]

Son I have something to say to you of concernment, pray (now we are alone) speak freely, how do you like this *Isabella* ? (setting aside the name of a Mother-in-Law).

Theodore. I like her, what does he mean ?   *[Aside.]*

Gold. Yes, her Air ! her Shape ! her Beauty ! her Wit.

Theodore. Faith Sir (to speak the truth) she is not what she appear'd to me, she has no Air or Spirit in her Face, her Shape's very indifferent, her Motion awkward, and her Wit little or none, but I like her well enough for a Mother-in-Law.

Gold. You talked at another rate to her to day.

Theodore. I only made some few complements to her in your name, I meant not one of 'em, I assure you.

Gold. Do yeu think you could have no kind of inclination for such a kind of woman ?

Theodore. No not I Sir, if there were none but such women, I should be out of danger of Gun Shot.

Gold. I am sorry to find this, because it breaks a resolution I had made : I had reflected with my self upon *Isabella*'s youth and my age ; which are so disproportionable, that I have made choice of another, a Countess too of about thirty years old, that's worth five hundred Pounds more than she.

Thaodore. How has *Cheatly* wheadled him already ! I'le try him further : Sure Sir you cannot be in earnest.

Gold. By Heaven I am, and (but for this aversion I find in you) I would have married *Isabella* to you.

Theodore. To me Sir ?

Gold. Yes, to you.

Theodore. 'Tis a thing I must confess I have no inclination in the world to ; but I will obey your commands in any thing.

Gold. No no, mistake me not, I'le not force your inclination.

Theodore. Sir, I am easily inclined to any thing you please to impose upon me.

Gold. No Sir, I will impose nothing ; those Marriages can never be happy where affections do not meet.

Theodore. I'le sacrifice my affection to interest, and your commands.

Gold. No no, if you had loved her, you should have married her in my stead ; but (since you have such an aversion) I'll follow my first design, and marry her my self.

Theodore. Then Sir I must speak freely to you, I love her infinitely, and designed to ask your consent at the same time you declared your intention to marry hear your self, and you might easily have perceived how that declaration surprised me.

Gold. 'Tis very well, & did you ever reveal your love to her?

Theodore. I have Sir, and she received it very kindly; and her Mother too, if you will quit her of her engagement, will freely dispose of her to me.

Gold. And has the Daughter consented to this, say you?

Theodore. She has Sir, and I am extreamly happy that you are pleased to give your consent; nothing else could be wanting to compleat my happiness.

Gold. I will give you my consent to hang your self, but not to marry her, I assure you.

Theodore. How's this?

Gold. 'Slife I had been finely serv'd, to have been bob'd of my Mistriss, for a story of a Countess of I know not what, this was a fine conspiracy.
                                                                    [*Aside.*]

Theodore. Sir, Your are very mysticall, pray let me understand you.

Gold. I speak plainly: Do not dare once to think of loving this Lady: Have you the impudence to pretend to one whom I reserve for my selfe?

Theodore. This makes me mad. Sir, since you provoke me thus, I doe pretend to her, and will never quit those pretentions but with my life.

Gold. Impudent villaine! to speak thus to your Father.

Theodore. In other things I respect you as my Father, but love knows no body.

Gold. I will make you know me, or I'le cut your throat.

Theodore. A lover, and afraid of threats?

Gold. And shall I that am a lover endure this insolence?

Theodore. I will not make use of my plot yet, things are not ripe.

Gold. Out of my doores you Rascall.

Theodore. Fare you well Sir.   [*Exit* Theodore.

Gold. This designe was well scaped; but I'le watch your waters I warrant you.   [*Exit* Goldingham.

[*Squeeze, Lettice,* and *Cheatly.*]

Squeeze. My dear, I doubt not thy constancy, so pretty a creature cannot be false to one that loves her as I do.

Lettice. Indeed I can think of no body but you; the thoughts of you are the last that leave me at night, and the first that salute me in the morning.

Cheat. I am sure I am sufficiently troubled with her, she talkes and thinks of nothing but you; if I ask her a question about business, she answers me something about you, and is so out of humour when you are absent. I hear some body knock.   [*Knocking at the dore.*]   *Exit* Cheatly.

Squeeze. Alas poor thing! my dear pretty *Lettice!*

Lettice. My dear Mr. *Squeeze,* I can find no satisfaction but in thy conversation, 'tis so charming and pleasant.   [*She stroaks his cheeks.*]

Squeeze. Thou art the rarest woman upon earth. Let me kiss thy hand upon my knees; [*He kneels.*] I know thou lovest me, and art true to me, for which I'le reward thee to the full: There's ne're a one of 'em all shall keep his Mistriss better than I do; go to the Goldsmiths, and chuse a hundred pounds worth of Plate, I'le send money for't by an unknown hand.

Lettice. Alas how can I deserve it? I can return nothing but my thanks, nor can I desire any thing from you but your constancy.

[*Aside,*] upon these Termes.

Squeeze. I will be as constant to thee, as the Sun and Moon are to their courses.

Lettice. But I shall have you get a young Wife, and forget me.

Squeeze. If I should marry, my Dear, it should be for money, that I might spare the more for thee: besides, what married man loves not his Mistriss better than if he were single; a Wife is but a foyle to a Mistriss.

Lettice. 'Tis true, this is the fashionable opinion, but you would be of another mind I feare.

Squeeze. Prethee believe me, if I had a Wife, thou shouldst have power to turne her out of doors at thy pleasure, thou shouldst ride in my glass Coach when she took a Hackney; thou shouldst have my purse, my heart, and every thing: are Wives to be compar'd to Mistrisses, that would be a fine age i faith.

Lettice. This is extreame kind, you are a good man: I could never endure that a Wife should share affection with me; especially from thee my Deare.   [*She stroaks him on the head.*]

Squeeze. Nay, prethee my dear, do not stroak my head, 'tis bald, but 'tis not with age, for I am not above eight and thirty, but the hair came off with a sicknesse.

Lettice. 'Tis no matter, I like it, I hate them that wear much hair upon their heads, 'tis greazy, and smells ill; but this is so sweet, and clean, and pretty, I could kiss it now.

[*Enter* Cheatly.]

Cheatly. Oh Daughter, here has been the young Knight you know of; he was so importunate to see you, I thought I should never have got rid of him.

Squeeze. What's that, pray let me know?

Lettice. Nothing Sir.

Squeeze. Prethee my Dear tell me.

Lettice. Pray Sir do not aske, it signifies nothing.

Squeeze. I shall take it unkindly if you do not tell me.

Lettice. Nay, there is nothing I can keep from you: The truth is, my Taylor came to dun me, but the Rascall shall stay I warrant him.

Squeeze. How much is the Debt?

Cheatly. Twenty pounds.

Squeeze. As I am an honeſt man, but he shall not ſtay, here's the money, give it him immediately.

[*Enter a Servant of* Cheatly's.]

Servant. Sir *Jeffery Smelsmock* is coming up to see Miſtriss *Lettice ;* she was denied below, but he would not be answered.

Cheatly. Oh heaven ! we are undone, if I ſtop him not.

[*Ex.* Cheatly *and Servant.*]

Squeeze. What's the matter, is it another Dun ? Prethee have comfort, I'll send thee fifty Pounds to morrow morning to discharge all little driblets.

Lettice. I could not expeĉt this from you.

[*Enter* Cheatly.]

Cheatly to *Lettice,* softly.   I have got ride of Sir *Jeffery,* much adoe ! Well, this Mercer's a sawcy fellow, here's a ſtir for a little money indeed !

Lettice. Hang him Rascall, he shall not have it these six Moneths for his insolence, and I'le have him kickt besides.

Servant within. Sir, I tell you she is not within.

Bully within. Hold your tongue you insolent Rascal ! I'le break open the door. Where's *Lettice?* Where is your Ladyship ? Let me in, or by Heaven I'le break the door.

Lettice. For heaven's sake Sir get into the Closset till I get rid of this roaring fellow, I know not who it is.

Squeeze. Ay with all my heart, where is it ? I tremble every joynt of me.

Bully. What Madam, your Ladyship is grown coy, and deny your selfe : [*Bully bounces and breaks open the Dore, and enters.*] What you do this for an old Rascal they say that keeps you ; If I can learn his name, or catch him here once, I'le cut off his ears, and his nose, both his arms, and both his leges, I will mangle the old dog so.

Squeeze. Oh defend me heaven from this roaring *Bully,* he puts me in a cold sweat.

Lettice. Let me beg of you to go into another Room, and I'le satisfie you.

Bully. Come on, now you are civil.   [*Exit Bully and Lettice.*]

Cheatly. Would this *Bully* were hang'd, he'l ruine my daughter.   Come Mr. *Squeeze,* all's clear, come out.

Squeeze. Is he gone, he has put me in a dreadful fright, this was a Dragon of a *Bully.*

Cheatly. You see Sir what she suffers for your sake, because she will not yield to the temptations of men.

Squeeze. Ay poor heart, but whither is she gone ? Pray heaven she be true to me.   [*Aside.*]

Cheatly. She must give him faire words till she gets him out, and then she'l wait on you.

Squeeze. Oh me ! where is she ? she stayes long, pray heaven all be well.

Cheatly. What is this Girle doing ?   [*To her selfe.*]

Squeeze. Gad forgive me, will she never come, what is the matter ? I am afraid the *Bully* is not gone.

Cheatly. Why *Lettice*, will you never come ?

Squeeze. I hope in Gad she's honest, but I do not like this.

[*Enter* Lettice.]

Cheatly. Oh fie upon you, you have been naught with this *Bully*, look how you are Ruffled ?

Lettice. Mum, not a word, I have sent him away much adoe, I'll have him clapt by the heeles if he comes to affront me again like an insolent Fellow as he is.

Squeeze. Heaven, what noyse is that there ?   { *A noise without of singing* there are more roaring *Bullies* abroad.   Let {   *and roaring, and Fidlers.* us retire quickly to bed, and bolt the dore upon our selves, my dear *Lettice ;* quickly Mrs. *Cheatly* barre the dores of the house.

               [*Exeunt* Cheatly, Lettice, *and* Squeeze.]

Rant, Hazard, Tim. *with a Sword, two Servants, and Fidlers playing,*
         they singing and roaring, Drunk, breaking windowes.

Tim. Hey let's break windowes in abundance.

Haz. Ah brave *Timothy*, thou art as gallant a *Bully* as a man shall see in a summers day.

Tim. Here's the Constable, don't you use to beat him alwayes when you see him ?

Haz. Yes, and will now.

Constab. Stand in the King's Name.

Tim. I can stand in ne're a King's name in Christendom, but we will beat you in the King's name very exceedingly.

Constab. Knock 'em down, fall on Fellowes of the Watch.

Rant. Have at you Rogues that disturbe the King's Peace, and will not let honest fellows give serenades, and break windowes in quiet, have at ye.   [*They fight, the Constable and Watchmen*
                        are driven up into a corner.]

Tim. Hey, have we conquer'd you ye Rogues ? Lay down your armes.

Rant. Lay downe your Weapons, or wee'l cut your throats.

Constab. Well Sir, 'tis done.   [*They lay down their Halberts.*]

Haz. Do you mutiny ye Rogues against *Bully Rocks*, your Commanders ?

Rant. Are you offended at the noyse of Fiddles ? Strike up, and sound an alarm in the eares of 'em.

Haz. Come Rogues, here are just eight of you ; either dance to these fiddles, or we will slice you into steaks.

[*They play with their Fiddles at their ears.*

Constab. Ha ha, come fellowes of the watch, we'l please them for once, they are very merry Gentlemen I fack.

Rant. 'Tis very well done, there's a Crown to drink for you : I, like *Julius Cæsar*, am generous to foes o're come.

Haz. Here's another for you to make ye as drunk as we are.

Tim. And I'll be outdone by no man, there's a Broad Piece for you, now I have beaten you.

Rant. Hee's plaguy liberal of our Money.   Stay watch, and be our guard.

Constab. We thank ye Gentlemen, and will live and dy with ye.

Haz. Strike up here, faith wee'l see *Lettice* before we have done : *Cheatly* open the door.   [*They play.*

Cheatly within. We are all abed : What Ruffians are those ?

Tim. Bounce at the door, break the windowes, hey. [*They bounce at the doores.*]

Squeeze *at window, in his cap, and undressed.*

Squeeze. Heart ! If I be discovered in this condition I am ruined for ever, my credit in the City will be quite lost : Heaven ! they have almost broke the door, I must venture to escape at this window.   [*He leaps down.*] Death ! I have broke my bones ; oh, oh !

Constable. How now, what noyse is that ?

Rant. Some body leaped out of a window : let's see what old Rogue's this.

Tim. Ay, what old Rogue's this, ha ?

Squeeze. I was frighten'd out of my Lodging by these Roaring Blades, and I thought to have escaped out of a window.

Constable. Speak to me, I represent the King's Person, who are you ? What make you here ?

Tim. Hang him, take him away to the Round-House.

Squeeze. My Son here drunk with *Bullies !* then all my shame comes together.

Constable. What's here, he has been in bed with a woman, and for hast has mistaken a red silk stocking of hers for his own.

Hazard. 'Tis true, away with him, an old whoring Rogue.

Tim. Ay away with him, an old Rogue, in bed with a whore ! away with him, away with him.

Constable. We must secure the woman too.

Rant. Wee'l secure her, carry him away.

Squeeze. What a dreadfull miſtake was this, I am for ever undone, I am for ever ruined, what shall I do ?   *Ex. Conſtable and Watch with* Squeeze.

Hazard. If you will *Rant,* let's firſt give *Isabella* a serenade, and then come hither again.   It will be time too, to bring our bubble to Mrs. *Joyce* againe.

Rant. Come along Fiddles, ſtrike up.

Haz. Rank your selves here, ſtrike up, and put out the lights that we may not be discover'd.   [*They go off, and come in at another door.*]

[*Enter* Theodore *and* Robin.]

Rant. Faire *Isabella,* sweet *Isabella !* look out and shine upon your Servants.

Theodore. How now, what Rascals are these : *Robin* fall on.

Haz. Are you so briske ?   ⎧ *They fight, and* Theodore *is driven back:*
Bell. This muſt be *Theodore* and ⎪ *Enter* Bellamour *and Joyns with* Theo-
his man that are engaged, I parted ⎬ dore, *and they beat the other off the*
from 'em but juſt now.   ⎪ *Stage.*

Tim. Fly, shift for your selves, the day is loſt.

Theodore. Who's this that is so kind to draw his Sword for us ? My dear Brother, is it you ? A thousand thanks to you.

Bell. No words, but let's pursue the Rogues.

ACT V. SCENE I.

[*Enter* Theodore, Bellamour.]

Theodore. I Wonder who those Fellows were we rancounter'd laſt night.
    Bell. Very aċtive nimble Youths, they ran like *Irish* Footmen.
    Theo. If we had catch'd 'em, we would have paid 'em for scouring under that Window : But now I can think of nothing else but love.   Revenge has given place to that.   Yeſter-night I got a promise from my Miſtress, and am within this hour to meet her, and marry her privately in the City ; this day will make me richer than the *Indies* can.

Bell. I congratulate your good Fortune, but cannot envy any man, since I am happy in my *Theodora*'s love.

[*Enter* Roger *with a Letter.*]

Roger. Here's a Letter Mr. *Bellamour* came by the Poſt for you.
Bell. For me !   [*He reads it, and seems aſtonished.*]
Theodore. What is it that diſturbs you ?

(79)

Bell. News that nothing could make tollerable to me, but that it puts me into a condition of serving my *Theodora* better than I could before.

Theodore. How's that?

Bell. My Father has been dead these nine months, and died without a Will; my younger Brother is at present possess'd of the Estate, and has inhumanly put my Mother and Sister out of the house, who live privately in this Town, somewhere about *Coven garden.* This account I have received from my man, who is hasting up to Town to me.

Theodore. In good faith such news would break a mans heart; but pray bear it with a manly fortitude; if my Father should knock off, I could have no other remedy.

Bell. I have now no time to railly with you, I'le to my my dear *Theodora,* and hope to get her into so good a humour, that we shall not be long after you in Marriage: Adieu.   [*Ex.* Bellamour.]

Theodore. What ever you are in that, I am sure you are before hand with me in the death of a Father. How now Bullies, are you up so early? Sure you have lain rough, or have not slept to night.

[*Enter* Rant *and* Hazard.]

Rant. How now Lover that are, and Whore-master that was, you are full of your bobs.

Haz. What, I warrant you, you are got up early to write a fashionable *Sonnet,* without sense, upon the Divine *Isabella.*

Rant. How many Stars, Moons, Suns, Alablasters, Roses, Pearls, and Rubies, have you made use of for similies?

Haz. Come, prethee communicate, let's see the labour of thy Muse.

Theodore. As I live, drunk still: But, Gentlemen, I hate the name of a Muse, as I do that of a Baud; were I a Poet, I would invoke *Creswell* or *Gifford* before any Muse in Christendom.

Haz. Faith, thou art in the right, for they two can supply our necessities better than all the nine Muses.

Rant. But this is not our business, here is a young Gentleman at the door call'd Mr. *Timothy Squeeze,* that comes to wait on you.

Theodore. Hang him Rascal, keep him to your selves, he's fitter for your purpose; have you fleec'd him soundly?

Haz. Very sufficiently I assure you, but he is come upon a pleasant occasion; he says, he has done you and your Family such an injury.

Theodore. Pox on him, I will forgive him any but the trouble of his company.

Rant. Thou shalt see him, and when he tells thee his condition, thou wilt find we have Reveng'd thee to the full; I'll fetch him in.   [*Ex.* Rant.]

Theodore. How have you us'd the Rogue? You have won all his money.

Haz. That's not all, but I'll not forestall you, you shall be surprised into your pleasure ; he begg'd of us to make him friends with you, for fear you should kill him, he fears not your Father.

[*Enter* Rant *and* Timothy.]

Tim. Are you sure he will do me no hurt ?

Rant. I am, speak to him.

Tim. Sir, your Servant.

Theodore. Sir, Yours.

Tim. I beg your pardon from the bottom of my heart, for an injury I have done you, and your Family.

Theodore. What's that ?

Tim. Pray Sir, be not in passion, and I'le tell you ; You know Sir I should have been your Brother-in-Law Sir ; and last night it seems I was overtaken in *Campaigne*, and as these Gentlemen tell me (for I vow I remember not a word on't) I married one Mrs. *Joyce*, Mr. *Hazards* Cousin Sir : But your Sister sent me word she would have me kick'd out of the house, Sir, last night, or I should not have done it on my conscience Sir ; I find I did it in passion really.

Theodore. Oh brave Bullies, now you have Revenged me sufficiently.

Tim. Now Sir, I hope in God you will please to forgive me since I married in drink ; and I vow to God Sir, as I am an honest man, I meant no more hurt in't Sir, than I do at this present ; for I wak'd this morning Sir, and found my self in Bed with the said Mrs. *Joyce*, de' understand me, (and I vow she's a pure Bed-fellow, that's the truth on't) but at first I was frighted, and wondr'd what a dickens was the matter, when these Gentlemen came up with a Cawdle to me, and fac'd me down I was married Sir, and at last shew'd me the Ring, the License, and the Parsons Certificate Sir.

Theodore. No more Sir, I forgive you freely Sir.

Tim. Sir, I am beholding to you ; but if there be an offence, you must blame those Gentlemen ; for I protest and vow I intended to marry Mrs. *Thea*, or would I might ne're stir out of this place alive. But I tell you in private, if I had not married the aforesaid Mrs. *Joyce*, I believe they would have forc'd me to it ; for my part Sir, I don't like 'em ; for between you and I, they won above forty Pound on me. But to give the Devil his due, the Gentlewoman is a pretty Gentlewoman, and they say has a good Portion.

Theodore to Hazard *and* Rant. This Relation pleases me, but pray take away your Fool, for I have business of great concernment.

Rant. This was all we had to say to you. Fare you well.

Haz. Tim, come along, dear soul.

Tim. Ay, come Cousin ; [*To* Theodore.] Sir, your Servant to command.

[*Exeunt all but* Theodore.]

[Enter Robin.]

Robin. Sir, I have a Present for you, but let us begon Sir, and take it in another place ; pray follow me, I am weary with carrying it.

Theodore. What means the Fellow ?

Robin. Here is a Chest of money of your Father's that was hid in the Garden.

Theodore. Of my Fathers ! how camest thou by it ?

Robin. Not very honestly Sir, but this is no place to ask questions in, now I am Reveng'd on him for calling me thief ; follow me Sir.

Theodore. This is a lucky supply. [*Exeunt* Robin *and* Theodore.]

Enter at another door William, Cheatly, *and* Bridget,
with a Page.

Cheatly. Is Madam *Theodora* within ?

Will. She is gone out with Mr. *Bellamour.*

Cheatly. Is not your Master within ?

Will. We expect him every minute Madam. [*Ex.* Will.]

Cheatly. Now Mrs. *Bridget,* can you represent a Stately Countess ?

Bridget. Never fear me ; *Page,* hold up my Train Sirrah, I can beare my head as high as any Lady in Christendom.

Cheatly. Remember when any body Salutes you, to turn your Cheek to him, as great Ladies use ; that's very convenient too, for concealing a tainted breath.

Bridget. Mine is not so, but I'le not forget it.

Cheatly. But thou hast so used to offer thy mouth, that thou wilt forget it.

[Enter Goldingham.]

Oh Sir, your Servant, the Countess of *Puddle-Dock* is come to see Mrs. *Theodora.*

Gold. [*Aside.*] Countess of *Puddle-Dock !* I never heard of that Title, it may be 'tis some *Scotch* or *Irish* Title.

To Bridget. Madam, I kiss your Honour's hand : Where is my Daughter that she comes not to wait on her Honour ?

Cheatly. Not within. This is the Countess I spoke of. [*Softly.*]

Gold. Let me see ; if this be a Countess, and has such a Fortune, no more then of *Isabella ;* but I must into the Garden to my dear Gold. Madam, I'le wait on your Honour presently. [*Ex.* Goldingham.]

Cheatly. Is not this an amiable old Gentleman ?

Bridget. As bad as he is, I am not so nice, but I could make shift with him.

Golding. within.] Murder, murder, Oh Thieves, Thieves !

Cheat. What's the meaning of this, is the man mad ?

[*Enter* Goldingham.]

Gold. Thieves, thieves, murder, murder, death, devils, damnation, Hell and Furies, Thieves, thieves, I am undone, undone, they have cut my Throat, they have murder'd me, they have stole my money! Where is it! what's become on't? where are the Thieves? where have they hid themselves? whither shall I go to find 'em? what shall I do? shall I run? shall I stay? are they here? are they there? where are they?

Cheat. What is it transports you thus?

Gold. Oh, are you here, give me my money; [*He tugs and hales* Cheatly.] Where's my Gold? confess, or I'le rack you. Where is my dear Gold, my poor Gold? Give it me, conceale it no longer.

Cheat. Help, help, will you murder me?

Bridget. Are you Mad? 'tis Mrs. *Cheatly.*

Gold. Another! is there more of your number? I'll hang ye all, where is my money, Money, Money?

James. What's the Matter, Sir?

[*Enter* James, Roger, Will.]

Cheat. Come Countess, 'tis time to shift for our selves.

Goldingham falls on 'em with his Caine.] Oh you thieves, my Gold, my Gold, give me my Gold; I'le hang ye, I'le drown ye, I'le murder ye all; Oh my Gold, must I lose thee?

James. He raves help to hold him. [*He breaks from them, they run away.*]

Gold. I have lost my money, my life, my blood, my entrails, my heart, my vitals, I dye, I am dead, I am buried; will no body save my life, and help me to it? Oh, I am mad; what say you, will you? Hum; alas, I am mad, there's no body: Oh my money, my soule Justice, Justice, I will hang all the Towne; if *Isabella* has a hand in't, I will hang her; I will beg the help of Constables, Beadles, Church-wardens, Baylies, Sergeants, Justices, Aldermen, Judge, Gibbet, Gallowes, and Hangmen: I will hang my son and daughter if they be guilty: And if I find not my Money, I will hang my self.

James. My Master, Sir, is mad, be pleased to command him in His Majesties name to keep his worships wits.

Gold. Oh neighbour Justice, you are come in season, I am robb'd, undone, make me a Mittimus.

Justice. For whom neighbour *Goldingham?*

Gold. For all *Coven garden*, I will hang every body, oh my Gold!

Justice. You'l spoyl all, if you be thus outragious; we must examine such things privately, or you will never have notice of your money.

Gold. Oh my money, I cannot contain my self, but if you will assist me, I'le endeavour.

(83)

James. Ha, is my Master robb'd ? Now I may be fully revenged of our *dominus factotum* for my beating, and other things.

[*To Goldingham.*]   I am mistaken, or I can give you some light into this business.

Goldingham. Speake what you can say, if you do not discover it, I will hang you.

James. I do certainly believe that Mr. *Bellamour* has it.

Gold. What, he that appear'd so true and faithfull to me ?

James. The same Sir, I believe 'tis he that has robb'd you.

Gold. Pray Sir make his Mittimus, I'le hang him if there were no more of the race of all mankind.

Justice. But why do you believe it Sir !

James. Why do I believe it Sir ?

Just. Yes.

James. Why, why, why, because I do believe it.

Just. But I must have some proofs.

Gold. Did you see him dig where my money was hidden ?

James. Oh yes Sir, why should I say so else ? Where did you lay your money ?

Gold. In the Garden.

James. Ay, there I saw him digging : What was your money in ?

Gold. In a Chest.

James. Why there's the business now, I saw him have a Chest, and the very same Chest you mean.

Justice. What manner of Chest is it ?

James. What manner of one : 'Sdeath I shall be snap'd !   [*Aside.*

Justice. How is it made ?

James. Why 'tis made——'tis made very like a kind of a Chest : extraordinary like a Chest.

Justice. But how ?

James. Why 'tis a great Chest.

Gold. Mine is a little one.   Oh my Gold !

James. Ay so was this in it self, but for what it contained it was a great one, and was so heavy, that I am sure it made him puffe and blow to carry it.

Gold. It must be the same, mine is very heavy.

Justice. Hold a little, pray what Colour is it of ?

James. Of what Colour ?

Justice. Yes.

James. Why it is of a Colour, a certain Colour, I know not what a deus they call it, but really it is a very pretty Colour for a Chest, that's the truth on't.

James. Was it not a red.

Gold. No, no, mine's a green one.

James. Lord, you are so hasty, a reddish green I was going to say.

Gold. The same Sir; pray make his mittimus, and let him be hang'd.

[*Enter* Bellamour.]

James. Here he comes, let him not discover this of me; perhaps he'l confess it.

Gold. Come you Villain, come near and confess your wickednesse, your abominable action.

Bell. What do you mean Sir?

Gold. Oh horrid traytor, do you not blush?

Bell. Has he heard any thing of his daughter and me; for what should I blush Sir?

Gold. Oh impudence, as if he knew not what I meant; but all your villany is discovered: Oh wretch, to come into my house to betray me, and abuse my goodness with so infamous an action!

Bell. Sir, since you have discover'd me, I'l make no more excuses.

[*Aside.*]

James. That I should guess so right when I swear at a venture: I told you, Sir, he'd confess. [*To the Justice.*]

Justice. He ha' confess'd in part, but we must have more yet.

Bell. It was my design to tell you of this, but I stay'd for a happier opportunity, and I beseech you be not angry till I give my reasons.

Gold. Oh abominable insolence, he would be giving me reasons for his infamous theft, like an impudent Thiefe.

Bell. These Titles are none of mine, and you'l find, if you examine it, that my crime is pardonable.

Gold. Oh devill, pardonable, to take away my soul, my life, my blood!

Bell. I am in a condition to do your blood no wrong, and to make full reparation for this pretended injury.

Gold. Oh you overjoy me! will you make restitution?

Bell. Your honour shall be fully satisfyed.

Gold. Pox on my honour, I don't talk of my honour. But what could incite you to such action?

Bell. Love.

Golding. A pox on your love, admirable love indeed, love of my broad pieces.

Bell. No Sir, it is not your Gold that I care for, let me but enjoy what I have already, and I care for nothing in the world beside.

Gold. Oh intollerable insolence! he justifies his theft, and would keep what he has stollen. He distracts me; Sir, you shall be hang'd, drawn, and quarter'd, before you shall keep the least part of it.

Just. No Sir, you must not keep what you have got, by your favour.

Bell. With your favour Sir, but I must; we have mutually engaged our faiths, and are now married, and nothing but death shall part us.

Golding. Engaged his faith, and married to my Chest!　　　[*Aside.*]
'Tis enough, make his Mittimus, that he may be hang'd, and so be divorced from it.

Just. Here is some mystery: Where is this Treasure you have taken?

Bell. Here in the house.

Just. Have you not broke it up?

Bell. Broke her up! better words Sir, or I shall forget my respect to you; I assure you shee's too honest.

Gold. How, my Chest of money too honest.　　　[*Aside.*]

Bell. Her fair eyes have inspir'd in me a more refined passion.

Gold. The Faire eyes of my chest.　　　[*Aside.*]

Bell. I see Sir 'tis in vain to conceale the truth any longer. 'Tis not a quarter of an Houre since your Daughter and I were married in *Coven garden;* and without a Portion.

Gold. Oh devil, is that affront added to my losse?

Bell. Without portion, consider that Sir.

Gold. Make his Mittimus, you shall be hang'd you Villaine, send him to the Gatehouse quickly.

Bell. How, be hang'd! I assure you, though I stole your daughter, 'twas with her own consent.

Just. But you have confess'd a more capital theft; or if you had not, 'tis sworn against you, and I must send you to the *Gaol.*

[*Enter* Theodora.]

Theodora. Oh Heaven! what do I hear? Sir, if ever you had any affection for me, hear me now; this Gentleman is a Man of Quality and Fortune.

Gold. A curse on him, he has rais'd his Fortune on my ruines, and for his Quality 'twill bring him to the Gallows.

Theodora. For Heaven's sake Sir use no extremity on him, I consented to all he did; if there be a fault committed against you, I am equally guilty, and will suffer with him.

Gold. Heaven! my own Daughter guilty of such an action, she shall be hang'd, send her to the Gaol immediately; no less than six thousand Broad Pieces at a time.

Theodora. Sir, I understand you not.

Gold. Oh cunning Baggage! look you Mr. *Justice,* she understands me not; I'le have her hang'd, my own Daughter Rob me.

Theodora. Rob you! I am amaz'd.

Bell. Sure Sir, you are not *compos mentis.*

Justice. I am sorry to find ye guilty of so great a Fellony, I must send ye both to the Gaol without Bail or Mainprize.

[*Enter Theodore.*]

Theodore. Brother, I heard you were in this condition, and came to rescue you.

Gold. Oh Villain! are you come to heighten my affliction with the sight of you?

Theodore. Sir, I come about a little business that concerns you.

Gold. Business with me? you insolent Rebel, what can that be.

Theodore. Sir, the money is right.

Gold. What money you impertinent Ass?

Theodore. The broad pieces that were in the Garden, they are just Six thousand; and I'le give you an Acquittance under my Hand for them.

Gold. O Devil, had you them?

Theodore. They were received by my order, to my own proper use and behoof; *I say Received* per me *Theodore.*

Goldingham
strikes at } O Barbarous insolence, I will cut your Throat.
Theodore.

Justice. Nay, good Neighbour keep the peace.

Gold. I cannot keep the peace, I will not keep the peace, let the peace keep its self; 'tis impossible to keep the peace.

Justice. By your leave Sir, you must keep the peace, and not be Judge in your own case.

Gold. Send him to Gaol then presently.

Justice. Be patient, and I will.

Theodore. Why would you have the Conscience to hang your Son?

Gold. Give me my Gold, and I'le spare your life.

Theodore. No Sir, your Gold is in sure hands, 'tis held in Mortmain.

Gold. Then I will hang you Rogue, make his *Mittimus.*

Theodore. You may please to remember, that there is a *Colledge* Lease of 4 hundred Pounds a year, that you hold only by my life; you will lose that (if you hang me) besides your broad pieces, of which you shall never have one by Heaven.

Gold. Nay then, I cannot be in a worse condition than I am; make hast Sir with his *Mittimus.*

Justice. 'Tis a making.

Theodore. Hold Sir; you must not make it, I did not Steal the Gold; I did but Seize upon't for the King's use.

Gold. By Heaven, I owe the King not a farthing, I paid the last assessment, it went to my heart I am sure; and yet, to say the truth, the Assessors have stretch'd their consciences against the King all over

England, God bless them: Have you the impudence to say I owe the King Money?

Theodore. Assist me Brother. [*To Bellamour*.]
[*To Gold*.] Do you think Sir the King will let you commit [*Softly*.] Treason for nothing?

Gold. Treason.

Theodore. There are Arms and Ammunition in the Vault Sir, if you be pleas'd to remember.

Bell. Have a care what you do Sir, Treason will fall heavy upon a rich man; you will be an excellent morsel for a Courtier.

Gold. Have ye the impudence to speak of a Plot ye drew me into, ye brace of Traitors and Villains?

Theodore. Sir I know nothing of a Plot, not I, but my Brother and I can swear we saw Arms and Ammunition put in a Vault; and we know from whom they were Receiv'd, and the consideration too. We shall find friends Sir.

Bell. Sir Release the Gold, and make no more ado; if it should be found out that we know of the Plot, we should be pardon'd, for bringing in so rich and Capital an offender; but you would find no more mercy, than ever you shew'd to one that forfeited a Morgage.

Gold. A curse on these Villains, I am caught in my own snare; they are in the right, I shall be sure to be hang'd, but if I were sure they were to be hang'd with me, it were no matter: But Son, are you in earnest? Will you not give me some of my Gold again?

Theodore. Not one piece by heaven, and pray Sir believe I deal fairly with you, that I ask no more; you know, I have not had a shilling of you these dozen years, 'tis time now to gather my Arrears.

Gold. What will become of me? I must either lose my money or my life, I know not which is best; I think I must go hang my self, for fear of being hang'd.

Justice. What shall I send him to Gaol?

Gold. No, let it alone, I must forgive the Rogue for this time.

Theodore. And do you release me of the money, before all these witnesses?

Gold. Yes, yes, but you cursed Villain I will be reveng'd on you, I'le marry *Isabella*, get Children, and disinherit you of all the rest of my Estate.

Theodore. Now since you have Releast me, look in your Chests in the Vault, and you will find nothing but Lumber.

Gold. And was it no Plot you drew me into?

Theodore. No by Heaven, I but pretended it, and your hard usage forced me to these extreamities.

Gold. Oh unheard of Villain, I will go marry *Isabella* instantly, and I hope you will hang your self.

Theodore. Stay Sir, I have one thing more to ask of you. This Lady and I are Married; and beg your pardon, and your blessing.

[*Enter Isabella.*]

Isabella. Sir I beg your blessing and your pardon; Heaven would have it thus, and I could not help it.

Gold. 'Sdeath and Hell! Married! you two Married!

Theodore. 'Tis now too late to perplex your self.

Gold. Oh Treacherous Wretches! Oh this Engine of the Devil, *Cheatly* with her damn'd Countess of *Puddle-Dock*.

Theodore. Will you give us your blessing Sir? we kneel for it. [*They kneel.*]

Gold. Yes, I will give you my blessing.

Isabella. I shall receive it joyfully.

Gold. May all the curses e're attended Marriage fall on you.

Isabella. Oh impious wish.

Theodore. We are obliged to you Sir.

Gold. May invincible impotence possess you, raging Lust her, and tormenting jealousie both of ye.

Justice. For shame Neighbour be not so wicked.

Gold. May the perpetual spirit of contention wait on ye, may ye never in your lives agree in one thing; may the name of quiet ne're be heard betwixt ye; and to compleat all, may ye never be assunder: and so Farewel. [*Ex. Gold.*]

Justice. I'le after him, and try if I can mollifie him.

Theodora. Dear Sister, I am infinitely happy in my Relation to you.

Bellamour [*To himself.*] It must be so. Oh heaven! it is my sister (though I have not seen her these nine years) yet she has so much of her former Countenance remaining, that I am sure 'tis she.

Theodore. Dear *Isabella*, here is a worthy Gentleman you must call Brother.

Bell. I have a neerer Title to her than what you can give me, she's my own Sister *Isabella*.

Theodore. This is wonderful.

Isabella. Indeed I had an Elder Brother beyond Sea, but we (having not seen him in nine years, nor heard from him these fifteen Months) concluded him dead.

Bell. (To his great grief) my younger Brother will find it otherwise.

Isabella. But is it possible! are you my Brother? indeed you have some resemblance of my Father, when he was living.

Bell. If you be Sir *William Raines* his Daughter of the *North* (as I am sure you are) I am your Brother; but thou wert too young when I left *England*, to have any impressions left of me now.

Isabella. My dear Brother, I am convinced, this is a happy hour, this will revive my dear Mother, who has kept her Chamber ever since my Fathers death.

Theodore. My dear Brother, now you are doubly so, but friendship yet shall be the stricter tye.

Theodora. This is a wonderful and happy union of our Families.

Bell. To shew you more clearly I am your Brother, (though my Father died without a Will) I know it was his intention to give you five thousand Pounds, which upon my honour you shall have.

Theodore. This is generosity in the highest point; but I was rich in the possession of my *Isabella*, beyond the thoughts of Dowry; but if I live to have my Father's Estate, faith I'le be even with you.

Isabella. This noble offer confirms me, you are my Brother; but why did you so long conceal your self?

Bell. That my dear *Theodora* can best tell you. But let us haste to see my afflicted Mother.

[Enter Constable and Watch, with Squeeze.]

Constable. They say the Justices Worship is here Gentlemen.

Theodore. The *Constable* with *Squeeze!* pray let's stay a moment after our Comedy, that ends so pleasantly, in hopes to see a Farse.

Squeeze. Heaven! what confusion am I in, and besides my bones are all loose with the fall last night.

Theodore. What's the matter Mr. *Constable?*

Constable. Why Sir, this old Gentleman (not having the fear of God before his Eyes) by the malice and instigation of the Devil, did yesternight *vi & armis*, contrary to the Peace of our Sovereign Lord the King, his Crown and Dignity; commit carnal copulation with one Mrs. *Lettice*.

Bell. The Style of an *Inditement*.

Theodore. How now Mr. *Squeeze*, is the snare fallen upon you? can you help a man to three or four hundred Pound at fifty in the hundred, with good security?

Squeeze. You are very merry Sir, 'tis well if you have cause. Oh! Mrs. *Cheatly* what shall I do? my reputation is ruin'd, I am undone for ever.

[Enter Mrs. Cheatly.]

Cheatly. Oh Sir, there is more affliction for you yet, your Son lost fifty Pound last night, and Married a Wench, one Mrs. *Joyce*, that was kept by Alderman *Do-Little*.

Squeeze. Oh Heaven! all my misfortunes come together; this added to the other, will distract me.

Theodore. This is for your damn'd Brokeage and Use.

Cheatly. Could you not have brib'd the *Constable?*

Squeeze. He durſt not let me go for fear of the *Bullies?* what shall I do; what shall I do?

Cheatly. I would be loath to put you to inconvenience, but if you would own my Daughter for your wife it would soon preserve or at leaſt repair your credit.

Squeeze. She says true.   [*Aside.*]

Cheatly. And if you would really make her your wife, you would be fully reveng'd on your Son for his rash Marriage.

Squeeze. Ha, that's true again directly.   [*Aside.*]

Cheatly. If you do it not, the poor Girle will be ruin'd for ever in her reputation; which you know is her support at present.

Squeeze. She is in the right, there is no way to save my reputation but this; if my disgrace should be published, no Godly Citizen will truſt me; old Men in this Town had as good marry their wenches, for they ſtand 'em in more money, and they keep 'em as long as if they were their wives.

[*Enter* Hazard *and* Lettice.]

Hazard. Mr. *Squeeze,* here's your Lady, pray reſtore her Red Stocking, and take your own Black one; Oh *Theodore,* thou art gone the way of all flesh, I hear thou't Married.

Theodore. I am Sir, for all your inſtructions to the contrary.

Hazard. Then thou art a loſt Man; yet faith 'tis as pretty a Girle for a fortnight's use, or so, as a Man could wish.

Bell. I find this *Bully* has the common place wit of all the young Fops in this Town; in Railing againſt Marriage.

Hazard. Now art thou, *Theodore,* for a year, condemn'd to eat and drink, go to Playes, to Church, and lie with thy own wife moſt unreasonable; But 'tis but having a little patience, and we shall have you amongſt us again, as honeſt a sinner as the beſt of us.

[*Enter* Rant, Timothy, *and* Joyce.]

Tim. O Lord, here's my Father, I am so affraid of him.

Rant. Bear up to him, you say you have Two hundred Pound a year left by an Aunt, which he can't touch.

Tim. Ay, I have so.

Rant. Stand up and own your wife to him; then besides 'twill vex the heart of *Theodora* to see how you have bob'd her.

Tim. Ay, I think so, (do you underſtand me?) I hope 'twill break her heart, de' see?

Rant. Sir, here's your Son and his Lady, come to ask your blessing.

Squeeze. Oh you infinite Rascal!

Tim. Rascal Sir, I am the Son of a Scrivener, and they say I take mightily like my Father too.

(91)

Squeeze. Oh Villain! marry a Whore, out of my sight.

Tim. A Whore Sir, I vow to God I scorn your words, do you mark me, she's as Pretty a civil young Lady, and I am sure I had her Maiden-Head, had I not my dear?

Joyce. Yes indeed my dear, the best I had for you.   [*Aside.*]

Squeeze. Oh infamous Villain! marry a Strumpet?

Joyce. Sir, I'd have you kick'd if you were not my Father-in-Law.

Hazard. Dare to speak one ill word more of my Cousin, and I'le cut your Throat, old Sot.

Squeeze. I am horrible affraid of this Hector; but I will be Reveng'd of the Rogue my Son.

Joyce. Now Madam *Lettice* I hope you'l own me to be equal at least with your Ladyship, Mr. *Tim.* has made me an honest woman; that's more than you are.

Rant. Farewel *Theodore*, thou art no more a man of this world; Marriage alters some men, and makes them forget their friends, as much as Perferment does.

Hazard. But I hope he has more grace.

Theodore. No more of your senseless Railing against Marriage, 'tis dull and common.

[*Enter Justice.*]

Justice. There is no mollifying of your Father, he's run out in a rage; he has shut himself in his Closset, and will not be spoke to; *Constable* what makes you here?

Constable. Sir we have brought an old Gentleman here before you, upon suspition of Fornication, an please your Worship.

Justice. Whom, Mr. *Squeeze!* can a man of your years be guilty of Fornication?

Constable. Sir, we took him leaping out of a Window half undress'd, and for haste he had put on a Red Silk-stocking of the Gentlewomans from whom he rose.

Justice. Is this true?

Squeeze. 'Tis true, I was in bed with this Gentlewoman, but she's my wife; and I hope that's no offence.

Justice. Your wife.

Squeeze. Yes, and before all this company I avow her to be so.

Tim. O fie for shame Sir, marry a Strumpet.

Squeeze. Peace you insolent Rascal.

Theodore. *Lettice*, I wish thee joy of thy old Rascal.

Lettice. I thank you Mr. *Theodore.* Now Mrs. *Joyce* I hope you think not your self my equal: Down on your knees huswife and ask me blessing.

Joyce. I scorn your words, I shall never endure to call you Mother-in-Law while I live.

Cheatly. Madam *Isabella*, I wish you much joy with this Gentleman, and he is young enough, and handsom enough to give you good store on't.

Theodore. Mrs. *Cheatly*, to shew my gratitude to you, I have a hundred pieces ready for you ; and *Robin*, you I will make my particular care.

Robin. Sir, to shew that I have taken some care of you, I have provided Fiddles for you.

Theodore. Let 'em enter, wee'l borrow my Fathers House for a Dance ; for perhaps we shall never come in it again.

[*Enter Fiddles.*]

Robin. What say you Mrs. *Cheatly*, shall you and I marry, or continue to love on as we did ?

Cheatly. I am very indifferent *Robin*, take thy own choice.

Robin. Why then as you were.

Cheatly. Content.

Bell. Strike up. [*They Dance.*]

Theodore. Now we have done, I must confess I have transgress'd in my duty to my Father, which I could not help ; unless I would have neglected a greater, which I ought to your Beauty my dear *Isabella*, and my Love ; and I hope

> *My passion will a just excuse be thought :*
> *What is urg'd on by love, can be no fault.*

F I N I S.

Epsom-Wells.

A

COMEDY,

Acted at the

DUKE'S THEATRE.

Written by

THO. SHADWELL.

Μεγάλως Ἀπολισθαίνειν ἁμάρτημα εὐγενές.

Licensed, Feb. 17, 167¾. *Roger L'Eſtrange.*

LONDON,

Printed by *J.M.* for *Henry Herringman,* at the Sign of the *Blew Anchor* in the Lower Walk of the New Exchange. MDCLXXIII.

Source.

THIS comedy, which paints contemporary life at a fashionable spa, seems to own no direct original for its intrigues, rather lazily pursued, as indeed such fleeting amours are apt to be engaged in at similar resorts, yesterday and to-day, and doubtless to-morrow.

The cuckoldom of the cits Bisket and Fribble might be fairly paralleled in Elizabethan comedy and in other Restoration plays, but Shadwell has invested the dissipations of the Wells, high and low, with great spirit and verve. Clodpate, as was recognized at the time, is an admirable character, drawn with excellent strokes.

It is doubtful whether the mock marriage of Mrs. Jilt with the footman officiating was suggested by the Earl of Oxford's deception of Roxolana, as related in Grammont's *Memoirs*. When at the conclusion of the piece Peg pulls off the false beard worn by Woodly's servant, who is in canonicals, and cries : " Look you, this is the first Parson I ever ordained," there may be a reminiscence of *The Silent Woman*, Act V, Dauphine's " I thank you good doctor Cutbeard and parson Otter." " *Pulls their false beards and gowns off.*"

Jonson's *Bartholomew Fair* has been mentioned in connexion with these scenes, but to me the suggestion is most inapposite. The two pieces are widely dissimilar.

Ignorance both of Molière and of Shadwell has prated about borrowings from *Le médecin malgre lui* in *Epsom Wells*.

Some five and thirty years after Shadwell's comedy had fallen out of the theatrical repertory that arch-wag Sam Foote conveyed Mr. and Mrs. Bisket, Mr. and Mrs. Fribble into his rollicking farce *The Mayor of Garrat*, and dubbed them Jerry Sneak, Mrs. Sneak, Bruin, and Mrs. Bruin. *The Mayor of Garrat* was produced at the Haymarket in July, 1763, with Weston as Jerry, in which rôle he made a great hit ; Mrs. Daly as the vixenish wife ; Davis as Bruin ; and Mrs. Osborne as Jane Bruin. Foote himself doubled Major Sturgeon and Matthew Mug.

It is true Foote's farce is slight, but 'tis merry, although his japeries are mere milk-and-water to Shadwell's lusty stingo.

The gossip of the day said that Shadwell was assisted by Sir Charles Sedley in *Epsom Wells*, and Dryden's *Mac Flecknoe* does not forget the taunt :

> But let no alien *S–dl–y* interpose
> To lard with wit thy hungry *Epsom* prose.

Shadwell has defended himself against this imputation with no little zest, and truth to tell Sedley wanted all his wit and more for his own comedies, which are none of the liveliest.

(97)

Theatrical History.

EPSOM WELLS, which ranks among Shadwell's best comedies, was produced at Dorset Garden on the 2 December, 1672, Charles II himself being present at the first performance. The King was so delighted with the fun that he again visited the theatre on the 4 December; and on the 27 of that month, during the Christmas revels, the play was given at Whitehall when the Queen also attended.

Downes in the *Roscius Anglicanus* records: " *Epsom-Wells*, a Comedy wrote by Mr. *Shadwell*. Mr. *Rains* was acted by Mr. *Harris* ; *Belvil*, by Mr. *Betterton* ; *Woodly*, by Mr. *Smith* ; Justice *Clodpole*, Mr. *Underhill* ; *Carolina*, Mrs. *Johnson* ; *Lucia*, Mrs. *Gibbs* ; Mrs. *Jilt* by Mrs. *Betterton* ; Mr. *Nokes*, Mr. *Bisket* ; Mr. *Angel Fribble*. This Play in general being admirably acted produced great profit to the company.

Note, Mrs. *Johnson* in this comedy, dancing a Jigg so charming well, Love's power in a little time after coerc'd her to dance more charming else where."

Of Underhill, Cibber says: " In the coarse, rustic humour of *Justice Clodpate* in ' Epsom Wells ' he was a delightful brute."

Epsom Wells, a high favourite with royalty—(it was, among other occasions, seen by Charles II 5 December, 1673, and 20 February, 1680)—remained in the repertory of the theatre, being very frequently acted and never failing of loud and generous applause.

There was a revival of particular importance in 1693 with music by Henry Purcell.

Originally the song *How pleasant is mutual love* (Act II) was set by Nicholas Staggins, and may be found in Playford's " *Choice Songs and Ayres . . . Composed by Several Gentlemen of His Majesties Musick*. The First Book," 1673. Here also is given, *Oh, how I abhor*, the county song (Act IV), set by Robert Smith. Clodpate's old song *Lay by your pleading* (Act II), with an anonymous tune is printed in volume V of the 1714 edition of *Pills to Purge Melancholy* ; edition 1720, VI, p. 190.

The erroneous statement, which has been loosely repeated, that Purcell in 1676 wrote music to *Epsom Wells*, seems due in the first place to Rimbault, who was misled by finding in the Second Book of *Thesaurus Musicus*, 1694, " A New Song in *Epsome-Wells* set by *Henry Purcell*." This is a two-part song " Leave these useless Arts in loving," and was written for the 1693 revival of *Epsom Wells*, being either an additional number or substituted for one of the original songs by Staggins and Smith. A tune called " Epsom Wells " which occurs in seventeenth-century MSS. has no connexion with the play. It is ascribed to Paisable, and the words are by D'Urfey. It is often known as " The Scotch Law at Epsom."

The instrumental music to *Epsom Wells* has not been traced.

11 July, 1702, *Epsom Wells* was given for the benefit of Mrs. Moor, when Pinkethman for the second time delivered his comical epilogue.

At Drury Lane 18 December, 1708, *Epsom Wells* is announced as " Not acted 10 years." Wilks appeared as Woodly; Powell Rains; Mills Bevil; Johnson Clodpate, a masterly performance; Bullock Bisket; Pinkethman Fribble, a rôle in which he excelled; Pack Cuff; Mrs. Oldfield Carolina; Mrs. Porter Lucia; Mrs. Moor Mrs. Jilt; Mrs. Saunders Mrs. Bisket; and Mrs. Baker Mrs. Fribble.

On Wednesday, 15 October, 1714, *The Spectator* (DX) advertised : " By Her Majesty's Company of Comedians. At the Theatre Royal in Drury Lane, this present Wednesday, being the 15th of October, will be presented a Comedy call'd Epsom Wells. The Part of Justice Clodpate by Mr. Johnson, Frible by Mr. Pinkethman, Brisket [*sic*] by Mr. Bullock, Sen., Kick by Mr. Pack, Cuff by Mr. Burkhead, Bevil by Mr. Mills, Woodly by Mr. Bowman, Rains by Mr. Bullock, Jun., Mrs. Woodly by Mrs. Knight, Carolina by Mrs. Bradshaw, Lucia by Mrs. Porter, Mrs. Bisket by Mrs. Saunders. By Her Majesty's Command no Persons are to be admitted behind the Scenes."

2 April, 1715, at Drury Lane, *Epsom Wells* is played for Pinkethman's benefit. Woodly Wilks; Bevil Mills; Fribble Pinkethman; Bisket Norris; Justice Clodpate Johnson; Mrs. Woodly Mrs. Bicknell; Carolina Mrs. Oldfield; Lucia Mrs. Porter; Mrs. Bisket Mrs. Margaret Saunders. During the winter season at the same theatre the play was given on 9 December.

Shadwell's comedy, however, began to fall out of the repertory, and it had not been seen for several years before Pinkethman, with whom it was a prime favourite, chose it as his benefit at Drury Lane 23 April, 1724. He was supported by a strong company, Wilks, Mills, Johnson, young Wilks, Norris, Harper, Mrs. Thurmond, Mrs. Younger, and Mrs. Heron. After Pinkethman's retirement in 1724 *Epsom Wells* was but seldom given. On 22 July, 1726, it was revived at Lincoln's Inn Fields. " Never acted there " with Milward as Bevil, Chapman Woodly, Bullock Bisket, and the performance was repeated with much applause. Yet it does not appear any longer to have kept the stage.

Dramatis Personæ.

Rains,
Bevil, } Men of Wit and Pleasure.
Woodly,

Clodpate, A Country Justice, a publick spirited, politick, discontented Fop, an immoderate Hater of *London*, and a Lover of the Country above measure, a hearty true *English Coxcomb*.

Toby, *Clodpate*'s Man.

Kick,
Cuff, } Two cheating, sharking, cowardly Bullies.

Bisket, A Comfit-maker, a quiet, humble, civil Cuckold, governed by his Wife, whom he very much fears and loves at the same time, and is very proud of.

Fribble, A Haberdasher, a surly Cuckold, very conceited and proud of his Wife, but pretends to govern and keep her under.

Two Country Fellows.

Foot-boy.

Mrs. *Woodly, Woodly*'s Wife, Jilting, unquiet, troublesom, and very Whorish.

Lucia,
Carolina, } Two young Ladies, of Wit, beauty and Fortune.

Mrs. *Bisket*, An impertinent, imperious Strumpet, Wife to *Bisket*.

Dorothy Fribble, Wife to *Fribble*, an humble, submitting Wife, who Jilts her Husband that way, a very Whore.

Mrs. *Jilt*, A silly, affected Whore, that pretends to be in Love with most men, and thinks most men in love with her, and is always boasting of Love-Letters and mens favours, yet a Pretender to Vertue.

Peg, Her Sister, Mrs. *Woodly*'s Maid.

Parson, Hectors, Constable and Watch, and Fiddlers.

To his G R A C E the

DUKE of *NEW-CASTLE*, &c.

May it please your Grace,

YOur Grace has, by so many and extraordinary favours, so entirely made me your own, that I cannot but think whatever is mine is so. This makes me bold to present you with this Comedy, which the Town was extremely kind to, and which, I confess, I am more fond of than of any thing I have ever wrote, and therefore think my self obliged to dedicate it to your Grace, since whatever I can value most among my small Possessions is your due. And though the return be in no measure proportionable to the obligations I have received ; yet I hope I shall not be thought ungrateful, since I offer the best I have to your Grace, who I think I may say are the only *Mecænas* of our Age, I am sure the only one that I can boast of.

You are he who still preserves and maintains the Magnificence and Grandeur of our ancient Nobility ; and being one that's truly great in Mind as well as Fortune, you take delight in the rewarding and encouraging of Art and Wit : And while others detract from Poetry, or at least neglect it, your Grace not only encourages it by your great Example, but protects it too. *Welbeck* is indeed the only place where the best Poets can find a good reception. Your Grace well understanding their noble Science, and admiring it, while some Men envy it, and others are grossly ignorant of it ; and indeed, none but the latter can slightly esteem it, who commonly are solid Block-heads, that value Business and Drudgery, which every industrious Fool is capable of, before refined Wit and Sence. It is a certain sign of a sordid and foolish Age, when Poetry is depressed ; Men, by reason of their Folly and loosness of Manners, either not caring to imitate the generous Characters represented by it, or fearing the Satyr of it.

Your Grace is above the imitating of generous Characters made by Poets, being your self an Original which they can but faintly copy ; nor are you less for your Greatness, Wisdom and Integrity above their Satyr. So that your Grace is fitly qualified in all particulars for the support of poor neglected Poetry. Your Excellence in the Art is enough to keep up the Dignity of it, and your Greatness to encourage and protect it. And accordingly, your Grace does so magnificently extend your Favours to

(102)

the Poets, that your great Example is enough to attone the neglect of all the Nation, and among all whom your Grace has obliged, there is none shall be more ready, upon all occasions, to testifie his Gratitude, than,

My Lord,

Your Grace's most obedient,

humble Servant,

Tho. Shadwell.

PROLOGUE

Written by Sir *C. S.*

POets and Thieves can scarce be rooted out,
Scarce ne're so hardly, they'll have th'other bout ;
Burnt in the hand the Thieves fall to't agen,
And Poets hiſt, cry they did so to Ben——— :
Like Boys, who have at School too oft been ſtript,
They have no feeling in the part that's whipt.
They're for your pity, not your anger, fit,
They're e'en such fools, they wou'd be thought t' have wit.
Elsewhere you all can flatter, why not here ;
You'll say you pay, and so may be severe :
Judge for your selves then Gallants as you pay,
And lead not each of you his Bench aſtray :
Let easie Citts be pleas'd with all they hear,
Go home and to their Neighbours praise our Ware.
They with good ſtomachs come, and fain wou'd eat,
You nothing like, and make them loath their meat.
Though some men are with Wine, Wit, Beauty cloy'd,
The Creatures ſtill by others are enjoy'd.
'Tis not fair Play, that one for his Half Crown
Shou'd judge, and rail, and damn for half the Town.
But do your worſt ; if once the Pit grows thin,
Your dear lov'd Masks will hardly venture in.
Then w' are reveng'd on you, who needs muſt come
Hither, to shun your own dull selves at home :
But you kind Burgers who had never yet,
Either your Heads or Bellies full of wit :
Our Poet hopes to please ; but not too well ;
Nor wou'd he have the angry Criticks swell.
A moderate Fate beſt fits his humble mind,
Be neither they too sharp, nor you too kind.

PROLOGUE to the King and Queen, spoken at *Whitehall*.

POets and Souldiers used to various chance,
Cannot expect they should each day advance ;
Sometimes their Wreaths they miss, sometimes obtain ;
But whensoe're one luckie hit they gain,
Loudly the triumphs of that day they boast,
And ne're reflect on all their Battels lost,
So, Royal Sir, the Poet of this night,
Since he contributed to your delight,
No thoughts of former losses does retain,
But boasts that now he has not liv'd in vain :
His tide of joy will to ambition swell,
He that would think his whole life managed well,
Once pleasing him———
T' whom all the labours of our lives are due,
Has now liv'd twice, since he has twice pleas'd you.
* (If this for him had been by others done,
  (After this honour sure they'd claim their own.
Yet, to compleat his wishes, does remain
This new addition, which he hopes to gain,
That you, the other glory of our Isle,
Would grace his labours with your Royal smile.
Though he has faults, yet, Madam, you will save
The Criminal your Royal Lord forgave ;
And that indulgence he will much prefer
To all th' applauses of the Theater.
A common Audience gives but common praise,
Th' applause of Princes must confer the Bays.

* These two Lines were writ in answer to the calumny of some impotent and envious Scriblers, and some industrious Enemies of mine, who would have made the Town and Court believe, though I am sure they themselves did not, that I did not write the Play ; but at last it was found to be so frivolous a piece of malice, it left an impression upon few or none.

Epsom-Wells.

ACT I. SCENE I.

Enter Mrs. Woodly, Bisket, *Mrs.* Bisket, Fribble *and his Wife,* Kick,
    Cuff, Dorothy *and* Margaret ; *to* Toby *and others, drinking at the Wells.*

Bisk. I Vow it is a pleasurable Morning ; the Waters tast so finely after
    being fudled last Night.   Neighbour *Fribble,* here's a Pint to you.
        Fribb. I'll pledge you, Mr. *Bisket,* I have drunk eight already.
    Mrs. *Bisk.* How do the Waters agree with your Ladyship ?
    Mrs. *Wood.* Oh Soveraignly ; how many Cups are you arriv'd to ?
    Mrs. *Bisk.* Truly six, and they pass so kindly——
    Mrs. *Wood.* 'Tis a delicious Morning.
    Cuff. Honest *Kick,* how is it ? you were drunk last night ; I was so,
and was damnably beaten.
    Kick. I was drunk, *Ned Cuff,* and was not beaten, but beat ; I am come
to wash away my Claret, but you'l scarce wash away your black Eye.
    Mrs. *Fribb.* I am glad to see your Ladyship this Morning, you look so
fresh and fair ; my service to you, Madam.
    Kick. How the white Aprons scuttle, and leap, and dance yonder ; some
of 'em are dancing the Hey.
    Kick. Many a *London* Strumpet comes to Jump and wash down her
unlawful Issue, to prevent shame ; but more especially charges.
    Cuff. Others come hither to procure Conception.
    Kick. Ay Pox, that's not from the Waters, but something else that
shall be nameless.
    Cuff. I have a great mind to run roaring in amongst 'em all.
    Kick. Thou hadst as good fling thy self among the Lyons in the Tower
when they are fasting. They'll tear thee in pieces, but wee'll have a course
as they are going from the Wells.
    Cuff. Agreed : we seldom use to miss of some kind good body to
supply our necessities that way.
    Fribb. Is your Ladyships Coach here ?
    Mrs. *Wood.* It goes before, I'll follow it on foot for the pleasure of
the walk.

Mrs. *Bisk.* Madam, good Morrow, have your Ladyships Waters pass'd well.

Mrs. *Wood.* Yes wonderfully, I'l be going.   [*Exit* Mrs. *Wood.*

Bisk. Mr. *Kick,* and Mr. *Cuff,* good Morrow to you, we shall have you at the Bowling-Green in the afternoon.

Kick. I play on your side.

Bisk. I know it, and I'l lay all I am worth on't.

Kick. I hope he will, *Cuff,* that we may ruine him.

Fribb. And I am on my Neighbour *Bisket*'s side all I can rap and rend.

Cuff. Let's be sure to bet all we can. I have known a great Bowler, whose Betters place was worth above 200 *l.* a year, without venturing a farthing for himself.

Kick. They begin to go homewards, let's be gone.

Enter Raines *and* Bevil.

Bev. Jack, how is't this Morning? we are late, the Company is going from the Wells; how does thy laſt nights work agree with thee?

Raines. Whether that agrees with me or no, I am resolv'd to agree with that; for no diſtemper can trouble me that comes from so generous a Cause, as luſty *Burgundy,* and good Company.

Bev. Thou art i'the right, we should no more be troubled at the Feavers we get in drinking, than the Honourable wounds we receive in Battle.

Raines. 'Tis true, the firſt are the effeſts of our pleasure, and the laſt of our honour; which are two things absolutely necessary to the life of a Gentleman.

Bev. Yet your dull spleenatick sober Sots will tell you, we shorten our lives, and bring Gouts, Dropsies, Palsies, and the Devil and all upon us.

Raines. Let 'em lye and preach on, while we live more in a week, than those insipid-temperate Fools do in a Year.

Bev. We like subtle Chymiſts extraſt and refine our pleasure; while they like Fulsom Galeniſts take it in gross.

Raines. I confess, a disorder got by Wine in scurvy Company, would trouble a Man as much as a Clap got of a Bawd; but there are some women so beautiful, that the pleasure would more than ballance the disaſter.

Bev. And as your honeſt Whore-maſter makes haſte to his cure only to be at it again; so do we take Pills and the Waters to prepare us for another heat.

Raines. For my part I hate to hoord up a great ſtock of health, as Misers do Gold, and make no use on't: I am resolv'd to lay it out upon my Friends as far as' twill go; and if I run my self out, I'll be a good Husband for a while to lay it out again when I have it.

Bev. But, *Jack,* there are duties to our she, as well as he-neighbours, which the Dull, Grave, and Wise say, is lighting our Candle at both ends.

Raines. Let 'em be light at both ends. Is it not better to let Life go out in a blaze than a snuff?

Bev. I see thou art a brave fellow, and not to be mov'd by the formal Fops of this World.

Raines. I will converse with grave fellows in their Books; but with such as thou art over a bottle, *Ned.* But where's *Woodly* this morning? I warrant he was drunk last night, and has had a tedious Lecture from his Impertinent Wife; who impudently rails at him, as she says, because she loves him.

Bev. He's an honest fellow, and ventures hard when he drinks with us; for to say truth, she's a damn'd Wife, but a very good Mistress.

Raines. Art not thou a Villain to Cuckold this honest fellow, and thy friend *Ned?*

Bev. Gad it's impossible to be a man of honour in these Cafes. But my intrigue with her began before my Friendship with him, and so I made a friend of my Cuckold, and not a Cuckold of my friend.

Raines. An admirable School distinction.

Enter Woodly.

Wood. *Raines* and *Bevil,* good Morrow to you.

Raines. O *Franck Woodly,* where wer't thou last night? you scap'd a bloody night on't.

Wood. Faith *Raines* there is no scaping, a Coward may be kill'd as well as a brave man; I ran away from you but to little purpose. See how my hand shakes this Morning.

Raines. O let me kiss that hand; he must be an illustrious Man whose hand shakes at 22.

Wood. You are pleas'd to say so, but faith I take pains and live as fast as I can, that's the truth on't.

Bev. Thou art in the right, and a Pox on them that live slowly, lazily, and soberly. I love riding Post in a Journey, I hate a damn'd dull Carriers pace.

Wood. But I was in damn'd Company with that Publick spirited Fool, and Country Justice, Mr. *Clodpate,* and one or two as bad.

Bev. Thou art often seduc'd by Fools, *Franck;* have a care of 'em I say, have a care of 'em.

Raines. He Counsels you well; for conversation is to the mind, as the air we live in is to the body; in the good we by degrees suck in health, and in the ill Diseases. Wit is improv'd in good Company; but there is a Contagion in Folly, that insensibly insinuates into one that often converses with Fools, let his constitution of mind be never so good.

Bev. But *Clodpate* is a Clownish-Country Fool. The Murrain among Cattle is not infectious to men, nor can his blunt folly ever insinuate it self into an honest debauchee.

Enter Clodpate, and Toby.

Raines. Here he comes, let's observe him a little.

Clodp. Did you call upon my Cozen *Spatter-Brain* for that Interest money due to me this Midsummer?

Toby. I have, Sir, every day since he came to *Epsom*, and yesterday he said upon his Honour he would pay me, and went immediately to *London*.

Clodp. Honour, a Pox on his Honour, I'l sooner trust the honour of a Country Horse-Courser, than one of the Publicans and Sinners of that odious Town.   They never pay so much as a Taylors Bill till it comes to Execution : But I'l have *Spatter-Brain* by the back the next Tearm, though he be my Sisters Son.   But how does my dapple Mare?

Toby. She's much discontented to hear her Neighbours Whiney over their Oats and Beans, while she is fain to mortify with a poor lock of Hay.

Clodp. You Rogue, you wou'd have her as fat, and as foggy, as my Landlady the Hostess.   I care not what I spend amongst my Neighbours in *Sussex*, but I'd not have a Rogue so near that damn'd Town of *London* get a farthing by me.

Wood. Besides some dull Encomiums upon a Country life, and discourse of his serving the Nation with his Magistracy, popularity, and House-keeping, you see the best and worst of him.

Bev. But is his hatred to *London* so inveterate as is reported?

Wood. Six times more.   Since 'twas burnt he calls it nothing but *Sodom ;* he is such a Villain, he swears the Frenchman that was hang'd for burning on't was a Martyr ; he was so glad at the burning of it, that ever since he has kept the second of *September* a Festival ; he thinks a Woman cannot be honest, scarce sound that comes within the smell on't, he is shock'd at the very name on't.

Bev. I have heard that the reasons of his hatred, are, because he has been beaten, clapt, and cheated there.

Rains. Pox on him, he has found us, and there's no avoiding him.

Clodp. O Mr. *Woodly*, how is it?   You drink no Waters ; but have you had your other Mornings draught yet.

Wood. Yes, I never leave off my Evenings draught till it becomes my Mornings draught.

Clodp. Mr. *Rains* and *Bevill,* gad save ye ; how de'e like the Country? is't not worth a hundred of old *Sodom* yonder? good Horses, good Dogs, good Ale, hah———

Rains. Good Wine, good Wit, and fine Women, may I take it, compare with them.

(110)

Clodp. I find you'l never leave that place of sin and sea-coal, give me drink for all that, that breeds no Gout; a wholsome plain Wench, that will neither bring my body to the Surgeons hands, nor my Land to the Scriveners: and for Wit, there is such a stir amongst you, who has it, and who has it not, that we honest Country Gentlemen begin to think there's no such thing, and have hearty Mirth and good old Catches amongst us, that do the business every whit as well.

Rains. He's in the right. The Wits are as bad as the Divines, and have made such Civil Wars, that the little Nation is almost undone.

Clodp. But Mr. *Woodly*, how do you like my Dapple Mare?

Wood. Not comparable to a Hackney Coach.

Clodp. But she shall run with e're a Hackney Coach in *England* for all that, or e're a Horse in your stable, weight him and inch him.

Wood. I would not keep a running horse, though a running horse would half keep me.

Bev. We are for *London* to morrow; shall we have your company?

Clodp. Ud's bud, I go to *London*! I am almost sick at *Epsom*, when the wind fits to bring any of the Smoak this way, and by my good will would not talk with a man that comes from thence till he hath ayr'd himself a day or two.

Wood. Why, there's no Plague.

Clodp. There's Pride, Popery, Folly, Lust, Prodigality, Cheating Knaves, and Jilting Whores; Wine of half a crown a quart, and Ale of twelve pence, and what not.

Rains. This is a terrible regiment you have muster'd; but neither the Priests nor the Women will ravish you; nor are you forc'd to take the Wine, as the *French* are their Salt, there are twelve penny Ordinaries.

Clodp. Ay, and Cards and false Dice, and Quarrels, Hectors and reform'd Officers to borrow a Crown, and beat a man that refuses it, or asks for't again; besides, I'le sum you up the beastly pleasures of the best of ye.

Wood. What are those?

Clodp. Why, to sit up drunk till three a clock in the morning, rise at twelve, follow damn'd French Fashions, get dress'd to go to a damn'd Play, choak your selves afterwards with dust in Hide-park, or with Sea-coal in the Town, flatter and fawn in the drawing-room, keep your Wench, and turn away your Wife, Gad-ooks.

Bev. The Rogue is a tart and witty whorson.

Clodp. I was at *Sodom* at eighteen, I thank' em, but now I serve my Country, and spend upon my Tenants what I get amongst them.

Rains. And so, indeed, are no better than their Sponge, which they moisten only to squeeze again. But what important Service do you do your Country?

Clodp. 'SBud, I——why, I am Justice of *Quorum* in *Sussex,* and this

County too, and I make the Surveyors mend the High-ways ; I cause Rogues to be whipt for breaking fences or pilling trees, especially if they be my own ; I swear Constables, and the like.

Bev. But is this all ?

Clodp. No : I call Over-seers for the Poor to an account ; sign Rates ; am a Game-keeper, and take away Guns and Grey-hounds ; bind Fellows to the peace ; observe my monthly Meeting ; am now and then an Arbitrator, and license Ale-houses, and make people bury in Flannel, to encourage the Woollen Manufacture, which never a Justice of Peace in *England* does but I.

Wood. Look you, what would you have ?

Clodp. Besides, I am drunk once a week at my Lord Lieutenant's, and at my own house spend not scurvy French kick-shaws, but much Ale, and Beef, and Mutton, the Manufactures of the Country.

Bev. The Manufactures of the Country, that's well.

Rains. Ay, and, I warrant, by the virtue of that, can bring as many wide-mouth'd Rogues to Ball and holloa for a Knight of the shire as any Man.

Clodp. Ay, gads-ooks can I.

Rains. That men should be such infinite Coxcombs to live scurvily to get reputation among thick-scull'd Peasants, and be at as great a distance with men of wit and sense, as if they were another sort of Animals.

Bev. 'Tis fit such Fools should govern and do the drudgery of the world, while reasonable men enjoy it.

Clodp. Mr. *Woodly*, I'le go now and wait upon your Cousin *Lucia*, and if I can get her to marry me, and fill up my pack of dogs, my two great works are over in this world. God-by, Gentlemen. Uds-bud, I had forgot, I have the rarest stand of Ale to drink out in the Afternoon, with three or four honest Country-fellows ; you shall be very welcom to it I fack, and we'l dust it away.

Bev. We thank you, Sir.

Clodp. I am now in haste to read a Gazette, this is the day, I am impatient till I see it—— Oh, I love Gazettes extreamly, and they are the only things I can endure that come from *London*. They are such pretty penn'd things, and I do so love to hear of *Winowisky, Potosky, General Wrangle*, and *Count Tot*, and all those brave Fellows——Gad save ye. *Exit.*

[*Six Women cross the Stage in great haste.*

Rains. Look how the women begin to trip it from the Wells ; I see some of 'em well dress'd in Masques ; Oh that admirable Invention of Vizor-masques for us poor Lovers ; Vizors are so provocative, the Devil take me, I cannot forbear 'em.

Bev. Thou art such a Termagant Fellow, thou art as eager at a Woman in a Vizor-masque, as thou wouldst be if she show'd all. [*Exit* Rains. 'Faith I'll not be behind hand with ye——

Enter Mrs. Woodly, *and pulls* Bevil *by the sleeve.*

How now, what am I boarded first?

Oh Mrs. *Woodly*, is it you?

    Mrs. *Wood.* I dare not stay a minute, read that Note, adieu.   *[Exit.*

    Bev. Short and sweet, let me see——

Reads. *My Husband staid up late, and was very drunk last night, and I have had a happy quarrel with him this morning, that has driven him from home, where I shall have the happiness not to see him till night, so that I safely may enjoy your sweet society most part of this day.*   Yours Woodly.

Well the sin's so sweet, and the temptation so strong, I have no power to resist it.   (*Ex.* Bevil.

Enter Carolina *and* Lucia, *and Footman.*

    Caro. Let the Coach walk up the Hill, we'll follow it.

    Foot. It shall, Madam.   *[Ex. Footman.*

    Caro. But as I was saying, *Lucia*, here's very scurvy company.

    Luc. We have no body near us here, but some impertinent ill-bred City-wives, where they have more trading with the youth of the Suburbs, than their Husbands with their Customers within the walls.

    Caro. Sometimes we have their tame Husbands, who gallop hither upon their Tits, to see their faithful Wives play a game at Ninepins, and be drunk with stum'd wine; and strait are gone to their several and respective couzening vocations. Therefore, prithee, let's go to *Tunbridge;* for *London* is so empty, 'tis a very Wilderness this Vacation.

    Luc. No, 'faith, *Carolina*, I have a project in my head shall stay me here a little longer, and thee too——

    Caro. What, you hanker after an acquaintance with *Rains* and *Bevil?* thou art a mad wench, but they are so very wild.

    Luc. An they be naturally wilder than I, or you either for all your simpering, I'll be condemn'd to Fools and ill company for ever.

    Caro. Do not wish that dreadful curse; we are already so much pester'd with gay Fools, that have no more sense than our Shock-dogs, that I long for an acquaintance with witty men as well as thou dost. But how can we bring it about without scandal?

    Luc. Let this brain of mine alone for that. I blush for my Sex, to see the Ladies of *London* (as if they had forsworn common sense) make insipid young Fools their greatest Favourites.

    Caro. 'Tis a shame that a company of young, wall-fac'd Fellows, that have no sense beyond Perruques and Pantaloons, should be the only men with the Ladies, whilst the acquaintance of witty men is thought scandalous.

    Luc. For my part, I am resolv'd to redeem the honour of our Sex, and love Wit, and never think a Fool a fine Gentleman.

Enter Cuff *and* Kick.

What Ruffins are these that come to interrupt us in our great design?

Kick. Ah, Ladies, have we catch'd ye i'faith; you shall go along with us.

Caro. What pitiful fellows are these?

Cuff. Pitiful fellows, Gad have a care what you say, we do not use to put up such words, either from man or woman.

Luc. What would you do you dowty Hectors?

Kick. Hectors? upon my honour, if we can find them out, we'll beat your Gallants for this.

Caro. If I had a Gallant that kept a Footman, that would not beat either of you, I'd disown the Master for the cowardise of the man.

Cuff. S'death, I could find in my heart to draw upon her.

Kick. Would you had two of the bravest Fellows in *Christendom* to defend ye, you shou'd see how wee'd swinge 'em.

Luc. Avaunt, you Hectors, we are not fit for you. I am sure, neither of you yet were ever honoured with a favour from a Chamber-maid.

Caro. Your acquaintance never rises higher than a Landress or an Hostess.

Cuff. Be not perverse and foolish, we are persons of quality, and have money. Look ye, let this tempt you.

Kick. Come faith, we'll pay you well upon my honour.

Caro. Upon my honour you shall be well paid with a couple of sufficient beatings, if you leave us not.

Cuff. Hilts and blades, men of honour beaten, ye proud Flirts.

Enter Rains *and* Bevil *following some Women who run cross the Stage.*

Luc. Gentlemen, ye look like men of quality; pray owne us to be of your acquaintance, and protect us from a couple of troublesome Ruffians.

Rains. Owne thee! that I will faith in any ground in *Christendom*, and I hope thou wilt be of my acquaintance before we part. I embrace the adventure as greedily as a Knight errand could.

Bev. to Caro. This is the Dame that I'll defend.

Rains. Gentlemen, have you any business with these Ladies?

Kick. Why, Sir, what if we have?

Cuff. May be we have not, Sir, may be we have.

Bev. Nay, Gentlemen, no huffing, know you're men and vanish.

Rains. You may else, unawares, pull down a beating upon your own heads.

Kick. Beating, Sir.

Cuff. We are Gentlemen of quality; never tell us of this, and that, I gad——

Rains. Do not provoke us, but be gone.

Kick. Well, Sir, fare ye well; who cares? I care no more for 'em.——

Cuff. No, nor I neither. What a pox care I; tell me —— fare ye well. But who the Devil thought they wou'd have come hither?

Kick. Pox on 'em for me.

Luc. softly. These are our Gallants: Gentlemen, let's see how you will swinge 'em.

Kick. 'Pshaw, prethee hold thy tongue, talk to me——fa, la, la.

[*Ex.* Kick, *and* Cuff *Singing.*

Luc. This is lucky, *Carolina,* for our design. Gentlemen, you have oblig'd us extreamly.

Rains. We are like Knights Errands, or Knights of the *Bath,* bound to relieve Ladies by our Order.

Bev. But if we have oblig'd you; pray let us see whom we have had the honour of obliging.

Caro. Generous men should be content with the Action, without knowing whom they have oblig'd. But let it satisfie you, we are women of no small quality.

Luc. This desire of knowing us, looks as if ye expected a reward; the seeing of our faces would be none; and upon my word, Gentlemen, we can go no farther if we would do that——

Caro. Besides, you may think us handsom now, and if we shew our faces, we shall convince you to the contrary, and make you repent the obligation.

Bev. I like thy shape and humour so well, that gad if thou'lt satisfie my Curiosity; I'll not repent, though you want that great ornament of a face, called a Nose.

Rains. I am sure mine's handsom; I have an instinct that never fails me.

Luc. Your infallable instinct has guess'd wrong now.

Bev. Come, Ladies, faith off with these Clouds and shine upon us.

Rains. We can never leave you till we see your faces; and if ye don't shew 'em us, we shall think you desire to keep us with ye.

Luc. Nay, rather than have that scandal upon us, we'll shew 'em.

Caro. With all my heart, but upon these terms; you shall promise, upon your honour, not to dog us, or inquire further after us at this time.

Luc. You hear the conditions.

Bev. The conditions are very hard—but I promise——

Rains. Come, Ladies, I find you are handsom, and think your selves so; or you would not be afraid of our dogging you, when we have seen you.

Luc. No seeing our Faces but upon these terms.

Rains. You are cruel Tigers——but since there's no remedy, I promise——

Luc. Look you, Sir, do you like it now?

Caro. You'l believe us another time.

Bev. By Heaven a Divine Creature !

Rains. Beyond all comparison ! where have I liv'd ?

Bev. Gad mine has kill'd me. Since they were so much too hard for us at Blunts ; we were fools to go to sharps with them.

Rains. I will never believe a Ladies word of her self again.

Luc. Come you flatter now.

Rains. To shew that I don't, I cannot help making my honour yield to my love ; and must beg the favour of you to know who you are ; and that I may wait on you home.

Bev. And, Madam, had I sworn by your self, I must have been perjur'd, the temptation is so powerful.

Caro. Have you seen so much Love and Honour upon the Stage, and are so little Judges of it here ?

Luc. In short, if you are men of Honour, you'll keep your words ; for we will never release you of 'em.

Bev. Shall we have hopes of seeing you hereafter ?

Caro. As you behave your selves now.

Rains. Give me hopes of once more seeing you——and I'll trust you, and let you carry my heart away with you.

Luc. You shall hear further from us, and suddenly.

Rains. Upon your Honour ?

Luc. Upon my Honour.

Caro. And mine.

Bev. Farewel then ; but let me tell you, 'tis very cruel.

Car. Why didst leave 'em so soon ? I could have stayed longer, with all my heart.

Luc. 'Tis enough at first——let me alone hereafter.

[*Ex*. Luc. *and* Caro.

Rains. This was a lucky Adventure, and so much the more lucky, that I lighted upon the Lady I love best, though they are both beautiful.

Bev. And I am even with you in that too.

Enter Woodly.

Here's *Woodly ;* the Intrigue is not ripe for his knowledge yet. Where have you been, *Franck ?*

Wood. I have had two damn'd unlucky Adventures. The first Vizor-masque I pursu'd after, I had followed her a Furlong, and importun'd her to show her Face ; when I thought I had got a Prize beyond my hopes, prov'd an old Lady of threescore with a wrinkl'd, pimpl'd Face, but one Eye, and no Teeth ; but which was ten times a worse disappointment, the next that I follow'd prov'd to be my own Wife.

Rains. This was for your good, *Franck ;* Heaven designs to keep you vertuous.

(116)

Wood. But I like not Vertue that springs from necessity. Mine is so noble, I'd have it try'd often.

Rains. Well, Gentlemen, where shall we waste the latter part of the day? for I must spend this former part on't with a convenient sort of Utensil, call'd a Citizen's Wife.

Wood. I must divert that design, and carry you to my Cousin whom you never saw, the prettiest Girl in *Christendom*, she has seen you, and likes you extreamly.

Rains. Prethee, *Woodly*, what should I do with her? I love thee and thy Family too well to lye with her, and my self too well to marry her; and I think a Man has no excuse for himself that visits a Woman without design of lying with her one way or other.

Wood. Why, *Jack*, eight thousand pound and a handsom Wench of seventeen were no ill bargain.

Rains. But here's eight thousand pound, there's Liberty, *Franck*. Would you be content to lye in *Ludgate* all your life time for eight thousand pound?

Wood. No, certainly.

Rains. Marriage is the worst of Prisons.

Bev. But by your leave, *Rains,* though Marriage be a Prison, yet you may make the Rules as large as those of the *King's-Bench,* that extend to the *East Indies.*

Rains. O hang it. No more of that Ecclesiastical Mouse-Trap.

Wood. Prethee, speak more reverently of the happiest Condition of Life.

Rains. A married man is not to be believ'd. You are like the Fox in the Fable that had lost his Tail, and would have persuaded all others to lose theirs; you are one of the Parsons Decoy Ducks, to wheadle poor innocent Fowls into the Net.

Wood. Why shouldst thou think so ill of my Wife to think I am not in earnest?

Rains. No application, *Franck,* I think thy Wife as good a Woman as a Wife can be.

Wood. She loves me extremely, is tolerable handsom, and, I am sure, vertuous.

Rains. That thou know'st, *Ned Bevil*. [*Aside.*

Wood. 'Tis true, she values her self a little too much upon her Vertue, which makes her sometimes a little troublesom and impertinent.

Rains. I never knew a Woman that pretended over-much to Vertue, that either had it, or was not troublesom and impertinent.

Enter Bisket.

Rains. Mr. *Bisket,* good morrow to you.

Bisk. Your humble Servant, Sir.

(117)

Bev. This is *Rains* his most obsequious humble Cuckold, his Wife is a pretty impertinent Strumpet, and scorns to have any other Pimp but her own Husband, who all the while thinks her the innocentest Creature.

Wood. A glorious Punk! but what a despicable thing a Cuckold is; they look as if they had the mark of *Cain* upon 'em. I would not be a Cuckold for the World.

Bev. How blind a thing a Husband is!   [*Aside.*

Bisk. Now, as I am an honest man, and I would I might ne're stir, if I have not had such a life about you with my pretty *Molly*, I would not have her so angry again for fifty pound, Cod-sniggs.

Rains. About me, what's the matter, man?

Bisk. Why I promis'd to bring you to her last night, and got a little tipsy'd, as they say, and forgot it. She says you play the best at Cribach of any body, and she loves gaming mightily, and is as true a Gamester, though I say it.

Rains. I know it, Man.

Bisk. Besides, she would fain learn that new Song of you; she says tis a rare one.

> Sings. *Thou shalt have any thing, thou shalt have me,*
> *And I have one thing that will please thee.*

Tis such a pretty little innocent Rogue, and has such odd Fancies with her, ha, ha, ha——

Wood. Lord, what a strange Creature a Cuckold is!   [*Aside.*

Bisk. But I swear, all that I could do to her could not please her this morning. I fackings no body can satisfie her but you; therefore as you tender the quiet and wellfare of a poor humble Husband, come and play at Cribach with her to day; for she loves Cribach most intemperately. I do wonder that a Woman should love Gaming so.

Rains. Faith I am half ingag'd.

Bisk. For Heavens sake, as you love me do not deny me. I shall have no quiet with her; besides, some *Cheapside* Neighbours of mine are to have a Game at Bowls, and a merry meeting this Afternoon, and she wishes the Waters may ne're go through her, if she'll give me leave to go to 'em, unless I bring you to her to keep her Company, and sing and play at Cards with her, therefore, dear Mr. *Rains.*

Wood. This is beyond all Example.

Rains. Well, there is not in Nature so tame and inoffensive a Beast as a *London* Cuckold, I'le say that for him.   [*Aside.*

Wood. Prethee, *Jack,* do not refuse to go to my Cousin for a little Strumpet.

Rains. I cannot be so inhumane to refuse a Husband that invites me to his own Wife Allons, Mr. *Bisket.*

(118)

Bisk. Come, good Sir, I thank you for this favour a thousand times; my Wife will be in a very good humour to day, Sir.

Rains. Go before, I'le follow you, and carry her this Kiss from me.

Bisk. I thank you, Sir, I'le carry it her, poor Rogue, she'll be overjoy'd; but pray don't ſtay long.   [*Exit* Bisket.

Enter a Boy with a Letter.

Boy. Are Mr. *Rains* and Mr. *Bevil* here?

Bev. Yes, we two are they.

Boy. Here's a Letter for you.

Wood. How now, Gentlemen, what an Assignation to both of you!

Rains. Upon my life, *Ned*, 'tis from the Ladies.

Reads. *You two have injur'd a couple of Gentlemen that will expeƈt you with your Swords in your hands, at eleven, in a Field on the North-side of the Church. If you fail, you shall not fail of being poſted. 'Till you meet us, you shall not know our names, but know that we are worth the meeting,* &c.

Bev. This is a business of another nature, *Rains.*

Rains. We muſt to Tilts and Turnaments, *Ned*, sure they are the Bullies we saw juſt now.

Bev. From whom did you bring this, Boy?

Boy. From a couple of Gentlemen in Buff Belts, Red Coats, and Shammey Breeches.

Rains. 'Tis from them; sure they'l not fight.

Bev. But we muſt try whether they will or no: tell 'em we'll not fail.

Boy. I shall, Sir.   *Exit Boy.*

Rains. I have a business of another nature to dispatch, *Ned;* I'll meet you before eleven at your lodging.

Bev. I have juſt such another business too; but I'll not fail to meet you —— But how can you relish Mrs. *Bisket* after the Lady you saw this Morning?

Rains. I am not sure of her I saw this morning; besides, if I were, is it reasonable that a man that has a good ſtomack should refuse Mutton to day, because he expeƈts Quails to morrow? but how can you in conscience think of Concupiscence, when for ought you know, we may venture our lives within two hours?

Bev. Since, for ought I know, my life may be in danger, I'll make use on't while it is not.

Rains. Adieu, *Woodly*, let's meet on the Bowling green in the afternoon.
                                                    [*Ex. Rains.*

Wood. You are happy men, Gentlemen, but I am going to visit one that I love more than my eyes, and would give both of them to enjoy.

Bev. Aside. That's not his own Wife; I shall be safe enough there. I have an engagement too, and muſt leave you.

Wood. Adieu, we'll meet about five.

Bev. Agreed; —— *Ex.* Bevil.

Wood. Now for my dear *Carolina.* ——
Thus all the world by several ways does move,
But all the Mighty business ends in love. Exit.

ACT II. SCENE I.

Enter Clodpate, Lucia, *and* Carolina.

Luc. PRethee ſtay with me, that I may be no longer peſter'd with this Country Coxcomb.

Caro. Would'ſt thou have me so barbarous to interrupt Lovers.

Luc. He a Lover! yes, of a clear Title in his next Purchace, his Dapple Mare, a dear year of Corn, or so.

Caro. Come, he has as violent a subſtantial country passion for you, as one would wish; and I will leave you to him.

Luc. You mischievous creature, I'll be reveng'd on you.

[*Exit* Carolina.

Clodp. If my propositions be not reasonable, I'll ne'r pretend to serve my Country more.

Luc. A pretty Country to be serv'd by such fellows. *Aside.*

Clodp. In that noble Brick-house, moted round with Turrets and fine things, that I now spoke of, in the beſt hunting Country in *Europe*, with a thousand pounds a year will I joynture you.

Luc. 'Tis not profit, but honour I respeƈt; and I have vow'd never to Marry one that cannot make me a Lady, and you are no Knight.

Clodp. A Knight, no I thank you; why I have known a Fishmonger Knighted: Knighthood's a pretty bawble for a fellow to play with that is no Gentleman. But what needs he that is a Gentleman desire to be more?

Luc. But, methinks, the name of *Clodpate* does not sound well without a title.

Clodp. I thank you heartily; my name is now *Hugh Clodpate*; and I should give two or three hundred pounds to add three letters to it, Sir *Hugh Clodpate*: no, no, I can't make so much on't again.

Luc. Oh, a Knight is such a thing!

(120)

Clodp. Such a thing! has he more hands or legs, or more brains than another man?

Luc. But if I could be content without being a Lady, I have vow'd to spend all my life in *London.*

Clodp. Pox on her; live in *London* did she say?   [*Aside.*
Death, have you vow'd to live in *London* say you?

Luc. Yes, is that so wonderful? why people do really live no where else; they breath, and move, and have a kind of insipid, dull being; but there is no life but in *London.*

Clodp. *London!* that sink of Sin.

Luc. I believe there is no Village but sins as much, in proportion to the bigness; only your Country sins are something the more block-headed sins.

Clodp. Madam, give me leave to ask you one question.

Luc. You may.

Clodp. Do you resolve to live honest?

Luc. 'Tis a familiar question; you had need ask my leave first.

Clodp. Why you may as reasonably expect to preserve your Health in a Pest-house, as your Chastity in that damn'd lascivious Town.

Luc. You are rude, Sir.

Clodp. Come, Madam, plain-dealing is a Jewel. But can you prefer an idle, scandalous *London*-life before a pretty, innocent, huswifely-life in the Country, to look to your Family and visit your Neighbours.

Luc. To see my Ducks and Geese fed, and cram my own Chickens.

Clodp. Ay.

Luc. To have my Closet stink, like a Pothecaries shop, with Drugs and Medicines, to administer to my sick Neighbours, and spoil the next Quack's practice with the receipt-book that belongs to the Family.

Clodp. Very well.

Luc. And then to have one approved Green-salve, and dress sore Legs with it; and all this to deserve the name of as good a neighbourly body as ever came into *Sussex.*

Clodp. Very good.

Luc. Never to hear a Fiddle, but such as sounds worse than the Tongs and Key, or a Gridiron; never to read better Poetry than *John Hopkins* or *Robert Wisdom*'s vile Metre; nor hear better singing than a company of Peasants praising God with doleful, untunable, hoarse voices, that are only fit to be heard under the Gallows.

Clodp. However you make bold with the Country, be not prophane. Is not this better than any thing in that stinking Town?

Luc. Stinking Town! I had rather be Countess of *Puddle-Dock,* than Queen of *Sussex.*

Clodp. Oh foh———but ah, the excellent fresh air upon the Downs.

Luc. So there's fresh air in a Wilderness, if one could be contented with

(121)

Bears and Wolves for her companions. But, sir, in short, I am resolv'd to live at *London*, and at or very near the Court too.

Clodp. 'sDeath the Court! I shall not only be Cuckolded, but lose all my Country interest; Madam, I beg your pardon, I shall take my leave; I am not cut out for a *Londoner* or a Courtier; fare you well, good Madam, though I like your Person pretty well, I like not your Conditions; I'd not marry a *London* Cherubin.

Luc. Farewel, Sir; but I'le not be wholly ungrateful for the Address you have honoured me with: know then my Friend *Carolina* is the most averse to *London*, and most infatuated with the Love of the Country.

Clodp. Uds bud, infatuated; pray change that word if you please.

Luc. You know my meaning by it: she and I are parting, because she will not with patience hear of returning to *London*; she calls it nothing but vain, obscene, wicked, filthy, Popish place.

Clodp. Ha! how's this? I did not think she had so much sense.   [*Aside*.

Luc. She often says, she had rather marry a Country Justice of five hundred pounds a year, than a Man of five thousand pounds a year in *London*; nay than a Duke at Court.

Clodp. She's an ingenious Woman, Guds-sooks.   [*Aside*.
I had rather marry her naked than you with all your portion, Madam. But a pox on't, I had damn'd ill luck to make my application to you first, as the Devil would have it.

Luc. This is a very Country Courtier——   [*Aside*
Here she comes, let's withdraw; I will tell you more, and we'll consult about this business.

Clodp. Your servant, Madam.   [*Ex*. Clodpate *and* Lucia.

Enter Carolina *and* Woodly.

Wood. How can you mistrust a man in so credible a thing?

Caro. As what?

Wood. As that he should love the prettiest, sweetest, dearest Creature he ever saw——

Caro. So far from that, I believe he will love all the prettiest, sweetest, dearest Creatures, as he calls 'em, that he ever shall see: but you have paid that Tribute already to vertuous Madam *Woodly*, and are Marry'd.

Wood. I am so; and there's the less danger in my Love; I should else be tempting you to accept me for better for worse till death us depart, *&c*. Now, Madam, take my heart upon its good behaviour, as much as you have use on, and the rest again and no hurt done.

Caro. Where there are so many free; why should I venture upon a heart with so manifest a flaw in the title as a marry'd man's.

Wood. 'Faith, there are none without their incumbrances; your fashionable Spark has his Miss in the Play-house; your Lady's eldest Son his Mother's Chamber-maid; the Country Gentleman his Tenant's Daughter; a handsom young Fellow that is to make his fortune, some elderly Sinner that keeps him fine; so that Marriage is the least engagement of all, for that only points out where a Man cannot love.

Caro. Since Marriage obliges men so little and women so much, I wonder we endure the cheat on't.

Wood. Y'are in the right, 'tis worse than cross I win, pile you lose: but there are some left that can love upon the square.

Caro. A Woman may be undone upon the square, as well as a Gamester, if she ventures too much.

Wood. Never, so long as you play for nothing but what you have about you; and, upon my honour, I would engage you no deeper at this time; 'tis tick and after-reckonings that ruine Lovers as well as Gamesters; and, gad, if you mistrust me, I am ready to make stakes; and because y'are a young beginner, I'le play three to one.

Caro. Not so fast, good Sir, you'll make me quit the few good thoughts I had of you if you persist.

Wood. Persist in loving you I must till death; but the methods and ceremonies I leave to you to prescribe. I guess'd you would not care for a whining Lover.

Caro. Nor do I care for one in your extreamity the other way.

Wood. Take your choice, I can make love from the stiff, formal way of the year 42, to the gay, brisk way of this present day and hour.

Caro. Since I suppose it is for diversion, pray let me see how that is.

Wood. Look you, thus.   [*Sings, dances and combs his Peruque.*

Caro. Is this it? why, you don't mind me.

Wood. I mind my self though, and make you fall in love with me, after a careless way, by the bye.

Car. When do you begin?

Wood. Begin? why, I am at it all this while. [*Sings and Dances again.* Now have at you: These Breasts are not hard to speak on; no, nor this Neck white; nor those Eyes black. Lord, how you look to day! that ever a Man should love such a Creature; what will you give me for a piece when you are mother of the maids?

Caro. Must I answer you like a Lady of the times too?

Wood. Ay, by all means, Madam.

Caro. This Mr. *Woodly* is the strangest Man, he would make one die to hear him, I vow, ha, ha, ha——

Wood. Lord, what a set of teeth you shew when you laugh! if they were mine I'd pull 'em out; sure your breath can't be sweet, let me see. [*Offers to kiss her.*

Caro. Well, I vow you're a pleasant man; but you go too fast.

Wood. For your Lover of the laſt Age, I grant you ; but the World is well mended since, fair Ladies and fortified Towns yield upon easier terms now adays.   [*Offers to kiss her agen.*
Now I see you dare not ſtand the tryal, 'tis even so ; I'le be hang'd if you ha'n't crooked Legs too.   [*Offers to lift up her Coats.*

Caro. I had rather you should think so than take the pains to satisfie you ; but I vow you'd make one burſt, you have such a way with you, ha, ha, ha——

Wood. I hate to live in doubt ; you have a pretty Face, but an ill Breath and crooked Legs, gad, are insufferable.

Caro. Is this your new way ? I have enough on't, no more ; drinking my health in a Beer-glass, and quarrelling with the man that can't pledge ; Scribling your passion in Glass-windows, and wearing my Colours continually I can better endure ; but now I talk of scribling, divert me a little better, and give me the Song you promis'd me.

Wood. I have taught it your Woman, who I conceive has some thing a better Voice than I, she's here too.

Caro. Sing that Song Mr. *Woodly* taught you.

She Sings.

How pleasant is mutual Love that is true,
Then Phillis *let us our affeЛions unite ;*
For the more you love me, the more I love you,
The more we contribute to each others delight :
For they that enjoy without loving firſt,
Still eat without ſtomach, and drink without thirſt.

Such is the poor Fool who loves upon duty,
Because a Canonical Coxcomb has made him,
And ne'er taſtes the sweets of love and of beauty,
But drudges because a dull Prieſt has betray'd him ;
But who in enjoyment from love take their measure,
Are rap't with delight, and ſtill ravish'd with pleasure.

Each night he's a Bridegroom, and she is a Bride.
When their minds and their bodies shall both so agree ;
That neither shall pleasure from the other divide,
But both at one inſtant shall satisfy'd be ;
Let Fools for convenience be drawn to their love,
But this is the way real pleasure to prove.

Enter Clodpate *and* Lucia.

Luc. So, you are pleasant here, Mr. *Clodpate,* how do you like this Song ? 'tis a *London* Song.

Clodp. Ay, Pox on't, I hate it for it; when I had the misfortune to know that damn'd Town first, they had better Songs by half; they put no wit in their Songs now adays.

Caro. Pray do us the favour to Sing one of those you speak of.

Clodp. Faith, Madam, I have but an ordinary voice, but I cannot disobey you.

Sings ridiculously this old Song.

> *Lay by your pleading,*
> *Law lies a bleeding,* &c.

Wood. What an incomprehensible block-head is this.

Clodp. This pleases us in the Country; I know you like it ne're the worse, Madam.

Caro. Nor much the better.

Clodp. Come, Madam, I am sure you love a Country Life, and hate that vile Town of *London;* and I honour you for't.

Caro. I hate *London !*

Clodp. I knew you would dissemble it, but I know your heart; 'tis true, indeed, 'tis a vain obscene, wicked, filthy, popish place.

Caro. What means the Worshipful Fop.

Clodp. And a Virtuous Lady had better Marry a Country Justice of five hundred pounds a year, than one in *London* of five thousand pounds; nay, than a Duke at Court —— 'tis granted, Madam, 'tis granted.

Caro. It may be granted by you, but not by me.

Clodp. There are some such fools to refuse good offers; but there are others have more wit, Heaven be prais'd.

Caro. Sure you have been at cross purposes of late, Mr. *Clodpate*.

Clodp. No, Madam, but I know you hate *Sodom* yonder; foh —— methinks I smell it hither; let me tell you in private; I would not marry Mrs. *Lucia* if she had fifty thousand pounds; Ud's bud, marry one that would live at *London*, nay at Court; No, I had rather go to Sea in a Fire-ship; but I'll shew you the finest seat in *Sussex* which you shall call your own.

Caro. What do you mean by this?

Clodp. All this I know very well, and though by the Sot her Uncle I was misguided to Mrs. *Lucia*, 'tis to you, Madam, my affection first inclin'd.

Caro. Ah mischief, have you contriv'd this? you thought to punish me much, but I had rather have such a fellow to Fool with, than a lap Dog, or a Squirrel; abusing of a Fool is almost as pleasant as conversing with a witty Man.

Luc. 'Tis true, now I consider it, and he that's laugh'd at is oft-times as good Company as he that laughs, nay some have rais'd their fortunes by it; but you forget our appointment; pray let's go?

(125)

Caro. Ay, prithee.   My dear, Gentlemen, we must leave you; your servant.

Wood. Will you not let me wait on you?

Caro. By no means 'tis a private affair.

Clodp. Shall not I wait on you?

Caro. I shall not refuse the favour another time, but now I must beg your pardon.

Luc. Allons, let's meet the Duellists, I warrant you they are men of honour.

Clodp. Come, I am going a setting, will you go?

[*Ex.* Luc. *and* Caro.

Wood. No, I must go home.   [*Ex.* Clodpate.

Enter Fribble, *and* Dorothy *his Wife.*

Fribb. Whither are you a going Mr. *Woodly?* will you not go to the Bowling-Green to day?

Wood. Yes, perhaps in the Afternoon,——Adieu.   [*Ex.* Woodly.

Fribb. Why do you follow me with your Impertinence?

Doro. My dear honey, how have I offended thee? did I not with my own hands put thee to Bed when thou wert fudled last night? did I not set thy Bottle of small Beer by thy Bedside? did I not rise early and make thee a Caudel when thou wer't puking, and gave thee *Aqua Mirabilis,* to fetch up the Water off thy Stomach?

Fribb. All this you did, and 'twas your Duty, but you are strangely troublesom.

Dor. Think not my love a trouble, Dear; I speak for thy good, prethee do not go abroad to day, thou'lt kill thy self with drinking, and thy Death will be sure to kill me.

Fribb. You are impertinent, I'le go, let that suffice.

Dor. You are shrewdly mistaken, if you think I desire your Company. But I am sure this is the way to be rid on't.   [*Aside.*

Frib. I am to meet Mr. *Bisket* and some *Cheapside* Neighbours; be silent, my will is like the Laws of the Maids and Parsons.

Dor. I cannot hide my love and fears from thee; prethee, dearest, kiss me.

Frib. I say again, Peace; I shall be much offended.

Dor. Thou art a naughty Man, and always abroad, while I am languishing for thee; and I have thee but two days in a week at *Epsom.*

Frib. Know your Lord and Master, and be subject to my Government; I though but a Haberdasher will be as absolute a Monarch over you, as the great Turk over his Sultan Queen.

Dor. Well, I can but submit and weep for thy absence.

Frib. Can't you keep Company with Mrs. *Bisket?*

Dor. What thou pleasest, my Dear.

So you'll go and not hinder me from better Company.   [*Aside.*

Frib. Well, I have the most Virtuous, and best Govern'd Wife in all the Ward; but I must observe Discipline, and keep a strict hand over her.

Dor. I am an unfortunate Woman not to have thy Company; so I am.

Enter Mrs. Bisket.

Mrs. *Bisk.* What, in tears, Mrs. *Fribble!* this is that naughty man; out on thee, thou art a shame to all Husbands, thou wou'dst be so insolent to command thy own Wife; wou'dst thou use thy own flesh, thy own rib so, out upon thee.

Frib. I am my own Master, and will be hers.

Mrs. *Bisk.* Ah, thou art a good one 'ifaith; and thou wer't mine, I'd teach thee better manners.

Fribb. Dorothy, Listen not to this lewd Woman, her Husband is a sneaking, sniveling Cuckold; if you should be like her, I would make you such a terrible Example! Mrs. *Bisket,* you are impertinent, were I your Husband, I would swinge you much.

Mrs. *Bisk.* Swinge me, say you, I could tear thy Eyes out. Death, if you provoke me, I'll show you what the Courage of an inraged Woman can do.

Doro. Nay, good Mrs. *Bisket,* Mr. Fribble is a good Man for all his passion.

Mrs. *Bisk.* Swinge me——

Frib. This Woman is as outragious as a Milch Bear that wants her Breakfast. Fare you well.   [*Ex.*

Mrs. *Bisk.* Come, Neighbour, you are a shame to all Wives to be so tame and foolish; pluck up a Spirit, and order him as I do my *Bisket.*

Dor. This is the only way to order a surly Husband.

Mrs. *Bisk.* I am asham'd of you, you betray our cause; submit to a Husband; I'd fain see that Husband that I'd crouch to. I say again, pluck up a Spirit; I keep a strict hand of Discipline over mine.

Enter Bisket.

Here he comes, you shall see how I order him.

Bisket. How now, my pretty Dear, poor Duck.

Mrs. *Bisk.* Duck, you Widgeon; how came you and I so familiar? observe me now.   [*Aside.*

Bisk. Well, Mrs. *Fribble,* 'tis such a pretty Rogue, and has such pleasant Fancies with her, ha, ha, ha. I protest and vow, I could kiss the very ground she goes on. If she would eat Gold, nay, Pearls and Diamonds, she should have them, I vow and swear.

Mrs. *Bisk.* You Beast, you had best be drunk agen, 'ifaith I'll order you,

I'll keep you in better awe, you shall neither have Caudel nor Custard for't this week.

Bisk. Nay, good Dear, be not so cruel, I protest and vow I could not help it : my Neighbour *Fribble* is a very merry man, I could not forbear, we were at it, Tory Rory, and sung old Rose, the Song that you love so, Duck.

Thou shalt have any thing, thou shalt have me, &c.

Mrs. *Bisk.* Ay, Mr. *Fribble* maintains his Wife like a Lady, and she has all things about her as well as any Woman in the Parish, he keeps her the prettiest pacing Nag with the finest Side-saddle of any Womans in the Ward, and lets her take her pleasure at *Epsom* two months together.

Doro. Ay, that's because the Air's good to make one be with Child ; and he longs mightily for a Child ; and truly, Neighbour, I use all the means I can, since he is so desirous of one.

Bisk. All this thou shalt do, my Dear ; I'le omit nothing that shall please thee.

Mrs. *Bisk.* Yes, you Nicompoop, you are a pretty Fellow to please a Woman indeed.

Bisk. But prethee, my Dear, let me go to the Bowling-green to my Neighbours : would I might ne're stir, if I drink above a pint of Wine, or a quart of Mum for my share at most.

Mrs. *Bisk.* You impertinent Puppy, I wonder you have the impudence to ask me such a question.   [*She gives him a slap on the face.*

Bisk. Mrs. *Fribble*, my pretty *Mollie* has some humours, but this is the worst you'll see of her.

Doro. How rarely she orders a Husband ; I vow I think I must pluck up a spirit as she does, that's the truth on't.

Mrs. *Bisk.* Where's Mr. *Rains*, you Lolpoop ? Do you think you shall go, and he not here ?

Bisk. O Duck, he'll be here presently, and sent thee a kiss by me.

Mrs. *Bisk.* Yes, I warrant he'd kiss such a Fellow as thee.

Bisk. I vow he did ; prethee take it of me, my Dear.

Mrs. *Bisk.* I'le swear he's a fine person. Well, because it comes from him, I'le take it ; he's the compleatest Man, and so courteous and well-behav'd.

Bisk. Now thou'lt let me go.

Mrs. *Bisk.* No, not till he comes.

Bisk. Nay, good Dear.

Mrs. *Bisk.* I tell you, you shall not ; get you in.

Bisk. Pray, Duck, now.

Doro. I never saw any thing so admirable as this Discipline of hers ; I am resolved to try my *Fribble*, that's once.

Bisk. Why, look here he is now already.

Enter Rains.

Doro. Oh me ! is he acquainted with her ?   [*Aside.*

Mrs. *Bisk.* Does he know her ?   [*Aside.*

Bisk. I'le ſteal away and say nothing.   [*Ex.* Bisket.

Mrs. *Bisk.* Come, Mr. *Rains*, let's in.   Mrs. *Fribble*, your Servant.

Doro. Madam, I'le wait on you in ; Mr. *Rains* will not think my Company troublesom.

Mr. *Bisk.* Ah, shame on her.   [*Aside.*
We shall entertain you but ill.   Mr. *Rains* is pleased to come and play at Cribage with me, 'twill be no sport to look on.

Doro. I'll make one at Gleek, that's better than any two-handed Game.

Mrs. *Bisk.* I do not think so, by your leave, Madam *Fribble*, Oh Impertinence !

Doro. Well then, I'le be content to be a looker on for once.   She would fain have him to her self, but I'le look to her for that.   [*Aside.*
[*Exeunt* Rains, Dorothy, *Mrs.* Bisket.

Enter Mrs. Woodly *in a Dining-room.*

Mrs. *Wood.* Mr. Bevil ſtays mighty long, pray Heaven he be not diverted by some paltry Citizen's Wife ; here are such a Company of them that lye upon the snap for young Gentlemen, as Rooks and Bullies do for their Husbands when they come to Town.

Enter Bevil.

Bev. Madam, your Servant.

Mrs. *Wood.* O Mr. *Bevil*, are you come ?   I vow, I was afraid I had loſt you.   A Woman that's apt to be jealous as I am, should not make such a person the objeſt of her affeſtions.

Bev. Words are the common payment of those that intend no other. There is no such sign of having been long faſting, as falling to with a good ſtomach.

Mrs. *Wood.* I am so afraid you should be seduc'd by some of these naughty Women at *Epsom*.   A shame take 'em, I hate a lewd Woman with my heart, I vow, I do now.

Bev. Madam, I have a very pressing affair that requires some speedy conference with you in your Bed-Chamber.

Mrs. *Wood.* No, Sir, no——I wonder you have the confidence to ask me, when you were so rude to me there laſt time.

Bev. I do not know what she calls rude.   I am sure I oblig'd her as often as I could there.

Mrs. *Wood.* One can't be private with you, but you are so uncivil presently.   I can scarce forgive you ; I wonder who learnt you such tricks, for my part.

Bev. If I were ne're so backward, she'd soon inſtruct me. I am not so ill-bred, but I know what I owe to a Lady. Come, Deareſt.

Mrs. *Wood.* Do not ask me; I vow, I won't. You are the ſtrangeſt Man that I ever met with, you won't let one alone; nay, pish, fie, Mr. *Bevil*, aren't you asham'd?

Bev. No more, nay, Dear, come in, come in.

Mrs. *Wood.* Nay, pish, ha, ha, ha, ha. I vow, you make me blush; get you gone, you naughty man, you.

Bev. You'll make me outragious; I shall force you, have a care.

Mrs. *Wood.* Well, I vow you are a parlous man. Will you promise me then to sit ſtill when you are there, and not ſtir hand or foot.

Bev. Ay, ay, come, come.

Mrs. *Wood.* Nay, but will you swear?

Bev. Yes, yes, come allons, my Deareſt, she'll soon dispense with that Oath.

Mrs. *Wood.* Well, I am so asham'd, I vow, I would not go, but that you said you would force me, and swore too besides.

[*As they are going into the Bed-Chamber, enter* Peg.

Peg. Madam, here's my Maſter juſt coming in a doors.

[*Ex.* Peg. *inſtantly.*

Mrs. *Wood.* Heaven! What shall I do?

Bev. I told him I had private business, to get rid of him, and he'll discover all.

Mrs. *Wood.* Go into the Bed-Chamber, I'le lock it.

Bev. But how will you get rid of him?

Mrs. *Wood.* Let me alone, this is an unlucky surprise, in quickly.

Bev. If I should be locked up so long till I fail *Rains*, and our fighting appointment, I shall get much honour, I take it.   [Bev. *goes in.*

Mrs. *Wood.* In, in.

Enter Woodly.

O you unworthy Fellow; have you the impudence to appear before me after your beaſtly usage?

Wood. I thought your fit might have been off by this time.

Mrs. *Wood.* No, it shall never be off, thou inhumane Beaſt; to sit up anights late, and come home drunk and wake me, and lye like a Statue by me all the reſt of the night, flesh and blood can't bear it; you make me cry my Eyes out, to see that you'll kill your self by your villainous debauchery.

Woodly *while she scolds sings.* Fa, la, la, la, fa.

Mrs. *Wood.* Fa, la, la, la, fa—— Is that the notice you take of me? If I were not the beſt Woman in the World, and did not love thee, thou base Fellow, 'twould not trouble me. Oh that I should be so unfortunate, so bewitch'd, to love such a monſter of a Man!

(130)

Wood. Fa, la, la, la, Oh, Impudence!

Mrs. *Wood.* I wonder what I should see in thee to love thee so, out on thee, for a Villain. Oh, that I could withdraw my affection from thee, thou Brute! but I can't for my life, 'tis that makes me miserable, thou barbarous wicked Wretch.

Wood. If to seek quiet abroad, when one can't have it at home, is a sin, Heaven help the wicked, but pox on't.

Mrs. *Wood.* Ay, now you ban and curse, you Wretch; this you get by keeping Company with Wits, as you call them, a Company of wicked Fellows, the Scum of the Nation, Fellows that have no Religion in 'em, that swear and drink, and wench, and never consider me that am disconsolate at home.

Wood. Oh the incomprehensible blessings of Matrimony!

Mrs. *Wood.* If I were so perfidious and false to take pleasure in a Gallant in the absence of my Husband; but I am too honest, too virtuous for thee, thou ingrateful Wretch: besides, if my Conscience would give me leave, I love you too well for that, you barbarous base Fellow.

Wood. A Pox on her troublesom Vertue, would to Heaven she were a Whore, I should know then what to do with her.   [*Aside.*

Mrs. *Wood.* Other Women can be happy, and have their Husbands carry 'em abroad and delight in their Company, and be proud to be seen with them; but I have such an inhumane ingrateful Creature to mine!

Wood. Come, come, I confess I am behind hand with you, but I'le pay thee all thy arrears, I have a stock in bank.   [*Embraces her.*

Mrs. *Wood.* Heaven, what shall I do?

Wood. Where's the Key, I'le break open the door.

Mrs. *Wood.* Let the Key alone, go get you gone, I am not so impatient; but I'le trust you till night, I should leave open the door, and let all my things be lost; go get you gone, you naughty man, I love you too well to hold out long.

Wood. Well, now you'r come to your self, and speak reason, and have left off railing, I'll go and incourage my self with eating and drinking well, and return and pay you the aforesaid sum with interest.   [*Exit.*

Mrs. *Wood.*] Are you gone? Joy be with you, and more with me,
opens the door.] Mr. *Bevil.*

Enter Bevil.

Bev. Madam, is he gone?

Mrs. *Wood.* Yes, now I hope we shall be safe from further interruption.

Bev. s'Death, this accident has frighted me so, that I am afraid to venture, lest I should be taken Pris'ner agen, and disappoint the Duellists.
                    [*Aside.*

And yet I will; come, Madam.

(131)

Enter Peg.

Peg. Madam, here's Mrs. *Jilt* coming up to give you a Visit.

Mrs. Wood. Why did you not deny me, Huswife, must that vain silly Wench come to trouble us at such a time too. [*Aside.*

Bev. That is she that reports every man that she sees is in love with her, and wou'd marry her, and has been a Whore these seven years. I will take my leave, I see this is an unfortunate day.

Mrs. Wood. No, I'le get rid of her soon by some Trick or other.

Bev. 'Tis impossible. I'll wait on you an hour or two hence, but now I am ingag'd upon my reputation, and must not break my ingagement. Your Servant. [*Ex.* Bevil.

Mrs. Wood. In such haste there must be something more than ordinary in't, I long to know it. *Peg,* go and dog Mr. *Bevil* at a distance, till you have fixt him somewhere, and let me have an account of the reason of his haste.

Peg. I'le not fail. [*Exit.*

Enter Rains *in the Field.*

Rains. I wonder *Bevil* stays so long, this Mrs. *Woodly* has no mercy on him, there's some cross accident or other; for methinks after a year or two's Intrigue, he should not be so very Termagant a Fellow; if these Roguy Bullies should come; but methinks they are a little slow too. Oh, *Bevil,* are you come?

Enter Bevil.

Bev. I beg your pardon, *Jack,* I have been lock'd up to save the Honour of a Lady, whose Husband came in most uncivilly without giving us warning enough of it.

Rains. Was that it? But the Rogues begin to think 'twill come to Battaille, and their hearts misgive 'em.

Bev. I was afraid of this. A Hector dares no more fight than be honest, and yet 'tis strange they should make it their Trade when they are so little fit for't.

Rains. 'Tis so in all Mankind, they are most violently bent upon the things they are least capable of, as if it were in spite of Nature.

Bev. 'Tis true, so I have observ'd while a wise-man that's fit for imployment is restrained by his modesty; your pragmatick dull Fool thrusts himself forward into policy and business.

Rains. Great dulness qualifies men for great business, there's nothing but order and road in it; your Mill-Horse is a Creature of great business. The methodical Block-head that is as regular as a Clock, and as little knows why he is so, is the man cut out by Nature and Fortune for business and government.

(132)

Enter Carolina *and* Lucia *disguised.*

Hold, here come two sprightly Girls, this may prove the softer and pleasanter encounter of the two.

Caro. I see they are men of Honour, and will answer a Challenge.

Luc. Now are they meditating on blood, what a disappointment they'll have. Well, men that are so punctual in their anger, would sure be so in their love.

Bev. Ladies, having the Honour to meet you in so solitary a place, we cannot but offer you our Service.

Luc. You look as if you ftay'd here to make Ladies ftand and deliver.

Enter Peg.

Rains. If you should deliver your beft Jewel, I'de be very honeft and make but a little use on't for the present, and you should carry it away with you ne'ere the worse.

Luc. I know the Law too well to compound a Felony. If you should take any thing of mine, you should e'en keep it as long as you live, but I'd prosecute you for't.

Peg. 'Tis enough, this is Mr. *Bevil*'s ingagement, that's *Carolina*, and the other is Mrs. *Lucia*.   [*Exit.*

Caro. Ye don't look as if you would make Love, but War ; ye have long Swords, and your hair tuck'd up.

Bev. If we were never so much inclin'd to War, you have power to soften us into Peace.

Rains. They are pleasant Wenches ; if they are handsom, we are undone.   [*To* Bevil.

Bev. Twice in a day catch'd with Vizor Masks !

Caro. What wild Fellows hands are we fallen into ? they run at all, you see, they know us not.   [*To* Lucia.

Luc. Oh, if witty men had but the conftancy of Fools, what Jewels were they ?   [*To* Carolina.

Rains. Ladies, pray, lay by your disguises, and let's converse upon the square.

Caro. You make all Prize, Gentlemen ; but I'll venture to show my face to you, Sir, if you'll give me your word not to discover it to your Friend.   [*To* Rains.

Rains. I do, Madam.

Luc. And you shall see mine upon that condition.   [*To* Bevil.

Bev. Upon my Honour, I will not discover you.   [*They pull off their Masks.*

Rains. Ha, who's this ? this is a Trick.   [*Aside.*
Madam, I confess you are very beautiful. I had the misfortune to lose a Heart this morning in your Company, but I think, Madam, you did not take it up ; but my Friend has something to accuse you of.

Bev. I cannot invade the propriety of my Friend, though I muſt confess the great temptation would excuse the crime.

Rains. This is the Lady I muſt apprehend.   [*To* Lucia.

Bev. And, Madam, I muſt seize upon you.   [*To* Carolina.

Caro. Who says they are not a couple of conſtant men?

Bev. What, I warrant, you think we did not know you?

Luc. O yes, as *Falſtaff* did the true Prince by inſtinſt. You are brisk men, I see you run at all.

Rains. The wilder we are, the more honour you'll have in reclaiming us.

Bev. 'Tis in our own power to make us a couple of as conſtant dull Fellows as ye could wish.

Caro. Ye have conſtancy enough of all conscience, for the use we shall have of it.

Luc. And for dulness, for our own sakes we do not wish it you, since I find ye are resolv'd to be acquainted with us, whether we will or no.

Caro. Is it not pity that witty men should be so scandalous, that if we converse with them, we muſt do it with the same privacy that Statesmen debauch.

Bev. If wit be a scandalous thing, you are the moſt scandalous Women I have met with him; but methinks, Fools should rather be scandalous, since they can have but one way of passing their time with you.

Luc. You rally well, but your wit is never without extravagancy; you drink *Burgundy* perpetually, and Scower as you call it.

Bev. We hate debauching, but love complaisance, Madam. And can no more deny a Friend that calls for another Bottle, than you can deny to turn up a Card at *Ombre*.

Rains. We use Wine, Madam, to elevate our thoughts; but Love has don't for me a pleasanter way.

Bev. And, Madam, your Beauty has already reclaim'd me.

Luc. If y'are as soon drunk as y'are in love, y'are the weakeſt Drinkers in Chriſtendom.

Rains. You see, Madam, the ſtrength and spirit of your Beauty.

Luc. For love I bar you, can't we converse without remembring we are of different Sexes.

Caro. If you will accept of such conditions, we may sometimes admit you into our Privy-Council.

Rains. Would you have us spend our time like some visiting Fools, that never aspire at more, than playing at *Langtriloo* with Women, all days of their lives.

Bev. Our communication would then be as dull and insipid, as the mirth of Statesmen.

Enter Cuff *and* Kick.

Luc. Yonders Company coming; such scandal has want of discretion brought upon your wit, that we dare not ſtay with you.

Rains. Let's have the honour to know your Names and Lodgings before you go?

Caro. Our Names are *Carolina* and *Lucia;* our Lodging's next House to Mr. *Woodly*'s nearer the Wells.

Bev. The Rogues are come at laſt.   [Car. *and* Luc. *retire.*

Cuff. Let's make to the Bowling-Green, we shall be too late to begin to engage and bubble the Citizens.

Kick. Who are these make toward us?

Luc. What do *Rains* and *Bevil* make up to yon two for?

Caro. We have done finely, if our feigned Challenge should occasion a real Duel——Let's ſtay and observe.

Rains. Come, Gentlemen, you are very late.

Cuff. I hope we shall be time enough there.

Bev. Y'have done scurvily to make us wait so long, we are not us'd to it.

Kick. What the Devil do they mean, *Cuff?*

Bev. Come, prepare.

Cuff. Prepare, to what?

Rains. s'Death, ye Rascals, do you trifle with us? Come, Draw.

Kick. Draw, Sir, why should we draw, Sir?

Cuff. What, this is for the Ladies in the morning, ne're be jealous of us, Gad take me, we resign to ye.

Rains. Why, what impudent Rascals are ye, did not you send this Challenge?

Kick. We send a Challenge, Sir!

Rains. Y'are a couple of harden'd Cowards.

Kick. Cowards, Gad take me, ye were never so much in the wrong in your life.

Cuff. But I believe if you did not think us Cowards, you'd scarce call us so.

Bev. Ye shall be very much kick'd.

Kick. We scorn to be kick'd, Sir.

Cuff. I see some body behind the Trees, *Kick;* draw, and be valiant. Kick'd, d'ye say? I'd fain see that.   [*They draw, and fight retiring.*

Enter Lucia *and* Carolina.

Luc. Hold, hold, Gentlemen.

Caro. Hear us, what do you do?

Luck. Hold for Heaven's sake.

Rains. Oh you nimble footed Rogues! we cannot run so faſt forward as you do backward.

Caro. What's the matter, Gentlemen?

Bev. These Fellows sent us a Challenge, and then disown'd it.

Kick. As Gad mend me, not we : But if we be not reveng'd on 'em, *Cuff.*

Cuff. What a Pox ail they, we ne're trouble such as they are, if they'll be quiet, we know our men.

Luc. No, to our knowledge they did not send the Challenge.

Caro. The Challenge was sent by better Friends of yours, but such as would be as loth to engage with you at this Weapon, as they are, and would not have discovered this, but to prevent blood-shed.

Rains. Oh, is it so, Ladies?

Bev. 'sDeath, what dull Rogues were we. Gentlemen, ye may go.

Kick. Well, Sir, fare you well.

Cuff. Who cares, you may pay for this though—— [*Ex. Cuff and* Kick.

Rains. Had you a mind to try our courage? Gad we would have met ye in any ground in Christendom, without being dar'd to't.

Luc. We did send the Challenge, and are here to answer ye ; make your best on't.

Bev. Faith, Ladies, if you shrink from us now, we shall think ye have as little Honour as yon Bullies have.

Caro. We did not doubt your Honour, and, pray, don't you doubt ours.

Luc. We know you have too much wit to be vain upon this, and too much generosity to impute it to our weakness. We told ye you should hear from us, and we kept our words, not thinking of this accident.

Caro. We had no way to quit the obligations you did us in the morning, but this.

Rains. But, Ladies, I hope you'll give us leave now, to meet without these preparations, though we should be glad to meet you upon any terms.

Bev. Shall we have free admittance?

Caro. So long as you use your freedom wisely.

Luc. But let us now part in the next Field, and when you see us, still take this rule with you.

> *Think not what's pleasant, but what's just and fit,*
> *And let discretion bridle in your wit.*

ACT III. SCENE I.

Enter Mrs. Woodly *and* Peg.

Mrs. *Wood.* ARE you sure *Bevil* met with *Carolina?*

Peg. I am sure 'twas one in her dress, and Mr. *Rains* walk'd with Mrs. *Lucia;* but I do not know but they might meet by accident.

Mrs. *Wood.* I'll soon try that. Find some means to convey this Note to *Bevil*, as from *Carolina.*

Peg. I will, Madam, and give you an account of it.   [*Ex.* Pegg.

Mrs. *Wood.* If he be false, I shall soon turn my love into revenge.

Enter Mrs. Jilt.

Jilt. Madam, I beg your Ladiships pardon, I have staid too long within ; my Maid brought me a Love-Letter from a sweet fine person indeed, and I vow, I could not but answer it.

Mrs. *Wood.* No doubt, you had reason.
Am I sacrific'd to *Carolina ?*   [*Aside.*

Jilt. He's in the saddest condition for me, just for all the world like a man in a Consumption ; I'll swear 'twould grieve your heart to see him : I'll swear it would, Madam——

Mrs. *Wood.* And why were you so cruel ?

Jilt. I vow, I am the strangest person for that in the whole world ; I could not marry a Prince if I did not like his person strangely, and I have a world of choice, upon my word that's all, I'll swear it is.

Mrs. *Wood.* Since you have such choice, why are you unmarried two days ?

Jilt. I have such an odd fancy, Madam, I am so nice and hard to please, and I vow, I don't care for Marriage, but that I would be a little setl'd in the World, that's all ; there's Mr. *Bevil*, Oh, he loves me dearly !

Mrs. *Wood.* Love her, how she stabs me.   [*Aside.*

Jilt. And I'll swear he's a fine person, I have the prettiest, sweetest, delicate Letters from him every day.

Mrs. *Wood.* What says she ?   [*Aside.*

Jilt. Your Ladiship will be secret, I know : he has a strange passion for me ; upon my word, he sighs and sits with his Arms a-cross, and makes *Doux yeux* upon me ; I'll swear 'twould do your Ladiship good to see him. Now I think on't, I'le show your Ladiship the kindest Letters from him. I have so many Love-letters, I vow, I can scarce find it. I have twice as many come to me in a week.   [*She pulls out a great bundle of Letters.*

Mrs. *Wood.* Vain, silly Creature !

Jilt. Oh, here's one of his hand !

Mrs. *Wood.* Heaven, it is his hand.
      Mrs. *Jilt.*

Mrs. *Wood.* Reads, *I wonder at the occasion of your mistrust, unless you have been tampering with some body else ; I am very well, and drink much Hockamore, and perhaps have given you more occasion for a Midwife than a Surgeon.*

July 22. 72.   Bevil.

O perfidious Wretch! this is since my Intrigue with him. This will distract me; I could tear him in pieces.

Jilt. Your Ladiship is disturb'd at something.

Mrs. *Wood.* No, no; but this is a very familiar Love-letter, as you call it.

Jilt. Oh, mischief! that I should put this among the rest of my Letters; but I'll face her down in it, ha, ha, ha.

Mrs. *Wood.* What's the cause of your laughter?

Jilt. Ha, ha, ha, to see what a ridiculous mistake this was. It seems there's a Wench in *Coven-garden* of my Name, and Mr. *Bevil's* man brought this Note to me instead of her; I'll swear he did, ha, ha, ha.

Mrs. *Wood.* Oh, Impudence!

Jilt. We had such a quarrel about it; I did not speak to him for three days after, I vow, I did not. [*Enter* Peg.

Mrs. *Wood.* How now, *Peg*, what News of *Bevil?*

Peg. I got a Maid of my acquaintance to deliver the Note to him, which he received with the greatest Joy imaginable, and said, he would wait on her instantly.

Mrs. *Wood.* Oh perfidious Wretch! I'll to him immediately. Excuse me, Mrs. *Jilt,* I am in great haste. [*Ex. Mrs.* Woodly.

Jilt. Your Servant, sweet Madam. She's strangely nettl'd about something. Well, now we are alone, Sister, I'le owne thee: I hope your Lady knows not that we are of Kin.

Peg. No, nor any body else here.

Jilt. Prethee keep it secret still, that I may be taken for a greater person than I am; it will further my designs.

Peg. But I wonder you will not bend all your designs upon Mr. *Clodpate.*

Jilt. I have baits ready for him, I can humour him to a hair; but I'le lay by no design that can get me any manner of Husband, that's once. But 'tis strange *Clodpate* and I should not meet, I lying in this house too where he comes often.

Peg. Next time he comes to visit my Master, I'le give you notice.

Enter Clodpate.

Jilt. Oh, me! he's here to our wish, and we alone; remember your Cue.

Clodp. Mr. *Woodly* is not here I see.

Jilt. Oh that villainous lewd Town of *London!* how happy am I that am out on't, nothing shall ever perswade me thither again.

Peg. Why? Sir *William* your Father, sent you thither for Breeding.

Jilt. Breeding, yes; could I not play, *I am the Duke of* Norfolk, *Green-Sleeves,* and the *fourth Psalm* upon the Virginals; and did I not learn, and could play six Lessons upon the Viol *de Gambo,* before I went to that nasty, stinking, wicked Town; out on't?

Clodp. Ud's bud, this is an ingenious Woman.

(138)

Peg. Besides, Madam, though you be a Person of Quality, and have a good portion, yet *London* is the properest place to get a Husband in.

Jilt. Oh foh——I'le swear I had rather marry a Farmer of forty pound a year in the Country, than a vain, idle, fluttering, foolish *London*-Fellow of two thousand pound a year. Oh the pleasure of a pretty, innocent Country-life !

Clodp. Ud'sooks she's i'th right; as Gad judge me, she's a judicious person.

Peg. Oh, hang a dull silly Country-life.

Clodp. A Pox on that Carrion, how I could beat her.

Jilt. Out on thee for a foolish Wench; were I thy Lady, I'de turn thee away for that word.

Peg. Pray, pardon me, Madam, I am sorry I offended your Ladiship.

Jilt. Can'st thou talk so after the Song the Fidler sung this morning in praise of the Country ? Oh that he were here, I should never be weary of hearing that Song.

Peg. I see him yonder, I'le call him to you.   [*Ex.* Peg.

Clodp. Madam, I have over-heard and admired your excellent Discourse upon the Country.

Jilt. Who are you, some bold, jeering, fleering *Londoner?* avoid my presence.

Clodp. Ud's bud, you wrong me, I am a Country Justice, Gad'sooks.

Jilt. Pray be gone, and leave me, you are some rude *London*-Fellow; foh, you smell rank on't.

Clodp. As Gad shall save me, she's a fine Person : if I were not ingag'd to *Carolina*, I should like her strangely.

Enter Peg *and* Fidler.

Peg. Here's the honest Fellow that sings the Song, Madam.

Jilt. I have nothing to say to him, I am troubled with an impertinent Fellow here, and he shall not sing.

Clodp. By your leave, Madam, 'tis in praise of the Country, and he shall sing. Sing, dear Rogue.

Fidler Sings.

Oh, how I abhor
The tumult and smoak of the Town,
The Clamours of War,
The glittering Court, the fraudulent Gown,
The Suburb debauches,
The Cheats of the City,
The ratling of Coaches,
And the noise of the men they call witty.

(139)

Clodp. Admirable.

> *But give me the man from all vanity free,*
> *with good store of Land,*
> *And a Country Command,*
> *who honest dares be.*
> *Who Justice dares do, and the Nation will serve,*
> *And ne're from his true Country principle swerve.*
> *This, this is the man for me.*

Jilt. Very fine.

> *While the fluttering vain Gallant in* London *consumes*
> *His Estate in rich Cloaths and Perfumes,*
> *And with drinking and swilling corrupts all his health;*
> *Or in Punk and on Bawd spends his youth and his wealth,*
> *While such shall his wit and his bounty applaud.*

Clodp. Admirable.

> *Give me the good man that lives on his own grounds,*
> *And within his own bounds*
> *Has room for his Hawks and his Hounds.*
> *Can feast his own Tenants with Fowls and with Fishes,*
> *And from his own plenty with good store of Dishes,*
> *And not with damn'd Wine, but with good* English *Ale*
> *O'er their faithful hearts can prevail,*
> *And nothing to others does owe.*
> *But from his own house hears his own Oxen low,*
> *And his own Sheep bleat,*
> *While the grateful sounds sweet Echoes repeat.*
> *This, this is the man that is truly call'd great.*

Jilt. Excellent, there's a Crown; pray, come and sing this to me twice a day, as long as I stay in *Epsom.*

Fid. I will, Madam.

Clodp. 'Tis incomparable, let me embrace thee, there's ten shillings for thee; and if thou wilt live with me in *Sussex,* thou shalt never see *London* again.

Fid. Pardon me, Sir, I was born and bred in *London,* and would not live out on't for five hundred pound a year.

Jilt. Out on you, you scurvy Fellow.

Clodp. aside. A pox on him for a Rascal. Thou art a very honest Fellow, give me my ten shillings agen, and I'll make it a Guinny.

Fid. There 'tis and please you.

Clodp. Ay, and here 'tis, and shall be. Do you think I'll let a *London* Rogue carry away ten shillings of my money?

Fid. Why, you will not take it away thus?

Clodp. Yes, I will, and you may thank Heaven that it is unseemly in a Magistrate to break heads. Be gone, you insolent Rascal, lest you should tempt me to condescend to break yours.

Fid. What the Devil, are they both mad? farewel. [*Ex.*

Clodp. An insolent *London* Rogue, to sing against his Conscience; but pray, Madam, let me salute you, you're a fine person.

Jilt. No, Sir, fare you well; Sir, you're a stranger, fare you well, I am none of those. [*Ex.* Jilt.

Clodp. Who's this, Mrs. *Margaret?*

Peg. She's a Person of Quality comes to *Epsom* for her pleasure, I must wait on her. [*Exit* Peg.

Clodp. She's a fine Lady, but I must to *Carolina*. [*Exit* Clodp.

Enter Bevil *in a Field.*

Bev. Carolina writ to me to meet her alone? She's very frank; let me see, she says meet me alone, that we may confer about an affair which nearly concerns us both. 'sDeath I have dropt my Letter, unlucky accident, I must go back for it. I cannot now, she's here.

[*Enter Mrs.* Woodly *disguised.*

'Tis a solitary place, and I hope no body will find it.

Mrs. Wood. Ah, false wretch! how punctual he is. [*Aside.*

Bev. Ah, my dear *Carolina.*

Mrs. Wood. Ah, my cursed *Bevil.* [*Aside.*

Bev. I have not words enough to acknowledge and thank you for this favour.

Mrs. Wood. Nor I words enough to upbraid you for this injury. [*Aside.*

Bev. How now, what is she dumb? Madam, you see how conscientious I am in my duty of assignation; you shall always find me a man of Honour.

Mrs. Wood. Yes, I thank you, you are a man of Honour. [*Unmasks.*

Bev. 'sDeath, Mrs. *Woodly!* how unlucky is this, she'll stay too, and prevent my meeting with *Carolina;* I am undone, I must conceal the Intrigue. Nothing but impudence can bring me off. [*Aside.*

Mrs. Wood. Unworthy man.

Bev. You do well, pray, who was this assignation made to? I can watch your private haunts, you see, Madam.

Mrs. Wood. Are you past all sense of modesty?

Bev. We shall soon see your Lover here, I suppose.

Mrs. Wood. Have I caught you, and do you accuse me? I have been as virtuous and as constant to my Intrigue as any Woman breathing: have

I not had as many Addresses made to me by the fine persons of the Town and Court as any Lady has?

Bev. And have refus'd as few, I'll say that for you.   [*Aside.*

Mrs. *Wood.* Have I not deny'd all, to be constant to you?

Bev. Gad, I hate constancy in a Woman, after a little while; especially in an impertinent one, as much as constancy in a Quartane-Ague.

Mrs. *Wood.* And all this to be betrayed to *Carolina!* perfidious man!

Bev. Ha, ha, ha——I knew I should catch you; there was no way I knew to make you shew your face, but my pretending to another: *Carolina*, I think, I call'd her.

Mrs. *Wood.* Oh, abominable treachery! I forged that Letter from *Carolina*, which you even now received with the greatest joy imaginable: Ungrateful man!

Bev. Well, give me your little Punck, for Marriage is not so troublesome as the imperiousness of your Whore of Honour.   [*Aside.*

Mrs. *Wood.* Have I deserv'd this from you?

Bev. Well, I confess you have catcht me. I was indeed amaz'd at the Letter, having only heard of *Carolina*, and had a curiosity to see the meaning on't.

Mrs. *Wood.* Yes, 'twas curiosity made you walk with her in the Forenoon, in a Field beyond the New-Inn.

Bev. 'sDeath, how came she to know it?   [*Aside.*
Was that *Carolina?*   [*To her.*

Mrs. *Wood.* As if you did not know it, inhumane Creature. Nor is this all; I saw a Letter just now to one Mrs. *Jilt*, wherein you tell her you have given her more occasion for a Midwife than a Surgeon.

Bev. 'sDeath, how come she to see that, she deals with the Devil?

Mrs. *Wood.* You shall find, ungrateful man, that love does as naturally degenerate into revenge, as Wine into Vinegar: do you abuse me, a virtuous Lady, a Lady of Honour, for such a Creature, without any consideration of my Quality?

Bev. Pox on her Quality. This is all a mistake, Madam.

Mrs. *Wood.* I know your Hand too well for that: you might use your little tawdry, mercinary Creatures so, that flutter about the Town in their short-liv'd bravery: but a Woman of my Quality——

Bev. Well, however 'tis in other things, I would have no liberty of Conscience in whoring: I would have none but those Women hold forth that are in lawful Orders, 'tis the more setled way, and has more the face of Discipline.

Mrs. *Wood.* If I be not reveng'd for this——

Enter Woodly *with a Note in his hand.*

Wood. How the Devil came *Bevil* to lose this Note in the Fields, *Carolina*

appoint to meet him privately? I thought he ne're had seen her——
Death how she Jilts me.

   Reads. *That we may freely confer about an Affair which nearly concerns*
   us both.   Carolina.

Hell and Devil he's with her there; I'll steal behind 'em and surprize 'em.
So, *Bevil*, is this your private business?

 Mrs. *Wood.* My Husband, I dye, I dye.

 Bev. You have done well, you have frighted a Lady into a swound;
Heaven knows what will become of her.

 Wood. I knew she would be surpriz'd.

 Bev. Unlucky man.

 Wood. Death, *Ned*, you'll stifle her, pull off her Mask, and give her more
air.

 Bev. Pray forbear, Sir, you are not to see her; she recovers.

 Mrs. *Wood.* Give her more air, quoth a'? how he frighted me?

 Wood. Good, Sir *Pol*, make a secret on't no longer; she may as well
unmask, she and I are no strangers to one another.

 Mrs. *Wood.* What says he?   [*Aside.*

 Bev. You may have seen her, but you are not acquainted with her.

 Wood. Ad autre, prethee leave fooling.

 Bev. Upon my Honour you are not——
A Gentleman ought in Honour to lye for his Mistress.   [*Aside.*

 Wood. I could sooner believe a Country Gentleman that swears and
lyes for the honour of his Horse, when he is selling him.

 Mrs. *Wood.* He knows me; I am lost, undone for ever.

 Bev. Whatever happens, do not discover your self.

 Wood. I am oblig'd to you, you can be kind to others.

 Mrs. *Wood.* Can any thing be more plain?

 Bev. Prethee, *Woodly*, trouble us no farther; I assure you, you neither do,
nor shall know this Lady.

 Wood. Is it so? Fare you well. I will let 'em alone at present.
                    [*Ex.* Woodly.

 Bev. He'll go home, and discover that 'tis you.

 Mrs. *Wood.* As good luck would have it, I have the Key of the back
Gate, and can be there before him: I hope I shall bear him down that it
was not I.   [*Exit Mrs.* Woodly.

 Bev. I doubt not. Oh Woman, Woman! impudence and invention
never fail thee at a pinch.   [*Exit.*
   [*A noise within of rub, rub, narrow, short, gone a thousand yards,*
     and such like words of Bowlers.]

    Enter Bisket, Fribble, Cuff, *and* Kick.

 Cuff. Come, Mr. *Bisket*, let's hold 'em t'other Game.

       (143)

Bisk. As I am an honest man, I have lost all my money.

Frib. And so have I, and yet you bowl'd like an Emperour, Neighbour *Bisket*, the two last Games, but Mr. *Cuff*'s hand was quite out.

Bisk. A Duce take it, we ne're won one Game since Mr. *Kick* laid against us, and in my Conscience and Soul he is a Witch, for Mr. *Cuff* ne're plaid well after.

Cuff. I'll make you amends if you'll play again.

Frib. But we have no Money.

Kick. I have 40 or 50 *l*. to spare, you shall have it betwixt you.

[*Mrs.* Bisket *and Mrs.* Fribble *look out at the Window.*

Bisk. No, we'll drink a Bottle first and rest, my thighs ake with bowling, Cods me, yonder are our Wives looking out at the Window to see us bowl ; poor Rogues, i'fack we'll have a Bottle with them. I warrant you, they have been dancing in a Barn yonder, with some Neighbours, I hear their Fiddles.

Dor. Mr. *Rains* is not yonder ; I'll swear he's rare company.

Mrs. *Bisk.* A Murrain take you ; and you had not troubled us with your impertinence, he had been better company to me to day than he was.

[*Aside.*

Dor. Yonder are our Husbands, I am resolv'd as you have advis'd me to pluck up a spirit. But let's down to 'em now, for fear we lose 'em.

[*They go down.*

Bisk. Now here's my Wife, I'll be bold to say, I'll shew you the handsomest Woman in *Epsom*.

Frib. It must be my Wife then, I'll tell you that.

Bisk. Your Wife handsomer than mine ! that's pleasant, ha, ha.

Cuff. This may prove as good as bowling with them.

Kick. I never saw two so cut out for honest tame suffering Cuckolds.

Cuff. There are many as fit here, if their Wives be as handsome as they say theirs are.

Frib. Come, I'll hold you 20 *s*. to be spent, and these Gentlemen shall be Judges here.

Bisk. With all my heart. But I am sure mine is the prettiest, neatest, titest Woman in the Ward.

Frib. I have seen our Minister stare at my Wife in her Pew, 'till he has been out in his Sermon, she's so pretty. And you shall see, Gentlemen, what discipline I keep her in ; 'tis the obedientest poor Creature !

Bisk. Nay, mine has some humours, but they become her so prettily, and 'tis the sweetest little Rogue ! I vow she has had more temptations than any Woman in *Cheapside*, ne're stir.

Frib. More temptations than my Wife, I scorn your words. There are a company of the bravest Gallants come to my Shop to see her, and she'll not speak to any of them——i'faith not she.

Bisk. I have known Knights, nay, Lords in love with my Wife, and she does make such Fools of 'em all. Poor Rogue, ha, ha, ha, my dear Lamb, art thou come?

Enter Mrs. Bisket *and* Dorothy.

Mrs. *Bisk.* Yes, you Sot; but is't not time for you to come home? Mr. *Rains* has been gone this three hours.

Bisk. I told you she had some humours. Pretty Duck, i'fack now, I have catch'd you, I'll give you a Bottle of Wine and a Quart of Mum.

Frib. These are my Friends, Gentlemen, an please you.
                              [*He presents them to his Wife and they salute her.*
Bisk. This is my Duck, Gentlemen.   [*They salute Mrs.* Bisket.
Has not my Lamb a rare way of kissing? I warrant you for the Wager, Neighbour.

Frib. I fear you not.

Cuff. What admirable Cuckolds and Bubbles have we met with.

Frib. Now, Gentlemen, observe here's a stately forehead.

Bisk. But here's a delicious Eye-brow, and sweet rowling wanton Eye: She's my *Cacara camouchi*, my pretty Pigs nye, as *Mamamouchi* notably has it.

Kick. Excellent fine.

Mrs. *Bisk.* Alas, alas! I, but what do you mean by this, you are always fooling thus before Company.

Bisk. Peace, I have laid a Wager on thy head against Mrs. *Fribble.*

Frib. Here are pretty plump red lips.

Bisk. But see my Ducks teeth, and smell her sweet breath. Breath on 'em, Duck.

Frib. Here's pure red and white; here's a shape.   [*He turns her round.*

Cuff. Most admirable.

Frib. 'Tis your goodness, Sir.

Kick. These Fools praise their Wives, as Horse-Coursers do their Horses, to put 'em off.

Bisk. Prethee Dear, do but shew them a little of your Foot and Leg, good Duck, now if thou lovest me, do prethee now.

Mrs. *Bisk.* Well, well, so I can: there 'tis.

Bisk. A little higher, but up to your Garter, good Lamb.

Mrs. *Bisk.* You are such a simple Fellow.

Cuff. Oh, 'tis charming!

Mrs. *Bisk.* You are so obliging really.

Frib. Here's a fine round small white hand.

Kick. Extreme fine.

Mrs. *Frib.* You are pleased to Complement.

(145)

Frib. Now you shall see how obedient my Wife is, she durſt as well eat her Nails as refuse what I command. *Doll,* pray kiss these two Gentlemen immediately. Now you shall see.

Dor. Pray, Dear, what do you mean?

Frib. How now, Huswife, dare you dispute my Commands, Hah?

Dor. Be not angry, I muſt obey.

Kick. Your Servant, dear Madam.   [*They kiss her.*

Cuff. Your humble Servant.

Frib. Look you, did I not tell you what discipline she was under?

Bisk. Good sweet dear Lamb, do thee as much if thou lov'ſt me do.

Mrs. *Bisk.* Not for your bidding: but they shall find I am not behind Mrs. *Fribble* in good breeding.

Bisk. Gentlemen, my Dear shall salute you too.

Frib. Ay, it won't do.

Kick. Your Servant, dear Lady.

Cuff. Sweet Madam, your humble Servant.

Frib. Come now, let's in, and be very merry, and decide the Wager.

Kick. Allons, this is the moſt extraordinary adventure, but you know we have a weighty Affair in hand; our Bullies will be all ready immediately.

Cuff. We'll swinge the Rascals, *Rains* and *Bevil:* but we muſt make haſte, this is the time they use to come to the Bowling-Green, we'll meet them.

Kick. There is another weighty affair. *Clodpate* is to duſt his Stand of Ale, and he muſt be bubbled; we have not long to ſtay with 'em.

Cuff. We muſt borrow our selves of 'em for a while.

Frib. Gentlemen, will you please to walk in?

Cuff. Come on.   [*Ex. omnes.*

Enter Rains *and* Lucia.

Luc. A man of wit and make love, leave off this foolish old fashion'd subjeſt: I'd have all discourse between us tend to something.

Rains. 'Tis as unseasonable for a young Lady not to entertain love, as for a Judge or a Bishop to make love.

Luc. Love is so foolish and scandalous a thing, none now make use of any thing but ready money.

Rains. Methinks, ready Love is a pretty thing.

Luc. But there are few in this Age have it about 'em.

Rains. I have as good a Stock, and am as full of love, Madam——

Luc. That you squander it away upon every one you see, as a young Prodigal newly of age, treats and pays reckonings for every body.

Rains. How prodigal soever I have been, I am resolv'd to take up in my expences, and reserve all my love for you.

Luc. For me? I am as hard to be fixt as you: I love liberty as well as any of ye.

Rains. Say you so ? Faith let's make use on't.

Luc. Not the lewd liberty you mean : Come, to divert us better, go a little further, and try the Eccho, here is an extraordinary one that will answer you to as much purpose as I can.

Rains. 'Tis a fine Eccho, but, Madam———— [*Ex.* Rains *and* Lucia.

Enter Woodly *and* Carolina.

Caro. Nothing but love, love : always one Note like a Cuckow.

Wood. Fine *Jilt*, I can no more restrain my self, than a Fanatick full of new lights and revelations can himself.

Caro. Can I suffer this any longer without prejudice to my virtue and honour ; let me hear no more, you will not suffer me to use you like a Gentleman.

Wood. I am too loyal to rebel against you, but I may attack your evil Counsellors, your virtue and honour.

Caro. You'll find them impregnable.

Wood. Virtue and Chastity unsociable foolish qualities ! I hope to live till every such Woman shall be thought vicious, or at least as much scandalous as a Lawyer with a tatter'd Gown out of practice : We are in a fair way to it.

Caro. If you resolve to persist in this subject, I will ask the advice of your Lady before I treat further.

Wood. Say you so, Madam ? there is a pleasant Field behind my Lodgings, 'tis delicate walking there at this time o' day, especially if you have one you like there.

Caro. What say you, Sir ?

Wood. No, no, Madam, you were not there, you know not what I mean.

Caro. What Riddle's this of yours ?

Wood. But the Lady was not so ill to pull off her Mask, and discover her Face, tho' for more Air.

Caro. You are mad, that I confess is one sign of a Lover.

Wood. Oh Woman-kind, the Original of all lying, I confess he said upon his Honour, I did not know her, but I could read her Note, it would not do.

Caro. This is so extravagantly ridiculous, it deserves no serious answer.

Enter Bevil.

Wood. Here's *Bevil*, I'le not show her Note till I have an opportunity to push this business home. I knew you were not far off, *Ned*, come.

Caro. Does he know of our interviews ? [*Aside.*

Bev. What mean'st thou, *Franck* ?

Wood. You are not acquainted with this Lady, no.

Bev. I wish nothing more than the acquaintance of so fine a Lady.

[*Rains and* Lucia *appear.*

Wood. What impudence is this that makes thee fool with me any longer thus? Yonder's *Rains*, he is not acquainted with my Cousin *Lucia* neither. No, no, come, *Rains*, you may show your self, your Intrigue is discovered.

Rains. What Intrigue, *Franck?*

Wood. Cousin *Lucia*, your Servant; I see, Sir, you can serve your self without the help of your Friends.

Rains. Is this his Cousin *Lucia?*

Luc. Oh! Is that the Intrigue? These two Gentlemen rescu'd us this morning from the insolence of two Hectors.

Caro. Yes, and with their Swords protected us from their violence, and reveng'd the affront.

Luc. We are not so ungrateful to disown those that had oblig'd us so much.

Caro. This morning was the first time they ever saw us.

Wood. You are grown very familiar already, Madam.

Caro. If I be, you are not concern'd, I assure you.

Wood. I fear too much. But how do you like *Lucia*, *Jack?* have you a design of lying with her one way or other?

Rains. Mum, *Woodly*, or I will discover all your Rogueries to your Lady Bright at home; be satisfied I like her too well to dishonour her. But to divert this. [*He whistles, and the Fiddles flourish.*

Wood. What a Devil's this?

Bev. We are fallen into an Ambuscade of Fiddlers.

Luc. Do you conjure?

Caro. You charm the Air to give us Sounds.

Rains. The truth is, Madam, 'tis a Trap I have laid for you, and you have no way but to dance your self out on't.

Caro. No, then I am resolv'd to free my self as soon as I can. Play a Jigue. [*She dances.*

Enter Clodpate *with a Dog.*

Clodp. What you are merry with your Fiddles. I have been hunting up and down for Madam *Carolina*; I came to present you with some Country Partridges; here's dear *Tray*, a *Sussex*-Dog, set 'em for you, Oh he ranges with such mettle, and points so true. Poor *Tray*, Gad I love and honour him.

Bev. That *Tray* is the better qualifi'd Beast of the two.

Clodp. Pray, Madam, kiss him a little.

Caro. Kiss a Dog?

Clod. A Dog, Ud'sooks he has as sweet a breath as any man, I won't say

(148)

Lady has.   Your scurvy *London*-Ladies feed their Dogs at their Tables, and have Joynts of Mutton roasted on purpose for 'em, and make them their Bed-fellows for want of better.   But since you don't love a Dog, Madam, I'll be bold to say, yonder's the beautifull'st Dapple Mare of mine that my Man leads there.   There's a Buttock, Madam, how clean she treads upon her Pasterns.   There's a Body round as a Barrel; there's a Head and Neck finely rais'd, a delicate broad Chest.   Gads'ooks she's the finest forehanded Mare in Christendom, there's Beauty, and you talk of Beauty.

Rains. He describes his Mare so passionately, I shall begin to suspect her vertue.

Clodp. But I must desire some words with you in private.

Caro. I am going to visit now; but shortly I will hear you.

Clodp. I had waited on you sooner, but that I have been giving out Warrants, and binding some *London* Rogues to the Peace, and the like. Thus I represent the Kings Person, I.

Caro. You are the worst Picture of him that ever I saw.

Clodp. I am content, Madam, to imploy my self in business, and to serve my Country, while your *London* Sparks, lascivious, libidinous Swines follow their beastly lusts and sensual pleasures.   Poor Fools, I pity 'em.

Wood. Why, we have Justices of the Peace that serve the Nation at *London*.

Clodp. What, honest ones? thank you for that; they are the greatest Malefactors there; they make a pretty Trade on't in the Suburbs with Bribes received from Pads, Pick-pockets, and Shop-lifts, with the Taxes they raise from labouring Whores, and Contributions from Tributary Bawds; but Gentlemen, will you dust a Stand with me?

Enter Kick *and* Cuff *with six more.*

Rains. We are all engag'd.

Kick. Here they are, they shall find that none shall affront any of our Gang unpunisht.

Cuff. As long as we Bullies hold together, we defie the World, we'll chastise their insolence: fall on.

   [*They fight, and* Lucia *and* Carolina *shreek and run away.*

Kick. Come, have at you.

Rains. How now. ⎫
Bev. Rogues. ⎬
Wood. You Dogs. ⎭

Clodp. Hold, I command you in the King's Name, keep the Peace.   I am a Justice of *Quorum*, and represent the King's Person.   I say, keep the Peace, or I'll bind you all over to the Sessions.   [*The Bullies are beaten off.*

Wood. Let's pursue the Rogues, and now we have won the field, take them Prisoners.

Rains. Dam 'em, they are not worth our pursuit; I know two of 'em, and shall find out the rest.

Clodp. Go, I say, and bring 'em before me, and I will bind 'em to the Peace, and make 'em be of good abearing till the next Sessions, or they shall forfeit their Recullisence.

Bev. We are oblig'd to you for your help, you fought bravely.

Clodp. 'Tis very indecent for a Magistrate to fight, I will give you Law.

Wood. 'Pox of his Cowardize; but what mean these Rogues?

Rains. Let's find the Ladies, I'le tell you as we go.   [*Exeunt*.

ACT IV. SCENE I.

Enter Clodpate, *two Country-Fellows*, Cuff, *and* Kick *in Country Habits*.

Kick. THese Disguises have done us Knights Service.

Cuff. He'll begin to be drunk by and by, preach the Parson upon him, or try Coal under the Candlestick, even or odd with a Witness, or the grand Game at Put, for I find he hates Dice.

Clodp. Come, Gentlemen, put about a Cup of Ale. 'Tis stingo i'faith; is not this better than your foolish *French* kickshaw Claret? This is of the growth and product of our own Country, and we encourage the noble Manufacture of Ale. How say you? come fill all.   [*Drinks*.

1 *Count*. His Worship is a notable man in the Politicks as e'er a Justice of *England*, no dispraise——

2 *Count*. He has a brave Head-piece of his own.

Clodp. Fill again once, Oh Gentlemen, things do not go well. There's the *Streights* Trade I was speaking of, why, it signifies not a Farthing to us; for, look you, if the Manufacture or Commodity exported, be not equal to the Commodity imported, we must ruine our Trade, that's clear demonstration. Now we send them money in specie for foolish superfluities, for Currans to make Mince-pyes with; it grieves my heart to think on't: but come, dust it away.

Kick. Your Worship speaks like an Oracle.

Clodp. Then there is your Canary Trade takes away not one of our Manufactures. Well, no more to be said, I am not thought worthy, but here's to you.   [*Drinks*.

Cuff. A very politick Coxcomb.   [*Aside*.

1 *Count*. What News is there in the Gazette, an't please you?

Clodp. Why, there 'tis. We keep a puther about the honest *Dutch*, I say

(150)

nothing, but I hate *French* Fricasies and Ragousts, and *French* Dances too; but no more to be said, fill agen.   Gud'sooks, here's your true *English* Ale and your true *English* Hearts.   [*He Drinks.*

2. *Count.* I purtest he's incomparable man.

Clod. In the mean time poor *Poland*'s in danger, and yet *Sobieski*'s a pretty man, and *Wisnowiski*, and *Lubomirski*, and *Potoski* too pretty men, very pretty men; but, alas! they are but men, we ne're think of assisting 'em, and poor *Poland* may be lost, and we are in a fine condition; but here's t'other Pot.   [*All drink.*

Kick. Excellent Coxcomb! but what hurt can the loss of *Poland* do us, Sir?

Clodp. Lord, that you should ask such a question, why 'twill spoil our Trade of Tin, no people in the World can make Lattin Ware, or work our Tin well, but they; the *Germans* indeed pretend to it: this would trouble a man that loves his Country as I do.

2 *Count.* What Religion are they of in *Poland*, an't please your Worship?

Clodp. Why, they are Christians, they are not within the Pale indeed, but they are very good out-liers.

Cuff. Let's ply him hard.   Come, here's a Health to all your Deputy Lieutenants.

Clodp. Come on, I hope to be one my self, I serve the Nation upon a true Country-principle, and have as many friends as any man upon a National account.

1 *Count.* Here's News from *Ditto*; an't please your Worship, what place is that?   I ask'd our Minister, and he could not tell me.

Clodp. Fy upon him; why *Ditto* is a Town in *Pomerania*, a very fine Town: but fill agen.

Kick. Here's a Health to the Bishop of *Munster*.

Clodp. Excuse me, Sir, he's a Popish Bishop, and I'le drink ne're a Papists Health on 'em all; he a Clergy-man, and run up and down souldiering and fighting! truly he may be asham'd on't; and he were a godly man, he'd stay at home and preach; I hate a lazy Bishop that won't preach; but here's my Cup.   Come on, Udsooks, I begin to be fox't.

Cuff. That's good News, *Kick*.

Clodp. Well, *Poland*'s a brave Nation, and they have a Company of the fiercest magnanimous Fellows, your *Iskies, Oskies, Irskies, Ouskies, Erskis,* and the *Cossacks* upon the *Ukrain*, there's a Monarchy as it should be, every thing governed by the great Council.   Uds bud they have the best Diet in Christendom.

2 *Count.* Nay, with his Worships leave, an' they have better Diet than *English* Beef.   I'le be sacrific'd——

1 *Count.* An't please your Worship we'll present you with a Country-dance; we have Companions without, if you please, Sir.

Clodp. With all my heart.

[*Dance of two Clowns and two Country Wenches.*
Uds bud, my head begins to turn round ; but let's into the House. 'Tis dark. we'll have one *Bellarmine* there, and then *Bon Nouscius*, I must to my Mistress, she's the prettiest Rogue——

Sings. *Her Lips are two Brimmers of Claret,*
Where first I began to miscarry,
Her Breasts of delight
Are two Bottles of white,
And her Eyes are two Cups of Canary.   [*Ex. omnes.*

Enter Rains.

Rains. Mrs. *Jilt* appointed to meet me here, she's handsome, and I hope sound. I love *Lucia* even to the renouncing of Wine and good Company ; but flesh and blood is not able to hold out her time without some refreshment by the bye.

Enter Mrs. Jilt.

Jilt. O are you here ! well you think me a strange confident person to meet you thus ; but if I had not known you to be a fine sweet man, and 'tis dark, and you cannot see my blushes, Sir, I would have suffered all the extremities in the World before I would have done it, I'le swear I wou'd.

Rains. What extremities can you suffer, pretty Mrs. *Jilt.*

Jilt. No, 'tis no matter what I suffer, Alas ! Alas !

Rains. What's the matter ?

Jilt. I am the most unhappy Lady in the whole World, I'll swear, ah, ha ; but 'tis no matter, I may thank my self for't, I vow.

Rains. What have you lost Friends or Money ?

Jilt. No, no, I have something nearer my heart than all that. 'Tis not money that I care for, I'le swear, not I.

Rains. I find that some body has catch'd you, you are in Love.

Jilt. If I were not in Love, I were a happy Woman ; but now I am the most unfortunate Maid in the whole World, I'll swear, oh, oh.

Rains. Fy on't, young and pretty, and despair in this Age.

Jilt. Oh, but this is so fine, so excellent a Person, he'll ne're love me, I am ruin'd, oh, oh.

Rains. Who is this bewitching Man ?

Jilt. Oh it's no matter, alas ! who cares what becomes of me ? a poor inconsiderable person, tho' none can say I am not a Gentlewoman, and well bred, but 'tis no matter. Oh, oh, but the Gentleman is no ill Friend of yours, upon my word, now.

Rains. Prithee who is it ?

Jilt. A great acquaintance of Mr. *Bevil*'s, a *Norfolk* Gentleman.

(152)

Rains. S'death, she won't put this upon me at laſt, he's acquainted with none of my Country but my self.   [*Aside.*

Jilt. He's the wittieſt, fineſt, handsomeſt well-bred Gentleman in the whole World, I'le swear.

Rains. Prithee tell his Name, I can be secret.

Jilt. The firſt Letter of his Name is R. but why should I say so much? I am a loſt Woman, he'll never love me, oh, oh.

Rains. Though not by your fine description, yet by my Country and my Name you wou'd perswade me, that I am the happy Man.

Jilt. She kisses his hand.] Now shall I never see you agen, you'll hate me for my confidence. Oh that my Tongue should betray me thus! Oh that I had bit it out before I had said this! Oh my heart will break, I'le swear.

Rains. Gad, her Tears have mollifi'd me : it shall ne're be said a Woman shall dye under my hands ; but she might have brought it about without all these Circumſtances.   [*Aside.*

Jilt. Oh unfortunate Woman! I know you'll hate me for this, oh, oh.

Rains. No, my Dear, I am none of those, do but ſtep into my Lodging where there's a good Convenience as can be ; and if I do not give you as good proof of my affeƈtions——

Jilt. Good Sir, you miſtake me ; do you take me for a Strumpet ? No, Sir, I'de have you to know I am no such, I swear.

Rains. I know you are modeſt ; but Lovers should lay by that.

Jilt. I lay by my modeſty! Heaven forbid, you are a wicked libidinous person ; I wonder you have the confidence to affront one of my Birth and Breeding thus like a base man.

Rains. Oh, oh, all this talk of love is a trick, is it ? you might have plac'd it better, good Madam *Jilt.*

Jilt. No, Sir, it is no trick, and that you should find, if you would but——

Rains. But what ?

Jilt. But marry me, that's all I swear.   [*Cries.*

Rains. All, in the Devils name! Marry, quoth she, Zounds what a word was that ?

Jilt. I knew how I should be us'd by an ungrateful man ; oh that I should betray my weakness, oh, oh!

Rains. Fare you well, good Mrs. *Jilt :* 'Sbloud, marry ? ha, ha, ha, ha.

Jilt. Miserable Woman, how unlucky am I ? but I am resolv'd never to give over 'till I get a Husband, if I live and breath.   [*Exit* Jilt.

Enter Mrs. Woodly, Lucia, *and* Carolina.

Lucia. This is your Husband's ſtory.

Mrs. *Wood.* No, 'tis their own, I assure you : why did you intend your acquaintance with *Rains* and *Bevil* should be a secret? that's pleasant, they have only proclaim'd it in the Town, yet no where else.

Caro. They cannot be so base; we saw 'em but by accident.

Mrs. *Wood.* By accident! you are pleasant, Madam, ha, ha, ha.

Luc. What's the cause of your unseemly mirth, Cousin?

Mrs. *Wood.* By accident, Mr. *Rains* applys himself wholly to you, and by accident Mr. *Bevil* makes love to you, Madam; by accident ye all met in a Field this forenoon; by accident, Madam, Mr. *Bevil* expected you to meet him alone in a Field on the backside of my Lodging.

Caro. Me: you drive a jest too far, do you intend to affront me?

Mrs. *Wood.* I have no mind to fall under the lash of their malicious tongues; but I walked over that Field in a Masque, *Bevil* meets me, calls me, dear *Carolina*, said he had obeyed my summons, and that I was punctual in my assignation, thank'd me for the favour of my Note——

Caro. Heaven! what do I hear? this is your project, you must be acquainted with witty men.

Luc. Unworthy men! have they no sense of honour?

Enter Mr. Woodly.

Mrs. *Wood.* Yonder, I believe, comes one of them; I'le leave ye lest I should be suspected to tell this.   [*Ex. Mrs.* Woodly.

Wood. I love *Carolina* so, I must undermine *Bevil*, whom I fear she's inclin'd to; I must render *Rains* suspected too, lest they should clear one another.

Luc. If this be true, we have been finely mistaken.

Wood. Oh, Ladies, are you here, you're punctual, are your new Gallants come yet——Perhaps I may guess right.   [*Aside.*

Curo. What Gallants?

Wood. Nay, perhaps it may be a mistake; but I was told by 5 or 6 Gentlemen, upon Clay-Hill, that you were to meet with *Rains* and *Bevil* privately this night here in *Mawses* Garden; that's all.

Caro. O base, perfidious men!

Luc. We meet 'em?

Wood. Why, did you think it had been a secret, so is a Proclamation, they themselves have bragg'd on't.

Caro. Do they already boast of our easiness, vile men! Well, I see we must condemn our selves to the conversation of dull sober Fools.

Luc. Or which is as bad, confine our selves to the impertinence of our own Sex.

Wood. I profer'd to day to bring *Rains* acquainted with you, Cousin; but he refus'd it, and said he would not marry you for his own sake, nor lie with you for mine; and that a man had no excuse for himself, that visited a Woman without design of lying with her one way or other.

Luc. Oh Impudence!

Wood. They are men of wit and good company, but not so fit for young Ladies that love reputation; but I hope my Cousin is not so intimate with *Rains*, as you are with *Bevil*, Madam?

Caro. I intimate with him, what mean you?

Wood. You are pleasant, Madam; I mean she does not meet him alone, as you do *Bevil*.

Caro. Had he the impudence to say this? or have you so little honour to believe the words of a vain idle fellow?

Wood. But I must believe my eyes: did I not see you with him mask'd? and speak to you, by the same token you fell into a swound at the surprize?

Caro. You are mad, Sir, or would make me so.

Wood. To shew you I am not mad, there's the Note you wrote to *Bevil*.

Caro. That I wrote? Heaven! *Lucia*, do you hear what Monsters of men our ill fate, or your worse Conduct have thrown us upon? Let's in and read this Note.

Lucia. How am I amazed?

Wood. All this confidence won't clear her with me; I know Womankind too well.   [*Exeunt.*

Enter Rains *and* Bevil.

Rains. *Lucia* and *Carolina* are slipt into the House, or some Arbour, I see a Hackney-Coach, for they resolv'd not to bring their own.

Bev. Death, that we lewd young fellows shou'd be catch'd thus; I ne're had any love yet, that I could not satisfy with Gold, or wash away with *Burgundy;* but to be content to leave all the numerous Ladies of the Game in *London*, for two that on my conscience are foolishly honest.

Rains. But by your leave, *Bevil*, *London* is overstock'd with Wenches, that like too many Hares in a Hare-Warren, they cross our hunting, and we can make no work on't; the difficulty of finding is one part of the Game.

Bev. I love these Women the more, for declaring against Fools, contrary to most of their Sex.

Rains. I hate a Woman that's in love with a fulsom Coxcomb, she's a foul feeder, and I can no more have an appetite to her, when I think of her diet, than to a tame Duck, when I think it feeds on Toads.

Bev. Well, I love *Carolina* beyond all sense of modesty, so much, that I am resolv'd if she will, to turn recreant and marry her, let what will be the consequence.

Rains. To forbear pleasing our selves to day, for fear of being troubled to morrow, were to adjourn life and never to live.

Bev. I am sure of the present pleasure, and but venture the future pain.

Rains. But I am resolved to venture, though the Gallies were the consequence.

Bev. And I too. I will live 50 years in that one night I first enjoy her; and care not if I were to be a Slave all the rest of my life. Yonder I believe they are.

Enter Carolina *and* Lucia.

Caro. Ungrateful men!

Luc. 'Tis not too late to retreat from this adventure.

Bev. Ladies, your humble Servant: I see you are to be trusted.

Caro. But you are not, you treacherous ungrateful men!

Bev. How's this, Madam?

Luc. Your infamous dealing with us, exceeds all barbarousness, *Indians* and *Cannibals* would have us'd us better.

Rains. What mean they? do you think, Madam, we would eat you? we have a pleasanter way of using Ladies.

Luc. Do you make our anger your mirth?

Caro. We may thank our selves to trust such perfidious men.

Bev. You amaze us, you are just declaring War, when we thought to have concluded a Peace with you.

Caro. Avoid our sight, thou vain man.

Luc. And take thy lewd Companion with thee.

Rains. Ladies, you have so much wit that I cannot think you are in earnest.

Bev. Our love is not so dull, that it needs to be spurr'd with anger.

Rains. I hope this is only to make us relish your kindness the better. Anger is a Sawce to Love, as Sickness is to Health.

Bev. For my part, I love so violently, that every look of yours charms me, your anger pleases, I am in love with your frowns.

Caro. It seems so, you would not else so justly have provok'd 'em.

Rains. 'Tis some honour, Madam, to be thought worth your anger. I cou'd never be angry with those I despis'd.

Luc. But you shall find I can. Let's leave 'em, *Carolina*.   [*Exit* Lucia.

Rains. Death, this is madness; I'll not leave you so.   [*Exit* Rains.

Caro. I write Letters, and make private appointments with you? perfidious man! to blast my reputation thus——

Bev. This is Mrs. *Woodly*'s malice——   [*Aside.*
Pray hear me, Madam——

Caro. No, Sir. Farewel.

Enter Woodly *as they are going out.*

Wood. There go *Bevil* and *Carolina*.   [*Ex.* Bev. *and* Carolina.
Now jealousie assist me, I may o'rehear something, 'tis not so like a Gentleman, but 'tis like a wise and jealous Lover: I'll follow.

                                             [*Exit* Woodly.

(156)

Enter Mrs. Woodly *at the door on the right hand of the Stage.*

Mrs. *Wood.* I long to hear what my information has wrought upon 'em. Mischief enough, I hope.

[*Enter* Bevil *and* Carolina *at the door on the left hand, at which Mrs.* Woodly *starts back and conceals her self.*]

Here are the two whom I am most concern'd in; 'tis dark, and I shall easily conceal my self.

[Woodly *enters a little after* Bevil *and* Carolina, *and stands close.*]

Caro. Why do you follow me thus far? begone, inhumane Creature!

Mrs. *Wood.* Oh, it works finely.

Bev. Hear me but one word: if you condemn me then, I will own my self the Rascal you speak of.

Caro. What can you say in defence of your treachery? I write Notes to you.

Bev. I know who is my Accuser, and the reason of my Accusation.

Caro. Who is your Accuser besides your self——

Bev. I have had the misfortune to be pursu'd by the love and jealousy of a Woman, cholerick, haughty, and revengeful, Mrs. *Woodly*, I am sure she is my Accuser.

Mrs. *Wood.* Heaven! what says the Villain? I will tear him in pieces.

Wood. Death, Hell, and the Devil! the love of my Wife. But I will hear further.

Caro. Is this possible?

Bev. 'Tis true, I assure you; she wrote that Letter as from you to me, and met me in the Field; I was amaz'd at the Letter, and resolv'd to see the event on't: but I found her instead of you.

Wood. Damnation on this Woman.

Mrs. *Wood.* I cou'd stab the Traytor: but I'll yet have pat ence.

Bev. Her Husband came by in the mean time, and as I believe took her for you, said he knew her, and seem'd to be much concern'd; and she swounded.

Caro. Now the Riddle's clear'd.

Wood. I will yet hear farther.

Caro. But how came you to part with the Note which I have now? I see you are not to be trusted with a Ticket.

Bev. I am glad you have it, Madam, I unluckily dropt it I know not how; and have been afraid of the effects a strangers finding it might have produc'd. With all my diligence I cou'd not find it; but how came you by it?

Caro. You have told a plausible Story, and I will let you know, but I conjure you to take no notice of it.

Bev. You shall command me, Madam——

Caro. Know then I have been perpetually importun'd since I came to *Epsom*, by the love of Mr. *Woodly*, and I suppose he having the same jealousie of me, that his virtuous Lady has of you, though there's no danger, gave me this Note, with an excellent character of Mr. *Rains* and you——

    [*Woodly and his Wife both ſtart, as surprised at the News.*

Wood. Hell and Devils! now all's out.   [*Both appear, and ſpeak together.*

Mrs. *Wood.* Where's the Traytor that has abus'd me thus?

Wood. Madam *Carolina*, I thank you, you have oblig'd me much.

Mrs. *Wood.* My Husband! I am undone.

Wood. 'Sdeath, is she here?

Caro. Heaven! what will this come to?

Bev. Unlucky accident!

Mrs. *Wood.* Oh let me ſtab this perjur'd Man!

Caro. Hold, Madam.

Wood. Sir, I muſt have a farther account of you.

Bev. Let it suffice to tell you my anger againſt your Wife; for contriving this mischief againſt me, made me say more than was true : She's innocent of any Intrigue with me, only the Letter she did write, what made her I know not.

Wood. But, Sir——

Bev. But, Sir, I muſt demand an account of you, concerning the Letter and the fair Character you gave me; 'twas not so like a Gentleman.

Wood. 'Sdeath, not like a Gentleman.   [*Lays his hand on his Sword.*

Caro. Hold, Gentlemen.

Wood. Oh, Madam, I thank you for your favours.

Caro. If I have any power with you, follow me, or I shall diſtruſt all you have said.

Mrs. *Wood.* Oh base inhumane Villain! so falsly to asperse my Honour.

Bev. Madam, I muſt obey you.   *Monsieur ne mettez vous pas en peine, je trouver l'occasion de vous voir demain au Matin.*

Wood. *Et Bien Monsieur si faites.*

Caro. None of your French to shew your breeding; come along.

    [*Ex.* Car. *and* Bevil.

Mrs. *Wood.* I am basely abus'd by a forsworn Wretch. If you have honour in you bear it not. Heaven knows, I know nothing of the Letter, nor have I seen him this day before.

Wood No! what can provoke him to so injurious an accusation.

Mrs. *Wood.* Do you wonder at the malice of base lascivious men, that cannot have their ends : I was loth to make a quarrel between you, not knowing how fatal it might be : but I have never reſted from the importunity of his love—

Wood. I know how to deal with him; but for you, Madam——

Mrs. *Wood.* For me! Heaven knows I am innocent and virtuous; but 'tis too apparent thou art false; *Carolina* speaks truth certainly: besides I have heard this day that you are pleased to keep a Wench too, nay one that was a Bawd, and you pervert the use of her, and turn her into a Whore; an honest Gentleman complain'd on't; I'le not endure it.

Wood. 'Tis well invented: but methinks, Madam, you shou'd have too much to do to clear your self, to think of accusing me.

Mrs. *Wood.* If thou hadst courage in thee, thou wouldst revenge me of this false Rascal. But why should I expect such honour from you? you are one of those keeping Coxcombs; that rather than not keep will keep a Bawd: Nay, your Mistress, forsooth, has turn'd from Bawd to Punk, from Punk to Bawd, as often as they say *Thames* Water will stink and grow sweet again at Sea.

Wood. 'Sdeath, none of your foolery, clear your self, or I'le make you an example. [*Ex.* Woodly.

Mrs. *Wood.* Now all the power of revengeful rage assist me: here's company I'le away. [*Exit Mrs.* Woodly.

Enter Rains, Lucia, *and* Roger, *as Mrs.* Woodly *is going out.*

Rains. There can be nothing plainer than that the jealousie and malice of Mrs. *Woodly* contriv'd this. Can you believe we can be such Rascals without provocation?

Luc. 'Tis probable *Woodly* has done this for Love and Jealousie of *Carolina*, and his Wife for Love and Jealousie of *Bevil*. [*Aside.* But if you were not monstrously lewd, the freedom of *Epsom* allows almost nothing to be scandalous.

Rains. Do you know, Madam, there is no such thing as scandal in this Age. Infamy is now almost as hard to get as preferment.

Enter Clodpate.

Clodp. Who's here, Mr. *Rains?* Udsbud I am almost fox't, we have dusted it away, Gudsooks; but there were two Country-Fellows there that I never saw before, won above forty pound of me at Put, but they are honest Country-Fellows; one of 'em is a chief Constable, a very honest Fellow. But where's Madam *Carolina?* I have been at her Lodging.

Luc. Oh Mr. *Clodpate!* I am glad I have found you, I sent all up and down the Town for you.

Clodp. Udsbud, Madam, what's the matter, is my Mistress not well?

Luc. Her Brother is come this Evening to Town, with a resolution to force her to *London*, to marry one, he has provided for her: the poor

Lady is almoſt diſtracted, and bid me tell you, if you'll relieve her from this diſtress, she'll be for ever yours.

Clodp. Udsooks, does he take her *vi & armis*, I'll send my Warrant for him, and ſtop his Journey.

Luc. No, she has design'd a better way; her Brother has carried her in his Coach to see a Kinſwoman that lodges near the Church, and intends to sup there, and not to come home till eleven of the Clock.

Clodp. Good.

Luc. If you'll go and ſtay for her in the Church-yard, and have your man with Horses juſt by, she'll ſteal away and come to you, and go where e're you'll dispose of her, she'd rather dye than live in *London*.

Clodp. As Gad judge me, she's a fine person; but why the Church-yard? that's a place to meet in when we are dead, not while we are living, there are Sprights and dead Folks walk: I tremble to think on't.

Rains. This Fellow has not yet out-grown the belief of Raw-head and Bloody-bones.

Luc. There is now no remedy; if you omit this opportunity, you will for ever lose her.

Clodp. Nay, rather than that I'le venture; but I'll take my Practice of Piety in my Pocket.

Luc. Do so, and then let 'em walk their hearts out.

Clodp. Well, Gad save you, I'le marry her to night.　　[*Exit* Clodpate.

Luc. If I had not sent him away, we had been peſter'd with him all night.

Rains. Since you have gone thus far with him, I'll have my share in the sport.

Luc. If he should see *Bevil* and *Carolina*, 'twould spoil all.

Enter Foot-Boy.

Foot-Boy. Madam, my Lady sent me to tell you, that she is gone home with Mr. *Bevil*, and desires your Company.

Luc. I'le follow her.　　　　　　　　　　　　　　[*Exit Boy.*

Rains. Roger, you heard what pass'd, pray go you with my Valet de Chambre, and take each of you a Sheet, and wait in the Church-porch till *Clodpate* comes into the Church-yard, and then sally out upon him and fright him to purpose.

Rog. I will, Sir, and am glad of the imployment: let us alone for mischief.

Rains. He believes in Spirits and dead Folks walking, as ſtedfaſtly as in his Creed.

Luc. This may make excellent Sport.

Rog. I'll about it inſtantly; if we do not fright him out of that little wit his Juſticeship has, I am miſtaken.　　　　　　　　[*Exeunt.*

Enter Fribble, *Mrs.* Frib. *and* Bisket.

Frib. Where's Mr. *Kick* and *Cuff, Doll,* we left 'em here but even now when we went to drink with our Neighbours.

Mrs. Frib. They were sent for upon extraordinary business, they paid the Reckoning.

Bisk. I vow they are very civil fair condition'd Gentlemen as one would wish to drink or bowl with; but I vow there were some Bullies there, swore so bloodily, I was afraid the Bowling-Green would have fallen upon our heads; but where's my Lamb?

Mrs. Frib. She's stept to a Neighbour in the Bowling-green, she'll come instantly.

Frib. Come, Neighbour *Bisket,* will you go? our friends expect us to be merry with them, I could be so brisk to night, fa, la, la, &c.

Brisk. Ay, and I too, fa, la, la; we'll sing old Rose, faith, hey Boys.

Mrs. Frib. Why, have you the confidence to offer to leave me when the Gentlemen are gone, and you in this condition?

Frib. How, what say you?

Mrs. Frib. I have been too tame; 'tis time now to pluck up a spirit, you scurvy Fellow.

Frib. As Gad judge me, the Jade's drunk.

Mrs. Frib. 'Tis you are drunk, Beast, every night; you are sipping off your half pints all day long, and one has no more comfort of you at night, than of a Bed-staff, nay, not so much.

Frib. Oh monstrous impudence! the Woman's possess'd, as I hope to breathe.

Bisk. Pish, this is nothing, my Duck says more to me than this every day; they will have these humours with 'em, mine has abundance, pretty Rogue, ha, ha.

Frib. But if you be a fool, Neighbour, I'le be none, I'll not endure it. Know your Lord and Master.

Mrs. Frib. I am my own Mistress. Did I marry a foolish Haberdasher to be govern'd by him? out upon thee, Nickcompoop, I'le order thee, i'faith.

Bisk. Just, my Duck, to a hair, ha, ha, ha.

Frib. Oh unheard of impudence!

Mrs. Frib. All my Neighbours cry out on me, for suffering you in your impudence. Shall I endure a Fellow to be drunk and loose, and spend that abroad that he should spend with me at home; you villanous man, I'le not endure it.

Bisk. Just, my *Mollie,* for all the world, ha, ha, ha.

Frib. Nay then, 'tis time to be in earnest. Huswife, know your Lord and Master, I say, know your Lord and Master.

Mrs. Frib. My Lord and Master, I scorn thee, thou insolent Fellow,

(161)

know your Lady and Miſtress, Sirrah, I'le order you better, you scurvy Fellow.

Frib. Oh horrible! she's diſtraéted. Huswife get you home and sleep, and be sober, or I'le send you home with a Flea in your Ear.

Mrs. *Frib.* Get you home, you pitiful Fellow, or I'le send you home with a Flea in your Ear, and you go to that, thou fumbling Fool.

Frib. This is prodigious. Do you know, Huswife, that I will give you much correétion?

Dor. You give me correétion, you Coward?

Frib. The Law allows me to give my Wife due correétion. I know the Law, Huswife, consider and tremble.

Dor. You give me correétion, you Wittal; I'le teach you Law.
                    [*She gives him a dash on the Chaps.*

Frib. Oh Impudence! nay then have at you. If you be mad, I'll cure you without the help of *Bedlam.*   [*Beats her.*

Dor. Help, help, murder, murder.

Biſk. Nay hold, Neighbour, for Heaven sake.

Frib. Stand by, let me alone, or I will mischief you. Would you be so wicked as to part man and wife, a curse will follow you, if you do.

Biſk. Nay then, whom Heav'n has joyn'd I will not put asunder.

Frib. Come, Huswife, ask me pardon, or I will swinge you immoderately.
                    [Frib. *ſtrikes her again.*

Dor. Hold, I do ask you pardon.   [*She kneels.*

Frib. Will you never be so insolent agen?

Dor. No, I will never pluck up a spirit agen.

Frib. Go, get you home.

Dor. Yes I will; but if I do not make your head ake for't before to morrow morning.   [*Aside.*   [*Exit* Doro.

Frib. Caſtigo te, non quod odio habeam, sed quod amem, is an excellent Sentence I learnt in my Grammar.

Biſk. This is incomparable. Oh that I could govern my Wife thus! if I thought I could, I would swinge my Duck extreamly, I'de beat my Lamb inordinately.

Frib. I warrant you, try. This is the only way to govern her; let her feel, if she can't underſtand that you are her head.

Biſk. I vow and swear I have a good mind, really, though she is a pretty Rogue. She does lead me such a life sometimes, I proteſt and vow, flesh and blood is not able to bear it.

Frib. I tell you, Neighbour, 'tis a dishonourable thing to bear an affront from a Woman, especially our own Wife.

Biſk. Uds me, here she is, I tremble.

Frib. Bear up for shame.

(162)

Enter Mrs. Bisk.

Mrs. *Bisk.* Where have you been, you Fop Doodle?

Bisk. What's that to you Jilt-Flirts?

Mrs. *Bisk.* What says the Fellow?

Bisk. I say know your Lord and Master.

Mrs. *Bisk.* Oh Heaven! the Boar's drunk, and has lost his Senses.

Bisk. No, the Sow is drunk, and has lost her manners.

Mrs. *Bisk.* Oh horrid insolence! you Villain, I'le order you, I can hear you have lost all your money at Bowls. Get you home, Sirrah, you drunken Beast, you shall have money agen, you shall.

Bisk. Peace, you impertinent unseasonable Ass, or I shall grow passionate.

Mrs. *Bisk.* You scurvy Fellow, I'll tear your eyes out. I am amaz'd, what can this insolence mean?

Bisk. Stand by me, Neighbour, I have too long endur'd your impudence, I will give you a great deal of Correction: I am your head, Huswife.

Mrs. *Bisk.* You my head, you Cuckold; nay, then 'tis time to begin with you. I'le head you before I have done.

[*She gives him a douce on the Chaps.*

Frib. Now it begins.

Bisk. Nay then have at you. [*He strikes her.*

Mrs. *Bisk.* Strike your own Wife, I'le tear your Throat out.

[*She takes away the stick and beats him, he tumbles down.*

Bisk. Help, murder, murder, Neighbour, help, help, help.

Mrs. *Bisk.* I'le make an Example on you. Hah would you govern your own Wife? Lord and Master, Quoth a!

Bisk. Oh my Throat, Oh my Eyes!

Frib. Come of for shame, you'r an insolent Woman, and were you my Wife, I would take off your Woman-hood.

[Bisket *gets up and runs away as hard as he can drive.*

Mrs. *Bisk.* Oh you are one of the Rascals that put him upon this! I'le try a pluck with you, I'le tear your Eyes out, you Villain, you Cuckoldly Villain.

[*She beats* Fribble.

Frib. Hold, hold——Oh Cowardly Rogue! Has he left me in the Lurch?

Mrs. *Bisk.* I'le order all such Rascals.

Frib. Hold, hold, this is a She-Devil. [Fribble *runs from her, and Exit.*

Mrs. *Bisk.* So, are you routed? now the Field's my own; but I'le order my Cuckold. Attempt to conquer his own Wife——

I to my Husband scorn to be a Slave,
I ne're can fear the beast whose horns I gave.

(163)

ACT V. SCENE I.

Enter Kick *and* Cuff.

Kick. THis has been a lucky day ; but this last business you drew me into, frighted me devilishly.

Cuff. We that are to live by vertuous industry, ought to stand out at nothing.

Kick. But no more of this, if you please, yet 'twas well design'd to rob *Clodpate ;* a false Rogue to have threescore pounds in his Pocket, and leave us off at Put. He rob'd us of that first, and we took it by way of Reprisal.

Cuff. His Man is gagg'd and bound far enough from helping him.

Kick. And away the Horses are gone for *London.* The Rogue will neither go nor send to *London* for a discovery, he hates it so ; but what a Pox made the Sot in the Church-yard.

Cuff. Nay, I know not, unless he waited to kill some body, and then give him Christian Burial. I am sure it furnished me with a good invention.

Kick. If thou hadst not been a thorough-pac'd Rogue, thou could'st never have been so present to thy self. If we had only bound him, some body might have pass'd by by accident and unloos'd him ; but to tie his hands behind him, and take a sheet off the next Hedge, and tie him up in it like a Ghost, and gag him, was a Master-piece of Roguery.

Cuff. This way will not only secure us from present pursuit, for no body durst come near him to unbind his hands. But it will make excellent sport, he'll fright all the Town out of their wits.

Enter Rains *and* Roger.

Kick. There's *Rains,* let us retire for fear of broken heads.

[*Exeunt* Kick *and* Cuff.

Rains. How now, what news of *Clodpate ?*

Roger. Oh, Sir, we had like to have been frighted out of our wits our selves.

Rains. How so ?

Roger. When we expected to have frighted Mr. *Clodpate,* we saw another in a sheet, at which at first we cryed out for fear, which he (to our comfort) hearing, roar'd like a Bull at a Country Bear-bating, and run from us with all the speed he could.

Rains. 'Tis strange ! who should it be ?

Roger. We know not, Sir ; but the amazement made us soon pull off our Ghostly Habits, and come home.

Enter Woodly.

Rains. Who's here?

Wood. Mr. *Rains*, I am glad I have found you.

Rains. Oh, Sir, is it you? we are to thank you for the favour you did us in giving those excellent Characters of us to our Mistresses.

Wood. Your Mistresses? you are men of dispatch, you take Women as fast as the *French* Towns; none of 'em endure a Siege, but yield upon the first Summons to you.

Rains. You are in the wrong, such as we can buy or corrupt the Governours of, may be easily had; but there are your Nimmegen Ladies that will hold out, and pelt damnably. But, Sir, I must be a little more serious with you. Do you think you have us'd a couple of honest Fellows as you ought?

Wood. Why, I could do no less for the honour of my Kinswoman, or the securing my own love to *Carolina*, which was desperate; and let me tell you, it is a silly Honour that will hinder a man the satisfying of his love, and is never to be found but in foolish Rhiming Plays and Romances.

Rains. I could however be no rub in your way, since all my pretences are to your Cousin *Lucia*, and I'le assure you as honourable——

Wood. That's as she pleases; for you have no more honour in love than needs must. There's no trusting young Ladies now a-days *to the Invasion of Audacious men.*

Rains. But they may to the *men of easie Phlegm.*

Wood. You are no man of *easie Phlegm;* but this is not my business. I suppose you have heard of the Bustle at *Mawse's* Garden to night.

Rains. I have.

Wood. I have no more to say, but that you would tell *Bevil* I desire to see him with his Sword in his hand.

Rains. Sure you are too well grounded in the belief of your Wifes vertue, to entertain a slight suspition of her.

Wood. I am sure they ne'er shall know that I suspect her.   [*Aside.* Sir, since I do not question her honour, do not you make bold with it, 'tis for his false accusation that I require satisfaction.

Rains. The same love that provok'd you to accuse him falsly, made him do the same to your Wife; he loves *Carolina* almost to madness.

Wood. The Honour of my Wife is too nice a thing to be us'd at that rate, especially by one that rivall'd me in my Mistress, without further dispute I will fight with him; if he refuses to meet me, I shall think he dares not.

Rains. That you shall not think; since you are so brisk, provide one to entertain me, I am his Friend.

Wood. Such a one you shall not want instantly.

Rains. We cannot possibly meet to night, at 5 in the morning we'll meet you at *Box-Hill*.

Wood. I will expect you there, adieu.   [*Ex.* Woodly.

Rains. Goodnight.

Enter Fribble, Bisket *drunk, with Fidlers.*

Bisk. Come on Fiddlers, play us a Serenade ; a Serenade's a fine merry Tune ; we'll be as merry as the veryest Roysters of 'em all, and as drunk too, an we set upon't, Neighbour *Fribble.*

Frib. I warrant you, come we are choice Lads ; come play a Serenade at this Window, fa, la, la, la.

Bisk sings. Fa, la. Hold, can't you sing *Hey for Cavaliers, ho for Cavaliers, Dub, a dub, dub, have at old Belzebub,* Oliver *stinks for fear.*

Fid. No an't please you, Sir.

Frib. Ah brave Neighbour *Bisket,* you are a merry man i' fack.

Bisk. I, am I not ? I defie any man in *Epsom* to be merrier, i' fags. Come let's all be Musitioners, and all roar and sing,

> *Here's a Health unto his Majesty,*
> *With a Fal, la, la, la, la lero.*

Frib. Come on, hey Boys, strike up——

Bisk. Now have I as much courage as any man upon the face of the Earth, if my Sweeting were here I'd beat her extreamly, I'd Chastise my Pigsnye immoderately : I love her, poor Bird, but she's too unruly.

An old senseless Song.

> *If she prove constant, obliging, and kind,*
> *Perhaps I'll vouchsafe for to love her,*
> *But if pride or inconstancy in her I find,*
> *I'd have her to know I'm above her.*

Frib. Bravely resolv'd. But for all that you left me engag'd basely and scurvily.

Enter Mrs. Bisket *and Mrs.* Fribble.

Mrs. *Frib.* Mr. *Rains* shou'd be here by the Fiddles. O lamentable, our Husbands are drunk, and roaring, and serenading.

Mrs. *Bisk.* Oh, my fingers itch at 'em, I'll order my Rogue.

Bisk. 'Slife here they are ; now does my heart fail me : Fiddlers do you keep back ; they shall be the Reserve, you shall lead the Van, and I'll bring up the Rear : There's discipline for you.

Frib. We are fallen into an Ambush, bear thy self bravely.

(166)

Mrs. *Bisk.* Where's my drunken beast? do you sneak behind? I'll make you an example.

Bisk. *sings :*
> *But if pride or inconstancy in her I find,*
> *I'de have her to know I am above her.*

Mrs. *Bisk.* Above me! a pitiful Comfit-maker, above me! I'le have better men above me. Sirrah, I'le spoil your singing.

Enter Kick *and* Cuff, *with Fiddles.*

Kick. They are our Bubbles drunk, but not drunk enough, and their Wives with them to. Now for some stratagem to part 'em——

Cuff. Ladies, a word of consultation.

Mrs. *Bisk.* Your Servant, Sir.

Bisk. Oh Gentlemen, your Servant; now we'll be merry as Princes i'faith : who cares for you now, come, strike up Fiddlers.

Frib. Ay, come, fa, la, la, let 'em alone, who cares.

Bisk. Ay, come, let 'em alone, who cares.

Kick. Ladies, let me desire you to walk away, your Husbands are too drunk for your company; we'll carry 'em to our Lodgings, and they shall sleep till they be sober.

Cuff. And we'll come back and wait on you with our Fiddles.

Mrs. *Frib.* Your Servant, sweet Sir, you are very obliging.

Mrs. *Bisk.* We shall be proud to wait on you. Your humble Servant.

> [*Ex.*

Frib. Are you gone. Come, Gentlemen, let's join our forces, and away a serenading, fa, la, la, la.

Kick. Come on toward our Lodging.

Bisk. Strike up, fa, la, la, la.

Enter people crying the Devil, the Devil, Clodpate *with his hands bound behind him in a sheet like a Ghost.* Bisket *and* Fribble *run with the Fiddles, crying the Devil, the Ghost,* &c.

Kick. He's here, the Rogue has made haste ; now will our Ladies be afraid to lye alone to night.

Cuff. We must e'en be content to supply their Husbands places. Come along. [*Exeunt.*

Clodp. Oh, oh, oh, Udsooks there's my Gag broke at length, thanks to the strength of my teeth ; unmerciful Rogues, if it had been like *Dapper's* Gag of Ginger-bread, it would have melted in my mouth ; never man has been so unfortunate as I have been this night, I have been frighted out of my Wits, I saw two Ghosts in the Church-yard, I have almost sweat my self into a Consumption, my man's gone, for ought I know, murder'd ;

nay, which is worse, my Dapple Mare's lost, I am rob'd of Threescore Pounds, my hands ty'd behind me, every one takes me for a Ghost; oh, oh, oh.

Enter a Country-man.

Count. Oh, the Devil, the Devil! [*Exit.*
Clodp. Do you hear, I am no Devil, stay, stay. If I should run after him, he'd run ten times faster. If I go home they'll shut the doors upon me, no body will come near me this night, nor for ought I know, to morrow.

Enter Landlord and two more with him whistling.

Landl. Oh, here's the Ghost, the Ghost. [*Ex.*
Clodp. Stay, I am no Ghost, Landlord; Rogue, stay, I will pursue that Rascal. [*He runs out after him, and both run over the Stage again, and* Exeunt.

Enter Toby.

Toby. How luckily was I reliev'd? I had been sure for one night, if an honest Fellow had not come by, by Miracle; but he told me a dreadful story of a Spirit walking to night.

Enter Clodpate.

Who's this? my man *Toby?*
Toby. Oh the Devil, the Devil!
        [*He runs off the Stage,* Clodpate *follows him, and they enter again.*
Clodp. Why, *Toby*, Rogue, Rascal, I am your Master *Clodpate.*
[*As they run cross the Stage,* Clodp. *overtakes* Toby, *and strikes up his heels.* Justice *Clodpate,* Rogue, Rascal.
Toby. Devil I defie thee, and all thy works: Oh, oh, oh!
Clodp. Lye still, or I will stamp thy guts out, hear me, hear me; why, Rogue *Toby*, Rascal, I am thy Master.
Toby. Ha, I think it is my Master's voice.
Clodp. Oh, I am rob'd and abus'd, rise and unbind my hands.
Toby. Oh, it is he, let me recover the fright. Oh! how came you in this condition?
Clodp. Ask no questions, but unty my hands.
Toby. Oh, Sir, your Dapple Mare's gone.
Clodp. Oh, what shall I do? Oh miserable man! Oh poor Dapple——
I love her so, I could go into mourning for her. I had as good almost have lost *Carolina.*
Toby. Nay, you had better, Sir; she was in the Plot against you to night, and abus'd you all this while with a story of the Church-yard.
Clodp. Gudsooks, abuse me?
Toby. She has no Brother hates the Country, is an absolute vain *London*-Lady, and has made sport with you all this night.

Clodp. Now I reflect upon't, Ud'sbud, the Assignation in the Church-yard was very odd.

Toby. Mrs. *Woodly*'s Maid has told me all; she has been laughing at you, and her design upon you all this night.

Clodp. Gudsooks, laugh at me, a Magistrate? I could find in my heart to bind her to her good behaviour.

Enter Peg.

Toby. Ha, who's this, Mrs. *Margaret?* Look you, Sir, she's come in time. I have told my Master what you told me.

Peg. 'Tis true; but I shall be ruin'd, if he tells it again.

Clodp. Fear not that, Godsbud, I tell! but if I be not reveng'd on her. Hold, it comes into my head; what is become of the pretty Country-Lady I saw to day?

Peg. At her Lodging, the same we lie in; but why do you ask, Sir?

Clod. As Gad judge me, 'tis the finest Lady I ever saw.

Peg. I could tell you, Sir, but I dare not.

Clodp. What could'st thou tell me? Upon the honour of a Country-Justice, I'le be secret.

Peg. Sir, she is extremely taken with your Worship. Alas! she's a poor innocent Country thing.

Clodp. Nay, but is she, poor Rogue?

Peg. She loves your honest, true, *English* Country Gentlemen, and wonders what Ladies can see in foolish *London* Fellows, to charm 'em so.

Clodp. And so do I, a Company of Spindle-shank'd Pocky Fellows, that will scarce hold together: I am of your true tuff *English* heart of Oak, Gudsooks.

Peg. But, Sir, I am in haste, my Lady sent me of an Errant, and I must go.

Clodp. Hold, Mrs. *Margaret;* if you can bring about my Marriage with this Lady, I will give you 50 *l.*

Peg. That I know not whether I can do or no; but, Sir, I'le endeavour to serve you without a reward, if you be in earnest.

Clodp. I am, prepare a Visit for me presently.

Peg. I'le do what I can to serve you, but I must go, your Servant. [*Exit.*

Clodp. If I do not give *Carolina* such a bob, she shall repent it all her life time.   [*Ex.* Clodp. *and* Toby.

Enter Rains, Bevil, Lucia, *and* Carolina.

Caro. Good *Brisk;* Sir, you shall not meet with *Woodly* this night.

Luc. And you, Sir, shall pass your word for your self and him. I know you'll offer your help to commit a Gentleman-like murder for his Honour.

Rains. Faith, Ladies, there's no way to secure us but to take each of us and keep us in your several Chambers all night.

Luc. No, Sir, we shall be in more danger with that, than you'll be with fighting.

Caro. We shall find a better way with a Constable and Watch, if you will not pass your words to go home peaceably to night.

Bev. If I could think this care of me proceeded from a value you have for me, I would renounce my Honour for my Love.

Caro. Perhaps I have such a value for you, as in time might grow to a kind of Friendship. But that's the farthest point I shall ever stretch it to.

Bev. Friendship's a dull, foolish, flegmatick affection, which you might a had, being a Woman for the matter; but if it could ever grow to Love, I would renounce my dear Friends, the World, the Flesh, and the Devil for you.

Rains. A Lady will be little pleas'd with one that should renounce the Flesh for her sake.

Luc. Are not you angry in your heart to be kept from your belov'd Bottles?

Rains. The Devil take me, I love you so, that I could be content to abjure Wine for ever, and drink nothing but Almond-milk for your sake.

Bev. We never meet like Country-Sots to drink only, but to enjoy one another, and then Wine steals upon us unawares, as late hours do sometimes upon your selves at Cards.

Rains. And it makes your dull Fools sit hickupping, sneezing, drivelling, and belching, with their eyes set in their heads, while it raises men of heat and vigour to mirth, and sometimes to extravagance.

Bev. And which is most scandalous, witty extravagance, or drivelling, snivelling, sneaking dulness.

Enter Peg *with a Note.*

Peg. Is my Lady here, Ladies? 'tis past eleven, and she's not come home yet.

Luc. No, she's not here.

Peg. My Lady is at home, and bid me give you that Note.

[*Gives a Note to* Rains.

Not a word to Mr. *Bevil*, good night. I have taken order, the other Note shall be given to Mr. *Bevil*.   [*Aside.*

Caro. Gentlemen, we are not us'd to your late hours, we must retire; but if you will not promise to go home peaceably, I will send for the Constable.

Rains. Take my word, Madam, there shall be nothing done to night.

Luc. Gentlemen, your Servant.

Rains. I hope the noise of Fiddles under your Window, will not offend you.

(170)

Luc. In a Town where there are such vile noises all night long, we may suffer good Musick to come into the Consort.

Caro. Adieu.

Bev. Your Servant, dear, dear Madam.   [*Ex. Women.*

Enter Messenger with a Letter, and delivers it to Bevil.

Bev. Is this for me?

Mess. It was left in the house for you.

Rains. What's this? Reads, *I know you to be a gen'rous Person, and that you will succour a distressed Lady, who stands in need of your Advice immediately.*
                                Sarah Woodly.

Gad I believe she stands in need of something else than my Advice, she has a design on my Chastity shall I go? good Devil, do not tempt me, I must be constant, I will be constant: nay, Gad, I can be constant when I resolve on't, and yet I am a Rogue. But I hope I shall have Grace, and yet I fear I shall not; but come what will, I must suffer this tryal of my Vertue.

Bev. How now, *Jack*, an Assignation?

Rains. Peace, *Ned*, peace, go home, I'le be with you in half an hour.

Bev. Farewel Constancy.   [*Exit* Rains.
I am glad he's gone; *Woodly* has repented him of fighting in the morning, and wou'd dispatch the business to night, 'tis a Moon-light night, and we shall do't well enough. Reads, *Meet me in the Field behind my Lodging, and I will, Sir, since you are pleas'd to doubt whether I durst or no.*   [*Exit.*

Enter Clodpate *and Mrs.* Jilt.

Clodp. Udsooks, do you suspect me? my word will go for ten thousand pounds in *Sussex*.

Jilt. Alas! I am a poor innocent Country thing unexperienc'd in the World; do not go about to betray a harmless Maid as I am, God wot.

Clodp. As I am an honest Man, I am in earnest; here's a Parson lies in the House, and I'le marry you immediately.

Jilt. Alas! I am an inconsiderable person, and not worth your Love, though I have been offer'd the Love of Knights, nay Lords, upon my word; but they were scurvy *London* ones, and I swear I scorn 'em all.

Clodp. As Gad judge me, you are in the right.

Jilt. Oh I hate that Town, my Father forc'd me thither for Breeding, forsooth. Excellent Breeding is learnt there indeed, to wash, daub, paint, and be proud, and senseless; out on 'em for *Jezebels*.

Clodp. Very fine, she's an Angel, Gudsbud.

Jilt. I had rather wait upon a Lady in the Country, than be that vain thing at *London;* upon my word now.

Clodp. Leave all, and cleave to me, we'll into *Sussex* far enough off that lewd Town.

Jilt. Alas! I am a silly innocent poor Creature, I cannot abide Marriage, upon my word not I; yet I wou'd undergo any thing rather than live at *London;* I had rather milk Cows in the Country, than be a Maid of Honour there.

Clodp. Maid of Honour! I'le make you a Wife of Honour, if you'll go with me; that's better.

Jilt. Well, I vow I use to go sometimes for my pleasure to Milk a Cow; it is a very pleasant recreation to ſtroke the Cows Teats, I delighted in it extreamly.

Clodp. Admirable——

Jilt. Nay I have gone a Hay-making in a frollick, upon my word now; but my Father was ſtark mad with me, and forc'd me to *London*, to learn breeding, and to break me of those tricks as he call'd 'em.

Clodp. Gudsooks, he was too blame. If you'll be my Wife you shall milk and make Hay as much as you will.

Jilt. Sir, you are in a manner a ſtranger to me, though Mrs. *Margaret* has told me your condition and quality; yet an innocent simple thing as I am muſt take advice of Friends.

Clodp. Friends! Gad take me, I have 2000 *l.* a year, take advice of that, 'twill be the beſt Friend you can advise with.

Enter Mrs. Woodly.

Mrs. Wood. 'Tis ſtrange this Husband of mine is not come home yet; but I hope Mr. *Rains* will not fail his appointment.

Clodp. Here's Company, let us retire and discourse of this business. If I do not give *Carolina* such a bob as she never had in her life——

[*Ex.* Clodpate *and* Jilt.

Mrs. Wood. Mr. *Rains* seems to be a person of worth, and fitter to be truſted with an intrigue, than that Villain *Bevil.*

Enter Rains.

Rains. What a Rogue am I to run into temptation; but Pox on't, *Lucia* will ne'er miss what I shall lose. Madam, your humble Servant; I have obey'd your Summons.

Mrs. Wood. Sir, I hope you'll pardon the confidence of a ſtranger, that blushes for't, as I do.

Rains. I muſt thank you for the honour. I'le ne're ſtand out at serving such a Lady with my soul and body too; I Gad as far as it will go—I am a Rogue, poor *Lucia*, forgive me. [*Aside.*

Mrs. Wood. Your Friend *Bevil* is the falseſt of men, but I do not doubt your honour; you are fit to make a friend of, and advise a Lady in the dangerous actions of her life.

Rains. It was an unlucky embroilment you were in this night.

Mrs. *Wood.* It was, Sir; but I am the more easily appeas'd, since it has offer'd mean occasion of knowing, in some measure, so worthy a person as your self.

Rains. Why there it is——I see what it must come to.   [*Aside.*

Enter Peg.

Peg. Madam, Mr. *Bevil* is walking yonder, but my Master is coming in.

Rains. 'Sdeath, Madam, I shall be discover'd.

Mrs. *Wood.* Fear it not, go in.   [*Exit* Rains.
Peg, go down.

Enter Woodly.

Wood. So, Madam, does not your Ladiship blush, and tremble at my presence?

Mrs. *Wood.* You are an unworthy man to suspect my virtue, I am the most abus'd Woman upon the Earth.

Wood. Abus'd! it is impossible.

Mrs. *Wood.* I can clear my self, wou'd you cou'd do so, barbarous man!

Wood. You clear your self!

Mrs. *Wood.* That false Villain, *Bevil* has again had the impudence to sollicite my virtue, and after he had ask'd me a thousand pardons, he was so audacious to press me to a meeting, saying, he would defend me against all your rage, and that there was no way for me left, but to fling my self upon him for protection.

Wood. S'death and Hell, and I'le reward him for't.

Mrs. *Wood.* Lord, how I tremble, do not quarrel, good Dear; though you are a naughty man, I cannot but love you yet, and wou'd not have told you this, but to clear my honour; take two or three of your Servants, and beat him soundly; do not quarrel, good Dear.

Wood. I'le warrant you, let me alone.   [*Ex.* Woodly.

Mrs. *Wood.* I know he has too much honour not to meet him singly; if he kills *Bevil*, I am reveng'd, if *Bevil* kills him, he rids me of the worst Husband for my humour in Christendom; but I'le to Mr. *Rains*, he's a Gentleman indeed.   [*Ex. Mrs.* Woodly.

Enter Bevil *in the field.*

Bev. Where is this *Woodly?* 'Tis as fine a Moon-light night to run a man through the Lungs in, as one wou'd wish; 'Twas unlucky he shou'd over-hear me to night, but 'tis too late to retreat now.

[Rains *and Mrs.* Woodly *appear at the Window above.*

(173)

Rains. 'sLife yonder's *Bevil;* I muſt to him, for I gave my word to keep him from meeting your Husband to night.

Mrs. *Wood.* You need not fear, my Husband's gone another way.

Rains. However, Madam, I muſt secure him in my Lodgings, and I'le wait on you again presently.

Mrs. *Wood.* But, Sir, I have an immediate occasion for your assiſtance and advice.

Rains. Madam, I'le return immediately.

Mrs. *Wood.* My affair is so pressing and urgent, it muſt be dispatch'd inſtantly.

Rains. I'le not ſtay a moment from you.

Mrs. *Wood.* Stay but one minute; they'll not meet I tell you.

Rains. Madam, I pass'd my honour, and dare not venture it.

Mrs. *Wood.* Excellent honour, to leave a Lady that has such occasion for you as I have.

Rains. I have as much occasion, Madam, for you; but those old Enemies Love and Honour will never agree.

Mrs. *Wood.* Sir, you shall not ſtir, for a reason I have to my self.

Rains. For a reason I have to my self, I muſt, madam.

[*Breaks from her and Exit.*

Mrs. *Wood.* Farewel you ill-bred, rude, unworthy Fellow: Heaven! how unlucky this is? I am ruin'd. [*Ex. Mrs.* Wood.

Enter Woodly.

Wood. All's true she has said, he's here.

Bev. Oh, Sir, are you come, I have waited sufficiently for you.

Wood. Oh, cunning! how ready he's at a lye to excuse himself? Do you think to carry it off thus?

Bev. Carry what off? you see, Sir, I dare meet you.

Wood. Rare impudence, meet me! have at you, Sir. [*Draws.*

[*They fight,* Woodly *falls and is disarm'd.*

Bev. Your Life——

Wood. Take it——I deserve to lose it Since I defended it no better.

Bev. No, Sir——live——and live my Friend if you please; and know your Lady's innocent: I had not gone so far, but that you were pleased to make a queſtion to *Rains,* whether I durſt meet you or no.

Enter Rains.

Rains. How, Gentlemen, you have put a fine trick upon me, to engage me, and then leave me out at this business.

Wood. He came hither to meet another, Sir, not me.

Bev. Another, you are mad, Sir.

Enter Lucia *and* Carolina *in Night-Gowns.*

Luc. So Gentlemen, you are men of honour, you keep your words well, but we would not trust you——we had you dogg'd——

Caro. This will redound much to our reputation, to have our names us'd in one of your quarrels.

Rains. There's a mistake, Madam, hear it out.

Wood. Did not you come to meet a Lady of my acquaintance?

Bev. I receiv'd a Challenge from you, there 'tis——

Wood. From me? I sent none. Ha, this must be my damn'd Wife. 'sDeath and Hell; but no more, I am resolv'd. Ladies and Gentlemen, do me the favour to go into my Lodgings with me, and you shall see I will behave my self like a man of honour, and doubt not but to have all your approbations.

Rains. What does he mean?

Luc. Come, let's in.   [*Exeunt.*

Enter Bisk *and* Fribble *in the Hall.*

Bisk. A duce take Mr. *Cuff* and Mr. *Kick*, for locking us up. I'le take him up roundly for't to morrow: it's well his Landlord took pity on us and releas'd us.

Frib. Well, I am so loving in my drink, I'le go to bed to my Dear, and forgive her all.

Bisk. I can hold out no longer, I'le go to bed and make peace with my Bird, there's no such peace as that concluded between a pair of sheets. Prithee, Neighbour, go you first gently into her Chamber, and try to appease her, a little to prepare my way.

Frib. Well, I'le venture a Broken-head for you once.

Bisk. Gently, gently.

Frib. 'sdeath, what do I see?   [*Peeps in.*

Bisk. Be not afraid, man, what's the matter?

Frib. Mr. *Kick* is in a very indecent posture upon the Bed with your Wife.

Bisk peeps in. 'Slife what do you say? Oh, 'tis true, 'tis true, what shall I do? If I should go in, he'd grow desperate at the discovery, and for ought I know, kill me.

Frib. You must get a Constable and apprehend him; but for my Jade I'd maul her, If I should find her at it.

Bisk. I will, I will, come along with me, Neighbour.

Frib. Stay but a minute till I see how my poor Rogue does, and I'le go with you; I beat her damnably, and am very sorry for't, i'fack.

Bisk. Oh make haste, make haste!

Frib. Oh, Lord! Oh, Lord!   [*Peeps.*

Bisk. What's the matter?

Frib. Oh, Lord!

Bisk. What's the matter, come away?

Frib. As Gad judge me, my Jade's at the same recreation with Mr. *Cuff.* Oh look, look, Neighbour, that you may be my witness as well as I am yours.   [*Bisk peeps.*

Bisk. She has given you occasion to maul her, Neighbour.

Frib. This I may thank you for; you must be bringing Fellows acquainted with your Wife, ye Sot.

Frib. And you must be laying wagers upon your Wife's head. Come, come, let's fetch a Constable, the World shall know what lewd Creatures they are.   [*Exeunt.*

Enter Rains, Bevil, Lucia, *and* Carolina.

Rains. Since Mr. *Woodly* is so busie within, setling his great affair with his Lady, let us mind our business. Ladies, our Loves to you two are so violent, they must end in Marriage.

Luc. Your Love is violent indeed, it is a hot Spur *French* Love.

Bev. I am sure I have lov'd out a year of ordinary Love in this one day.

Caro. Marriage! that were time to talk of when we have known you seven years.

Rains. 'sDeath, would you have a man have the patience of a Patriarch?

Luc. Methinks 'twere enough to arrive at Platonick Love at first.

Bev. The pretence to that is more out of fashion in this active Age, than Ruffs and Trunk-breeches are.

Caro. If we hear one word of Marriage more, we'll discard you. We may perhaps admit of a little harmless Gallantry.

Luc. This is no Age for Marriage; but if you'll keep your distance, we will admit you for a Couple of Servants as far as a Country Dance, or Ombre, or so.

Enter Clodpate.

Clodp. So, Ladies, I thank you for the Tricks you have put upon me; but, Madam, I am even with you for your *London* Tricks, I have given you such a bob.

Caro. Me?

Clodp. You have lost me, Madam, you have. I have married a pretty innocent Country-Lady worth fifty of you. Come in, my Dear. Here's the Parson too, that dispatch'd the business for us. I think I have met with you now.

Enter Jilt *with a Parson.*

Rains. Mrs. *Jilt.*

Bev. Old Acquaintance.

(176)

Clodpate. How's this!

Jilt. I have got a Husband at last, though much a ado, I'le swear.

Enter Peg.

Peg. Sister, I wish you Joy. Now I hope I may be own'd by you.

Clodp. Is she her Sister? Curs'd Instrument of Hell, I am cheated, abus'd.

Bev. Is this your Country-Lady? she has liv'd in *London* all her life.

Clodp. Udsbud, is this true?

Jilt. I was never so far out of *London*, nor ever will be agen, I'le swear.

Clodp. Nay, now I am sure she has liv'd in *London*, she could not have been so impudent else.

Caro. I wish you happy in her, Sir, though it was not my good Fortune to be made so by you; but let's in and hear *Woodly's* resolution.

[*Ex*. Rains, Bevil, Lucia, *and* Carolina.

Jilt. Did you think I would be mop'd up in a house in *Sussex?* Sister, take a place in the Coach, and go to morrow to *London*, get my Brother to bespeak me a fine Coach and Horses, and to hire me a House in *Lincolns-Inn-Fields*, I shall find Credit for Furniture; but now I think on't, my Dear, you shall go with me. You are so strangely Rustical, I swear, you must be better bred, if you think to please me; upon my word you must.

Clodp. Gudsooks, Gudsbud, I'le go hang my self.

Jilt. A person of your Quality keep Company with Boars and Rascals, it's a shame. I'le ha'you to *London*, and bring you acquainted with Wits and Courtiers upon my word, and you shall learn such breeding of 'em. I am belov'd and courted at a high rate by 'em all, I'le swear.

Clodp. Oh, miserable man! I have not only married a *Londoner*, and consequently a Strumpet, and consequently one that is not sound, but the most audacious of her Sex, a *Mall* Cutpurse, a *Doll* Common.

Jilt. My Dear, you are strangely unkind upon your Wedding night. We'll to *London* together to morrow, you'll find great respect there for my sake. I have had so many Lovers I have been cruel to, that I'le swear you'll be the most envi'd man in the whole World, upon my word you will.

Clodp. I am distracted, I know not what to do or say.

Jilt. Why are you troubled, my Dear? you shall find I have interest at Court, and can keep you from being Sheriff; nay, I believe I could get you Knighted.

Clodp. Knighted with a Pox; would you had interest enough with the Parson, and wou'd get me unmarry'd, I wou'd willingly give a Leg or an Arm.

Jilt. Unmarried; nay, Sir, an' you despise me, I scorn such a pitiful

Fellow as you are; matters are not gone so far, but upon good terms I can release you.

Clodp. How, Gudsbud, what say you?

Peg. Leave it to me, give me a handsome reward, and her some consideration for the loss she shall have in such a Husband, and I'le do't.

Clodp. I will, any thing that you can in reason demand.

Jilt. We'll in, and consult about the business.

                        [Ex. Jilt, *and* Peg, *and* Parson.

Clodp. 'Sbud I'de give half of my Estate to be rid on her.

Enter Bisket *and* Fribble, *with a Constable and Watch, bringing in Mrs.* Fribble, *Mrs.* Bisket, Kick, *and* Cuff.

Bisk. Sir, an please your Worship, I have brought a Malefactor before you here, that in most unseemly manner did make an assault upon the body of my Wife.

Frib. And I another, that committed the same insolence upon mine.

Clodp. Ha, Rogues! I'le vent some of my anger upon them: Hah, you were the Rogues in Country Habits, to day, that won my money at Putt: I'le make you Examples, cheating Villains; you, for ought I know, rob'd me, bound me, and stole my Dapple Mare.

Kick. Shameless Rascals, to publish thus your own disgraces.

                        [To Bisk. *and* Frib.

Cuff. Rogues! we shall meet with you.

Clodp. Away with 'em, cheating Slaves! adulterous Rogues!

Cuff. Mr. Justice, you are a Coxcomb; and I shall find a time to cut your Nose.

Kick. And I will make bold to piss upon your Worship.

Clodp. Oh impudence! Constable secure 'em to night, and I'le send 'em in the morning to *Kingstone* Goal without Bail or Mainprize.

Cuff. Pheu, our Party is too strong for that, here in Town.

                        [Ex. Constable, Cuff, *and* Kick.

Clod. Oh this cursed Match of mine! I'le see what they do within.

                        [Ex. Clodp.

Mrs. *Frib.* Good Dear, forgive me: I will never do the like again.

Frib. Again, quoth she! no she had not need——   *[They Kneel.*

Mrs. *Bisk.* Good Duck, now forgive me; I will never commit Adultery again, nay I will never pluck up a spirit against thee more. Thou shalt command me for ever, if thou'lt say no more of this business.

Bisk. Well, my heart melts——I cannot deny my Lamb when she begs any thing upon her Knees. Rise, poor Bird——but i'fack you were too blame, Duck.

Mrs. *Bisk.* I was; but I will never do so again.

Bisk. But will you swear, as you hope to be sav'd.

Mrs. *Bisk.* Ay, as I hope to be sav'd.

Mrs. *Frib.* Pray, Dear, forgive me.

Frib. Ay, now you are upon your Knees ; but you were in another posture just now.

Mrs. *Frib.* And I wish I may never stir out of this place alive, if I e're do so again. Pray forgive me.

Frib. Well, I'le pass it by for once ; but I'le not fail to sue *Cuff* upon an Action of Assault and Battery.

Bisk. And I'le sue *Kick* too. If we order our business wisely and impannel a good substantial Jury, of all married men, they'll give us vast damages.

Frib. I have known a man recover 4 or 500 *l.* in such a Case, and his Wife not one jot the worse.

Bisk. No, not a bit. But shall I always command you ?

Mrs. *Bisk.* Yes, you shall, you shall.

Bisk. Why then this is the first day of my reign.

Enter Woodly, *Mrs.* Woodly, Rains, Bevil, Lucia, *and* Carolina.

Wood. I desire you all here to stay, and be Witnesses of what I now shall do.

Rains. Be not rash, consider 'till to morrow.

Wood. I have consider'd, disswade me not : next to the obligation she did me to let me enjoy her when I lik'd her, is the giving me occasion to part with her when I do not like her.

Bev. I am extream sorry, Madam, that I was the occasion, though unwillingly, of this breach.

Mrs. *Wood.* You are not the occasion, he believes you not ; but if you were, I should thank you ; for you would rid me at once of him and your self too : but the business is, we like not one another, and there's an end on't.

Wood. But let's execute our Divorce decently ; for my part I'le celebrate it like a Wedding.

Mrs. *Wood.* To me 'tis a more joyful day.

Enter Clodpate, Jilt, Peg, *and Parson.*

Peg. Do but sign this Warrant, to confess a Judgment to my Sister, and this Bond to me ; and I'le null your Marriage, or declare these Writings before all these Witnesses to be void.

Clodp. Give me the Writings, I will do't with all my heart.

Luc. What's here another Divorce ? *Clodpate* begins betimes.

Clodp. Here they are, take 'em.

Peg. Well now, Sir, know the Parson would not marry you, because the hour was not Canonical, but I was fain to steal a Cassock, and counterfeit a Beard for Mr. *Woodly*'s man. Look you, this is the first Parson I ever ordain'd. *[Pulls his Beard off.*

Jilt. I release you of your Marriage and thank you, you have qualified me to marry one I like better, for I am resolv'd to marry upon my word, and suddenly too.

Clodp. 'Sdeath and Hell, if ever I come so near *London* agen, I'le commit Treason, and have my head and quarters set upon the Bridge. [*Ex.* Clodpate.

Wood. Now listen, and be witnesses to our agreement.

Mrs. *Wood.* This I think is the first time we e'er agreed since our Wedding.

Wood. Imprimis, I *Francis Woodly,* for several causes me thereunto especially moving, do declare I will for ever separate from the company of *Sarah* my now Wife.

Mrs. *Wood.* Your lewd disorderly life made you separate before. The said *Sarah* having for this two years scarce seen you by day-light.

Wood. And that I will never hereafter use her like a Wife.

Mrs. *Wood.* That is scurvily. Also all Obligations of conjugal affections, shall from henceforth cease, be null, void, and of none effect.

Wood. Then, that I am to keep what Mistress I please, and how I please, after the laudable custom of other Husbands.

Mrs. *Wood.* And that I am to have no Spies upon my company or actions, but may enjoy all Priviledges of other separate Ladies, without any lett, hindrance, or molestation whatsoever.

Wood. And if at any time I should be in drink, or otherwise in a loving fit, and should be desirous to visit you, it shall and may be lawful for you to deny me ingress, egress, and regress.

Mrs. *Wood.* Yes, though you serve me as you do others, and break my Windows.

Wood. I restore you all your Portion, and add 2000 *l.* to it for the use I have had on you.

Mrs. *Wood.* So, it is done.

Wood. Is not this better than to live and quarrel, and to keep a pother with one another. Faith take a Kiss at parting for old acquaintance.

[Kisses her.

Mrs. *Wood.* Farewell, dear Husband.

Wood. Adieu, dear Wife.

Frib. to his Wife. This 'tis to marry a Gentleman, forsooth; if you had marry'd one, you certainly had been turn'd away for the prank you plaid to night.

Bisk. Ay, but we Citizens use our Wives better: let me tell you, Neighbour *Fribble,* I would not part from my Lamb for all the World, let her do what she will, she is such a pretty Rogue.

Luc. See what Matrimony comes to——

(180)

Rains. Madam, since we cannot agree upon better tearms, let me claim your Promise, and admit me for your Servant.

Luc. I do receive you upon tryal.

Caro. And I you upon your good behaviour: I think you have gone far enough in one day.

Luc. If you should improve every day so, what would it come to in time?

Rains. To what it should come to, Madam.

Bev. 'Twill come to that, *Jack;* for one Fortnights conversing with us will lay such a scandal upon 'em, they'll be glad to repair to Marriage.

Wood. To shew you, that there was never yet so decent a Divorce, I have Fiddles to play at it, as they use to do at Weddings.

Mrs. Wood. And to shew you I am extreamly pleas'd, I'le dance at it.

Wood. How easie and how light I walk without this Yoak! methinks 'tis air I tread——Come let's Dance, strike up.

Dance.

Marriage that does the hearts and wills unite,
Is the best state of pleasure and delight:
But——
When Man and Wife no more each other please,
They may at least like us each other ease.   [*Ex. omnes.*

F I N I S.

Epilogue.

A Play without a Wedding, made in *spight*
    Of old Black-Fryars ; *'tis a fine way they write ;*
    They please the wicked Wenchers of the Age,
And scoff at civil Husbands on the Stage :
To th' great decay of Children in the Nation,
They laugh poor Matrimony out of fashion.
A young man dares not marry now for shame,
He is afraid of losing his good name.
If they go on thus, in a short time we
Shall but few Sons of honest Women see :
And when no virtuous Mothers there shall be,
Who is't will boast his ancient Family ?
Therefore, for Heavens sake, take the first occasion,
And marry all of you for th' good o' th' Nation.
Gallants, leave your lewd whoring and take Wives,
Repent for shame your Covent-Garden lives :
Fear not the fate of us, whom in the Play
Our bawdy Poet Cuckolded to day ;
For ours are Epsom Water-drinking Wives,
And few in that lewd Town lead stricter lives :
But for the rest, he'd have it understood
By representing few ill Wives he wou'd
Advance the value of the many good.
He knows the wise, the fair, the chaste, the young.
A party are so numerous and strong,
Would they his Play with their protection owne,
They might each day fill all this House alone.
He says, none but ill Wives can ever be
Banded in faction 'gainst this Comedy.
Therefore come all, who wish to have it known,
Though there are scurvy Wives, that they are none.

THE
TEMPEST,

OR THE

Enchanted Island.

A

COMEDY.

As it is now Acted at His Highness the Duke of *York's*

THEATRE.

LONDON,

Printed by *T. N.* for *Henry Herringman*, at the *Blew Anchor* in the *Lower Walk* of the *New Exchange.*
MDCLXXIV.

Source.

TIECK pointed out the resemblance between Shakespeare's *The Tempest* and the German play *Comedia von der schönen Sidea* by Jakob Ayrer, where the parallels are indeed so striking that it almost seems there must have been some common original, unless perchance Shakespeare knew of the play from the English comedians who visited Nürnburg, Ayrer's native town, in 1604 and 1606. Moreover, English actors performed a *Sidea* " in good German " in 1613. Jakob Ayrer died 26 March, 1605, so he cannot in any case have been the borrower. Yet even if Shakespeare did thus glean certain incidents from theatrical gossip of *Sidea*, that bare hint cannot have been his main source for *The Tempest*. The poet Collins gave a misleading clue when he spoke of *Aurelio and Isabella*, but none the less I am inclined to believe the poet was indebted to some lost romance. This seems to me supported by the fact that there are several loose threads in *The Tempest* such as might well be left in a play founded upon a romance, and, although they have been remarked, in my opinion the significance of these has been overlooked. For example, we are never told what was the one thing Sycorax did for which they would not take her life—it was assuredly not the fact of her pregnancy ; the whole business of the marriage of Claribel to the King of Tunis seems insufficiently introduced, either some other motive for the voyage should have been suggested or more should have been made of this episode,— Dryden, it will be noted, represents Alonzo as returning from Portugal, where he has very Christianly fought the Barbary foe. These are slight, but remarkable, points.

There is some faint trace of such a romance in a Spanish tale by Antonio de Eslava, which forms part of the collection *Las noches de invierno*, published at Madrid in 1609.

Here we have a dispossessed king, Dardanus, who is a beneficent magician, who raises an ensorcelled palace amid the seas, and provides his daughter, Seraphina, with a royal bridegroom. A tempest helps to unravel the plot of the story, and Sirens, Dryads, Nymphs, Tritons, minister the will of the kindly thaumaturge.

No doubt various records of Jacobean voyaging and adventure, relations of the expedition of Sir Thomas Gates and Sir George Somers, published in 1610, supplied Shakespeare with suggestions of which he made most excellent use. To endeavour to locate the enchanted isle seems the crassest folly, an ineptitude of that kind well-beloved of many Shakespearean commentators.

Since the Masque of Iris, Ceres, and Juno does not appear in the Shadwell opera, it were impertinent to discuss it here. There are certain noodle sciolists, who have piddled about with *The Tempest*, that would deny it to be Shakespeare's writing. One can but feel sorry for the poor naturals.

Some of Shakespeare's names, Ferdinand, Alonzo, Sebastian, Gonzalo, were probably suggested by Eden's *History of Travaile*, 1577, whence was also taken the name *Setebos*, a great devil.

Caliban is generally considered to be a metathesis of Canibal, *i.e.*, Caribee ; and Shakespeare's source here was indisputably Florio's *Montaigne*, published 1603, Book I, c. 30 *Of the Caniballes*.

Various ingenious, but hardly satisfactory, derivatives have been advanced for the name Sycorax, in whose figure at least one ingenious editor, with more historical perception of truth than fact and gallantry, sees an allegorization of that " bright Occidental star " Queen Elizabeth.

In his preface to *The Tempest*, 4to, 1670, Dryden explicitly states that the character of Hippolito is due to Davenant. Herman Grimm, *Fünfzehn Essays*, Berlin, 8vo, 1785, once made a futile, and indeed ridiculous, attempt to show that Hippolito is borrowed from Calderon's *En esta vida todo es verdad, y todo mentira*. H. H. Furness in his very faulty edition of *The Tempest, Variorum Shakespeare*, 1892, jumped at the suggestion, and absurdly wrote that " the mutilations, or rather the additions, for which Dryden took to himself credit as the author, are wholesale ' conveyances ' from a play of Calderon." It is obvious that Furness had no acquaintance with the play in question. *En esta vida todo es verdad, y todo mentira* is a play of strange and beautiful fantasy, which save for the merest chance resemblance of some half a dozen lines, has absolutely nothing in common with *The Tempest*. The error, however, was unfortunately repeated by Strunk, who relied upon the incorrect and blundering Furness, in his amateurish editing of *All for Love*, Introduction, p. xvii, no date, but presumably published about 1910. In my *Shakespeare Adaptations*, 1922, when I reprinted the Dryden-Davenant *Tempest*, I have dealt with this whole question in detail, and by an analysis of the Spanish play I show that Davenant has taken nothing from Calderon.

Theatrical History.

THE various complicated problems connected with the Davenant-Dryden alteration of *The Tempest* and the question of an operatic version by Shadwell have been fully discussed in the Introduction, and therefore do not require to be further dealt with here.

The Davenant-Dryden *The Tempest ; or, The Enchanted Island* was produced on Thursday, 7 November, 1667. Pepys, who was present, found himself among " a great many great ones. The house mighty full ; the King and Court there : and the most innocent play that ever I saw ; and a curious piece of musique is an echo of half-sentences, the echo repeating the former half, whilst the man goes on to the latter ; which is mighty pretty." This is the song sung by Ferdinand in Act III, 3, where Ariel echoes *Go thy way*. It was set by Banister, who with Pelham Humphreys supplied the music in 1667. All, Pepys tells us, " were mightily pleased with the play." The diarist saw the comedy several times, and on one occasion was admitted behind the scenes, and " had the pleasure to see the actors in their several dresses, especially the seamen, and monster, which were very droll."

No list of actors was printed with the quarto, but we know that Henry Harris played Ferdinand ; Edward Angel, " an incomparable Comedian," Stephano ; Cave Underhill, Trincalo. Moll Davis was also in the original cast, her rôle perhaps being Hippolito, for the " right Heir of the Dukedom of *Mantua* " was assigned to a woman, and little Miss Davies in breeches parts had already proved an irresistible attraction. After she left the stage she was succeeded in *The Tempest* by Mrs. Gosnell, who, according to Pepys, was a sorry substitute. Betterton himself did not appear in the play.

The Davenant-Dryden comedy was printed quarto, 1670, the preface by Dryden being dated 1 December, 1669. It was for the first time edited by myself in my volume *Shakespeare Adaptations*, 1922. Downes records : " In 1673 [rather 1674] *The Tempest ; or Inchanted Island ;* made into an Opera by Mr. *Shadwell :* having all new in it ; as Scenes, Machines ; particularly, one scene painted with myriads of *Ariel* Spirits ; and another flying away with a table, furnisht out with fruits, sweet-meats, and all sorts of viands, just when Duke *Trincalo* and his companions were going to dinner ; all things perform'd in it so admirably well, that not any succeeding opera got more money." Mr. W. J. Lawrence in his *Did Thomas Shadwell write an Opera on " The Tempest "* (*Elizabethan Playhouse*, I, p. 203) fixes "the date of production of the Shadwell *Tempest* at *circa*, 30 April, 1674, probably a sound approximation." This operatic version was printed quarto, 1674; 1676 (*bis*); 1690; 1695; and 1701. With the exception of the folio Dryden, 1701, this is the text which has been given in all editions of Dryden's work.

The first alteration of *The Tempest* seems immediately to have been absorbed in the opera, which was extraordinarily popular, indeed few pieces upon the Restoration stage proved so great and so continued an attraction. The Opera was seen by the King on Tuesday, 17 November, 1674; upon the following day, upon Saturday, 28 of that month; upon Monday, 5 November, 1677; and apparently again ten days later.

There are innumerable contemporary allusions to *The Tempest*, to the elaborate *mise-en-scène* and effects; to Duke Trincalo and the sailors; to Caliban and Sycorax; to the singing and dancing; to the spirits and devils; to the Terminal Masque; all of these having fairly ensorcelled the Town.

For the Opera new instrumental music was written by Matthew Lock, and new vocal music by Pietro Reggio and J. Hart. The dances were composed by Giovanni Battista Draghi. In a private letter to myself the late Mr. W. Barclay Squire wrote (1922): "Excepting Draghi's dances I think we now have the whole of the music for Shadwell's version." The song *Arise, arise! ye subterranean winds*, at the end of the second act will be found, duly ascribed to Shadwell, "A Song in The Tempest. The Words by Mr. Shadwell," in the work advertised in the *London Gazette*, 1680, as "A choice collection of Songs set by Signior Pietro Reggio to be engraved on copper in an extraordinary manner in very large folio, most of them out of Mr. A. Cowley's excellent Poems." This beautiful book is embellished with a copper-plate title representing Arion upon the dolphin, carried safe over a swelling sea. There are commendatory verses by Flatman; Ayres; Laurence Maidwell, a Latin copy, for Maidwell was a schoolmaster; one T. B.; and Shadwell himself. To Shadwell, whom he hails as "Cigno Immortal," Reggio replied in a "Soneto Al' Signor Tomaso Shadwel, Poeta Digmissimo." A MS. copy of the same setting is ascribed to Grabu, but this is obviously an error. For a second MS. copy corrected bears Reggio's name.

The Operatic *The Tempest*, doubtless as being one of the most splendid spectacles known to the London stage, took the chief place of the three magnificent productions seen by the Morocco Ambassador at Dorset Garden early in 1682. His Excellency declared himself "extreamly pleased" at the performances.

Edward Angel had died in the spring or early summer of 1673, and it is doubtful if Henry Harris was acting in 1682, but Cave Underhill played Trincalo, his original part, it was in fact one of his most eminent rôles.

There were special revivals of *The Tempest* in 1690 and 1691, and it was probably for these that the opera, with additions, was wholly re-set by Henry Purcell. Towards the close of 1695 a song for Dorinda, "Dear Pretty Youth," not to be found in the quarto, was published in Book III of *Deliciæ Musicæ* as "A New Song in *The Tempest*, sung by Miss *Cross* to her Lover who is supposed Dead. Set by Mr. Henry Purcell."

A performance of *The Tempest* with "all the original Flyings and Musick" is announced in the *Daily Courant*, 13 February, 1707-8, "Dorinda by Mrs. *Cross* with the Song of 'Dear Pretty Youth.'" Letitia Cross, as notorious for her amours as admired for her beauty, had been the mistress of Peter the Great during his stay in England.

It is, of course, only possible to chronicle a very few performances of *The Tempest*, which, it is interesting to note, we find frequently advertised in *The Spectator*. At Drury Lane, 4 June, 1714, Powell played Prospero; Johnson Caliban; Ryan Ferdinand; Mrs. Mountfort Hippolito; Mrs. Santlow Dorinda; whilst Bullock had succeeded Underhill as Trincalo.

2 January, 1729, at the same theatre, John Mills was Prospero; Wilks Ferdinand; Joe Miller Trincalo; Mrs. Cibber Hippolito; Mrs. Booth Miranda; Miss Robinson Ariel; and Kitty Raftor, a young nymph of seventeen, who afterwards became Kitty Clive, Dorinda.

31 January, 1746, Garrick revived *The Tempest* as by Shakespeare. Luke Sparks acted Prospero; Macklin Stephano; and Kitty Clive Ariel. None the less the Masque of *Neptune and Amphitrite*, for which Arne had written new music, was appended.

In December of the following year *The Tempest*, loosely announced as "Not acted 7 years," was given at Drury Lane with Berry as Prospero; Macklin Trincalo; Isaac Sparks Caliban; Taswell, a great farceur, Sycorax; Peg Woffington Hippolito; Mrs. Mozeen Miranda; Kitty Clive Ariel; and Mrs. Green Dorinda. The whole concluded with the Masque.

There is an interesting and detailed account of the production of *The Tempest* at Dublin on 13 January, 1748-9, at the Theatre Royal, Smock-alley.

Sheridan had got together for the season of 1748-9 an exceptionally strong company, including Mr. and Mrs. Macklin, Mrs. Bland, Mr. and Mrs. Lampe, Mr. Sullivan, Mrs. Mozeen, Mrs. Storer, Mr. Howard, and Signor Pasquali. In the Dublin papers he announced that, in order to do full justice to the musical plays and operas, he had engaged an orchestra consisting of ten violins, a tenor, a 'cello, two hautbois, two bassoons, two double-basses, two French horns, a trumpet, and a harpsichord. At the request of several patrons, in December, the Drury Lane revival of *The Tempest* was put in rehearsal by Macklin, who played Trincalo, and was duly produced on Friday, 13 January, 1749.

The *Dublin Courant* of 3–7 January, 1748–9, announced that on Friday, 13 January, would be revived *The Tempest*, with the original songs " and Musick, compos'd by Mr. Purcell." This advertisement was repeated in the issue of 7–10 January, and the play was given to a crowded house. Its success was assured, and the second performance followed on 19 January. The advertisement for this repeat performance contains the announcement that the play was now performed " for the second time in the present Manner in this Kingdom." A later advertisement, in the issue for 14–17 January, informs the public that the original " Musick by the celebrated Purcell " would be given, and that the whole was to conclude with " a Grand Masque of Neptune and Amphitrite." In the announcement of the third performance, which took place on 25 January, the advertisement held out as a lure " the original Musick composed by Purcell," as well as " Sinkings, Flyings, and other Decorations," and " an extraordinary Piece of Machinery representing the Rising Sun."

On 11 February, 1756, Garrick put on an operatic version of *The Tempest* prepared by himself. Hippolito and Dorinda, it is true, have disappeared ; but there were wholesale conveyances from *Tyrannic Love ;* Trincalo, Stephano, and Ventoso indulge in a trio ; and there are many other impertinent interpolations, whilst Shadwell's *Arise, arise ! ye subterranean winds* is sung by Milcha. New music had been composed by John Christopher Smith. With not unmerited sarcasm did Theophilus Cibber write of " *The Tempest* castrated into an opera. Oh ! what an agreeable Lullaby might it have prov'd to our Beaus and Belles to have heard Caliban, Sycorax, and one of the Devils, trilling of trios."

Shakespeare's *The Tempest* without adulteration was revived by Garrick on 20 October, 1757, and announced as " Not acted 14 years."

Bell's acting edition of Shakespeare " regulated from the prompt-books by permission of the managers " (1773–1775) supplies a " pure and unmixed," if greatly abridged, text of *The Tempest*, and Shakespeare alone held the stage until 13 October, 1787, when Kemble at Drury Lane restored Hippolito, played by Mrs. Goodall, and Dorinda Miss Farren.

31 October, 1812, Young attempted Prospero at Covent Garden, but it is said that the performance, though intelligent and correct, suffered by comparison with Kemble. Mrs. Henry Johnston was the Hippolito, and Miss Booth Dorinda.

Hippolito and Dorinda did not, indeed, finally disappear from the theatre until 13 October, 1838, when at Covent Garden Macready gave his sumptuous and extremely successful production of *The Tempest* " from the text of Shakespeare." This ran for fifty-five nights. The music was " selected from the works of Purcell, Linley, and Dr. Arne, and arranged by Mr. T. Cooke." Macready appeared as Prospero ; Anderson Ferdinand ; Phelps Antonio ; G. Bennett Caliban ; Harley Trincalo ;

Bartley Stephano; Miss Faucit Miranda; and Priscilla Horton Ariel. On 29 November and 1 and 4 December Miss Vanderhoff was the Miranda.

Probably Shadwell's songs have not been heard in *The Tempest* since 1756, and it must be remembered that Hippolito and Dorinda wholly belong to Sir William Davenant and Dryden.

Some account of Thomas Duffett's amusing skit *The Mock-Tempest ; or, The Enchanted Castle*, which was written for the rival company to burlesque the operatic *Tempest*, will be found in the Introduction. As Langbaine says, this farce was penned " on purpose to draw Company from the other Theatre, where was great resort about that time to see that reviv'd Comedy call'd *The Tempest*, then much in vogue." *The Mock-Tempest* was given at Drury Lane in November, 1674, and printed quarto, 1675 ; *Term Catalogues*, Hilary (15 February), 1675. It was republished, for the first time, and edited by myself, in my *Shakespeare Adaptations*, 1922.

PREFACE

TO THE

Enchanted Island.

THE *writing of Prefaces to Plays, was probably invented by some very ambitious Poet, who never thought he had done enough : Perhaps by some Ape of the French Eloquence, which uses to make a business of a Letter of Gallantry, an examen of a Farce ; and, in short, a great pomp and ostentation of words on every trifle. This is certainly the Talent of that Nation, and ought not to be invaded by any other. They do that out of gaiety, which would be an imposition upon us.*

We may satisfie our selves with surmounting them in the Scene, and safely leave them those trappings of writing, and flourishes of the Pen, with which they adorn the borders of their Plays, and which are indeed no more than good Landskips to a very indifferent Picture. I must proceed no farther in this argument, lest I run my self beyond my excuse for writing this. Give me leave therefore to tell you, Reader, that I do it not to set a value on any thing I have written in this Play, but out of gratitude to the memory of Sir William Davenant, *who did me the honour to join me with him in the alteration of it.*

It was originally Shakespear's : *a Poet for whom he had particularly a high veneration, and whom he first taught me to admire. The Play it self had formerly been acted with success in the* Black-Fryers : *and our excellent* Fletcher *had so great a value for it, that he thought fit to make use of the same Design, not much varied, a second time. Those who have seen his* Sea-Voyage, *may easily discern that it was a Copy of* Shakespear's *Tempest : the Storm, the Desart Island, and the Woman who had never seen a Man, are all sufficient Testimonies of it. But* Fletcher *was not the only Poet who made use of* Shakespear's *Plot : Sir* John Suckling, *a profess'd admirer of our Author, has follow'd his footsteps in his* Goblins ; *his* Regmella *being an open imitation of* Shakespear's Miranda ; *and his Spirits, though counterfeit, yet are copied from* Ariel. *But Sir* William Davenant, *as he was a Man of quick and piercing imagination, soon found that somewhat might be added to the design of* Shakespear, *of which neither* Fletcher *nor* Suckling *had ever thought : and therefore to put the last hand to it, he design'd the Counter-part to* Shakespear's *Plot, namely, that of a Man who had never seen a Woman ; that by this means those two Characters of Innocence and Love might the more illustrate and commend each other. This excellent Contrivance he was pleas'd to communicate to me, and to desire my assistance in it. I confess, that from the very first moment it so pleas'd me, that I never writ any thing with more delight. I must likewise do him that justice to acknowledge, that my writing received daily his amendments, and that is the reason why it is not so faulty, as the rest which I have done, without the help or correction of so judicious a Friend. The Comical parts of the Saylers were also of his invention, and for the most part his writing, as you will easily discover by the Style. In the time I writ with him, I had the opportunity to observe somewhat more nearly of him than I had formerly done, when I had only a bare acquaintance with him: I found him then of so quick a fancy, that nothing was propos'd to him, on which he could not suddenly produce a thought extreamly pleasant and surprising: and those first thoughts of his, contrary to the old Latine Proverb, were not always the least happy. And as his fancy was quick, so likewise were the products of it remote and new. He borrowed not of any other; and his imaginations were such as could not easily enter into any other Man. His Corrections were sober and judicious: and he corrected his own writings much more severely than those of another Man, bestowing twice the time and labour in polishing, which he us'd in invention. It had perhaps been easie enough for me to have arrogated more to my self than was my due, in the writing of this Play, and to have pass'd by his name with silence in the Publication of it, with the same ingratitude which others have us'd to him, whose Writings he hath not only corrected, as he hath done this, but has had a greater inspection over them, and sometimes added whole Scenes together, which may as easily be distinguish'd from the rest, as true Gold from counterfeit by the weight. But besides the unworthiness of the Action which deterred me from it (there being nothing so base as to rob the dead of his reputation) I am satisfi'd I could never have receiv'd so much honour, in being thought the Author of any Poem, how excellent soever, as I shall from the joining my imperfections with the Merit and Name of* Shakespear *and Sir* William Davenant.

Decemb.
1669.

John Driden.

PROLOGUE to the *TEMPEST*,

or the *Enchanted Island*.

AS when a Tree's cut down, the secret Root
    Lives under ground, and thence new branches shoot ;
    So, from old Shakespear's honour'd dust, this day
Springs up and buds a new reviving Play.
Shakespear, who (taught by none) did first impart
To Fletcher Wit, to labouring Johnson Art.
He, Monarch-like, gave those his Subjects Law,
And is that Nature which they paint and draw.
Fletcher reach'd that which on his heights did grow,
Whilst Johnson crept and gather'd all below.
This did his Love, and this his Mirth digest :
One imitates him most, the other best.
If they have since out-writ all other Men,
'Tis with the drops which fell from Shakespear's Pen.
The Storm which vanish'd on the neighb'ring shore,
Was taught by Shakespear's Tempest first to roar.
That Innocence and Beauty which did smile
In Fletcher, grew on this Enchanted Isle.
But Shakespear's Magick could not copy'd be,
Within that Circle none durst walk but he.
I must confess 'twas bold, nor would you now
That liberty to vulgar Wits allow,
Which works by Magick supernatural things :
But Shakespear's Powe'r is Sacred as a King's.
Those Legends from old Priesthood were receiv'd,
And he then writ, as People then believ'd.
But, if for Shakespear we your grace implore,
We for our Theatre shall want it more :
Who by our dearth of Youths are forc'd t' employ
One of our Women to present a Boy.
And that's a transformation, you will say,
Exceeding all the Magick in the Play.
Let none expect in the last Act to find,
Her Sex transform'd from Man to Woman-kind.
What e'r she was before the Play began,
All you shall see of her is perfect Man.
Or if your fancy will be farther led
To find her Woman, it must be a-bed.

(195)

SECOND PROLOGUE.

WEE, as the ffathers of the Stage have said,
   To treat you here a vast expense have made ;
   What they have gott from you in chests is laid,
Or is for purchas'd Lands, or houses paid,
You, in this house, all our estates may find,
Wch for your pleasures wholly are design'd.
'Twas foolish, for we might, we must confesse,
Value ourselves much more, & you much lesse ;
And like those reverend men, we might have spar'd
And never for our Benefactors car'd ;
Still made your Treatment, as they do, more Coarse,
As if you did, as fast as they, grow worse :
But we young men, are apt to slight advice,
One Day we may decrepid grow and wise :
Then, hoping not to time to get much more,
We'll Save our money, & cry out wee'r poore.
Wee're young, & look yet many yeares to live,
& by your future Bounty hope to thrive ;
Then let us laugh, for now no cost wee'l spare
And never think we're poor, while we your favours share,
Without the good old Playes we did advance,
And all ye stages ornament enhance ;
To splendid things they follow in, but late :
They ne're invent, but they can imitate :
Had we not for yr. pleasure found new wayes
You still had rusty Arras had, & thredbare playes ;
Nor scenes nor Woomen, had they had their will,
But some with grizl'd Beards had acted Woomen still,
Some restive horses, spight of Switch & spurre,
Till others strain agst 'em, will not stirr.
Envying our Splendid house, & prosp'rous playes,
They scoff at us, & Libell the high wayes.
Tis fitt we, for our faults, rebukes shou'd meet.
The Citty ought to mend those of ye street,
With the best poets' heads our house we grac'd
Wch we in honour to ye Poets plac'd.
Too much of the old witt They have, Tis true :
But they must look for little of ye new.

Dramatis Personæ.

ALonzo Duke of *Savoy*, and Usurper of the Dukedom of *Mantua*.
 Ferdinand his Son.

Prospero right Duke of *Millain*.

Antonio his Brother, Usurper of the Dukedom.

Gonzalo, a Nobleman of *Savoy*.

Hippolito, one that never saw Woman, right Heir of the Dukedom of *Mantua*.

Stephano Master of the Ship.

Mustacho his Mate.

Trincalo Boatswain.

Ventoso a Mariner.

Several Mariners.

A Cabbin-Boy.

Miranda and
  Dorinda } (Daughters to *Prospero*) that never saw Man.

Ariel an aiery Spirit, attendant on *Prospero*.

Several Spirits, Guards to *Prospero*.

Caliban
Sycorax his Sister } Two Monsters of the Isle.

THE
Enchanted Island.

The Front of the Stage is open'd, and the Band of 24 Violins, with the Harpsicals and Theorbo's which accompany the Voices, are plac'd between the Pit and the Stage. While the Overture is playing, the Curtain rises, and discovers a new Frontispiece, join'd to the great Pilasters, on each side of the Stage. This Frontispiece is a noble Arch, supported by large wreathed Columns of the Corinthian Order; the wreathings of the Columns are beautifi'd with Roses wound round them, and several Cupids flying about them. On the Cornice, just over the Capitals, sits on either side a Figure, with a Trumpet in one hand, and a Palm in the other, representing Fame. A little farther on the same Cornice, on each side of a Compass-pediment, lie a Lion and a Unicorn, the Supporters of the Royal Arms of England. In the middle of the Arch are several Angels, holding the Kings Arms, as if they were placing them in the midst of that Compass-pediment. Behind this is the Scene, which represents a thick Cloudy Sky, a very Rocky Coast, and a Tempestuous Sea in perpetual Agitation. This Tempest (suppos'd to be rais'd by Magick) has many dreadful Objects in it, as several Spirits in horrid shapes flying down amongst the sailers, then rising and crossing in the Air. And when the Ship is sinking, the whole House is darken'd, and a shower of Fire falls upon 'em. This is accompanied with Lightning, and several Claps of Thunder, to the end of the Storm.

ACT I.

Enter Mustacho *and* Ventoso.

Vent. What a Sea comes in?
Must. A hoaming Sea! we shall have foul weather.

Enter Trincalo.

Trinc. The Scud comes against the Wind, 'twill blow hard.

Enter Stephano.

Steph. Bosen !

Trinc. Here, Master, what say you ?

Steph. Ill weather ! let's off to Sea.

Must. Let's have Sea room enough, and then let it blow the Devils
Head off.

Steph. Boy ! Boy !   [*Enter Cabin Boy.*

Boy. Yaw, yaw, here, Master.

Steph. Give the Pilot a dram of the Bottle.   [*Exeunt* Stephano *and Boy.*

Enter Mariners, and pass over the Stage.

Trinc. Bring the Cable to the Capstorm.

Enter Alonzo, Antonio, Gonzalo.

Alon. Good Bosen have a care ; where's the Master ?
Play the Men.

Trinc. Pray keep below.

Anto. Where's the Master, Bosen ?

Trinc. Do you not hear him ? you hinder us : keep your Cabins, you
help the storm.

Gonz. Nay, good Friend be patient.

Trinc. I, when the Sea is : hence ; what care these roarers for the
name of Duke ? to Cabin ; silence ; trouble us not.

Gonz. Good Friend, remember whom thou hast aboard.

Trinc. None that I love more than my self : you are a Counseller, if
you can advise these Elements to silence, use your wisdom : if you cannot,
make your self ready in the Cabin for the ill hour.   Cheerly good hearts !
out of our way, Sirs.   [*Exeunt* Trincalo *and Mariners.*

Gonz. I have great comfort from this Fellow ; methinks his complexion
is perfect Gallows ; stand fast, good fate, to his hanging ; Make the Rope
of his Destiny our Cable, for our own does little advantage us ; if he be
not born to be hang'd, we shall be drown'd.   [*Exit.*

Enter Trincalo *and* Stephano.

Trinc. Up aloft, Lads.   Come, reef both Topsails.

Steph. Make haste, let's weigh, let's weigh, and off to Sea.   [*Ex.* Steph.

Enter two Mariners, and pass over the Stage.

Trinc. Hands down ! man your Main-Capstorm.

Enter Mustacho *and* Ventoso *at the other door.*

Must. Up aloft ! and man your Seere-Capstorm.

Vent. My Lads, my Hearts of gold, get in your Capstorm-Bar : Hoa up,
hoa up, &c.   [*Exeunt* Mustacho *and* Ventoso.

Enter Stephano.

Steph. Hold on well! hold on well! nip well there;
Quarter-Master, get's more Nippers.   [*Exit* Steph.

Enter two Mariners, and pass over again.

Trinc. Turn out, turn out all hands to Capstorm.
You dogs, is this a time to sleep? lubbord.
Heave together, Lads.   [Trincalo *whistles.*
                              [*Exeunt* Mustacho *and* Ventoso.

Must. within. Our Vial's broke.
Vent. within. 'Tis but our Vial-block has given way.   Come heave,
Lads! we are fix'd again.   Heave together, Bullyes.

Enter Stephano.

Steph. Cut down the Hammocks! cut down the Hammocks!
Come, my Lads: Come, *Bullyes*, chear up! heave lustily.
The Anchor's a peek.
Trinc. Is the Anchor a Peek?
Steph. Is a weigh! Is a weigh.
Trin. Up aloft, my Lads, upon the Fore-castle!
Cut the Anchor, cut him.
All within. Haul Catt, Haul Catt, *&c.*   Haul Catt, haul:
Haul Catt, haul.   Below.
Steph. Aft, aft, and lose the Misen!
Trinc. Get the Misen-tack aboard.   Haul aft Misen-sheet.

Enter Mustacho.

Must. Loose the Main-top-sail!
Steph. Let him alone, there's too much Wind.
Trink. Loose Fore-sail! Haul aft both sheets! trim her right afore
the Wind.   Aft! aft! Lads, and hale up the Misen here.
Must. A Mackrel-gale, Master.
Steph. within. Port hard, port! the Wind veeres forward, bring the
Tack aboard Port is.   Star-board, star-board, a little steady; now steady,
keep her thus, no nearer you cannot come, till the Sails are loose.

Enter Ventoso.

Vent. Some hands down: the Guns are loose.   [*Ex.* Must.
Trin. Try the Pump, try the pump.   [*Ex.* Vent.

Enter Mustacho *at the other door.*

Must. O Master! six foot water in Hold.
Steph. Clap the Helm hard a weather!   Flat, flat, flat in the Fore-sheet
there.

Trinc. Over haul your fore boling.

Steph. Brace in the Lar-board. [*Exit.*

Trinc. A Curse upon this houling. [*A great Cry within.* They are louder than the Weather. [*Enter* Antonio *and* Gonzalo. Yet again, what do you here? shall we give o'r, and drown? ha' you a mind to sink?

Gonz. A pox o' your Throat, you bawling, blasphemous, uncharitable Dog.

Trinc. Work you then and be pox't.

Anto. Hang, Cur, hang, you Whorson insolent Noise-maker, we are less afraid to be drown'd than thou art.

Trinc. Ease the Fore-brace a little. [*Exit.*

Gonz. I'll warrant him for drowning, though the ship were no stronger than a Nut-shell, and as leaky as an unstanch'd Wench.

Enter Alonzo *and* Ferdinand.

Ferd. For my self I care not, but your loss brings a Thousand Deaths to me.

Alonz. O name not me, I am grown Old, my Son; I am tedious to the World, and that, by use, is so to me: But, *Ferdinand,* I grieve my Subjects loss in thee: Alas, I suffer justly for my Crimes, but why thou shouldst——O Heaven! [*A cry within.* Heark, Farewel, my Son, a long farewel!

Enter Trincalo, Mustacho, *and* Ventoso.

Trinc. What must our Mouths be cold then?

Vent. All's lost. To prayers, to prayers.

Gonz. The Duke and Prince are gone within to prayers. Let's assist them.

Must. Nay, we may e'en pray too; our case is now alike.

Ant. Mercy upon us! we split, we split.

Gonz. Let's all sink with the Duke and the Young Prince. [*Exeunt.*

Enter Stephano, *and* Trincalo.

Trinc. The Ship is sinking. [*A new Cry within.*

Steph. Run her ashore!

Trinc. Luff! luff! or we are all lost! there's a Rock upon the Star-board-Bow.

Steph. She strikes, she strikes! All shift for themselves. [*Exeunt.*

SCENE II.

In the midst of the Shower of Fire the Scene changes. The Cloudy Sky, Rocks, and Sea vanish; and when the Lights return, discover that Beautiful part of the Island, which was the Habitation of Prospero ; *'Tis compos'd of three Walks of Cypress-trees, each Side-walk leads to a Cave, in one of which* Prospero *keeps his Daughters, in the other* Hippolito : *The Middle-Walk is of a great depth, and leads to an open part of the Island.*

Enter Prospero *and* Miranda.

Prosp. Miranda, where's your Sister ?

Miran. I left her looking from the pointed Rock, at the Walk's end, on the huge Beat of Waters.

Prosp. It is a dreadful Object.

Mir. If by your Art, my dearest Father, you have put them in this roar, allay 'em quickly.

Prosp. I have so ordered, that not one Creature in the Ship is lost :
I have done nothing but in care of thee,
My Daughter, and thy pretty Sister :
You both are ignorant of what you are,
Not knowing whence I am, nor that I'm more
Than *Prospero*, Master of a narrow Cell,
And thy unhappy Father.

Mir. I ne'r endeavour'd to know more than you were pleas'd to tell me.

Prosp. I should inform thee farther.

Mir. You often, Sir, began to tell me what I am,
but then you stopt.

Prosp. The Hour's now come ;
Obey and be attentive.   Canst thou remember a time before we came into this Cell ?   I don't think thou canst, for then thou wert not full three years old.

Mir. Certainly I can, Sir,

Prosp. Tell me the Image then of any thing which thou dost keep in thy remembrance still.

Mir. Sir, had I not four or five Women once that tended me ?

Prosp. Thou hadst, and more, *Miranda :* what seest thou else in the dark back-ward, and abyss of Time ?
If thou remember'st ought e'r thou cam'st here, then how thou cam'st thou may'st remember too.

Mir. Sir, that I do not.

Prosp. Fifteen years since, *Miranda,* thy Father was the Duke of *Milan,* and a Prince of Power.

Mir. Sir, are not you my Father ?

Prosp. Thy Mother was all Vertue, and she said, thou wast my Daughter, and thy Sister too.

Mir. O Heavens ! what foul Play had we, that we hither came, or was't a Blessing that we did ?

Prosp. Both, both, my Girl.

Mir. But, Sir, I pray proceed.

Prosp. My Brother, and thy Uncle, call'd *Antonio*, to whom I trusted then the manage of my State, while I was wrap'd with secret Studies : That false Uncle,
Having attain'd the craft of granting suits, and of denying them ; whom to advance, or lop, for over-topping, soon was grown the Ivy which did hide my Princely Trunk, and suck'd my verdure out : thou attend'st not.

Mir. O good Sir, I do.

Prosp. I thus neglecting worldly ends, and bent to closeness, and the bettering of my mind, wak'd in my false Brother an evil Nature :
He did believe
He was indeed the Duke, because he then did execute the outward Face of Soveraignty.   Dost thou still mark me ?

Mir. Your Story would cure Deafness.

Prosp. This false Duke needs would be absolute in *Millan*, and confederates with *Savoy's* Duke, to give him Tribute, and to do him Homage.

Mir. False Man !

Prosp. This Duke of *Savoy*, being an Enemy,
To me inveterate, strait grants my Brother's Suit,
And on a Night,
Mated to his Design, *Antonio* opened the Gates of *Milan*, and i' th' dead of darkness, hurri'd me thence, with thy young Sister, and thy crying self.

Mir. But wherefore did they not that hour destroy us ?

Prosp. They durst not, Girl, in *Milan*, for the Love my people bore me ; in short, they hurri'd us away to *Savoy*, and thence aboard a Bark at *Nissa's* Port : bore us some Leagues to Sea, where they prepar'd a rotten carcass of a Boat, not rigg'd, no Tackle, Sail, nor Mast ; the very Rats instinctively had quit it.

Mir. Alack ! what trouble was I then to you ?

Prosp. Thou and thy Sister were two Cherubins, which did preserve me : you both did smile, infus'd with Fortitude from Heaven.

Mir. How came we ashore ?

Prosp. By Providence Divine.
Some food we had, and some fresh Water, which a Nobleman of *Savoy*, called *Gonzalo*, appointed Master of that black design, gave us ; with rich Garments and all necessaries, which since have steaded much : and of his Gentleness (knowing I lov'd my Books) he furnish'd me from my own Library, with Volumes which I prize above my Dukedom.

Mir. Would I might see that Man.

Prosp. Here, in this Island we arriv'd, and here have I your Tutor been. But by my Skill I find, that my Mid-heaven doth depend on a most happy Star, whose Influence if I now court not, but omit, my Fortunes will ever after droop : here cease more Questions, thou art inclin'd to sleep : 'tis a good dulness, and give it way ; I know thou canst not chuse.

[She falls asleep.

Come away, my Spirit *:* I am ready now, approach,
my *Ariel*, Come.   *Enter* Ariel.

Ariel. All hail, great Master, grave Sir, hail, I come to answer thy best pleasure, be it to fly, to swim, to shoot into the Fire, to ride on the curl'd Clouds ; to thy strong bidding, task *Ariel* and all his Qualities.

Prosp. Hast thou, Spirit, perform'd to point the Tempest that I bad thee ?

Ariel. To every Article.
I boarded the Duke's Ship, now on the Beak, now in the Waste, the Deck, in every Cabin ; I flam'd amazement, and sometimes I seem'd to burn in many places on the Top-mast, the Yards, and Boresprit ; I did flame distinctly.   Nay once I rain'd a shower of Fire upon them.

Prosp. My brave Spirit !
Who was so firm, so constant, that this coil did not infect his Reason ?

Ariel. Not a Soul
But felt a Feaver of the Mind, and play'd some tricks of Desperation ; all, but Mariners, plung'd in the foaming Brine, and quit the Vessel ; the Duke's Son, *Ferdinand*, with Hair upstaring (more like Reeds then Hair) was the first man that leap'd ; cry'd, Hell is empty, and all the Devils are here.

Prosp. Why that's my Spirit ;
But was not this nigh Shore ?

Ariel. Close by my Master.

Prosp. But, *Ariel*, are they safe ?

Ariel. Not a Hair perish'd.
In Troops I have dispers'd them round this Isle.
The Duke's Son I have landed by himself, whom I have left warming the Air with sighs, in an odd Angle of the Isle, and sitting, his Arms he folded in this sad Knot.

Prosp. Say how thou hast dispos'd the Marriners of the Duke's Ship, and all the rest of the Fleet ?

Ariel. Safely in harbour
Is the Duke's Ship, in the deep Nook, where once thou called'st
Me up at Midnight to fetch Dew from the
Still vext *Bermoothes*, there she's hid,
The Mariners all under Hatches stow'd,
Whom, with a Charm, joyn'd to their suffer'd Labour,
I have left asleep ; and for the rest o'th' Fleet,
(Which I disperst) they all have met again,
And are upon the *Mediterranean* Float,

Bound sadly home for *Italy ;*
Supposing that they saw the Duke's Ship wrack'd,
And his great Person perish.

    Prosp. *Ariel*, thy Charge
Exactly is perform'd ; but there's more Work :
What is the time o' th' day ?

    Ariel. Past the Mid-season.

    Prosp. At least two Glasses : the time 'tween six and now must by us both be spent most preciously.

    Ariel. Is there more Toyl ? since thou dost give me Pains, let me remember thee what thou hast promis'd, which is not yet perform'd me.

    Prosp. How now, *Moodie ?*
What is't thou can'st demand ?

    Ariel. My Liberty.

    Prosp. Before thy time be out ? no more.

    Ariel. I prethee !
Remember I have done thee faithful Service,
Told thee no Lies, made thee no Mistakings,
Serv'd without or Grudge, or Grumblings :
Thou didst promise to bate me a full Year.

    Prosp. Dost thou forget
From what a Torment I did free thee ?

    Ariel. No.

    Prosp. Thou dost,
And think'st it much to tread the Ooze of the salt Deep :
To run against the sharp Wind of the North,
To do my Bus'ness in the Veins of the Earth,
When it is bak'd with Frost.

    Ariel. I do not, Sir.

    Prosp. Thou ly'st, Malignant thing ! hast thou forgot the foul Witch *Sycorax*, who with age and envy was grown into a Hoop ? hast thou forgot her ?

    Ariel. No, Sir.

    Prosp. Thou hast, where was she born ? speak, tell me.

    Ariel. Sir, in *Argier*.

    Prosp. Oh, was she so !
I must once every Month recount what thou hast been, which thou forget'st. This damn'd Witch *Sycorax*, for Mischiefs manifold, and Sorceries too terrible to enter humane hearing, from *Argier* thou know'st was banish'd : but for one thing she did, they would not take her Life : is not this true ?

    Ariel. I, Sir,

    Prosp. This blew-ey'd Hag was hither brought with child,

And here was left by th' Sailers, thou, my slave,
As thou report'st thy self, wast then her servant,
And 'cause thou wast a Spirit too delicate
To act her Earthy and abhor'd commands ;
Refusing her grand Hests, she did confine thee,
By help of her more potent Ministers ;
(In her unmitigable rage) into a cloven Pine,
Within whose rift imprison'd, thou didst painfully
Remain a dozen Years ; within which space she dy'd,
And left thee there ; where thou didst vent
Thy Groans, as fast as Mill-Wheels strike.
Then was this Isle (save for two Brats,
Which she did litter here, the brutish *Caliban*,
And his Twin-Sister, two freckled hag-born Whelps)
Not honour'd with a humane Shape.

Ariel. Yes ! *Caliban* her Son, and *Sycorax* his Sister.

Prosp. Dull thing, I say so ; he, that *Caliban*, and she that *Sycorax*, whom I now keep in Service. Thou best know'st what torment I did find thee in ; thy groans did make Wolves houl, and penetrate the breasts of ever angry Bears, it was a torment to lay upon the damn'd, which *Sycorax* could ne'r again undo : It was my Art, when I arriv'd, and heard thee, that made the Pine to gape and let thee out.

Ariel. I thank thee, Master.

Prosp. If thou more murmurest, I will rend an Oak,
And peg thee in his knotty entrails, till thou
Hast houl'd away twelve Winters more.

Ariel. Pardon, Master,
I will be correspondent to command, and be
A gentle spirit.

Prosp. Do so, and after two days I'l discharge thee.

Ariel. Thanks, my great Master. But I have yet one request.

Prosp. What's that, my spirit ?

Ariel. I know that this day's business is important, requiring too much Toyl for one alone. I have a gentle Spirit for my Love, who twice seven years has waited for my freedom : Let it appear, it will assist me much, and we with mutual Joy shall entertain each other. This I beseech you grant me.

Prosp. You shall have your desire.

Ariel. That's my noble Master. *Milcha !*

Milcha *flies down to his Assistance.*

Milc. I am here my Love.

Ariel. Thou art free ! welcome, my dear ! what shall we do ? say, say, what shall we do ?

Prosp. Be subject to no sight but mine, invisible to every Eye-ball else. Hence with diligence, anon thou shalt know more.

> [*They both fly up, and cross in the Air.*

Thou hast slept well my Child.   [*To* Miranda.

Mir. The sadness of your story put heaviness in me.

Prosp. Shake it off; come on I'll now call *Caliban*, my Slave, who never yields us a kind Answer.

Mir. 'Tis a Creature, Sir, I do not love to look on.

Prosp. But as tis we cannot miss him; he does make our Fire, fetch in our Wood, and serve in Offices that profit us: what hoa! Slave! *Caliban!* thou Earth thou, speak.

Calib. within. There's Wood enough within.

Prosp. Thou poisonous Slave, got by the Devil himself upon thy wicked Dam, come forth.   [*Enter* Caliban.

Calib. As wicked Dew, as e'er my Mother brush'd with Raven's Feather from unwholesome Fens, drop on you both: A South-west blow on you, and blister you all o'er.

Prosp. For this, be sure, to night thou shalt have cramps, side-stitches, that shall pen thy Breath up; Urchins shall prick thee till thou bleed'st; thou shalt be pinch'd as thick as Honey-combs, each Pinch more stinging than the Bees which made 'em.

Calib. I must eat my Dinner: this Island's mine by *Sycorax* my Mother, which thou took'st from me. When thou cam'st first, thou stroak'st me, and mad'st much of me, would'st give me Water with Berries in't, and taught'st me how to name the Bigger Light, and how the Less, that burn by day and night; and then I lov'd thee, and shewed thee all the qualities of the Isle, the Fresh-springs, Brine-pits, barren places and fertile. Curs'd be I that I did so: All the Charms of *Sycorax*, Toads, Beetles, Bats, light on thee, for I am all the Subjects that thou hast. I first was mine own Lord; and here thou stay'st me in this hard Rock, whiles thou does keep from me the rest o' th' Island.

Prosp. Thou most lying Slave, whom stripes may move, not kindness: I have us'd thee (filth that thou art) with humane care, and lodg'd thee in mine own Cell, till thou didst seek to violate the Honour of my Children.

Calib. Oh ho, Oh ho, would't had been done: thou didst prevent me, I had peopled else this Isle with *Calibans*.

Prosp. Abhor'd Slave!

Who ne'er would any print of goodness take, being capable of all Ill: I pity'd thee, took pains to make thee speak, taught thee each hour one thing or other when thou didst not (Savage) know thy own meaning, but wouldst gabble, like a thing most Brutish, I endow'd thy Purposes with Words, which made them known: But thy wild race (though thou didst learn) had that in't, which good Natures could not abide to be with : therefore was thou deservedly pent up into this Rock.

Calib. You taught me language, and my profit by it is, that I know to curse : the red botch rid you for learning me your Language.

Prosp. Hag-seed hence !
Fetch us in fewel, and be quick
To answer other business : shrug'st thou (Malice)
If thou neglectest, or dost unwillingly what I command,
I'll wrack thee with old cramps, fill all thy bones with Aches,
Make thee roar, that Beasts shall tremble
At thy Dinn.

Calib. No, prethee !
I must obey.   His Art is of such power,
It would controul my Dam's God, *Setebos*,
And make a Vassal of him.

Prosp. So, Slave hence.   [*Exeunt* Prospero *and* Caliban *severally*.

Enter Dorinda.

Dor. Oh, Sister ! what have I beheld ?

Mir. What is it moves you so ?

Dor. From yonder Rock,
As I my Eyes cast down upon the Seas,
The whistling Winds blew rudely on my Face,
And the Waves roar'd ; at first I thought the War
Had been between themselves, but strait I spy'd
A huge great Creature.

Mir. O you mean the Ship.

Dor. Is't not a Creature then ? it seem'd alive.

Mir. But what of it ?

Dor. This floating Ram did bear his Horns above,
All ty'd with Ribbands, ruffling in the Wind ;
Sometimes he nodded down his head a while,
And then the Waves did heave him to the Moon ;
He clambring to the Top of all the Billows,
And then again he curtsi'd down so low,
I could not see him ; till at last, all side-long,
With a great crack his belly burst in pieces.

Mir. There all had perish'd,
Had not my Father's Magick Art reliev'd them.
But, Sister, I have stranger News to tell you ;
In this great Creature there were other Creatures,
And shortly we may chance to see that thing,
Which you have heard my Father call, a Man.

Dor. But what is that ? for yet he never told me.

Mir. I know no more than you : but I have heard
My Father say, we Women were made for him.

Dor. What, that he should eat us, Sister ?

Mir. No sure, you see my Father is a Man,
And yet he does us good.   I would he were not old.

Dor. Methinks, indeed it would be finer,
If we two had two young Fathers.

Mir. No, Sister, no, if they were young,
My Father said, that we must call them Brothers.

Dor. But, pray, how does it come, that we two are not Brothers then,
and have not Beards like him ?

Mir. Now I confess you pose me

Dor. How did he come to be our Father too ?

Mir. I think he found us when we both were little,
And grew within the ground.

Dor. Why could he not find more of us ?   Pray, Sister, let you and I
look up and down one day, to find some little ones for us to play with.

Mir. Agreed ; but now we must go in.   This is the hour
Wherein my Father's Charm will work,
Which seizes all who are in open air :
Th' effect of his great Art I long to see,
Which will perform as much as Magick can.

Dor. And I, methinks, more long to see a Man.   [*Exeunt.*

ACT II.   SCENE I.

The Scene changes to the wilder part of the Island, 'tis compos'd of divers sorts of Trees, and barren places, with a prospect of the Sea at a great distance.

Enter Stephano, Mustacho, Ventoso.

Vent. THE Runlet of Brandy was a loving Runlet, and floated after
us out of pure pity.

Must. This kind Bottle, like an old Acquaintance, swam
after it.
And this Scollop-shell is all our Plate now.

Vent. 'Tis well we have found something since we landed.
I prethee fill a soop, and let it go round.
Where hast thou laid the Runlet ?

Muſt. I' th' hollow of an old Tree.

Vent. Fill apace,
We cannot live long in this barren Island, and we may
Take a soop before death, as well as others drink
At our Funerals.

Muſt. This is Prize-Brandy, we ſteal Cuſtom, and it coſt nothing. Let's
have two rounds more.

Vent. Maſter, what have you sav'd?

Steph. Juſt nothing but my self.

Vent. This works comfortably on a cold ſtomach.

Steph. Fill's another round.

Vent. Look! *Muſtacho* weeps. Hang losses, as long as we have
Brandy left. Prithee leave weeping.

Steph. He sheds his Brandy out of his eyes : he shall drink no more.

Muſt. This will be a doleful day with old *Bess*. She gave me a gilt
Nutmeg at parting. That's loſt too. But, as you say, hang losses.
Prethee fill again.

Vent. Beshrew thy heart for putting me in mind of thy Wife,
I had not thought of mine else, Nature will shew it self,
I muſt melt. I prithee fill again, my Wife's a good old Jade,
And has but one Eye left : but she'll weep out that too,
When she hears that I am dead.

Steph. Would you were both hang'd for putting me in thought of mine.

Vent. But come, Maſter, sorrow is dry! there's for you agen.

Steph. A Marinner had e'en as good be a Fish as a Man, but for the
comfort we get ashore : O for an old dry Wench now I am wet.

Muſt. Poor heart! that would soon make you dry agen : but all is
barren in this Isle : Here we may lie at Hull till the Wind blow Nore
and by South, ere we can cry, A Sail, a Sail, at sight of a white Apron.
And therefore here's another soop to comfort us.

Vent. This Isle's our own, that's our comfort, for the Duke, the Prince,
and all their train, are perished.

Muſt. Our Ship is sunk, and we can never get home agen : we muſt
e'en turn Salvages, and the next that catches his Fellow may eat him.

Vent. No, no, let us have a Government ; for if we live well and
orderly, Heav'n will drive Shipwracks ashoar to make us all rich ; therefore
let us carry good Consciences, and not eat one another.

Steph. Whoever eats any of my Subjeċts, I'l break out his teeth with
my Scepter : for I was Maſter at Sea, and will be Duke on Land : you
Muſtacho have been my Mate, and shall be my Vice-Roy.

Vent. When you are Duke, you may chuse your Vice-Roy ; but I am a
free Subjeċt in a new Plantation, and will have no Duke without my voice.
And so fill me the other soop.

Steph. whispering. Ventoso, dost thou hear, I will advance thee, prithee give me thy voice.

Vent. I'll have no whisperings to corrupt the Election; and to show that I have no private ends, I declare aloud that I will be Vice-Roy, or I'll keep my voice for my self.

Must. Stephano, hear me, I will speak for the people, because there are few, or rather none in the Isle to speak for themselves. Know then, that to prevent the farther shedding of Christian bloud, we are all content *Ventoso* shall be Vice-Roy, upon condition I may be Vice-Roy over him. Speak, good people, are you well agreed? What, no Man answer? well, you may take their silence for consent.

Vent. You speak for the people, *Mustacho?* I'll speak for 'em, and declare generally with one voice, one and all; That there shall be no Vice-Roy but the Duke, unless I be he.

Must. You declare for the people, who never saw your Face! Cold Iron shall decide it.   *[Both draw.*

Steph. Hold, loving Subjects: we will have no Civil War during our Reign: I do hereby appoint you both to be my Vice-Roys over the whole Island.

Both. Agreed! agreed!

Enter Trincalo, *with a great Bottle, half drunk.*

Vent. How! *Trincalo* our brave Bosen!

Must. He reels: can he be drunk with Sea water?

Trinc. sings. I shall no more to Sea, to Sea,
        Here I shall die ashore.
This is a very scurvy tune to sing at a Man's Funeral,
But here's my comfort.   *[Drinks.*

Sings. The Master, the Swabber, the Gunner, and I,
        The Surgeon and his Mate,
    Lov'd *Mall, Meg*, and *Marrian*, and *Margery*,
        But none of us car'd for *Kate.*
    For she had a tongue with a tang,
    Wou'd cry to a Sailor, Go hang:
    She lov'd not the savour of Tar nor of Pitch,
    Yet a Taylor might scratch her where ere she did itch.

This is a scurvy Tune too, but here's my comfort agen.   *[Drinks.*

Steph. We have got another Subject now; Welcome, Welcome into our Dominions!

Trinc. What Subject, or what Dominions? here's old Sack, Boys: the King of good-fellows can be no subject. I will be old *Simon* the King.

Must. Hah, old Boy ! how didſt thou scape ?

Trinc. Upon a Butt of Sack, Boys, which the Sailors
Threw over-board : but are you alive, hoa ! for I will
Tipple with no Ghoſts till I'm dead : thy hand, *Muſtacho*,
And thine, *Ventoso ;* the Storm has done its worſt :
Stephano alive too ! give thy Bosen thy hand, Maſter.

Vent. You muſt kiss it then, for, I muſt tell you, we have chosen him
Duke in a full Assembly.

Trinc. A Duke ! where ? what's he Duke of ?

Must. Of this Island, Man.   Oh *Trincalo*, we are all made, the Island's
empty ; all's our own, Boy ; and we will speak to his Grace for thee,
that thou may'ſt be as great as we are.

Trinc. You great ? what the Devil are you ?

Vent. We two are Vice Roys over all the Island ; and when we are
weary of Governing, thou shalt succeed us.

Trinc. Do you hear, *Ventoso*, I will succeed you in both your places
before you enter into 'em.

Steph. *Trincalo*, sleep and be sober ; and make no more uproars in
my Countrey.

Trinc. Why, what are you, Sir, what are you ?

Steph. What I am, I am by free Election, and you, *Trincalo*, are not
your self ; but we pardon your firſt fault,
Because it is the firſt day of our Reign.

Trinc. Umph, were matters carried so swimmingly againſt me, whilſt
I was swimming, and saving my self for the good of the people of this
Island.

Must. Art thou mad, *Trincalo* ? wilt thou diſturb a setled Government,
where thou art a meer ſtranger
To the Laws of the Countrey ?

Trinc. I'll have no Laws.

Vent. Then Civil War begins.   [Vent. *and* Muſt. *draw.*

Steph. Hold, hold, I'll have no bloudshed,
My Subjeɛts are but few : let him make a Rebellion
By himself ; and a Rebel, I Duke *Stephano* declare him :
Vice-Roys, come away.

Trinc. And Duke *Trincalo* declares, that he will make open War where
ever he meets thee or thy Vice Roys.

[*Exeunt* Steph. Muſt. Vent.

Enter Caliban *with wood upon his back.*

Trinc. Hah ! who have we here ?

Calib. All the infeɛtions that the Sun sucks up from Fogs, Fens, Flats, on
Proſpero fall and make him by inch-meal a Disease : his Spirits hear me,

and yet I needs muſt curse, but they'l not pinch, fright me with Urchin
shows, pitch me i' th' mire, nor lead me in the dark out of my way, unless
he bid 'em : but for every trifle he sets them on me ; sometimes like
Baboons they mow and chatter at me, and often bite me ; like Hedge-hogs
then they mount their prickles at me, tumbling before me in my barefoot
way. Sometimes I am all wound about with Adders, who with their
cloven tongues hiss me to madness. Hah ! yonder ſtands one of his
spirits sent to torment me.

Trinc. What have we here, a Man, or a Fish ?
This is some Monſter of the Isle, were I in *England*,
As once I was, and had him painted ;
Not a Holy day Fool there but would give me
Six pence for the sight of him ; well, if I could make
Him tame, he were a present for an Emperour.
Come hither, pretty Monſter, I'l do thee no harm.
Come hither !

Calib. Torment me not ;
I'll bring thee Wood home faſter.

Trinc. He talks none of the wiseſt, but I'll give him
A dram o' th' Bottle, that will clear his underſtanding.
Come on your ways, Maſter Monſter, open your mouth.
How now, you perverse Moon-calf ! what,
I think you cannot tell who is your Friend !
Open your chops, I say.   *[Pours Wine down his throat.*

Calib. This is a brave God, and bears Cœleſtial Liquor ;
I'll kneel to him.

Trinc. He is a very hopeful Monſter ; Monſter, what sayſt thou, art
thou content to turn civil and sober, as I am ? for then thou shalt be
my Subjeﬆ.

Calib. I'l swear upon that Bottle to be true ; for the liquor is not
Earthly : did'ſt thou not drop from Heaven ?

Trinc. Only out of the Moon, I was the Man in her when time was.
By this light, a very shallow Monſter.

Calib. I'll shew thee every fertile inch i' th' Isle, and kiss thy foot :
I prithee be my God, and let me drink.   *[drinks agen.*

Trinc. Well drawn Monſter, in good faith.

Calib. I'l shew thee the beſt Springs, I'l pluck thee Berries,
I'll fish for thee, and get thee wood enough :
A curse upon the Tyrant whom I serve, I'l bear him
No more ſticks, but follow thee.

Trinc. The poor Monſter is loving in his drink.

Calib. I prithee let me bring thee where Crabs grow,
And I with my long nails will dig thee Pig-nuts,

Shew thee a Jays-nest, and instruct thee how to snare
The Marmazete ; I'll bring thee to cluster'd Filberds ;
Wilt thou go with me ?
   Trinc. This Monster comes of a good natur'd race ;
Is there no more of thy Kin in this Island ?
   Calib. Divine, here is but one besides my self ;
My lovely Sister, beautiful and bright as the Full Moon.
   Trinc. Where is she ?
   Calib. I left her clambring up a hollow Oak,
And plucking thence the dropping Honey-combs.
Say, my King, shall I call her to thee ?
   Trinc. She shall swear upon the Bottle too.
If she proves handsome she is mine : Here, Monster,
Drink agen for thy good news ; thou shalt speak
A good word for me.   *[Gives him the Bottle.*
   Calib. Farewel, old Master, farewel, farewel.

   Sings.   No more Dams I'll make for fish,
            Nor fetch in firing at requiring,
            Nor scrape Trencher, nor wash Dish,
            Ban, Ban, *Cackaliban*
            Has a new Master, get a new Man.
            Heigh-day ! Freedom, freedom !

   Trinc. Here's two Subjects got already, the Monster,
And his Sister : well, Duke *Stephano,* I say, and say agen,
Wars will ensue, and so I drink.   *[Drinks.*
From this Worshipful Monster, and Mistriss
Monster his Sister,
I'll lay claim to this Island by alliance :
Monster, I say, thy Sister shall be my Spouse :
Come away, Brother Monster, I'll lead thee to my Butt,
And drink her health.   *[Exeunt.*

         Scene Cypress Trees and Cave.

           Enter Prospero *alone.*

   Prosp. 'Tis not yet fit to let my Daughters know I kept
The Infant Duke of *Mantua* so near them in this Isle,
Whose Father dying, bequeath'd him to my care ;
Till my false Brother (when he design'd t' usurp
My Dukedom from me) expos'd him to that fate
He meant for me. By calculation of his birth
I saw death threat'ning him, if, till some time were

Past, he should behold the face of any Woman :
And now the danger's nigh : *Hippolito !*

Enter Hippolito.

Hip. Sir, I attend your pleasure.
Prosp. How I have lov'd thee from thy infancy,
Heav'n knows, and thou thy self canst bear me witness,
Therefore accuse not me for thy restraint.
Hip. Since I knew life, you've kept me in a Rock,
And you this day have hurri'd me from thence,
Only to change my Prison, not to free me.
I murmur not, but I may wonder at it.
Prosp. O gentle Youth, Fate waits for thee abroad,
A black Star threatens thee, and death unseen
Stands ready to devour thee.
Hip. You taught me not to fear him in any of his shapes :
Let me meet death rather than be a prisoner.
Prosp. 'Tis pity he should seize thy tender youth.
Hip. Sir, I have often heard you say, no Creature liv'd
Within this Isle, but those which Man was Lord of ;
Why then should I fear ?
Prosp. But here are creatures which I nam'd not to thee,
Who share Man's Sovereignty by Nature's Laws,
And oft depose him from it.
Hip. What are those Creatures, Sir ?
Prosp. Those dangerous Enemies of Men call'd Women.
Hip. Women ! I never heard of them before.
What are Women like ?
Prosp. Imagine something between young Men and Angels :
Fatally beauteous, and having killing Eyes,
Their Voices charm beyond the Nightingales,
They are all enchantment, those who once behold 'em,
Are made their slaves for ever.
Hip. Then I will wink and fight with 'em.
Prosp. 'Tis but in vain,
They'l haunt you in your very sleep.
Hip. Then I'll revenge it on 'em when I wake.
Prosp. You are without all possibility of revenge,
They are so beautiful, that you can ne'r attempt,
Nor wish to hurt them.
Hip. Are they so beautiful ?
Prosp. Calm sleep is not so soft, nor Winter Suns,
Nor Summer shades so pleasant.

Hip. Can they be fairer than the Plumes of Swans ?
Or more delightful than the Peacocks Feathers ?
Or than the gloss upon the necks of Doves ?
Or have more various beauty than the Rainbow ?
These I have seen, and without danger wondred at:
   Prosp. All these are far below 'em : Nature made
Nothing but Woman dangerous and fair :
Therefore if you should chance to see 'em,
Avoid 'em streight I charge you.
   Hip. Well, since you say they are so dangerous,
I'll so far shun 'em as I may with safety of the
Unblemish'd honour which you taught me.
But let 'em not provoke me, for I'm sure I shall
Not then forbear them.
   Prosp. Go in and read the Book I gave you last.
To morrow I may bring you better news.
   Hip. I shall obey you, Sir.   [*Exit* Hippolito.
   Prosp. So, so ; I hope this Lesson has secur'd him,
For I have been constrain'd to change his lodging
From yonder Rock where first I bred him up,
And here have brought him home to my own Cell,
Because the Shipwrack happen'd near his Mansion.
I hope he will not stir beyond his limits,
For hitherto he hath been all obedience :
The Planets seem to smile on my designs,
And yet there is one sullen Cloud behind,
I would it were disperst.

             Enter Miranda *and* Dorinda.

How, my Daughters ! I thought I had instructed
Them enough : Children ! retire ;
Why do you walk this way ?
   Mir. It is within our bounds, Sir.
   Prosp. But both take heed, that path is very dangerous.
Remember what I told you.
   Dor. Is the man that way, Sir ?
   Prosp. All that you can imagine ill is there,
The curled Lion, and the rugged Bear,
Are not so dreadful as that Man.
   Mir. Oh me, why stay we here then ?
   Dor. I'll keep far enough from his Den, I warrant him.
   Mir. But you have told me, Sir, you are a Man ;
And yet you are not dreadful.

Prosp. I Child! but I am a tame Man; old Men are tame
By Nature, but all the danger lies in a wild
Young Man.

Dor. Do they run wild about the Woods?

Prosp. No, they are wild within doors, in Chambers,
And in Closets.

Dor. But, Father, I would stroak 'em, and make 'em gentle,
Then sure they would not hurt me.

Prosp. You must not trust them, Child: no Woman can come
Near 'em, but she feels a pain, full nine moneths.
Well, I must in; for new affairs require my
Presence: be you, *Miranda*, your Sisters Guardian.   [*Exit* Prospero.

Dor. Come, Sister, shall we walk the other way?
The Man will catch us else: we have but two legs,
And he perhaps has four.

Mir. Well, Sister, though he have; yet look about you,
And we shall spy him ere he comes too near us.

Dor. Come back, that way is towards his Den.

Mir. Let me alone; I'll venture first, for sure he can
Devour but one of us at once.

Dor. How dare you venture?

Mir. We'll find him sitting like a Hare in's Form,
And he shall not see us.

Dor. I but you know my Father charg'd us both.

Mir. But who shall tell him on't? we'l keep each
Others Counsel.

Dor. I dare not for the World.

Mir. But how shall we hereafter shun him, if we do not
Know him first?

Dor. Nay, I confess I would fain see him too.   I find it in my
Nature, because my Father has forbidden me.

Mir. I, there's it, Sister, if he had said nothing, I had been quiet.   Go
softly, and if you see him first, be quick, and becken me away.

Dor. Well, if he does catch me, I'll humble my self to him,
And ask him pardon, as I do my Father,
When I have done a fault.

Mir. And if I can but scape with Life, I had rather be in pain nine
months, as my Father threaten'd, then lose my longing.   [*Exeunt.*

The Scene continues.   Enter Hippolito.

Hip. Prospero has often said, that Nature makes
Nothing in vain: why then are Women made?
Are they to suck the poison of the Earth,

(218)

As gaudy colour'd Serpents are ?   I'll ask that
Question, when next I see him here.

Enter Miranda *and* Dorinda *peeping.*

Dor. O Sister, there it is, it walks about like one of us.

Mir. I, just so, and has Legs as we have too.

Hip. It strangely puzzles me : yet 'tis most likely
Women are somewhat between men and spirits.

Dor. Heark ! it talks, sure this is not it my Father meant,
For this is just like one of us : methinks I am not half
So much afraid on't as I was ; see, now it turns this way.

Mir. Heaven ! what a goodly thing it is ?

Dor. I'll go nearer it.

Mir. O no, 'tis dangerous, Sister ! I'll go to it.
I would not for the World that you should venture.
My Father charg'd me to secure you from it.

Dor. I warrant you this is a tame man, dear Sister,
He'll not hurt me, I see it by his looks.

Mir. Indeed he will ! but go back, and he shall eat me first :
Fie, are you not asham'd to be so much inquisitive ?

Dor. You chide me for't, and wou'd give your self.

Mir. Come back, or I will tell my Father.
Observe how he begins to stare already.
I'll meet the danger first, and then call you.

Dor. Nay, Sister, you shall never vanquish me in kindness.
I'll venture you no more than you will me.

Prosp. within. Miranda, Child, where are you ?

Mir. Do you not hear my Father call ? go in.

Dor. 'Twas you he nam'd, not me ; I will but say my Prayers,
And follow you immediately.

Mir. Well, Sister, you'l repent it.   [*Exit* Miranda.

Dor. Though I die for't, I must have the other peep.

Hip. seeing her. What thing is that ? sure 'tis some Infant of the Sun,
dress'd in his Fathers gayest Beams, and comes to play with Birds : my
sight is dazl'd, and yet I find I'm loth to shut my Eyes.
I must go nearer it —— but stay a while ;
May it not be that beauteous Murderer, Woman,
Which I was charg'd to shun ?   Speak, what art thou ?
Thou shining Vision !

Dor. Alas, I know not ; but I'm told I am a Woman ;
Do not hurt me, pray, fair thing.

Hip. I'd sooner tear my Eyes out, than consent to do you any harm ;
though I was told a Woman was my Enemy.

(219)

Dor. I never knew what 'twas to be an Enemy, nor can I e'r prove so to that which looks like you : for though I have been charg'd by him (whom yet I never disobey'd) to shun your presence, yet I'd rather die than lose it ; therefore I hope you will not have the heart to hurt me : though I fear you are a Man, that dangerous thing, of which I have been warn'd. Pray tell me what you are ?

Hip. I must confess, I was inform'd I am a Man,
But if I fright you, I shall wish I were some other Creature.
I was bid to fear you too.

Dor. Ay me ! Heav'n grant we be not poison to each other !
Alas, can we not meet but we must die ?

Hip. I hope not so ! for when two poisonous Creatures,
Both of the same kind, meet, yet neither dies.
I've seen two Serpents harmless to each other,
Though they have twin'd into a mutual knot :
If we have any venome in us, sure, we cannot be more
Poisonous, when we meet, than Serpents are.
You have a hand like mine, may I not gently touch it ?   [*Takes her hand.*

Dor. I've touch'd my Father's and my Sister's hands,
And felt no pain ; but now, alas ! there's something,
When I touch yours, which makes me sigh : just so
I've seen two Turtles mourning when they met ;
Yet mine's a pleasing grief ; and so me thought was theirs :
For still they mourn'd, and still they seem'd to murmur too,
And yet they often met.

Hip. Oh Heavens ! I have the same sense too : your hand
Methinks goes through me ; I feel at my heart,
And find it pleases, though it pains me.

Prosp. within. Dorinda !

Dor. My Father calls again ; ah, I must leave you.

Hip. Alas, I'm subject to the same command.

Dor. This is my first offence against my Father,
Which he, by severing us, too cruelly does punish.

Hip. And this is my first trespass too : but he hath more
Offended truth than we have him :
He said our meeting would destructive be,
But I no death but in our parting see.   [*Exeunt several ways.*

SCENE III.   A wild Island.

Enter Alonzo, Antonio, Gonzalo.

Gonz. 'Beseech your Grace be merry : you have cause, so have we all, of joy, for our strange 'scape ; then wisely, good Sir, weigh our sorrow with our comfort.

Alonz. Prithee peace, you cram these words into my Ears, against my stomach; how can I rejoice, when my dear Son, perhaps this very moment, is made a meal to some strange Fish?

Anto. Sir, he may live, I saw him beat the Billows under him, and ride upon their backs; I do not doubt he came alive to Land.

Alonz. No, no, he's gone; and you and I, *Antonio*, were those who caus'd his death.

Ant. How could we help it?

Alonz. Then, then we should have help'd it, when thou betrai'dst thy Brother *Prospero*, and *Mantua*'s Infant Sovereign, to my power; and when I, too ambitious, took by force another's right: Then lost we *Ferdinand;* Then forfeited our Navy to this Tempest.

Ant. Indeed we first broke Truce with Heaven; you to the waves an infant Prince expos'd, and on the waves have lost an only Son. I did usurp my Brother's fertile Lands, and now am cast upon this Desart-Isle.

Gonz. These, Sirs, 'tis true, were crimes of a black die; but both of you have made amends to Heav'n by your late Voyage into *Portugal;* where, in defence of Christianity, your valour has repuls'd the Moors of *Spain.*

Alon. O name it not, *Gonzalo;*
No act but penitence can expiate guilt!
Must we teach Heav'n what price to set on Murder! what rate on lawless Power and wild Ambition! or dare we traffick with the Powers above, and sell by weight a good deed for a bad?   [*A flourish of Musick.*

Gonz. Musick! and in the air! sure we are Shipwrack'd on the Dominions of some merry Devil!

Ant. This Isle's Inchanted ground; for I have heard swift Voices flying by my Ear, and groans of lamenting Ghosts.

Alon. I pull'd a Tree, and bloud pursu'd my hand.
Heav'n deliver me from this dire place, and all the after-actions of my life shall mark my penitence and my bounty.   [*Musick agen lowder.*
Hark, the sounds approach us!   [*The Stage opens in several places.*

Ant. Lo the Earth opens to devour us quick.
These dreadful horrors, and the guilty sense of my foul Treason, have unmann'd me quite.

Alon. We on the brink of swift destruction stand;
No means of our escape is left. [*Another flourish of Voyces under the Stage.*

Ant. Ah! what amazing sounds are these we hear!

Gonz. What horrid Masque will the dire Fiends present?

Sung under the Stage.

1. Dev. *Where does the black Fiend Ambition reside,*
      With the mischievous Devil of Pride?

(221)

2. *Dev.* *In the lowest and darkest Caverns of Hell*
Both Pride and Ambition does dwell.
1. *Dev.* *Who are the chief Leaders of the damned Host?*
3. *Dev.* *Proud Monarchs, who tyrannize most.*
1. *Dev.* *Damned Princes there*
The worst of torments bear;
3. *Dev.* *Who in Earth all others in pleasures excel,*
Must feel the worst torments of Hell.
[They rise singing this Chorus.

Ant. Oh Heav'ns! what horrid Vision's this?
How they upbraid us with our crimes!
Alon. What fearful vengeance is in store for us!

1. *Dev.* *Tyrants by whom their Subjects bleed,*
Should in pains all others exceed;
2. *Dev.* *And barb'rous Monarchs who their Neighbours invade,*
And their Crowns unjustly get;
And such who their Brothers to death have betray'd,
In Hell upon burning Thrones shall be set.
3. *Dev.* } *——In Hell, in Hell with flames they shall reign,*
Chor. } *And for ever, for ever shall suffer the pain.*

Ant. Oh my Soul; for ever, for ever shall suffer the pain.
Alon. Has Heav'n in all its infinite stock of mercy
No overflowings for us? poor, miserable, guilty Men!
Gonz. Nothing but horrors do encompass us!
For ever, for ever must we suffer!
Alon. For ever we shall perish! O dismal words, for ever!

1. *Dev.* *Who are the Pillars of the Tyrants Court?*
2. *Dev.* *Rapine and Murder his Crown must support!*
3. *Dev.* *—— His cruelty does tread*
On Orphans tender breasts, and Brothers dead!
2. *Dev.* *Can Heav'n permit such crimes should be*
Attended with felicity?
3. *Dev.* *No, Tyrants their Scepters uneasily bear,*
In the midst of their Guards they their Consciences fear.
2. *Dev.* } *Care their minds when they wake unquiet will keep,*
Chor. } *And we with dire visions disturb all their sleep.*

Ant. Oh horrid sight! how they stare upon us!
The Fiends will hurry us to the dark Mansion.
Sweet Heav'n, have mercy on us!

1. Dev. *Say, Say, shall we bear these bold Mortals from hence?*
2. Dev. *No, no, let us show their degrees of offence.*
3. Dev. *Let's muster their crimes up on every side,*
    And first let's discover their pride.

Enter *Pride.*

Pride.   *Lo here is Pride, who first led them astray,*
    And did to Ambition their minds then betray.

Enter *Fraud.*

Fraud.   *And Fraud does next appear,*
     Their wandring steps who led,
     When they from vertue fled,
  They in my crooked paths their course did steer.

Enter *Rapine.*

Rapine.   *From Fraud to Force they soon arrive,*
    Where Rapine did their actions drive.

Enter *Murder.*

Murder.   *There long they could not stay;*
    Down the steep Hill they run,
  And to perfect the mischief which they had begun,
    To Murder they bent all their way.
     Around, around we pace,
Chorus   *About this cursed place;*
of all.   *While thus we compass in*
     These Mortals and their sin.   [*Devils vanish.*

Ant. Heav'n has heard me, they are vanish'd!
Alon. But they have left me all unmann'd?
I feel my sinews slacken with the fright;
And a cold sweat trills down o'r all my Limbs,
As if I were dissolving into water.
Oh *Prospero,* my crimes 'gainst thee sit heavy on my heart!
Ant. And mine 'gainst him and young *Hippolito.*
Gonz. Heav'n have mercy on the penitent.
Alon. Lead from this cursed ground;
The Seas in all their rage are not so dreadful.
This is the Region of despair and death.
Alonz. Beware all fruit, but what the Birds have peck'd.
The shadows of the Trees are poisonous too: a secret venom slides from

every branch! my Conscience does diftract me! O my Son! why do I speak of eating or repose, before I know thy fortune?

[*As they are going out, a Devil rises juft before them, at which they ftart, and are frighted.*

Alonz. O Heavens! yet more Apparitions!

Devil sings. *Arise, arise! ye subterranean winds,*
More to difturb their guilty minds.
And all ye filthy damps and vapours rise,
Which use t' infeft the Earth, and trouble all the Skies;
Rise you, from whom devouring plagues have birth:
You that i' th' vaft and hollow womb of Earth,
Engender Earthquakes, make whole Countreys shake,
And ftately Cities into Desarts turn;
And you who feed the flames by which Earths entrals burn.
Ye raging winds, whose rapid force can make
All but the fix'd and solid Centre shake:
Come drive these Wretches to that part o' th' Isle,
Where Nature never yet did smile:
Cause Fogs and Storms, Whirlwinds and Earthquakes there:
There let 'em howl and languish in defpair.
Rise and obey the pow'rful Prince o' th' Air.

Two Winds rise, Ten more enter and dance.
At the end of the Dance, Three winds sink, the reft drive *Alon. Ant. Gonz.* off.

Aft Ends.

ACT III.   SCENE I.

SCENE, *A wild Island.*

Enter Ferdinand, *and* Ariel *and* Milcha *invisible.*

Ariel. COme *unto these yellow sands,*
And then take hands,
Curtsi'd when you have, and kiss'd;
The wild waves whift.
Foot it featly here and there,
And sweet fprights the burthen bear.

Hark ! hark !
　Bow waugh, the Watch-dogs bark.
Bow waugh.　Hark ! hark ! I hear
The strain of strutting Chanticleer,
　Cry, Cock a doodle do.

Ferd. Where should this Musick be ? i' th' air, or earth ? it sounds no more, and sure it waits upon some God i' th' Island ; sitting on a Bank, weeping against the Duke ; my Father's wrack'd ; This Musick hover'd on the waters, allaying both their fury and my passion with charming Aires.　Thence I have follow'd it, (or it has drawn me rather) but 'tis gone :　No, it begins again.

Milcha sings.

Full fathom five thy Father lies,
　Of his bones is Coral made :
Those are Pearls that were his Eyes,
　Nothing of him that does fade.
But does suffer a Sea-change
Into something rich and strange :
Sea Nymphs hourly ring his knell ;
Hark ! now I hear 'em, ding dong Bell.

Ferd. This mournful Ditty mentions my drown'd Father. This is no mortal business, nor a sound which the Earth owns—— I hear it now before me ; however I will on and follow it.

[Exit Ferd. following Ariel.

SCENE II.　The Cypress-Trees and Cave.

Enter Prospero and Miranda.

Prosp. Excuse it not, *Miranda,* for to you (the elder, and I thought the more discreet) I gave the conduct of your Sisters actions.

Mir. Sir, when you call'd me thence, I did not fail to mind her of her duty to depart.

Prosp. How can I think you did remember hers, when you forgot your own ? did you not see the Man whom I commanded you to shun ?

Mir. I must confess I saw him at a distance.

Prosp. Did not his Eyes infect and poison you ? What alteration found you in your self ?

Mir. I only wondred at a sight so new.

Prosp. But have you no desire once more to see him ? Come, tell me truly what you think of him ?

Mir. As of the gayest thing I ever saw, so fine, that it appear'd more

(225)

fit to be belov'd than fear'd, and seem'd so near my kind, that I did think
I might have call'd it Sister.

Prosp. You do not love it?

Mir. How is it likely that I should, except the thing had first lov'd me?

Prosp. Cherish those thoughts: you have a gen'rous soul;
And since I see your mind not apt to take the light
Impressions of a sudden love, I will unfold
A secret to your knowledge.
That Creature which you saw, is of a kind which
Nature made a prop and guide to yours.

Mir. Why did you then propose him as an object of terrour to my
mind? you never us'd to teach me any thing but God-like truths, and
what you said, I did believe as sacred.

Prosp. I fear'd the pleasing form of this young Man
Might unawares possess your tender Breast,
Which for a nobler guest I had design'd;
For shortly, my *Miranda*, you shall see another of this kind,
The full-blown Flower, of which this Youth was but the
Op'ning Bud.   Go in, and send your Sister to me.

Mir. Heav'n still preserve you, Sir.   [*Exit* Miranda.

Prosp. And make thee fortunate.

Enter Dorinda.

O, Come hither, you have seen a Man to day,
Against my strict command.

Dor. Who I? indeed I saw him but a little, Sir.

Prosp. Come, come, be clear.   Your Sister told me all.

Dor. Did she? truly she would have seen him more than I,
But that I would not let her.

Prosp. Why so?

Dor. Because, methought, he would have hurt me less
Than he would her.   But if I knew you'd not be angry
With me, I could tell you, Sir, that he was much to blame.

Prosp. Hah! was he to blame?
Tell me, with that sincerity I taught you,
How you became so bold to see the Man?

Dor. I hope you will forgive me, Sir, because I did not see him much
till he saw me.   Sir, he would needs come in my way, and star'd, and
star'd upon my Face; and so I thought I would be reveng'd of him, and
therefore I gaz'd on him as long; but if I e'r come near a Man again——

Prosp. I told you he was dangerous; but you would not be warn'd.

Dor. Pray be not angry, Sir, if I tell you, you are mistaken in him;
for he did me no great hurt.

Prosp. But he may do you more harm hereafter.

Dor. No, Sir, I'm as well as e'r I was in all my life,
But that I cannot eat nor drink for thought of him.
That dangerous Man runs ever in my mind.

Prosp. The way to cure you, is no more to see him.

Dor. Nay pray, Sir, say not so, I promis'd him
To see him once agen; and you know, Sir,
You charg'd me I should never break my promise.

Prosp. Wou'd you see him who did you so much mischief?

Dor. I warrant you I did him as much harm as he did me;
For when I left him, Sir, he sigh'd so, as it griev'd
My heart to hear him.

Prosp. Those sighs were poisonous, they infected you:
You say, they griev'd you to the heart.

Dor. 'Tis true; but yet his looks and words were gentle.

Prosp. These are the Day-dreams of a Maid in Love.
But still I fear the worst.

Dor. O fear not him, Sir.

Prosp. You speak of him with too much Passion; tell me
(And on your duty tell me true, *Dorinda*)
What past betwixt you and that horrid Creature?

Dor. How, horrid, Sir? if any else but you should call it so, indeed I
should be angry.

Prosp. Go too! you are a foolish Girl; but answer to what I ask,
what thought you when you saw it?

Dor. At first it star'd upon me, and seem'd wild,
And then I trembled, yet it look'd so lovely, that when
I would have fled away, my feet seem'd fasten'd to the ground,
Then it drew near, and with amazement ask'd
To touch my hand; which, as a ransome for my life,
I gave: but when he had it, with a furious gripe
He put it to his mouth so eagerly, I was afraid he
Would have swallow'd it.

Prosp. Well, what was his behaviour afterwards?

Dor. He on a sudden grew so tame and gentle,
That he became more kind to me than you are;
Then, Sir, I grew I know not how, and touching his hand
Agen, my heart did beat so strong, as I lack'd breath
To answer what he ask'd.

Prosp. You have been too fond, and I should chide you for it.

Dor. Then send me to that Creature to be punish'd.

Prosp. Poor Child! thy Passion, like a lazy Ague,
Has seiz'd thy bloud, instead of striving, thou humour'st

And feed'st thy languishing disease : thou fight'st
The Battels of thy Enemy, and 'tis one part of what
I threatn'd thee, not to perceive thy danger.
    Dor. Danger, Sir ?
If he would hurt me, yet he knows not how :
He hath no Claws, nor Teeth, nor Horns to hurt me,
But looks about him like a Callow-bird,
Just straggl'd from the Nest : pray trust me, Sir,
To go to him agen.
    Prosp. Since you will venture,
I charge you bear your self reserv'dly to him,
Let him not dare to touch your naked hand,
But keep at distance from him.
    Dor. This is hard.
    Prosp. It is the way to make him love you more ;
He will despise you if you grow too kind.
    Dor. I'll struggle with my heart to follow this,
But if I lose him by it, will you promise
To bring him back agen ?
    Prosp. Fear not, *Dorinda ;*
But use him ill, and he'l be yours for ever.
    Dor. I hope you have not couzen'd me agen.   [*Exit* Dor.
    Prosp. Now my designs are gathering to a head.
My Spirits are obedient to my charms.
What, *Ariel !* my Servant *Ariel*, where art thou ?

Enter Ariel.

    Ariel. What wou'd my potent Master ?   Here I am.
    Prosp. Thou and thy meaner fellows your last service
Did worthily perform, and I must use you in such another
Work : how goes the day ?
    Ariel. On the fourth, my Lord, and on the sixth,
You said our work should cease.
    Prosp. And so it shall ;
And thou shalt have the open air at freedom.
    Ariel. Thanks, my great Lord.
    Prosp. But tell me first, my Spirit,
How fares the Duke, my Brother, and their Followers ?
    Ariel. Confin'd together, as you gave me order,
In the Lime-grove, which weather-fends your Cell ;
Within that Circuit up and down they wander,
But cannot stir one step beyond their compass.
    Prosp. How do they bear their sorrows ?

Ariel. The two Dukes appear like men diſtracted, their
Attendants brim-full of sorrow mourning over 'em;
But chiefly, he you term'd the good *Gonzalo* :
His Tears run down his Beard, like Winter-drops
From Eaves of Reeds, your Vision did so work 'em,
That if you now beheld 'em, your affections
Would become tender.

Proſp. Do'ſt thou think so, Spirit?

Ariel. Mine would, Sir, were I humane.

Proſp. And mine shall :
Haſt thou, who art but air, a touch, a feeling of their
Afflictions, and shall not I (a Man like them, one
Who as sharply rellish passions as they) be kindlier
Mov'd than thou art? though they have pierc'd
Me to the quick with injuries, yet with my nobler
Reason 'gainſt my fury I will take part;
The rarer action is in vertue than in vengeance.
Go, my *Ariel*, refresh with needful food their
Famish'd Bodies. With shows and cheerful
Musick comfort 'em.

Ariel. Presently, Maſter.

Proſp. With a twinkle, *Ariel*. But ſtay, my Spirit;
What is become of my Slave *Caliban*,
And *Sycorax* his Siſter?

Ariel. Potent Sir!
They have caſt off your service, and revolted
To the wrack'd Marriners, who have already
Parcell'd your Island into Governments.

Proſp. No matter, I have now no need of 'em.
But, Spirit, now I ſtay thee on the Wing;
Haſt to perform what I have given in charge :
But see they keep within the bounds I set 'em.

Ariel. I'll keep 'em in with Walls of Adamant,
Invisible as air to mortal Eyes,
But yet unpassable.

Proſp. Make haſt then.   [*Exeunt severally.*

SCENE III. *Wild Island.*

Enter Alonzo, Antonio, Gonzalo.

Gonz. I am weary, and can go no further, Sir.

Alonz. Old Lord, I cannot blame thee, who am my self seiz'd

With a weariness, to the dulling of my Spirits :   [*They sit.*
Even here I will put off my hope, and keep it no longer
For my Flatterers : he is drown'd whom thus we
Stray to find.
I'm faint with hunger, and must despair
Of food.   [*Musick without.*
What ! Harmony agen, my good Friends, heark !
   Ant. I fear some other horrid Apparition.
Give us kind Keepers, Heaven, I beseech thee !
   Gonz. 'Tis chearful Musick this, unlike the first.

Ariel and Milcha invisible, sing.

Dry those Eyes which are o'rflowing,
All your storms are overblowing :
While you in this Isle are biding,
You shall feast without providing :
Every dainty you can think of,
Ev'ry Wine which you would drink of,
Shall be yours ; all want shall shun you,
Ceres *blessing so is on you.*

   Alonz. This voice speaks comfort to us.
   Ant. Wou'd 'twere come ; there is no Musick in a Song
To me, my stomack being empty.
   Gonz. O for a Heavenly Vision of Boyl'd,
Bak'd, and Roasted !
           [*Dance of fantastick Spirits, after the Dance, a Table furnish'd with*
                 Meat and Fruit is brought in by two Spirits.
   Ant. My Lord, the Duke, see yonder.
A Table, as I live, set out and furnish'd
With all varieties of Meats and Fruits.
   Alonz. 'Tis so indeed ; but who dares taste this feast
Which Fiends provide, perhaps to poison us ?
   Gonz. Why that dare I ; if the black Gentleman be so ill-natur'd, he
may do his pleasure.
   Ant. 'Tis certain we must either eat or famish ;
I will encounter it, and feed.
   Alonz. If both resolve, I will adventure too.
   Gonz. The Devil may fright me, yet he shall not starve me.
                   [*Two Spirits descend, and flie away with the Table.*
   Alonz. Heav'n ! behold, it is as you suspected : 'tis vanish'd.
Shall we be always haunted with these Fiends ?
   Ant. Here we shall wander till we famish.

(230)

Gonz. Certainly one of you was so wicked as to say Grace : This comes on't, when Men will be godly out of season.

Ant. Yonder's another Table, let's try that—— [*Exeunt.*

Enter Trincalo *and* Caliban.

Trinc. Brother Monster, welcome to my private Palace. But where's thy Sister, is she so brave a Lass ?

Calib. In all this Isle there are but two more, the Daughters of the Tyrant *Prospero ;* and she is bigger then 'em both. O here she comes ; now thou may'st judge thy self, my Lord.

Enter Sycorax.

Trinc. She's monstrous fair indeed. Is this to be my Spouse ? well, she's Heir of all this Isle (for I will geld Monster). The *Trincalo's,* like other wise Men, have antiently us'd to marry for Estate more than for Beauty.

Syc. I prithee let me have the gay thing about thy neck, and that which dangles at thy wrist. [Sycorax *points to his Bosens Whistle and his Bottle.*

Trinc. My dear Blobber-lips ; this, observe my Chuck, is a badge of my Sea-office ; my fair Fuss, thou dost not know it.

Syc. No, my dread Lord.

Trinc. It shall be a Whistle for our first Babe, and when the next Ship-wrack puts me again to swimming, I'll dive to get a Coral to it.

Syc. I'l be thy pretty Child, and wear it first.

Trinc. I prithee, sweet Baby, do not play the Wanton, and cry for my goods e'r I'm dead. When thou art my Widow, thou shalt have the Devil and all.

Syc. May I not have the other fine thing ?

Trinc. This is a Sucking-bottle for young *Trincalo.*

Calib. Shall she not taste of that immortal Liquor ?

Trinc. Umph ! that's another question : for if she be thus flipant in her Water, what will she be in her Wine ?

Enter Ariel (*invisible*) *and changes the Bottle which stands upon the ground.*

Ariel. There's Water for your Wine. [*Exit* Ariel.

Trinc. Well ! since it must be so. [*Gives her the Bottle.*
How do you like it now, my Queen that [*She drinks.*
Must be ?

Syc. Is this your heavenly Liquor ?
I'll bring you to a River of the same.

Trinc. Wilt thou so, Madam Monster ? what a mighty Prince shall I be then ? I would not change my Dukedom to be great Turk *Trincalo.*

Syc. This is the drink of Frogs.

Trinc. Nay, if the Frogs of this Island drink such, they are the merriest Frogs in Christendom.

Calib. She does not know the virtue of this Liquor : I prithee let me drink for her.

Trinc. Well said, Subject Monster.   [*Caliban drinks.*

Calib. My Lord, this is meer Water.

Trinc. 'Tis thou hast chang'd the Wine then, and drunk it up, Like a debauch'd Fish as thou art.   Let me see't, I'll taste it my self.   Element ! meer Element ! as I live. It was a cold gulph, such as this, which kill'd my famous Predecessor, old *Simon* the King.

Calib. How does thy honour? prithee be not angry, and I will lick thy shoe.

Trinc. I could find in my heart to turn thee out of my Dominions for a Liquorish Monster.

Calib. O my Lord, I have found it out ; this must be done by one of *Prospero*'s Spirits.

Trinc. There's nothing but malice in these Devils, I would it had been Holy-water for their sakes.

Syc. 'Tis no matter, I will cleave to thee.

Trinc. Lovingly said, in troth : now cannot I hold out against her. This Wife-like virtue of hers has overcome me.

Syc. Shall I have thee in my arms ?

Trinc. Thou shalt have Duke *Trincalo* in thy arms : But prithee be not too boistrous with me at first ; Do not discourage a young beginner.   [*They embrace.* Stand to your Arms, my Spouse, And subject Monster ;

Enter Steph. Must. Vent.

The Enemy is come to surprise us in our Quarters. You shall know, Rebels, that I am marri'd to a Witch, And we have a thousand Spirits of our party.

Steph. Hold ! I ask a Truce ; I and my Vice-Roys (Finding no food, and but a small remainder of Brandy) Are come to treat a Peace betwixt us, Which may be for the good of both Armies, Therefore *Trincalo* disband.

Trinc. Plain *Trincalo*, methinks I might have been a Duke in your mouth ; I'l not accept of your Embassie without my Title.

Steph. A Title shall break no squares betwixt us : Vice-Roys, give him his style of Duke, and treat with him, Whilst I walk by in state.

      Ventoso *and* Mustacho *bow, whilst* Trincalo *puts on his Cap.*

Must. Our Lord and Master, Duke *Stephano*, has sent us
In the first place to demand of you, upon what
Ground you make War against him, having no right
To govern here, as being elected only by
Your own Voice.
    Trinc. To this I answer, That having in the face of the World
Espous'd the lawful Inheritrix of this Island,
Queen *Blouze* the First, and having homage done me,
By this Hectoring Spark her Brother, from these two
I claim a lawful Title to this Island,
    Must. Who that Monster? he a Hector?
    Calib. Lo! how he mocks me, wilt thou let him, my Lord?
    Trinc. Vice-Roys! keep good tongues in your heads,
I advise you, and proceed to your business.
    Must. First and foremost, as to your claim that you have answer'd.
    Vent. But second and foremost, we demand of you,
That if we make a Peace, the Butt also may be
Comprehended in the Treaty.
    Trinc. I cannot treat with my honour, without your submission.
    Steph. I understand, being present, from my Embassadors, what your
resolution is, and ask an hours time of deliberation, and so I take our
leave; but first I desire to be entertain'd at your Butt, as becomes a Prince,
and his Embassadors.
    Trinc. That I refuse, till acts of hostility be ceas'd.
These Rogues are rather Spies than Embassadors;
I must take heed of my Butt. They come to pry
Into the secrets of my Dukedom.
    Vent. *Trincalo*, you are a barbarous Prince, and so farewel.
                                        [*Exeunt* Steph. Must. Vent.
    Trinc. Subject Monster! stand you Centry before my Cellar; my Queen
and I will enter, and feast our selves within.   [*Exeunt.*

Enter Ferdinand, Ariel *and* Milcha (*invisible*).

    Ferd. How far will this invisible Musician conduct
My steps? he hovers still about me, whether
For good or ill, I cannot tell, nor care I much;
For I have been so long a slave to chance, that
I'm as weary of her flatteries as her frowns,
But here I am——
    Ariel. Here I am.
    Ferd. Hah! art thou so? the Spirit's turn'd an Eccho:
This might seem pleasant, could the burthen of my

Griefs accord with any thing but sighs.
And my laſt words, like those of dying men,
Need no reply.   Fain I would go to shades, where
Few would wish to follow me.
   Ariel. Follow me.
   Ferd. This evil Spirit grows importunate,
But I'l not take his counsel.
   Ariel. Take his counsel.
   Ferd. It may be the Devil's counsel, I'll never take it.
   Ariel. Take it.
   Ferd. I will discourse no more with thee,
Nor follow one ſtep further.
   Ariel. One ſtep further.
   Ferd. This muſt have more importance than an Echo.
Some Spirit tempts to a precipice.
I'll try if it will answer when I sing
My sorrows to the murmur of this Brook.
                He sings.

	Go thy way.
Ariel.	*Go thy way.*
Ferd.	*Why shouldſt thou ſtay?*
Ariel.	*Why shouldſt thou ſtay?*
Ferd.	*Where the winds whiſtle, and where the ſtreams cre,*
	Under yond Willow-tree, fain would I sleep.
	Then let me alone,
	For 'tis time to be gone,
Ariel.	*For 'tis time to be gone.*
Ferd.	*What cares or pleasures can be in this Isle?*
	Within this desart place
	There lives no humane race;
	Fate cannot frown here, nor kind fortune smile.
Ariel.	*Kind Fortune smiles, and she*
	Has yet in ſtore for thee
	Some ſtrange felicity.
	Follow me, follow me,
	And thou shalt see.

   Ferd. I'll take thy word for once ;
Lead on Musician.   *[Exeunt and return.*

SCENE IV.   *The Cypress-trees and Caves.*

Scene changes, and discovers Prospero *and* Miranda.

   Proſp. Advance the fringed Curtains of thine Eyes, and ſay what thou
seeſt yonder.

Mir. Is it a Spirit?
Lord! how it looks about! Sir, I confess it carries a brave form.
But 'tis a Spirit.

Prosp. No, Girl, it eats, and sleeps, and has such sences as we have.
This young Gallant, whom thou seest, was in the wrack; were he not
somewhat stain'd with grief (beauty's worst cancker) thou might'st call
him a goodly person; he has lost his Company, and strays about to find 'em.

Mir. I might call him a thing Divine, for nothing natural I ever saw
so noble.

Prosp. It goes on as my Soul prompts it: Spirit, fine Spirit. I'll free
thee within two days for this.

Ferd. She's sure the Mistriss on whom these Airs attend. Fair Excellence, if, as your form declares, you are Divine, be pleas'd to instruct me
how you will be worship'd; so bright a beauty cannot sure belong to
humane kind.

Mir. I am, like you, a Mortal, if such you are.

Ferd. My language too! O Heaven's! I am the best of them who speak
this Speech when I'm in my own Countrey.

Prosp. How, the best? What wert thou if the Duke of *Savoy* heard
thee?

Ferd. As I am now, who wonders to hear thee speak of *Savoy*: he does
hear me, and that he does I weep, my self am *Savoy*, whose fatal Eyes
(e'r since at ebb) beheld the Duke my Father wrack'd.

Mir. Alack! for pity.

Prosp. At the first sight they have chang'd Eyes, dear *Ariel*,
I'll set thee free for this——young, Sir, a word.
With hazard of your self you do me wrong.

Mir. Why speaks my Father so urgently?
This is the third Man that e'r I saw, the first whom
E'r I sigh'd for, sweet Heaven move my Father
To be inclin'd my way.

Ferd. O! if a Virgin! and your affections not gone forth,
I'll make you Mistriss of *Savoy*.

Prosp. Soft, Sir! one word more.
They are in each others powers, but this swift
Bus'ness I must uneasie make, lest too light
Winning make the prize light——one word more.
Thou usurp'st the name not due to thee, and hast
Put thy self upon this Island as a Spy to get the
Government from me the Lord of it.

Ferd. No, as I'm a Man.

Mir. There's nothing ill can dwell in such a Temple,
If th' evil Spirit hath so fair a House,

Good things will strive to dwell with it.

Prosp. No more.   Speak not for him, he's a Traitor.
Come! thou art my Pris'ner, and shalt be in
Bonds.   Sea-water shalt thou drink, thy food
Shall be the fresh-Brook Muscles, wither'd Roots,
And Husks, wherein the Acorn crawl'd; follow.

Ferd. No, I will resist such entertainment,
Till my Enemy has more power.   [*He draws, and is charm'd from moving.*

Mir. O dear Father! make not too rash a trial
Of him, for he's gentle, and not fearful.

Prosp. My Child, my Tutor! put thy Sword up, Traytor,
Who mak'st a show, but dar'st not strike: thy
Conscience is possess'd with guilt.   Come from
Thy Ward, for I can here disarm thee with
This Wand, and make thy Weapon drop.

Mir. 'Beseech you, Father.

Prosp. Hence: hang not on my Garment.

Mir. Sir, have pity,
I'll be his Surety.

Prosp. Silence! one word more shall make me chide thee,
If not hate thee: what, an Advocate for an
Impostor? sure thou think'st there are no more
Such shapes as his?
To the most of men this is a *Caliban*,
And they to him are Angels.

Mir. My affections are then most humble,
I have no ambition to see a goodlier Man.

Prosp. Come on, obey:
Thy Nerves are in their infancy again, and have
No vigour in them.

Ferd. So they are:
My Spirits, as in a Dream, are all bound up:
My Father's loss, the weakness which I feel,
The wrack of all my friends, and this Man's threats,
To whom I am subdu'd, would seem light to me,
Might I but once a day through my prison behold this Maid:
All corners else o' th' Earth let liberty make use of:
I have space enough in such a Prison.

Prosp. It works: come on:
Thou hast done well, fine *Ariel*: follow me.
Heark what thou shalt more do for me.   [*Whispers* Ariel.

Mir. Be of comfort!
My Father's of a better nature, Sir,

(236)

Than he appears by Speech : this is unwonted
Which now came from him.

Prosp. Thou shalt be as free as Mountain Winds :
But then exactly do all points of my command.

Ariel. To a syllable.   [*Exit* Ariel.

Prosp to Mir. Go in that way, speak not a word for him :
I'll separate you.   [*Exit* Miranda.

Ferd. As soon thou may'st divide the Waters
When thou strik'st 'em, which pursue thy bootless blow,
And meet when 'tis past.

Prosp. Go practise your Philosophy within,
And if you are the same you speak your self,
Bear your afflictions like a Prince———That door
Shews you your Lodging.

Ferd. 'Tis vain to strive, I must obey.   [*Exit* Ferd.

Prosp. This goes as I would wish it.
Now for my second care, *Hippolito.*
I shall not need to chide him for his fault,
His passion is become his punishment.
Come forth, *Hippolito.*

Hip. entring. 'Tis *Prospero*'s voice.

Prosp. *Hippolito !* I know you now expect I should severely chide you :
you have seen a woman in contempt of my commands.

Hip. But, Sir, you see I am come off unharm'd ;
I told you, that you need not doubt my Courage.

Prosp. You think you have receiv'd no hurt ?

Hip. No, none, Sir.
Try me agen, when e'r you please I'm ready :
I think I cannot fear an Army of 'em.

Prosp. How much in vain it is to bridle Nature !   [*Aside.*
Well ! what was the success of your encounter ?

Hip. Sir, we had none, we yielded both at first,
For I took her to mercy, and she me.

Prosp. But are you not much chang'd from what you were ?

Hip. Methinks I wish and wish ! for what I know not,
But still I wish———yet if I had that Woman,
She, I believe, could tell me what I wish for.

Prosp. What wou'd you do to make that Woman yours ?

Hip. I'd quit the rest o' th' World, that I might live alone with
Her, she never should be from me.
We two would sit and look till our Eyes ak'd.

Prosp. You'd soon be weary of her.

Hip. O, Sir, never.

(237)

Prosp. But you'l grow old and wrinkl'd, as you see me now,
And then you will not care for her.

Hip. You may do what you please, but, Sir, we two can never possibly
grow old.

Prosp. You must, *Hippolito*.

Hip. Whether we will or no, Sir, who shall make us ?

Prosp. Nature, which made me so.

Hip. But you have told me her works are various ;
She made you old, but she has made us young.

Prosp. Time will convince you,
Mean while be sure you tread in honours paths,
That you may merit her, and that you may not want
Fit occasions to employ your virtue, in this next
Cave there is a stranger lodg'd, one of your kind,
Young, of a noble presence, and, as he says himself,
Of Princely birth, he is my Pris'ner, and in deep
Affliction : visit, and comfort him ; it will become you.

Hip. It is my duty, Sir.   [*Exit* Hippolito.

Prosp. True, he has seen a Woman, yet he lives ; perhaps I took the
moment of his birth amiss, perhaps my Art it self is false : on what
strange grounds we build our hopes and fears, Man's Life is all a mist, and
in the dark, our Fortunes meet us.
If fate be not, then what can we foresee ?
Or how can we avoid it, if it be ?
If by free-will in our own paths we move,
How are we bounded by Decrees above ?
Whether we drive, or whether we are driven,
If ill, 'tis ours ; if good, the act of Heaven.   [*Exit* Prospero.

Scene, a Cave.

Enter Hippolito *and* Ferdinand.

Ferd. Your pity, noble youth, doth much oblige me,
Indeed 'twas sad to lose a Father so.

Hip. I, and an onely Father too, for sure you said
You had but one.

Ferd. But one Father ! he's wondrous simple !   [*Aside.*

Hip. Are such misfortunes frequent in your World,
Where many men live ?

Ferd. Such are we born to.
But, gentle Youth, as you have question'd me,
So give me leave to ask you, what you are ?

(238)

Hip. Do not you know ?

Ferd. How should I ?

Hip. I well hop'd I was a Man, but by your ignorance
Of what I am, I fear it is not so :
Wel!, *Prospero !* this is now the second time
You have deceiv'd me.

Ferd. Sir, there is no doubt you are a Man :
But I would know of whence ?

Hip. Why, of this World, I never was in yours.

Ferd. Have you a Father ?

Hip. I was told I had one, and that he was a Man, yet I have been so much deceived, I dare not tell't you for a truth ; but I have still been kept a Prisoner for fear of Women.

Ferd. They indeed are dangerous, for since I came, I have beheld one here, whose beauty pierc'd my heart.

Hip. How did she pierce, you seem not hurt.

Ferd. Alas ! the wound was made by her bright Eyes,
And festers by her absence.
But, to speak plainer to you, Sir, I love her.

Hip. Now I suspect that love's the very thing, that I feel too ! pray tell me, truly, Sir, are you not grown unquiet since you saw her ?

Ferd. I take no rest.

Hip. Just, just my disease.
Do you not wish you do not know for what ?

Ferd. O no ! I know too well for what I wish.

Hip. There, I confess, I differ from you, Sir :
But you desire she may be always with you ?

Ferd. I can have no felicity without her.

Hip. Just my condition ! alas, gentle Sir,
I'll pity you, and you shall pity me.

Ferd. I love so much, that if I have her not,
I find I cannot live.

Hip. How ! do you love her ?
And would you have her too ? that must not be :
For none but I must have her.

Ferd. But perhaps we do not love the same :
All Beauties are not pleasing alike to all.

Hip. Why are there more fair Women, Sir,
Besides that one I love ?

Ferd. That's a strange question. There are many more besides that Beauty which you love.

Hip. I will have all of that kind, if there be a hundred of 'em.

Ferd. But, noble Youth, you know not what you say.

Hip. Sir, they are things I love, I cannot be without 'em :
O, how I rejoyce ! more Women !
    Ferd. Sir, if you love, you must be ty'd to one.
    Hip. Ty'd ! how ty'd to her ?
    Ferd. To love none but her.
    Hip. But, Sir, I find it is against my nature.
I must love where I like, and I believe I may like all,
All that are fair : come ! bring me to this Woman,
For I must have her.
    Ferd. His simplicity   [*Aside.*
Is such, that I can scarce be angry with him,
Perhaps, sweet Youth, when you behold her,
You will find you do not love her.
    Hip. I find already I love, because she is another Woman.
    Ferd. You cannot love two Women both at once.
    Hip. Sure 'tis my duty to love all who do resemble
Her whom I've already seen.   I'll have as many as I can,
That are so good, and Angel like, as she I love.
And will have yours.
    Ferd. Pretty Youth, you cannot.
    Hip. I can do any thing for that I love.
    Ferd. I may, perhaps, by force, restrain you from it.
    Hip. Why do so if you can.   But either promise me
To love no Woman, or you must try your force.
    Ferd. I cannot help it, I must love.
    Hip. Well you may love, for *Prospero* taught me Friendship too : you
shall love me and other Men if you can find 'em, but all the Angel-women
shall be mine.
    Ferd. I must break off this Conference, or he will
Urge me else beyond what I can bear.
Sweet Youth ! some other time we will speak
Farther concerning both our loves ; at present
I am indispos'd with weariness and grief,
And would, if you are pleas'd, retire a while.
    Hip. Some other time be it ; but, Sir, remember
That I both seek and much intreat your friendship,
For next to Women, I find I can love you.
    Ferd. I thank you, Sir, I will consider of it.   [*Exit* Ferdinand.
    Hip. This stranger does insult, and comes into my
World to take those heavenly beauties from me,
Which I believe I am inspir'd to love,
And yet he said he did desire but one.
He would be poor in love, but I'll be rich :

I now perceive that *Prospero* was cunning;
For when he frighted me from Woman-kind,
Those precious things he for himself design'd.   [*Exit.*

ACT IV. SCENE I.

Cypress Trees and Cave.

Enter Prospero *and* Miranda.

Prosp. YOur suit has pity in't, and has prevail'd.
Within this Cave he lies, and you may see him:
But yet take heed; let Prudence be your Guide;
You must not stay, your visit must be short.   [*She's going.*
One thing I had forgot; insinuate into his mind
A kindness to that Youth, whom first you saw;
I would have Friendship grow betwixt 'em.
   Mir. You shall be obey'd in all things.
   Prosp. Be earnest to unite their very souls.
   Mir. I shall endeavour it.
   Prosp. This may secure *Hippolito* from that dark danger which my Art
forebodes; for Friendship does provide a double strength t' oppose the
assaults of Fortune.   [*Exit* Prospero.

Enter Ferdinand.

   Ferd. To be a Pris'ner where I dearly love, is but a double tye, a Link
of Fortune joyn'd to the Chain of Love; but not to see her, and yet to be
so near her, there's the hardship: I feel my self as on a Rack, stretch'd
out, and nigh the ground, on which I might have ease, yet cannot reach it.
   Mir. Sir! my Lord! where are you?
   Ferd. Is it your Voice, my Love? or do I dream?
   Mir. Speak softly, it is I.
   Ferd. O Heavenly Creature! ten times more gentle then your Father's
Cruel, how, on a sudden, all my griefs are vanish'd!
   Mir. How do you bear your Prison?
   Ferd. 'Tis my Palace while you are here, and love and silence wait upon
our wishes; do but think we chuse it, and 'tis what we would chuse.
   Mir. I'm sure what I would.
But how can I be certain that you love me?
Look to't; for I will die when you are false.
I've heard my Father tell of Maids, who dy'd,
And haunted their false Lovers with their Ghosts.

Ferd. Your Ghost must take another form to fright me,
This shape will be too pleasing : do I love you?
O Heaven! O Earth! bear witness to this sound,
If I prove false——

Mir. Oh hold, you shall not swear;
For Heav'n will hate you if you prove forsworn.

Ferd. Did I not love, I could no more endure this undeserv'd captivity, than I could wish to gain my freedom with the loss of you.

Mir. I am a fool to weep at what I'm glad of : but I have a suit to you, and that, Sir, shall be now the only trial of your love.

Ferd. Y'ave said enough, never to be deny'd, were it my life; for you have far o'rbid the price of all that humane life is worth.

Mir. Sir, 'tis to love one for my sake, who for his own deserves all the respect which you can ever pay him.

Ferd. You mean your Father : do not think his usage can make me hate him; when he gave you being, he then did that which cancell'd all these wrongs.

Mir. I meant not him, for that was a request, which if you love, I should not need to urge.

Ferd. Is there another whom I ought to love?
And love him for your sake?

Mir. Yes such a one, who, for his sweetness and his goodly shape, (if I, who am unskill'd in forms, may judge) I think can scarce be equall'd; 'Tis a Youth, a Stranger too as you are.

Ferd. Of such a graceful feature, and must I for your sake love?

Mir. Yes, Sir, do you scruple to grant the first request I ever made? he's wholly unacquainted with the World, and wants your Conversation. You should have compassion on so meer a stranger.

Ferd. Those need compassion whom you discommend, not whom you praise.

Mir. Come, you must love him for my sake : you shall.

Ferd. Must I for yours, and cannot for my own?
Either you do not love, or think that I do not :
But when you bid me love him, I must hate him.

Mir. Have I so far offended you already,
That he offends you onely for my sake?
Yet sure you would not hate him, if you saw
Him as I have done, so full of youth and beauty.

Ferd. O poison to my hopes!   [*Aside.*
When he did visit me, and I did mention this
Beauteous Creature to him, he did then tell me
He would have her.

Mir. Alas, what mean you?

Ferd. It is too plain : like most of her frail Sex, she's false,
But has not learn'd the art to hide it ;
Nature has done her part, she loves variety :
Why did I think that any Woman could be innocent,
Because she's young ?   No, no, their Nurses teach them
Change, when with two Nipples they divide their
Liking.
    Mir. I fear I have offended you, and yet I meant no harm :
But if you please to hear me——   [*A noise within.*
Heark, Sir ! now I am sure my Father comes, I know
His steps ; dear Love, retire a while, I fear
I've staid too long.
    Ferd. Too long indeed, and yet not long enough : Oh Jealousie !
Oh Love ! how you distract me ?   [*Exit* Ferdinand.
    Mir. He appears displeas'd with that young man, I know
Not why : but, till I find from whence his hate proceeds,
I must conceal it from my Father's knowledge,
For he will think that guiltless I have caus'd it ;
And suffer me no more to see my Love   [*Enter* Prospero.
    Prosp. Now I have been indulgent to your wish,
You have seen the Prisoner.
    Mir. Yes.
    Prosp. And he spake to you ?
    Mir. He spoke ; but he receiv'd short answers from me.
    Prosp. How like you his converse ?
    Mir. At second sight.
A Man does not appear so rare a Creature.
    Prosp, aside. I find she loves him much because she hides it.
Love teaches cunning even to innocence.   Well go in.
    Mir. aside. Forgive me, truth, for thus disguising thee ; if I can make
him think I do not love the stranger much, he'l let me see him oftner.
                           [*Exit* Miranda.
    Prosp. Stay ! stay——I had forgot to ask her what she had said
Of young *Hippolito !* Oh ! here he comes ! and with him
My *Dorinda.* I'll not be seen, let

              Enter Hippolito *and* Dorinda.
Their loves grow in secret.   [*Exit* Prospero.
    Hip. But why are you so sad ?
    Dor. But why are you so joyful ?
    Hip. I have within me all the various Musick of
The Woods.   Since last I saw you, I have heard brave news !
I'll tell you, and make you joyful for me.

Dor. Sir, when I saw you firſt, I, through my Eyes, drew
Something in, I know not what it is;
But ſtill it entertains me with such thoughts,
As makes me doubtful whether joy becomes me.

Hip. Pray believe me;
As I'm a Man, I'll tell you blessed news,
I have heard there are more Women in the World,
As fair as you are too.

Dor. Is this your news? you see it moves not me.

Hip. And I'll have 'em all.

Dor. What will become of me then?

Hip. I'll have you too.
But are not you acquainted with these Women?

Dor. I never saw but one.

Hip. Is there but one here?
This is a base poor World, I'll go to th' other;
I've heard Men have abundance of 'em there.
But pray where is that one Woman?

Dor. Who, my Siſter?

Hip. Is she your Siſter? I'm glad o' that: you shall help me to her,
and I'll love you for't.   [*Offers to take her hand.*

Dor. Away! I will not have you touch my hand.
My Father's counsel which enjoyn'd reservedness,   [*Aside.*
Was not in vain, I see.

Hip. What makes you shun me?

Dor. You need not care, you'l have my Siſter's hand.

Hip. Why, muſt not he who touches hers, touch yours?

Dor. You mean to love her too.

Hip. Do not you love her?
Then why should not I do so?

Dor. She is my Siſter, and therefore I muſt love her:
But you cannot love both of us.

Hip. I warrant you I can:
Oh that you had more Siſters!

Dor. You may love her, but then I'l not love you.

Hip. O but you muſt;
One is enough for you, but not for me.

Dor. My Siſter told me she had seen another;
A Man like you, and she lik'd onely him;
Therefore if one muſt be enough for her,
He is that one, and then you cannot have her.

Hip. If she like him, she may like both of us.

Dor. But how if I should change and like that Man?

Would you be willing to permit that change?
Hip. No, for you lik'd me first.
Dor. So you did me.
Hip. But I would never have you see that Man;
I cannot bear it.
Dor. I'l see neither of you.
Hip. Yes, me you may, for we are now acquainted;
But he's the Man of whom your Father warn'd you:
O! he's a terrible, huge, monstrous Creature,
I am but a Woman to him.
Dor. I will see him,
Except you'l promise not to see my Sister.
Hip. Yes, for your sake, I needs must see your Sister.
Dor. But she's a terrible, huge Creature too; if I were not
Her Sister, she would eat me; therefore take heed.
Hip. I heard that she was fair, and like you.
Dor. No, indeed, she's like my Father, with a great Beard,
'Twould fright you to look on her,
Therefore that Man and she may go together,
They are fit for no body, but one another.
Hip. looking in. Yonder he comes with glaring Eyes, fly! fly! before
he sees you.
Dor. Must we part so soon?
Hip. Y' are a lost Woman if you see him.
Dor. I would not willingly be lost, for fear you
Should not find me. I'll avoid him.   [*Exit* Dorinda.
Hip. She fain would have deceived me, but I know her
Sister must be fair, for she's a Woman;
All of a kind that I have seen are like to one
Another: all the Creatures of the Rivers and
The Woods are so.

Enter Ferdinand.

Ferd. O! well encounter'd, you are the happy Man!
Y' have got the hearts of both the beauteous Women.
Hip. How! Sir? pray, are you sure on't?
Ferd. One of 'em charg'd me to love you for her sake.
Hip. Then I must have her.
Ferd. No, not till I am dead.
Hip. How dead? what's that? but whatsoe'r it be,
I long to have her.
Ferd. Time and my grief may make me die.
Hip. But for a Friend you should make haste; I ne'r ask'd

Any thing of you before.

Ferd. I see your Ignorance;
And therefore will instruct you in my meaning.
The Woman, whom I love, saw you, and lov'd you.
Now, Sir, if you love her, you'l cause my death.

Hip. Be sure I'll do't then.

Ferd. But I am your friend;
And I request you that you would not love her.

Hip. When Friends request unreasonable things,
Sure th' are to be deny'd: you say she's fair,
And I must love all who are fair; for, to tell
You a secret, Sir, which I have lately found
Within my self; they 're all made for me.

Ferd. That's but a fond conceit: you are made for one,
And one for you.

Hip. You cannot tell me, Sir,
I know I'm made for twenty hundred Women.
(I mean if there so many be i' th' World)
So that if once I see her, I shall love her.

Ferd. Then do not see her.

Hip. Yes, Sir, I must see her.
For I would fain have my heart beat again,
Just as it did when I first saw her Sister.

Ferd. I find I must not let you see her then.

Hip. How will you hinder me?

Ferd. By force of Arms.

Hip. By force of Arms?
My Arms perhaps may be as strong as yours.

Ferd. He's still so ignorant that I pity him, and fain
Would avoid Force: pray do not see her, she was
Mine first; you have no right to her.

Hip. I have not yet consider'd what is right, but, Sir,
I know my inclinations are to love all Women:
And I have been taught, that to dissemble what I
Think, is base. In honour then of truth, I must
Declare that I do love, and I will see your Woman.

Ferd. Wou'd you be willing I should see and love your
Woman, and endeavour to seduce her from that
Affection which she vow'd to you?

Hip. I wou'd not you should do it, but if she should
Love you best, I cannot hinder her.
But, Sir, for fear she shou'd, I will provide against
The worst, and try to get your Woman.

Ferd. But I pretend no claim at all to yours ;
Besides you are more beautiful than I,
And fitter to allure unpractis'd hearts.
Therefore I once more beg you will not see her.

 Hip. I'm glad you let me know I have such beauty,
If that will get me Women, they shall have it
As far as e'r 'twill go : I'll never want 'em.

 Ferd. Then since you have refus'd this act of friendship,
Provide your self a sword, for we must fight.

 Hip. A sword, what's that ?

 Ferd. Why such a thing as this.

 Hip. What should I do with it ?

 Ferd. You must stand thus, and push against me,
While I push at you, till one of us fall dead.

 Hip. This is brave sport ;
But we have no Swords growing in our World.

 Ferd. What shall we do then to decide our quarrel ?

 Hip. We'll take the Sword by turns, and fight with it.

 Ferd. Strange Ignorance ! you must defend your life,
And so must I ; but since you have no Sword,
Take this ; for in a corner of my Cave   [*Gives him his Sword.*
I found a rusty one ; perhaps 'twas his who keeps
Me Pris'ner here : that I will fit :
When next we meet, prepare your self to fight.

 Hip. Make haste then, this shall ne'r be yours agen.
I mean to fight with all the Men I meet, and
When they are dead, their Women shall be mine.

 Ferd. I see you are unskilful ; I desire not to take
Your Life, but, if you please, we'll fight on
These conditions ; He who first draws bloud,
Or who can take the others Weapon from him,
Shall be acknowledg'd as the Conquerour,
And both the Women shall be his.

 Hip. Agreed,
And ev'ry day I'l fight for two more with you.

 Ferd. But win these first.

 Hip. I'll warrant you I'll push you.   [*Exeunt severally.*

SCENE II. *The Wild Island.*

Enter Trincalo, Caliban, Sycorax.

Calib. My Lord, I see 'em coming yonder.
Trinc. Whom ?

Calib. The starv'd Prince, and his two thirsty Subjects,
That would have our Liquor.

Trinc. If thou wert a Monster of parts, I would make thee
My Master of Ceremonies, to conduct 'em in.
The Devil take all Dunces, thou hast lost a brave
Employment by not being a Linguist, and for want
Of behaviour.

Syc. My Lord, shall I go meet 'em? I'll be kind to all of 'em,
Just as I am to thee.

Trinc. No, that's against the fundamental Laws of my Dukedom: you
are in a high place, Spouse, and must give good Example. Here they
come, we'll put on the gravity of Statesmen, and be very dull, that we may
be held wise.

Enter Stephano, Ventoso, Mustacho.

Vent. Duke *Trincalo*, we have consider'd.

Trinc. Peace or War?

Must. Peace, and the Butt.

Steph. I come now as a private Person, and promise to live peaceably
under your Government.

Trinc. You shall enjoy the benefits of Peace; and the first fruits of
it, amongst all Civil Nations, is to be drunk for joy: *Caliban*, skink
about.

Steph. I long to have a Rowse to her Graces Health, and to the *Haunse
in Kelder*, or rather Haddock in *Kelder*, for I ghess it will be half
Fish.   [*Aside.*

Trinc. Subject *Stephano*, here's to thee; and let old quarrels be drown'd
in this draught.   [*Drinks.*

Steph. Great Magistrate, here's thy Sister's health to thee.
                                              [*Drinks to* Caliban.

Syc. He shall not drink of that immortal Liquor,
My Lord, let him drink Water.

Trinc. O Sweet-heart, you must not shame your self to day.
Gentlemen Subjects, pray bear with her good Huswifry:
She wants a little breeding, but she's hearty.

Must. *Ventoso*, here's to thee. Is it not better to pierce the Butt, than
to quarrel and pierce one another's bellies?

Vent. Let it come, Boy.

Trinc. Now would I lay greatness aside, and shake my heels, if I had
but Musick.

Calib. O my Lord! my Mother left us in her Will a hundred Spirits to
attend us, Devils of all sorts, some great roaring Devils, and some little
singing Sprights.

Syc. Shall we call? and thou shalt hear them in the air.

Trinc. I accept the motion: let us have our Mother-in-law's Legacy immediately.

Calib. sings. *We want Musick, we want Mirth,*
   Up, Dam, and cleave the Earth:
   We have now no Lords that wrong us,
   Send thy merry Sprights among us.

Trinc. What a merry Tyrant am I, to have my
Musick, and pay nothing for't?
   [*A Table rises, and four Spirits with Wine and Meat enter,*
      placing it, as they dance, on the Table: The Dance ended,
      the Bottles vanish, and the Table sinks agen.

Vent. The Bottle's drunk.

Muſt. Then the Bottle's a weak shallow Fellow, if it be drunk first.

Trinc. Stephano, give me thy hand,
Thou haſt been a Rebel, but here's to thee: [*Drinks.*
Prithee why should we quarrel? shall I swear
Two Oaths? By Bottle, and by Butt I love thee:
In witness whereof I drink soundly.

Steph. Your Grace shall find there's no love loſt,
For I will pledge you soundly.

Trinc. Thou haſt been a false Rebel, but that's all one;
Pledge my Grace faithfully.

Trinc. Caliban,
Go to the Butt, and tell me how it sounds:
Peer *Stephano,* doſt thou love me?

Steph. I love your Grace, and all your Princely Family.

Trinc. 'Tis no matter if thou lov'ſt me; hang my Family:
Thou art my Friend, prithee tell me what
Thou think'ſt of my Princess?

Steph. I look on her, as on a very noble Princess.

Trinc. Noble? indeed she had a Witch to her Mother, and the Witches are of great Families in *Lapland,* but the Devil was her Father, and I have heard of the Mounsor *De-Viles* in *France;* but look on her Beauty, is she a fit Wife for Duke *Trincalo?* mark her Behaviour too, shee's tipling yonder with the Serving-men.

Steph. An't please your Grace, she's somewhat homely, but that's no blemish in a Princess. She is virtuous.

Trinc. Umph! Virtuous! I am loath to disparage her;
But thou art my Friend, canſt thou be close?

Steph. As a ſtopt Bottle, an't please your Grace.

Enter Caliban *agen with a Bottle.*

Trinc. Why then I'll tell thee, I found her an hour ago under an Elder-Tree, upon a sweet Bed of Nettles, singing Tory, Rory, and Ranthum, Scantum, with her own Natural Brother.

Steph. O Jew! make love in her own Tribe?

Trinc. But 'tis no matter, to tell thee true, I marri'd her to be a great Man and so forth: but make no words on't, for I care not who knows it, and so here's to thee agen, give me the Bottle, *Caliban!* did you knock the Butt? how does it sound?

Calib. It sounds as though it had a noise within.

Trinc. I fear the Butt begins to rattle in the throat, and is departing: give me the Bottle.   [*Drinks.*

Muſt. A short life and a merry, I say.   [Steph. *whispers* Sycorax.

Syc. But did he tell you so?

Steph. He said you were as ugly as your Mother, and that he Marri'd you onely to get possession of the Island.

Syc. My Mothers Devils fetch him for't.

Steph. And your Fathers too, hem! Skink about his Graces health agen. O if you will but caſt an eye of pity upon me——

Syc. I will caſt two Eyes of pity on thee, I love thee more than Haws, or Black-berries, I have a hoard of Wildings in the Moss, my Brother knows not of 'em; but I'll bring thee where they are.

Steph. *Trincalo* was but my Man when time was.

Syc. Wert thou his God, and didſt thou give him Liquor?

Steph. I gave him Brandy, and drunk Sack my self; wilt thou leave him, and thou shalt be my Princess?

Syc. If thou canſt make me glad with this Liquor.

Steph. I'll warrant thee we'll ride into the Countrey where it grows.

Syc. How wilt thou carry me thither?

Steph. Upon a Hackney-Devil of thy Mothers.

Trinc. What's that you will do? hah! I hope you have not betray'd me? how does my Pigs-nye?   [*To* Sycorax.

Syc. Be gone! thou shalt not be my Lord, thou say'ſt I'm ugly.

Trinc. Did you tell her so —— hah! he's a Rogue, do not believe him, Chuck.

Steph. The foul words were yours: I will not eat 'em for you.

Trinc. I see if once a Rebel, then ever a Rebel. Did I receive thee into Grace for this? I will correct thee with my Royal Hand.

                                             [*Strikes* Stephano.

Syc. Doſt thou hurt my Love?   [*Flies at* Trincalo.

Trinc. Where are our Guards? Treason! Treason!

                              Vent. Muſt. Calib. *run betwixt.*

Vent. Who took up Arms first, the Prince or the People?

Trinc. This false Traitor has corrupted the Wife of my Bosom.

             [Whispers Mustacho *hastily.*

Mustacho, strike on my side, and thou shalt be my Vice-Roy.

 Must. I'm against Rebels! *Ventoso,* obey your Vice-Roy.

 Vent. You a Vice-Roy?   *[They two fight off from the rest.*

 Steph. Hah! Hector Monster! do you stand neuter?

 Calib. Thou wouldst drink my Liquor, I will not help thee.

 Syc. 'Twas his doing that I had such a Husband, but I'll claw him.

     [Syc. and Calib. *fight,* Syc. *beating him off the Stage.*

 Trinc. The whole Nation is up in Arms, and shall I stand idle?

    [Trincalo beats off Stephano *to the door. Exit* Stephano.

I'll not pursue too far,

For fear the Enemy should rally agen, and surprise my Butt in the Cittadel;

well, I must be rid of my Lady *Trincalo,* she will be in the Fashion else;

first, Cuckold her Husband, and then sue for a Separation, to get

Alimony.   *[Exit.*

SCENE III. *The Cypress-trees and Cave.*

Enter Ferdinand, Hippolito, *(with their swords drawn).*

 Ferd. Come, Sir, our Cave affords no choice of place,

But the ground's firm and even: are you ready?

 Hip. As ready as your self, Sir.

 Ferd. You remember on what conditions we must fight?

Who first receives a wound is to submit.

 Hip. Come, come, this loses time; now for the

Women, Sir.   *[They fight a little,* Ferdinand *hurts him.*

 Ferd. Sir, you are wounded.

 Hip. No.

 Ferd. Believe your bloud.

 Hip. I feel no hurt, no matter for my bloud.

 Ferd. Remember our Conditions.

 Hip. I'll not leave, till my Sword hits you too.

        [Hip. presses on, Ferd. *retires and wards.*

 Ferd. I'm loth to kill you, you are unskilful, Sir.

 Hip. You beat aside my Sword, but let it come as near

As yours, and you shall see my skill.

 Ferd. You faint for loss of bloud, I see you stagger.

Pray, Sir, retire.

 Hip. No! I will ne'r go back——

Methinks the Cave turns round, I cannot find ——

 Ferd. Your Eyes begin to dazle.

Hip. Why do you swim so, and dance about me?
Stand but still till I have made one thrust.　　[Hippolito *thrusts and falls*.
Ferd. O help, help, help!
Unhappy Man! what have I done?
　Hip. I'm going to a cold sleep, but when I wake,
I'll fight agen. Pray stay for me.　　　　　　　　　　[*Swounds*.
　Ferd. He's gone! he's gone! O stay, sweet lovely Youth!
Help! help!

Enter Prospero.

　Prosp. What dismal noise is that?
　Ferd. O see, Sir, see!
What mischief my unhappy hand has wrought.
　Prosp. Alas! how much in vain doth feeble Art endeavour
To resist the will of Heaven?　　　　　　　[*Rubs* Hippolito.
He's gone for ever; O thou cruel Son of an
Inhumane Father! all my designs are ruin'd
And unravell'd by this blow.
No pleasure now is left me but revenge.
　Ferd. Sir, if you knew my innocence ——
　Prosp. Peace, peace,
Can thy excuses give me back his life?
What, *Ariel?* sluggish Spirit, where art thou?

Enter Ariel.

　Ariel. Here, at thy beck, my Lord.
　Prosp. I, now thou com'st, when Fate is past and not to be
Recall'd. Look there, and glut the malice of
Thy Nature, for as thou art thy self, thou
Canst not but be glad to see young Virtue
Nipt i' th' Blossom.
　Ariel. My Lord, the *Being* high above can witness
I am not glad; we Airy Spirits are not of a temper
So malicious as the Earthy,
But of a Nature more approaching good.
For which we meet in swarms, and often combat
Betwixt the Confines of the Air and Earth.
　Prosp. Why did'st thou not prevent, at least foretel,
This fatal action then?
　Ariel. Pardon, great Sir,
I meant to do it, but I was forbidden
By the ill Genius of *Hippolito*,
Who came and threaten'd me, if I disclos'd it,

To bind me in the bottom of the Sea,
Far from the lightsome Regions of the Air,
(My Native Fields) above a hundred years.
 Prosp. I'll Chain thee in the North for thy neglect,
Within the burning Bowels of Mount *Heila :*
I'll singe thy airy Wings with sulph'rous flames,
And choak thy tender nostrils with blew smoak,
At ev'ry Hick-up of the belching Mountain,
Thou shalt be lifted up to taste fresh air,
And then fall down agen.
 Ariel. Pardon, dread Lord.
 Prosp. No more of pardon then just Heav'n intends thee
Shalt thou e'r find from me : hence ! fly with speed,
Unbind the Charms which hold this Murtherer's
Father, and bring him, with my Brother, streight
Before me.
 Ariel. Mercy, my potent Lord, and I'll outfly thy thought. [*Exit* Ariel.
 Ferd. O Heavens ! what words are those I heard ?
Yet cannot see who spoke 'em : sure the Woman
Whom I lov'd was like this, some aiery Vision.
 Prosp. No, Murd'rer, she's, like thee, of mortal mould,
But much too pure to mix with thy black Crimes ;
Yet she had faults, and must be punish'd for 'em.
Miranda and *Dorinda !* where are ye ?
The will of Heaven's accomplish'd : I have
Now no more to fear, and nothing left to hope,
Now you may enter.

    Enter Miranda *and* Dorinda.

 Mir. My Love ! is it permitted me to see you once agen ?
 Prosp. You come to look your last ; I will
For ever take him from your eyes.
But, on my blessing, speak not, nor approach him.
 Dor. Pray, Father, is not this my Sister's Man ?
He has a noble form ; but yet he's not so excellent
As my *Hippolito.*
 Prosp. Alas, poor Girl, thou hast no Man : look yonder ;
There's all of him that's left.
 Dor. Why, was there ever any more of him ?
He lies asleep, Sir, shall I waken him ?
      [*She kneels by* Hippolito, *and jogs him.*
 Ferd. Alas ! he's never to be wak'd agen.
 Dor. My Love, my Love ! will you not speak to me ?

I fear you have displeas'd him, Sir, and now
He will not answer me, he's dumb and cold too ;
But I'll run ſtreight, and make a fire to warm him. [*Exit* Dorinda *running.*

Enter Alonzo, Gonzalo, Antonio, Ariel (*invisible.*)

Alonz. Never were Beaſts so hunted into Toils,
As we have been pursu'd by dreadful shapes.
But is not that my Son ? O *Ferdinand !*
If thou art not a Ghoſt, let me embrace thee.

Ferd. My Father ! O siniſter happiness ! Is it
Decreed I should recover you alive, juſt in that
Fatal hour when this brave Youth is loſt in Death,
And by my hand ?

Ant. Heaven ! what new wonder's this ?

Gonz. This Isle is full of nothing else.

Proſp. You ſtare upon me as
You ne'r had seen me ; have fifteen years
So loſt me to your knowledge, that you retain
No memory of *Proſpero ?*

Gonz. The good old Duke of *Millain !*

Proſp. I wonder less, that thou, *Antonio,* know'ſt me not,
Because thou didſt long since forget I was thy Brother,
Else I never had been here.

Ant. Shame choaks my words.

Alonz. And wonder mine.

Proſp. For you, usurping Prince,   [*To* Alonzo.
Know, by my Art, you were Shipwrack'd on this Isle,
Where, after I a while had punish'd you, my vengeance
Wou'd have ended, I design'd to match that Son
Of yours, with this my Daughter.

Alonz. Pursue it ſtill, I am moſt willing to't.

Proſp. So am not I. No Marriages can prosper
Which are with Murderers made ; Look on that Corps,
This, whilſt he liv'd, was young *Hippolito,* that
Infant Duke of *Mantua,* Sir, whom you, expos'd
With me ; and here I bred him up, till that bloud-thirſty
Man, that *Ferdinand* ——
But why do I exclaim on him, when Juſtice calls
To unsheath her Sword againſt his guilt ?

Alonz. What do you mean ?

Proſp. To execute Heav'ns Laws.
Here I am plac'd by Heav'n, here I am Prince,
Though you have dispossess'd me of my *Millain.*

(254)

Bloud calls for bloud; your *Ferdinand* shall die,
And I, in bitterness, have sent for you,
To have the sudden joy of seeing him alive,
And then the greater grief to see him die.

Alonz. And think'st thou I, or these, will tamely stand,
To view the Execution?   [*Lays hand upon his Sword.*

Ferd. Hold, dear Father! I cannot suffer you
T' attempt against his life, who gave her being
Whom I love.

Prosp. Nay then appear my Guards —— I thought no more to use
their aid; (I'm curs'd because I us'd it)   [*He stamps, and many Spirits appear.*
But they are now the Ministers of Heaven,
Whilst I revenge this Murder.

Alonz. Have I for this found thee, my Son, so soon, agen,
To lose thee? *Antonio, Gonzalo,* speak for pity:

Ferd. to Mir. Adieu, my fairest Mistriss.

Mir. Now I can hold no longer; I must speak
Though I am loth to disobey you, Sir,
Be not so cruel to the Man I love,
Or be so kind to let me suffer with him.

Ferd. Recal that Pray'r, or I shall wish to live,
Though death be all the mends that I can make.

Prosp. This night I will allow you, *Ferdinand*, to fit
You for your death, that Cave's your Prison.

Alonz. Ah, *Prospero!* hear me speak. You are a Father,
Look on my Age, and look upon his Youth.

Prosp. No more! all you can say is urg'd in vain,
I have no room for pity left within me.
Do you refuse? help, *Ariel*, with your Fellows,
To drive 'em in; *Alonzo* and his Son bestow in
Yonder Cave, and here *Gonzalo* shall with
Antonio lodge.   [*Spirits drive 'em in, as they are appointed.*

Enter Dorinda.

Dor. Sir, I have made a fire, shall he be warm'd?

Prosp. He's dead, and vital warmth will ne'r return.

Dor. Dead, Sir, what's that?

Prosp. His Soul has left his Body.

Dor. When will it come agen?

Prosp. O never, never!
He must be laid in Earth, and there consume.

Dor. He shall not lie in Earth, you do not know
How well he loves me: indeed he'l come agen;

He told me he would go a little while,
But promis'd me he would not tarry long.
  Prosp. He's murder'd by the Man who lov'd your Sister.
Now both of you may see what 'tis to break
A Father's Precept; you would needs see Men, and by
That sight are made for ever wretched.
Hippolito is dead, and *Ferdinand* must die
For murdering him.
  Mir. Have you no pity?
  Prosp. Your disobedience has so much incens'd me, that
I this night can leave no blessing with you.
Help to convey the Body to my Couch,
Then leave me to mourn over it alone.

> [*They bear off the Body of* Hippolito.

Enter Miranda *and* Dorinda *again.* Ariel *behind 'em.*

  Ariel. I've been so chid for my neglect, by *Prospero,*
That I must now watch all, and be unseen.
  Mir. Sister, I say agen, 'twas long of you
That all this mischief happen'd.
  Dor. Blame not me for your own fault, your
Curiosity brought me to see the Man.
  Mir. You safely might have seen him, and retir'd, but
You wou'd needs go near him, and converse, you may
Remember my father call'd me thence, and I call'd you.
  Dor. That was your envy, Sister, not your love;
You call'd me thence, because you could not be
Alone with him your self; but I am sure my
Man had never gone to Heaven so soon, but
That yours made him go.   [*Crying.*
  Mir. Sister, I could not wish that either of 'em shou'd
Go to Heaven without us, but it was his fortune,
And you must be satisfi'd?
  Dor. I'll not be satisfi'd: my father says he'll make
Your Man as cold as mine is now, and when he
Is made cold, my Father will not let you strive
To make him warm agen.
  Mir. In spite of you mine never shall be cold.
  Dor. I'm sure 'twas he that made me miserable,
And I will be reveng'd. Perhaps you think 'tis
Nothing to lose a Man.
  Mir. Yes, but there is some difference betwixt
My *Ferdinand,* and your *Hippolito.*

Dor. I, there's your judgment. Your's is the oldest
Man I ever saw, except it were my Father.
 Mir. Sister, no more. It is not comely in a Daughter,
When she says her Father's old.
 Dor. But why do I stay here, whilst my cold Love
Perhaps may want me?
I'll pray my Father to make yours cold too.
 Mir. Sister, I'l never sleep with you again.
 Dor. I'll never more meet in a Bed with you,
But lodge on the bare ground, and watch my Love.
 Mir. And at the entrance of that Cave I'll lie,
And eccho to each blast of wind a sigh.
     [Exeunt severally, looking discontentedly on one another.
 Ariel. Harsh discord reigns throughout this fatal Isle,
At which good Angels mourn, ill spirits smile ;
Old *Prospero* by his Daughters robb'd of rest,
Has in displeasure left 'em both unblest.
Unkindly they abjure each others Bed,
To save the living, and revenge the dead.
Alonzo and his Son are Pris'ners made,
And good *Gonzalo* does their Crimes upbraid.
Antonio and *Gonzalo* disagree,
And wou'd, though in one Cave, at distance be.
The Seamen all that cursed Wine have spent,
Which still renew'd their thirst of Government ;
And wanting subjects for the food of Pow'r,
Each wou'd to rule alone the rest devour.
The Monsters *Sycorax* and *Caliban*,
More monstrous grow by passions learn'd from Man.
Even I not fram'd of warring Elements,
Partake and suffer in these discontents.
Why shou'd a Mortal by Enchantments hold
In Chains a Spirit of Ætherial mold?
Accursed Magick we our selves have taught,
And our own pow'r has our subjection wrought!   *[Exit.*

ACT V.

Enter Prospero *and* Miranda.

Prosp. YOU beg in vain ; I cannot pardon him,
He has offended Heaven.
 Mir. Then let Heaven punish him.
 Prosp. It will by me.
 Mir. Grant him at least some respite for my sake.
 Prosp. I by deferring Justice should incense the Deity
Against my self and you.
 Mir. Yet I have heard you say, The Powers above are slow
In punishing, and shou'd not you resemble them ?
 Prosp. The Argument is weak, but I want time
To let you see your errours ; retire, and, if you love him,
Pray for him.   [*He's going.*
 Mir. And can you be his Judge and Executioner ?
 Prosp. I cannot force *Gonzalo*, or my Brother, much
Less the Father to destroy the Son ; it must
Be then the Monster *Caliban*, and he's not here ;
But *Ariel* strait shall fetch him.

Enter Ariel.

 Ariel. My Potent Lord, before thou call'st, I come,
To serve thy will.
 Prosp. Then, Spirit, fetch me here my salvage Slave.
 Ariel. My Lord, it does not need.
 Prosp. Art thou then prone to mischief, Wilt thou be thy self the
Executioner ?
 Ariel. Think better of thy Aiery Minister, who,
For thy sake, unbidden, this night has flown
O'r almost all the habitable World.
 Prosp. But to what purpose was all thy diligence ?
 Ariel. When I was chidden by my mighty Lord, for my
Neglect of young *Hippolito*, I went to view
His Body, and soon found his Soul was but retir'd,
Not sally'd out : then I collected
The best of Simples underneath the Moon,
The best of Balms, and to the wound apply'd
The healing juice of vulnerary Herbs.
His onely danger was his loss of bloud, but now
He's wak'd, my Lord, and just this hour

(258)

He must be dress'd again, as I have done it.
Anoint the Sword which pierc'd him with this
Weapon-Salve, and wrap it close from Air till
I have time to visit him again.

    Prosp. Thou art my faithful Servant,
It shall be done, be it your task, *Miranda*, because your
Sister is not present here, while I go visit your
Dear *Ferdinand*, from whom I will a while conceal
This news, that it may be more welcome.

    Mir. I obey you, and with a double duty, Sir : for now
You twice have given me Life.

    Prosp. My *Ariel*, follow me.   [*Exeunt severally.*
            [Hippolito *discover'd on a Couch,* Dorinda *by him.*

    Dor. How do you find your self ?

    Hip. I'm somewhat cold, can you not draw me nearer
To the Sun ? I am too weak to walk.

    Dor. My Love, I'll try.   [*She draws the Chair nearer the Audience.*
I thought you never would have walk'd agen,
They told me you were gone away to Heaven ;
Have you been there ?

    Hip. I know not where I was.

    Dor. I will not leave till you promise me you
Will not die agen.

    Hip. Indeed I will not.

    Dor. You must not go to Heav'n, unless we go together ;
For I've heard my Father say, that we must strive
To be each others guide, the way to it will else
Be difficult, especially to those who are so young.
But I much wonder what it is to die.

    Hip. Sure 'tis to dream, a kind of breathless sleep,
When once the Soul's gone out.

    Dor. What is the Soul ?

    Hip. A small blew thing, that runs about within us.

    Dor. Then I have seen it in a frosty Morning run
Smoaking from my mouth.

    Hip. But, dear *Dorinda*,
What is become of him who fought with me ?

    Dor. O, I can tell you joyful news of him,
My Father means to make him die to day,
For what he did to you.

    Hip. That must not be, my dear *Dorinda ;* go and beg your
Father, he may not die ; it was my fault he hurt me,
I urg'd him to it first.

Dor. But if he live, he'll never leave killing you.

Hip. O no! I just remember when I fell asleep, I heard
Him calling me a great way off, and crying over me as
You wou'd do; besides we have no cause of quarrel now.

Dor. Pray how began your difference first?

Hip. I fought with him for all the Women in the World.

Dor. That hurt you had was justly sent from Heaven,
For wishing to have any more but me.

Hip. Indeed I think it was, but I repent it, the fault
Was only in my bloud, for now 'tis gone, I find
I do not love so many.

Dor. In confidence of this, I'l beg my Father, that he
May live; I'm glad the naughty bloud, that made
You love so many, is gone out.

Hip. My dear, go quickly, lest you come too late.   [*Exit*. Dor.

Enter Miranda *at the other door, with* Hippolito's
Sword wrapt up.

Hip. Who's this who looks so fair and beautiful, as
Nothing but *Dorinda* can surpass her? O!
I believe it is that Angel, Woman,
Whom she calls Sister.

Mir. Sir, I am sent hither to dress your wound;
How do you find your strength?

Hip. Fair Creature, I am faint with loss of bloud.

Mir. I'm sorry for't.

Hip. Indeed and so am I, for if I had that bloud, I then
Should find a great delight in loving you.

Mir. But, Sir, I am another's, and your love is given
Already to my Sister.

Hip. Yet I find that, if you please, I can love still a little.

Mir. I cannot be unconstant, nor shou'd you.

Hip. O my wound pains me.

Mir. I am come to ease you.   [*She unwraps the Sword.*

Hip. Alas! I feel the cold Air come to me,
My wound shoots worse than ever.   [*She wipes and anoints the Sword.*

Mir. Does it still grieve you?

Hip. Now methinks there's something laid just upon it.

Mir. Do you find no ease?

Hip. Yes, yes, upon the sudden all the pain
Is leaving me: Sweet Heaven, how I am eas'd!

Enter Ferdinand *and* Dorinda *to them.*

Ferd. (to Dor.) Madam, I must confess my life is yours,
I owe it to your generosity.

Dor. I am o'rjoy'd my Father lets you live, and proud
Of my good fortune, that he gave your life to me.

Mir. How? gave his life to her!

Hip. Alas! I think she said so, and he said he ow'd it
To her generosity.

Ferd. But is not that your Sister with *Hippolito?*

Dor. So kind already?

Ferd. I came to welcome life, and I have met the
Cruellest of deaths.

Hip. My dear *Dorinda* with another man?

Dor. Sister, what bus'ness have you here?

Mir. You see I dress *Hippolito.*

Dor. Y' are very charitable to a Stranger.

Mir. You are not much behind in charity, to beg a pardon
For a Man, whom you scarce ever saw before.

Dor. Henceforward let your Surgery alone, for I had
Rather he should die, than you should cure his wound.

Mir. And I wish *Ferdinand* had dy'd before
He ow'd his life to your entreaty.

Ferd. (to Hip.) Sir, I'm glad you are so well recover'd, you
Keep your humour still to have all Women.

Hip. Not all, Sir, you except one of the number,
Your new Love there, *Dorinda.*

Mir. Ah *Ferdinand!* can you become inconstant?
If I must lose you, I had rather death should take
You from me, than you take your self.

Ferd. And if I might have chosen, I would have wish'd
That death from *Prospero,* and not this from you.

Dor. I, now I find why I was sent away,
That you might have my Sister's Company.

Hip. *Dorinda,* kill me not with your unkindness,
This is too much, first to be false your self,
And then accuse me too.

Ferd. We all accuse each other, and each one denies their guilt,
I should be glad it were a mutual errour.
And therefore, first, to clear my self from fault,
Madam, I beg your pardon, while I say I onely love
Your Sister. [*To* Dorinda

Mir. O blest word!
I'm sure I love no Man but *Ferdinand.*
 Dor. Nor I, Heaven knows, but my *Hippolito.*
 Hip. I never knew I lov'd so much; before I fear'd
Dorinda's Constancy, but now I am convinc'd that
I lov'd none but her, because none else can
Recompense her loss.
 Ferd. 'Twas happy then we had this little trial.
But how we all so much mistook, I know not.
 Mir. I have only this to say in my defence: my Father sent
Me hither, to attend the wounded Stranger.
 Dor. And *Hippolito* sent me to beg the life of *Ferdinand.*
 Ferd. From such small errours left at first unheeded,
Have often sprung sad accidents in love:
But see, our Fathers and our Friends are come
To mix their joys with ours.

    Enter Prospero, Alonzo, Antonio, Gonzalo.

 Alon. (*to Prosp.*) Let it no more be thought of, your purpose,
Though it was severe, was just. In losing *Ferdinand*
I should have mourn'd, but could not have complain'd.
 Prosp. Sir, I am glad kind Heaven decreed it otherwise.
 Dor. O wonder!
How many goodly Creatures are there here!
How beauteous Mankind is!
 Hip. O brave new World, that has such People in't!
 Alon. (*to Ferd.*) Now all the blessings of a glad Father
Compass thee about,
And make thee happy in thy beauteous choice.
 Gonz. I've inward wept, or should have spoken e'r this.
Look down, sweet Heaven, and on this Couple drop
A blessed Crown. For it is you chalk'd out the
Way which brought us hither.
 Ant. Though penitence forc'd by necessity can scarce
Seem real, yet, dearest Brother, I have hope
My bloud may plead for pardon with you; I resign
Dominion, which, 'tis true, I could not keep,
But Heaven knows too, I would not.
 Prosp. All past crimes I bury in the joy of this
Blessed day.
 Alonz. And that I may not be behind in Justice, to this
Young Prince I render back his Dukedom,

(262)

And, as the Duke of *Mantua*, thus salute him.

Hip. What is it that you render back ? methinks
You give me nothing.

Prosp. You are to be Lord of a great People,
And o're Towns and Cities.

Hip. And shall these People be all Men and Women ?

Gonz. Yes, and shall call you Lord.

Hip. Why then I'll live no longer in a Prison, but
Have a whole Cave to my self hereafter.

Prosp. And that your happiness may be compleat,
I give you my *Dorinda* for your Wife, she shall
Be yours for ever, when the Priest has made you one.

Hip. How can he make us one ? shall I grow to her ?

Prosp. By saying holy words, you shall be joyn'd in Marriage
To each other.

Dor. I warrant you those holy words are charms.
My Father means to conjure us together.

Prosp. to his Daughters. My *Ariel* told me, when last night you quarrell'd,
You said, you would for ever part your Beds ;
But what you threaten'd in your anger, Heaven
Has turn'd to Prophecy.
For you, *Miranda*, must with *Ferdinand*,
And you, *Dorinda*, with *Hippolito* lie in
One Bed hereafter.

Alonz. And Heaven make those Beds still fruitful in
Producing Children, to bless their Parents
Youth, and Grandsires age.

Mir. to Dor. If Children come by lying in a Bed, I wonder you
And I had none between us.

Dor. Sister, it was our fault, we meant like Fools
To look 'em in the fields, and they, it seems,
Are only found in Beds.

Hip. I am o'rjoy'd that I shall have *Dorinda* in a Bed,
We'll lie all night and day together there,
And never rise again.

Ferd. (aside to him) *Hippolito !* you yet are ignorant of your great
Happiness, but there is somewhat, which for
Your own and fair *Dorinda*'s sake, I must instruct
You in.

Hip. Pray teach me quickly how Men and Women in your
World make love, I shall soon learn,
I warrant you.

Enter Ariel, *driving in* Stephano, Trincalo, Mustacho,
Ventoso, Caliban, Sycorax.

Prosp. Why that's my dainty *Ariel*, I shall miss thee,
But yet thou shalt have freedom.

Gonz. O look, Sir, look, the Master and the Saylors——
The Bosen too —— my Prophecy is out, that if
A Gallows were on land, that Man could ne'r
Be drown'd.

Alonz. (*to Trinc.*) Now, Blasphemy, what not one Oath ashore?
Hast thou no mouth by Land? why star'st thou so?

Trinc. What, more Dukes yet? I must resign my Dukedom;
But 'tis no matter, I was almost starv'd in't.

Must. Here's nothing but wild Sallads, without Oyl or Vinegar.

Steph. The Duke and Prince alive! would I had now our gallant Ship
agen, and were her Master, I'd willingly give all my Island for her.

Vent. And I my Vice-Roy-ship.

Trinc. I shall need no Hangman, for I shall e'n hang
My self, now my Friend Butt has shed his
Last drop of life. Poor Butt is quite departed.

Ant. They talk like Mad-men.

Prosp. No matter, time will bring 'em to themselves, and
Now their Wine is gone, they will not quarrel.
Your Ship is safe and tight, and bravely rigg'd,
As when you first set Sail.

Alonz. This news is wonderful.

Ariel. Was it well done, my Lord?

Prosp. Rarely, my Diligence.

Gonz. But pray, Sir, what are those mishapen Creatures?

Prosp. Their Mother was a Witch, and one so strong,
She would controul the Moon, make Flows
And Ebbs, and deal in her command without
Her power.

Syc. O *Setebos!* these be brave Sprights indeed.

Prosp. (*to Calib.*) Go, Sirrah, to my Cell, and as you hope for
Pardon, trim it up.

Calib. Most carefully. I will be wise hereafter.
What a dull Fool was I, to take those Drunkards
For Gods, when such as these were in the world?

Prosp. Sir, I invite your Highness and your Train
To my poor Cave this night; a part of which
I will employ, in telling you my story.

Alonz. No doubt it must be strangely taking, Sir.

Prosp. When the Morn draws, I'll bring you to your Ship,
And promise you calm Seas, and happy Gales.
My *Ariel*, that's thy charge : then to the Elements
Be free, and fare thee well.
    Ariel. I'le do it, Master.
    Prosp. Now to make amends
For the rough treatment you have found to day,
I'll entertain you with my Magick Art :
I'll, by my power, transform this place, and call
Up those that shall make good my promise to you.
                  [Scene changes to the Rocks, with the Arch of Rocks,
                       and calm Sea. Musick playing on the Rocks.
    Prosp. Neptune, and your fair *Amphitrite*, rise ;
Oceanus, with your *Tethys* too, appear ;
All ye Sea-Gods, and Goddesses, appear !
Come, all ye *Trytons ;* all ye *Nereides*, come,
And teach your sawcy Element to obey :
For you have Princes now to entertain,
And unsoil'd Beauties, with fresh youthful Lovers.
           [Neptune, Amphitrite, Oceanus *and* Tethys, *appear in a*
              Chariot drawn with Sea-Horses ; on each side of the Chariot,
              Sea-Gods and Goddesses, Tritons *and* Nereides.
    Alonz. This is prodigious.
    Ant. Ah ! what amazing Objects do we see ?
    Gonz. This Art doth much exceed all humane skill.

SONG.

Amph.

*M*Y *Lord : Great* Neptune, *for my sake,*
    Of these bright Beauties pity take :
    And to the rest allow
      Your mercy too.
Let this inraged Element be still,
    Let Æolus obey my will :
Let him his boystrous Prisoners safely keep
    In their dark Caverns, and no more
Let 'em disturb the bosome of the Deep,
    Till these arrive upon their wish'd-for Shore.

Neptune.
    So much my Amphitrites *love I prize,*
    That no commands of hers I can despise.
    Tethys *no furrows now shall wear,*
    Oceanus *no wrinkles on his brow,*
    Let your serenest looks appear !
    Be calm and gentle now.

Nep. & } *Be calm, ye great Parents of the Flouds and the Springs,*
Amph. } *While each Nereide and Triton Plays, Revels, and Sings.*

Oceanus.   *Confine the roaring Winds, and we*
                   Will soon obey you cheerfully.

Chorus of }   *Tie up the Winds, and we'll obey,*   { Here the Dan-
Tritons }   *Upon the Flouds we'll sing and play,*   { cers mingle with
and Ner. }   *And celebrate a Halcyon day.*   { the Singers.

                                                                           [Dance.

Nept.   *Great Nephew Æolus make no noise,*
               Muzzle your roaring Boys,   [Æolus appears.

Amph.   *Let 'em not bluster to disturb our ears,*
          Or strike these Noble Passengers with fears.

Nept.   *Afford 'em onely such an easie Gale,*
         As pleasantly may swell each Sail.

Amph.   *While fell Sea-Monsters cause intestine jars,*
         This Empire you invade with foreign Wars.
            But you shall now be still,
           And shall obey my Amphitrites will.

Æolus de- } *You I'll obey, who at one stroke can make,*
scends. }   *With your dread Trident, the whole Earth to quake.*
         Come down, my Blusterers, swell no more,
           Your stormy rage give o'r.   { Winds from the four
         Let all black Tempests cease ——   { Corners appear.
         And let the troubled Ocean rest:
         Let all the Sea enjoy as calm a peace,
         As where the Halcyon builds her quiet Nest.
           To your prisons below,
           Down, down you must go:
         You in the Earths Entrals your Revels may keep;
         But no more till I call shall you trouble the Deep [Winds fly down.
         Now they are gone, all stormy Wars shall cease:
         Then let your Trumpeters proclaim a Peace.

Amph.   *Tritons, my Sons, your Trumpets sound,*
         And let the noise from Neighbouring Shores rebound.

                  { *Sound a Calm.*
                  { *Sound a Calm.*
Chorus. { *Sound a Calm.*
                       a Calm.
                  { *Sound a Calm.*

[Here the *Trytons*, at every repeat of *Sound a Calm*, changing their Figure and Postures, seem to sound their wreathed Trumpets made of Shells. A Symphony of Musick, like Trumpets, to which four *Trytons* Dance.

Nept.	*See, see, the Heavens smile, all your troubles are paſt,*
	Your joys by black Clouds shall no more be o'rcaſt.
Amph.	*On this barren Isle ye shall lose all your fears,*
	Leave behind all your sorrows, and banish your cares.
Both.	{ *And your Loves and your Lives shall in safety enjoy ;*
	{ *No influence of Stars shall your quiet deſtroy.*
Chor. of all.	{ *And your Loves,* &c.
	{ *No influence,* &c.

[Here the Dancers mingle with the Singers.

Oceanus.	*We'll safely convey you to your own happy Shore,*
	And yours and your Countrey's soft peace we'll reſtore.
Tethys.	*To treat you bleſt Lovers, as you sail on the Deep,*
	The Trytons *and* Sea-Nymphs *their Revels shall keep.*
Both.	{ *On the swift Dolphins backs they shall sing and shall play ;*
	{ *They shall guard you by night, and delight you by day.*
Chor. of all.	{ *On the swift,* &c.
	{ *And shall guard,* &c.

[Here the Dancers mingle with the Singers.
[A Dance of twelve *Tritons.*

Miran. What charming things are these ?
Dor. What heavenly power is this ?
Proſp. Now, my *Ariel,* be visible, and let the reſt of your Aerial Train,
Appear, and entertain 'em with a Song ;
　　　[*Scene changes to the Rising Sun, and a number of Aerial Spirits in the*
　　　Air, Ariel *flying from the Sun, advances towards the Pit.*
And then farewel my long-lov'd *Ariel.*
Alon. Heaven ! what are these we see ?
Proſp. They are Spirits, with which the Air abounds
in swarms, but that they are not subjeƈt
to poor feeble mortal Eyes.
Ant. O wondrous skill !
Gonʒ. O Power Divine !
　　　Ariel and the reſt sing the following Song.

Ariel.	*Where the Bee sucks, there suck I,*
	In a Cowslips Bed I lie ;
	There I couch when Owls do cry.
	On the Swallows wings I fly
	After Summer merrily.

Merrily, merrily shall I live now,
Under the Blossom that hangs on the Bow.
　　　[*Song ended,* Ariel *ſpeaks, hovering in the Air.*

(267)

Ariel. My Noble Master!
May theirs and your blest Joys never impair.
And for the freedom I enjoy the Air,
I will be still your *Ariel*, and wait
On Aiery accidents that work for Fate.
What ever shall your happiness concern,
From your still faithful *Ariel* you shall learn.
 Prosp. Thou hast been always diligent and kind!
Farewel, my long-lov'd *Ariel*, thou shalt find,
I will preserve thee ever in my mind.
Henceforth this Isle to the afflicted be
A place of Refuge, as it was to me :
The promises of blooming Spring live here,
And all the blessings of the ripening Year.
On my retreat, let Heav'n and Nature smile,
And ever flourish the *Enchanted Isle.*   [*Exeunt.*

EPILOGUE.

GAllants, by all good signs it does appear,
That Sixty seven's a very damning year,
For Knaves abroad, and for ill Poets here.
Among the Muses there's a gen'ral rot,
The Rhyming Monsieur, and the Spanish Plot :
Defie or Court, all's one, they go to Pot.
 The Ghosts of Poets walk within this place,
And haunt us Actors wheresoe'r we pass,
In Visions bloudier than King Richard's was.
 For this poor Wretch, he has not much to say,
But quietly brings in his part o' th' Play,
And begs the favour to be damn'd to day.
 He sends me onely like a Sh'riff's Man here,
To let you know the Malefactor's near,
And that he means to die, en Cavalier.
 For if you shou'd be gracious to his Pen,
Th' Example will prove ill to other men,
And you'l be troubl'd with 'em all agen.

FINIS.

SECOND EPILOGUE.

WHEN feeble Lovers' Appetites decay
They, to provoke, and keep themselves in play,
Must, to their Cost, make ye young Damsells shine ;
If Beauty can't provoke, they'l do't by being fine ;
That pow'rfull charme, wch cannot be withstood,
Puts offe bad faces, & adornes ye good.
Oft an Embroider'd Damsel have we seen   ⎫
Ugly as Bawd, & finer then a Queen,   ⎬
Who by that splendor has victorious been.   ⎭
She, whose weake Eyes had nere one Victory gott
May conquer with a flaming petticoat ;
Witt is a Mistress you have long enjoy'd,
Her beauty's not impair'd but you are cloy'd !
And Since 'tis not Witt's fault that you decay,
You, for your want of appetite, must pay.
You to provoke your selves must keep her fine,
And she must now at double charges shine.
Old Sinners thus————
When they feel Age, & Impotence approach,
Double the charge of furniture and Coach ;
When you of Witt, and sence, were weary growne,
Romantick, riming, fustian Playes were showne,
We then to flying Witches did advance,
And for your pleasures traffic'd into ffrance.
From thence new Arts to please you, we have sought ⎫
We have machines to some perfection brought,   ⎬
And above 30 Warbling voyces gott.   ⎭
Many a God & Goddesse you will heare   ⎫
And we have Singing, Dancing, Devills here ⎬
Such Devills, and such gods, are very Deare. ⎭
We, in all ornaments, are lavish growne   ⎫
And like Improvident Damsells of ye Towne,   ⎬
For present bravery, all our wealth lay downe, ⎭
As if our keepers ever wou'd be Kind,   ⎫
The thought of future wants we never mind,   ⎬
No pittance is for your Old age disign'd.   ⎭
Alone ; we on your Constancy depend,
And hope your Love to th' stage will never end.
To please you, we no Art, or cost will spare
To make yr. Mrs. look, still young, still faire.

PSYCHE:

A

TRAGEDY,

Acted at the

DUKE'S THEATRE.

Written by

THO. SHADWELL.

LONDON,
Printed by *T. N.* for *Henry Herringman*, at the
Anchor, in the Lower Walk of the New Exchange.
1 6 7 5.

Source.

UNDERTAKEN at the direct suggestion of Betterton, Shadwell's *Psyche* is largely borrowed from the French tragedie-ballet *Psyché* which was produced with the utmost magnificence at the theatre of the Palais des Tuilleries in January, 1671, and at the theatre of the Palais-Royal on 24 July of the same year. There were no less than thirty-eight consecutive performances, and two revivals followed in 1672. Molière wrote the first act, the first scene of the second act, and the first scene of the third act; Quinault composed all that is sung with the exception of the Italian aria " Deh ! piangete al pianto mio," the first interlude, which is by Lulli; the remainder of the piece is the work of Corneille, who, it is said, gave a fortnight to perfecting it. Mlle. de Brie appeared as Vénus; Baron L'Amour; Mlle. Molière Psyché; Molière Zéphyre; Mlle. Beaupré Aglaure; and Mlle. Beauval Cidippe.

Psyché was adapted as an opera by Fontenelle.

The original (which Shadwell did not neglect) is, of course, the story of Psyche so exquisitely told by Apuleius in the *Metamorphoses*, Books IV, V, and VI, that he has captured the imagination of the world. Some consideration of the treatment of this lovely fantasy by poet and artist will be found in the Introduction.

The story was not new to the English stage, for Heywood's *Love's Mistris ; or, The Queene's Masque* had been produced in 1634, and within the space of eight days three times presented at Court before King Charles I and Henrietta Maria. It is probable that Queen Henrietta, who liked to visit the private theatres, had first seen the play as given by her company at the Phœnix, and was so well pleased that when she would entertain the King on his birthday, 19 November, in her own palace of Denmark House, she bade Inigo Jones embellish it with " rare decorements."

Love's Mistris was printed 4to 1636; and again 4to 1640.

Heywood's play was revived and proved popular after the Restoration. Saturday, 2 March, 1660–1, Pepys notes : " To Salsbury Court, where the house as full as could be; and it seems it was a new play ' The Queen's Maske,' wherein there are some good humours; among others, a good jeer to the old story of the Siege of Troy, making it to be a common country tale. But above all it was strange to see so little a boy as that was to act Cupid, which is one of the greatest parts in it."

On Monday, 25 March following, Pepys again saw the play, or some two acts of it, at Salisbury Court. A few days earlier, Monday, 11 March, he notes : " After dinner I went to the theatre, and there saw ' Love's

Mistress ' done by them, which I do not like in some things as well as their acting at Salsbury Court." Killigrew's company again played *Love's Mistris* on Saturday, 26 October, 1661. Monday, 15 May, 1665, Pepys records : "To the King's playhouse, all alone, and saw 'Love's Maistresse.' Some pretty things and good variety in it, but no or little fancy in it." Saturday, 15 August, 1668, Pepys went " to the King's play-house, and there saw ' Love's Mistresse ' revived, the thing pretty good, but full of variety of divertisement."

Theatrical History.

SHADWELL has himself informed us that the libretto of *Psyche* was written sixteen months before the opera actually came on the stage. His attention had been particularly directed to the subject by Betterton, who no doubt during his stay in Paris not only saw the French *Psyché*, but also studied it with minutest care from the practical point of view. Yet the interval was by no means wasted. It was employed in the business-like method of inspiring gossip and awaking curiosity. On 22 August, 1673, James Vernon, writing a letter from Court to Sir Joseph Williamson at Cologne mentions "that the Duke's house are preparing an Opera and great machines. They will have dansers out of France, and St. André comes over with them." *Letters to Sir Joseph Williamson at Cologne* (Camden Society), I, 179.

Accordingly after many weeks of preliminary rumour and cleverly-bruited talk, Shadwell's opera *Psyche* was produced with every circumstance of theatrical pomp and show at the magnificent new theatre in Dorset Garden, a house especially suited for splendid spectacle, on 27 February, 1674-5. Musician, scenic-artist, ballet-master, had all done their parts. The vocal music was composed by Matthew Locke; the instrumental music by Giovanni Baptista Draghi, the famous Italian maestro who was in Queen Catherine's service; the elaborate scenery was painted by the admired Stephenson; the dances were arranged and superintended by St. Andrée, the principal coryphæus of his time. The whole was under the most careful supervision of Betterton himself, who had but newly returned from a visit to Paris, whither he specially journeyed to study French stage decoration, machinery, and production at the fount.

There is little wonder that so gorgeous a *mise-en-scène* attracted vast crowds to the theatre. King Charles himself was present at the first performance, and again a day or two later on the 2 March.

Downes tells us: "In *February*, 1673, the long expected Opera of *Psyche* came forth in all her ornaments; new scenes, new machines, new cloaths, new French dances: this Opera was splendidly set out, especially in scenes; the charge of which amounted to above 800£. It had a continuance of performances about 8 days together; it prov'd very beneficial to the Company: yet *The Tempest* got them more money." The reason for this last is surely not far to seek when one compares the libretto of *Psyche* with *The Tempest*, however altered, beperiwigged, and rehandled.

As might have been expected, the rival company at the Theatre Royal, who were still severely suffering from the catastrophe of the tragic fire,

and did not open in their new house until 26 March, 1674, regarded anything but dispassionately these operatic glories, outvying in their grandeur
and glitter the sovran pageantry of the old Court masques themselves.
Some counter-attraction must be established, and accordingly they
essayed the somewhat obvious but undeniably effective weapon of burlesque.

Thomas Duffett, whose skits upon *The Empress of Morocco* and *The
Tempest* proved irresistibly funny in their day and have even now for us a
certain humour, coarse though it be, whilst they cannot be denied thrust
and vigour, was soon employed to try his practised hand upon a mock
Psyche. Accordingly a few months later, probably in April, there appeared
at Drury Lane the travesty *Psyche Debauch'd*. "This *Mock Opera*," says
Langbaine, "was writ on purpose to Ridicule Mr. *Shadwell's Psyche*, and
to spoil the Duke's House, which, as has been before observ'd, was then
more frequented than the King's." Since this extravaganza has been
dealt with in some detail in the Introduction 'twere superfluous to make
further mention of it here. One may merely repeat that it is far from
unamusing, and can hardly fail to have been very effective at the moment.

Psyche, largely no doubt for the sake of the spectacle,—such shows
could never glut the Town—remained in the repertory of the theatre for
at least a quarter of a century. With the growing vogue of Italian opera,
however, which may fairly be said to have been introduced in its entirety
about 1705, Shadwell's farce seems to have fallen out of favour, largely
because it was considered old-fashioned, and so when *Psyche* was revived
at Drury Lane for the benefit of Mills on 10 June, 1704, we are not surprised to find the announcement "Not Acted there 6 years." Since it was
a production entailing vast expense, whilst as an attraction it had palpably
ceased to draw an audience sufficiently numerous to pay the house, it does
not appear to have been given after this season.

To the most
Illustrious Prince,
J A M E S
D U K E of
M O N M O U T H, &c.

May it please your Grace ?

YOur Grace has so Nobly Patronized this Undertaking, that I should rob you of your due, if I should not humbly lay this Play at your Feet, since by your great and generous encouragement of it, you have made that and the Author eternally your own. But had I never received any Obligation, by my particular Inclination I am bound to your Grace, since I am the moſt humble admirer of your Heroick Virtues, who by your early and unimitable Example, and by your eminent Command, are the greateſt Patron of Arms ; and by your Government of the moſt famous of Universities, are become the greateſt Protector of Arts : of that University, which I can never mention without reverence ; and from which I have yet another Tie to your Grace, since I had once the honour to be a Member of that Illuſtrious Society, which though it be the moſt Learned in the World, can boaſt of no greater Honour then that of being commanded by so excellent a Prince ; one who is equally Valiant againſt his Enemies, and Courteous to his Friends ; whose boundless Courage is always ready to vanquish the one, and whose Princely Generosity is always ready to oblige the other.

I shall not here recite those Heroick Actions, which all *Europe* have celebrated, and none have equall'd : Those are too Great for an Epiſtle Dedicatory, and only fit for solid, laſting Hiſtory ; which certainly muſt do your Grace that right, to Enrol you in the foremoſt Rank of Fame. Nor can we doubt, but the memory of your Grace's Actions will laſt, when Time shall have devoured the Places where they were performed :

(277)

When *Maſtrick* shall be a heap of Rubbish, and the name might otherwise be swallow'd in the Ruine, it will be remembred by the greateſt Action in the World, done there by the Greateſt and the Earlieſt Hero, and by one, who for all his fierceness of Courage, has yet that Gentleness to Mankind, that he thinks that day loſt, in which he does not oblige. One who is not only infinitely bless'd in the moſt excellent Partner of his Joys and Cares, happy above measure in the Goods of Mind, the Perfections of Body, and the greateſt Splendour and Ornaments of Fortune, but he enjoys all these unenvied ; nay, is not onely free from every mans envy, but has his love.

I should be afraid of this boldness, in once mentioning things so much above my Pen, were I not assured of your Grace's Generosity, that enclines you to pardon, even a well-intended Errour, in your humble Creature, who begs Protection from you, and needs it too.

I have, by my misfortune, not my fault, met with some Enemies, who are always ready to do me the irreparable injury, to blaſt my Reputation with the King ; and when I have the Honour to please Him, (which is of all things in the World, my greateſt Ambition) endeavour to perswade him, that I do not write the Plays I own, or at leaſt, that the beſt part of them are written for me ; which is so malicious an aspersion, that I am sure they themselves believe it not, and they may as well accuse me of firing the City. I am sure (though I may want Wit to write a Play) I have more honeſty than to own what another man writes. But I am not yet so poor as to borrow ; if I should, I should find not many that are rich enough to lend, Wit being much a scarcer Commodity than Money, I am sure with some who have reported this of me ; who what ever they have of one, have scare enough of the other to supply their own necessities ; and therefore I should be but very slenderly furnished from them.

I can never enough acknowledge the Honour done me by your Incomparable Dutchess, in endeavouring to clear me of this Aspersion : And who would not be proud of being aspersed, to be so vindicated ? From this and some other injuries of my Enemies, I humbly beg your Grace's protection, who, I am sure, have Goodness and Greatness enough to defend me againſt them : And I had rather owe it to your Grace, than to any Man : For no Man is more then I,

My Lord,

    Your Grace's

        Moſt devoted humble Servant,

                    Tho. Shadwell.

PREFACE.

IN a good natur'd Countrey, I doubt not but this my first Essay in Rhime would be at least forgiven; especially when I promise to offend no more in this kind: But I am sensible, that here I must encounter a great many Difficulties. In the first place (though I expect more Candor from the best Writers in Rhime) the more moderate of them (who have yet a numerous party, good Judges being very scarce) are very much offended with me, for leaving my own Province of Comedy, to invade their Dominion of Rhime: But methinks they might be satisfied, since I have made but a small incursion, and am resolv'd to retire. And were I never so powerful, they should escape me, as the Northern People did the Romans, their craggy barren Territories, being not worth the Conqu'ring. The next sort I am to encounter with, are those who are too great admirers of the French Wit, who (if they do not like this Play) will say, the French Psyche is much better; if they do, they will say, I have borrow'd it all from the French. Whether the French be better, I leave to the Men of Wit (who understand both Languages) to determine; I will only say, Here is more variety, and the Scenes of Passion are wrought up with more Art; and this is much more a Play than that. And I will be bold to affirm that this is as much a Play, as could be made upon this Subject. That I have borrow'd it all from the French, can only be the objection of those, who do not know that it is a Fable, written by Apuleus in his Golden Ass; where you will find most things in this Play, and the French too. For several things concerning the Decoration of the Play, I am oblig'd to the French, and for the Design of two of the only moving Scenes in the French, which I may say, without vanity, are very much improv'd, being wrought up with more Art in this, than in the French Play, without borrowing any of the thoughts from them.

In a thing written in five weeks, as this was, there must needs be many Errors, which I desire true Criticks to pass by; and which perhaps I see my self, but having much bus'ness, and indulging my self with some pleasure too, I have not had leisure to mend them, nor would it indeed be worth the pains, since there are so many splendid Objects in the Play, and such variety of Diversion, as will not give the Audience leave to mind the Writing; and I doubt not but the Candid Reader will forgive the faults, when he considers, that the great Design was to entertain the Town with variety of Musick, curious Dancing, splendid Scenes and Machines: And that I do not, nor ever did, intend to value my self upon the writing of this Play. For I had rather be Author of one Scene of Comedy, like some of Ben. Johnson's, then of all the best Plays of this kind that have been, or ever shall be written: Good Comedy requiring much more Wit and Judgment in the Writer, than any Rhyming unnatural Plays can do: This I have so little valu'd, that I have not *alter'd six lines in it since it was first written, which, (except the Songs at the Marriage of* Psyche *in the last Scene) was all done Sixteen months since. In all the words which are sung, I did not so much take care of the Wit or Fancy of 'em, as the making of 'em proper for Musick; in which I cannot but have some little knowledge, having been bred, for many years of my Youth, to some performance in it.*

I chalked out the way to the Composer (in all but the Song of Furies *and* Devils, *in the Fifth Act) having design'd which Line I wou'd have sung by One, which by Two, which by Three, which by four Voices, &c. and what manner of Humour I would have in all the Vocal Musick.*

And by his excellent Composition, that long known, able, and approved Master of Musick, Mr. Lock, *(Composer to His Majesty, and Organist to the Queen) has done me a great deal of right; though I believe, the unskilful in Musick will not like the more solemn part of it, as the Musick in the Temple of* Apollo, *and the Song of the* Despairing Lovers, *in the Second Act; both which are proper and admirable in their hands, and are recommended to the judgement of able Musicians; for those who are not so, there are light and airy things to please them.*

All the Instrumental Musick (which is not mingled with the Vocal) was Composed by that Great Master, Seignior Gio. Baptista Draghi, *Master of the Italian Musick to the King. The Dances were made by the most famous Master of* France, Monsieur St. Andree. *The Scenes were Painted by the Ingenious Artist, Mr.* Stephenson. *In those things that concern the Ornament or Decoration of the Play, the great industry and care of Mr.* Betterton *ought to be remember'd, at whose desire I wrote upon this Subject.*

POSTSCRIPT.

I Had borrow'd something from two Songs of my own, which, till this Play was Printed, I did not know were publick; but I have since found 'em Printed in Collections of Poems, *viz.* part of the Song of the *Despairing Lovers*, in the Second Act, and about eight lines in the first Act, beginning at this line, *'Tis frail as an abortive Birth.* This I say to clear my self from Thiev'ry, 'tis none to rob my self.

PROLOGUE.

AS a young wanton when she first begins,
  With shame, and with regret of Conscience sins ;
  So fares our trembling Poet the first time,
He has committed the lewd sin of Rhime,
While Custom hardens others in the Crime.
It might in him that boldness too beget,
To lay about him without Fear or Wit :
But humbly he your pardon does implore ;
Already he repents, and says he'll sin no more.
His bus'ness now is to shew splendid Scenes,
T' interpret 'twixt the Audience and Machines.
You must not here expect exalted Thought,
Nor lofty Verse, nor Scenes with labor wrought :
His Subject's humble, and his Verse is so ;
This Theme no thund'ring Raptures would allow,
Nor would he, if he could, that way pursue.
He'd ride unruly Fancy with a Bit,
And keep within the bounds of Sense and Wit,
Those bounds no boisterous Fustian will admit.
And did not gentle Hearers oft dispence
With all the Sacred Rules of Wit and Sense ;
Such tearing Lines, as crack the Writers Brain,
And the laborious Actors Lungs o'r-strain,
Wou'd, on our Stages, be roar'd out in vain.
In all true Wit a due proportion's found,
To the just Rules of heighth and distance bound.
Wit, like a Faulcon tow'ring in its flight,
When once it soars above its lawful height,
Lessens, till it becomes quite out of sight.
But of such flights there is no danger now ;
He would not soar too high, nor creep too low :
Howe'r he hopes you will excuse his haste,
For he this gawdy Trifle wrote so fast ;
Five weeks begun and finish'd this design,
In those few hours he snatch'd from Friends and Wine ;
And since in better things h' has spent his time,
With which he hopes e're long t' atone this Crime.

But he, alas!   has several pow'rful Foes,
Who are unjustly so, and yet he knows,
They will, whate're he writes, though good, oppose.
    If he the honour has to please the best,
'Tis not his fault if he offends the rest :
But none of them yet so severe can be,
As to condemn this Trifle more then he.

PSYCHE:

ACT I.

The Scene is a very deep Walk in the midst of a mighty Wood,
through which, is seen a Prospect of a very pleasant Country.

Enter Psyche *and two Ladies.*

Psyc. HOW charming are these Meads and Groves !
    The Scene of Innocence and Artless Loves ;
    Where Interest no discord moves.
No stormy passions can the mind invade,
No Sacred Trust is violated here.
 1 *Lad.* Man does not here his own kind fear,
    Traps are for Wolves and Foxes made,
    And Toils for Beasts, not Men, are laid ;
    Man is not here by Man betray'd.
 2 *Lad.* Here no man's ruine is with baseness sought,
For in this happy place no Court-like Arts are taught.
 Psyc. How pleasant is this undisturb'd retreat,
    With harmless Joys, and Rural Sports,
Free from tumultuous Cares that trouble Courts,
And all the Factions which disturb the Great.
 1 *Lad.* How vain their gaudy Pomp and Show,
    To which the cheated vulgar bow !
    Their Splendor and their per'shing Pride,
Their shining Revels, their adult'rate Joys,
When in the midst of all this pomp and noise,
In their unquiet minds still anxious thoughts reside ?
 2 *Lad.* Their Triumphs are disturb'd with fears,
    Their Joys allay'd with griefs and cares :
    Envy and pride possess each Breast,
    And guilty dreams distract their Rest.
 Psyc. From Sleep to dang'rous Arts they 'wake ;

To undermine each other, all mean ways they take,
   Each ſtrives who shall his Monarch lead,
Though at the price of his own Father's Head :
Nor care they how much they their Prince misguide,
To serve their Luſt, their Avarice, and Pride.
  1 *Lad.* Yet there the Mighty are not prosp'rous long,
    Though ne'r so cunning, ne'r so ſtrong ;
    Though ne'r so much endear'd to th' Crown :
Fresh Favourites succeed and pull them down.
  Psyc. As a black Cloud which the gross Earth exhales,
    Swell'd and oppreſt with its own weight,
Down to the Earth rent with fierce Lightning falls :
So splendid Fav'rites in their envy'd height,
Big with the swellings of their Pride and Pow'r,
    Do seldom scape the dismal hour,
    When by some new-rais'd Meteors torn,
They from the higheſt pinacle of fate,
    Fall to the moſt dejeſted ſtate,
And, from the Idols of the World, become the scorn.
These troubles in my Father's Court I've seen,
    And ne'r can wish to be a Queen.
  1 *Lad.* Cannot so many pow'rful Princes move
    Psyche's obdurate heart to Love ?
  2 *Lad.* Not one who can a Prince in *Greece* be call'd,
    Who is not by your Eyes enthrall'd :
    Each Prince great *Psyche* does adore,
    And pity from her heart implore.
  1 *Lad.* But you with all their charms unmov'd remain,
And smile when every Captive shakes his Chain.
  Psyc. Not all the Pomp of Courts can e'r remove
Me from the Pleasures of the quiet Grove :
Each pretty Nymph to me her Tribute yields
Of all the fragrant Treasure of the Fields.
    Garlands and Wreaths they bring
    From the sweet bosom of the Spring.
And with their rural Numbers sing my Praise,
In soft delights passing their quiet days.
    Princes in all the Calms of Peace,
    Have no such powerful Charms as these :
Shall I for Courts abandon this soft life,
For splendid Beggary, and for smiling ſtrife ?
      [*A Symphony of Recorders and soft Musick.*
What Harmony is this which fills the Air ?

And does my Senses charm ?

2 *Lad.* Some Entertainment your poor Swains prepare,
Which they each day perform.

Enter *Pan* with his Followers, and sings in Recitative.

Pan
sings.
{ *Great* Psyche, *Goddess of each Field and Grove,*
Whom every Prince and every God does love :
To your all-commanding hand
Pan *yields his Sovereign Command.*
For you the Satyrs *and the* Fawns
Shall nimbly trip it o're the Lawns :
For you the Shepherd's Pipe and Sing,
And with their Nymphs Dance in a Ring.
Fruits shall they bring, and pretty Garlands weave,
And shall the Meads of all their Sweets bereave :
Vertumnus *and* Flora *their Tribute shall pay,*
And to Psyche *shall dedicate this happy day.*
The Sylvans *and* Dryads *shall Dance all around,*
And Psyche *dread Queen of this place shall be Crown'd.*
My Lov'd Syrinx *and* Eccho *shall Sing and shall Play,*
And to Psyche *shall dedicate this happy day.*

Chor.
And Pan *who before all here did command,*
Now resigns all his Empire to Psyche's *fair hand.*

[They all kneel and sing the *Chorus.*
While the following *Symphony's* playing, *Pan* Crowns her
with a Garland ; his Attendants present her with Fruits,
Flowers, &c.

A short *Symphony* of Ruſtick Musick, representing the Cries and Notes of
Birds. Then an Entry Danc'd by Four *Sylvans* and Four *Dryads* to
Ruſtick Musick. At the end of the Dance, the *Dryads,* upon their Knees,
present *Psyche* with Fruits and Flowers ; and the *Sylvans* present her
with Wreaths of Lawrel, Myrtle and Cyprus. Then *Exeunt* Sylv. *and*
Dryads. Then a short *Symphony* of Ruſtick Musick, representing an
Eccho. The *Dryads* and *Sylvans* presenting their Offerings. [*One sings.*

1 Voice. *Great* Psyche *shall find no such pleasure as here*
Eccho.   *no such pleasure as here,*
                                                      as here.

2 Voices. *Where her dutiful Subjects shall all ſtand in awe*
Eccho.   *shall all ſtand in awe*
                                                      in awe.

3 Voices. *Her Frowns and her Smiles shall give us all Law*
Eccho.   *shall give us all Law*
                                                      all Law.

(285)

4 Voices. *And from us of Rebellion she need have no fear*
Eccho.   *she need have no fear*
                                                                                            no fear.

Voices, Flajolets, Violins, Cornets, Sackbuts, Hoa-boys :
all joyn in *Chorus.*

[Here the Singers mingle with the Dancers.

Chor.   *How happy are those that inhabit this place,*
            Where a sigh is ne'r heard, where no falshood we meet,
            Where each single heart agrees with the face.
            No Climate was ever so calm and so sweet,
    Eccho.   *was ever so calm and so sweet,*
                                    so calm and so sweet,
                                                so sweet.
1 Voice. *To beauteous* Psyche *all Devotion is due,*
    Eccho.   *all Devotion is due,*
                                        is due.
2 Voices. *Our humble Offerings she will not despise,*
    Eccho.   *she will not despise,*
                                        despise.
3 Voices. *Since the Tribute is offer'd from hearts that are true,*
    Eccho.   *from hearts that are true,*
                                            are true.
4 Voices. *From hearts all devoted to* Psyche's *bright Eyes,*
    Eccho.   *to* Psyche's *bright Eyes,*
                                            bright Eyes.

Chor. *How happy are those,* &c.   [They Dance.

Psyc. Oh happy Solitude ! Oh sweet Retreat !
Free from the noise and troubles of the Great !
Not all the wealth of all the World shall charm
                    Me from this calm retirment here.
Where I enjoy all pleasure, know no fear,
No Joy can her surprize, nor Danger can alarm.

Enter four Women, personating Ambition, Power, Plenty *and* Peace.
What new unwelcom Guests are these,
                    That wou'd invade my Peace ?
    Amb. We come t' invite you from your vicious ease,
To Courts, where glorious Actions are perform'd.
Leave lazy Groves for active Palaces,
Where you by great *Ambition* may be warm'd ;
By me to noble thoughts may be inflam'd ;

(286)

To think of Ruling Kings, not silly Swains,
Each day your Beauty a new Captive gains,
And in all Courts no other Beauty's nam'd.
   Power. I from your Solitude do you invite,
And I am she for whom all Monarchs fight,
         Power, Mankind's supreme delight,
Fair *Psyche* to the Court, come follow me,
Numbers of Tributary Kings shall kneel to thee.
What e're can be within the prospect of thy Thought,
Shall instantly to thee by humble Slaves be brought.
   Plenty. Psyche, this lonely Desart quit,
The Scene of homeliness and poverty :
A splendid Palace does your state befit,
          Where you shall be adorn'd by me,
With all the Treasures of the East and West.
Thy life shall be but one continu'd Feast,
         And every Prince shall be thy Guest :
All delicates I'll find for thy content,
Which Luxury, inspir'd by Wit, can e'r invent.
   Peace.   And I to Crown all these,
   Will give you everlasting Peace ;
   Peace that no Fiends shall ever harm,
Nor the mad tumults of Mankind allarm :
My Olive still shall flourish where you are,
For Peace should always wait upon the fair.

   Psyc. Happy are they who know Ambition least.
I'm only safe and quiet, while my breast
Is not with base ambitious thoughts opprest,
Too turbulent to let poor mortals rest.

   O'er all my Tyrant Passions Power I have,
And scorn that Pow'r which can but rule a Slave.

   The use of mighty Riches is but small ;
Besides I, nothing coveting, have all.

   Peace, with such vain Companions never dwells,
She's only safe in humble Groves and Cells.

     Envy *with six Furies arise, at which* Ambition, Power, Plenty
        and Peace *run away affrighted.*

   1 *Lad.* What dreadful Vision does distract our sight !
Do not these Fiends your mighty mind surprize ?

Psyc. Their ugly shapes bring wonder to my eyes,
But nothing can my constant mind affright.

Envy sings. Envy 'gainst Psyche *such black storms shall raise,*
As all her pow'rful beams shall ne'r dispel :
Beyond her strength shall be her suffering ;
Her to the greatest misery I'll bring,
And e're I've done, I'll send her down to Hell.

1 Fury. *In Hell, too late she shall relent,*
And all her arrogance repent.

2 Fury. *We Furies will torment your Soul,*
And you shall weep and howl.

1 Fury. *And at the sight of ev'ry Snake,*
Tremble and quake.

2 Fury. *There you shall mourn eternally,*
And to the quick shall feel each lash we give :

1 Fury. *There you shall always wish to dye,*
And yet in spight of you shall always live.

Chor. of all. *There you shall always,* &c.

[*Envy* and *Furies* sink.

2 *Lad.* What horrid words are these we hear ?
I am amost dissolv'd with fear :
Can Envy this sweet dwelling find ?

1 *Lad.* Envy the greatest Bane to all Mankind.
What dreadful Fate does she foretel ?
What Prophecy is this ?
The gods will sure do much amiss,
Should they permit you to be snatch'd to Hell.

Psyc. Fate ! do thy worst, thou ne'r shalt trouble me,⎫
The Innocent within themselves are free :⎬
Envy, I can be valiant against thee.⎭

Enter Prince Nicander.

2 *Lad.* But see the Prince *Nicander* does appear :
Industrious Love pursues you every where.

Nican. Madam, I to this Solitude am come,
Humbly from you to hear my latest doom.

Psyc. The first Command which I did give,
Was, that you should not see me here :
The next Command you will receive,
Much harsher will to you appear.

Nican. How long, fair *Psyche,* shall I sigh in vain ?
How long of scorn and cruelty complain ?

Your eyes enough have wounded me,
You need not add your cruelty.
You against me too many weapons chuse,
Who am defenceless against each you use.
   Psyc. Shall no conceal'd retirement keep me free
From Loves vexatious importunity ?
I in my Father's Court too long endur'd
The ill which I by absence thought t' have cur'd ?
   Nican. Planets, that cause our Fates, cannot be long obscur'd,
      Though Comets vanish from our sense,
When they've dispers'd their fatal influence,
And nothing but the sad effects remain,
Yet Stars that govern us, wou'd hide themselves in vain.
The momentary Clouds must soon be past,
      Which wou'd their brightness overcast.
   Psy. Why should *Nicander* thus pursue in vain
Her, o'r whose mind he can no Conquest gain :
For though my Body thus abroad you fee,
My Mind shall stay within and keep its privacy.
   Nican. Blame not the passion you your self create,
Which is to me resistless as my Fate :
      Can *Psyche* own such Cruelties,
As vainly Priests impute to Deities ?
To punish the Affections they inspire,
As if they'd kindle to put out a fire.
If from the Gods we any gifts receive,
Our Appetites of Nature they must give.
Let Priests for Self-denial then contend,
If we 'gainst Nature go, we Heav'n offend,
Who made that Nature to pursue its end.
Nature's desires Heav'n's known prescriptions are,
Of greater certainty than others far :
Priests Inspirations may but Dreams be found,
Th' effects of Vapors or of Spleens unsound :
But Nature cannot err in her own way,
And though Priests may, she cannot lead astray.
   Psyc. Nature the Gods first uncorrupted made,
But to corruption 'twas by Man betray'd ;
Which when so much exorbitant they found,
What first they had made free, they justly bound.
   Nican. If Nature be not what the Gods first meant,
Then pow'rful Man defeated Heavens intent.
If the Gods Engine of the World must be

Mended by them, how did they then foresee ?
Must men, like Clocks, be alter'd to go right ?
Or though wound up by Nature, must stand still ?
Must we against our own affections fight,
And quite against the Bias bend the will ?
   Psyc. Against your self y' have pleaded all this time ;
If not to follow Nature be a crime,
Mine so averse to Love by Heav'n is made,
She above all by me shall be obey'd.

Enter Polynices.

   Nican. Nature incites all humane kind to love ;
Who deny that, unnatural must prove.
How, *Polynices*, my great Rival here !
This is the only way I him can fear :
His Arms are far less dreadful than his Love.
   Psyc. Sir, what could your injurious kindness move,
Thus to disturb the quiet of my life ?
In vain, great Princes, is your am'rous strife.
   Polyn. If I were singular, you might think me rude :
But I can many dang'rous Rivals find.
A violent Passion makes me thus intrude.
Be but to me as you're to others, kind ;
Let not my death alone be here design'd.
           Too fatal was the first surprise
            I suffer'd by your conqu'ring Eyes :
Your pow'rful Charms no Mortal can resist,
I in an instant lov'd, and never can desist.
   Nican. Such violent and sudden love
           Perhaps must soon remove :
           'Tis frail as an abortive Birth,
And as it soon approach'd, it soon may fly
           As when too early flowers come forth,
From the first moment of their birth they dye.
Mine by degrees did to perfection grow,
And is too strong to be resisted now.
   Polyn. That which I have for that illustrious face,
           Is Sympathy, not lazy Love,
The Steel the Loadstone does as soon embrace,
           And of it self will ne'r remove.
   Nican. The Steel you speak of may be snatch'd from thence
           With very little violence.
   Polyn. Who shall commit that violence on me ?

(290)

Nican. He who before has conquer'd thee :
Thou didſt my Empire, doſt my Love invade :
  My Love shall be my onely aid.
And I again thy Conqueror can be.
 Polyn. I was by Fortune then betray'd,
But now by Love am much more pow'rful made.
Oh that the way for *Psyche* to be won,
  Were for me to possess thy Throne,
  I wou'd believ't already done !
And when with ease I'ad triumph'd o'r thee,
Thou on thy Knees should'ſt beg her Love for me.
 Nican. Did not her Sacred Presence guard thy life,
This fatal place should soon decide our ſtrife :
  I on thy conquer'd Neck would tread,
And make thee forfeit soon thy useless head.
I'd put an end now to your Love and you :
And when, perhaps, I'd nothing else to do,
I might vouchsafe to take your petty Kingdom too.
 Polyn. Should my death soon ensue,
  Which never can be caus'd by you,
It might to you some bold presumptions give,
You dare not think such thoughts while yet I live.
   For what thou haſt already said,
  Shouldſt thou escape me with thy head,
Yet I will soon depopulate thy Land,
And leave thee none but Beaſts for thy command ;
Or may be, If thou fall'ſt into my hand,
I openly will thee in triumph lead :
Thy Cities into Desarts I will turn,
And thou in Chains shalt tamely see 'em burn.
 Nican. Gods——
 Psyc. Princes, let your untimely discord cease ;
If my eſteem you'd gain, conclude a Peace.
Each to the other muſt become a Fricnd :
   Though Rivals, yet you muſt agree ;
You but for something in the Clouds contend,
   If thus you think to conquer me.
 Polyn. So absolute is your command,
  That I my Rival will embrace ;
  Your will no Lover can withſtand.
I can do any thing but give my Rival place.
 Nican. Your Voice may ſtill the fury of the Winds,
  Or calm the moſt diſtemper'd minds :

Wild Beasts at your command in peace would be,
        When you make Rivals thus agree.   [*They embrace.*
    Psyc.   I ne'er can value Birth or State,
        'Tis virtue must my heart obtain :
        You may each other emulate.
In glorious actions ; but must quit all hate,
Ere either of you my esteem can gain.
        The next command I give, must be,
        Not to invade my privacy.
Princes, farewel, you must not follow me.
    Nican. So sacred are the dread commands you give,
From you my death I humbly wou'd receive.
        For I can scarce hear this and live.
    Polyn. Your breath mens minds to any thing may move,
When you make Rivals one another love.   [*Exit* Psyche.
But see ! her envious Sisters do appear,
        Whose anger less than love we fear.

        As they are going off in haste,
        Enter Cidippe *and* Aglaura.

    Cid. Great Princes, whither do you fly so fast ?
    Aglau. 'Tis to their Idol *Psyche* by their haste.
    Cid.   What Prince-like virtue can you find
        In her poor and groveling mind ?
    Aglau. Heav'n did her Soul for Cottages create,
And for some vulgar purpose did design :
Her mind's too narrow for a Prince's state,
She has no vertues which in Courts may shine.
    Cidip. Her Beauty like her Mind is vulgar too.
Like the dull off-spring of some Village-Pair,
She might perhaps some Shepherds heart subdue,
But should, poor Thing, of Princes looks despair.
    Aglau. A thousand times more charms they here might find,
Beauty, that's fit to attract great Princes eyes.
But silly Love, forsooth, hath struck them blind ;
For could they see, they would their Love despise.
    Nican. Farewel—— Such blasphemies we must not hear,
        Against the Goddess we adore.
    Poly. So beautiful to us she does appear,
        That none shall ever charm us more.
        [*Exeunt* Nicander & Polynices.
    Cidip. Blasted be her Beauty, and her charms accurst,
        That must our ruine bring ;

I am almost with Envy burst.
To see each day she can command a King.
  Aglau. And whilst she lives, we can no Lovers have :
Oh that her Cradle had become her Grave !
  Cid. She by each Prince is Idoliz'd,
Whilst our neglected Beauties may grow old,
And not be sought by them she has despis'd.
  Aglau. Oh that I live to hear this story told.
        This Theme has made my anger bold.
I on her Beauty will revenge our Cause.
        We are not safe whilst breath she draws.
Her Example of Revenge I'll make.
  Cidip. Must we be thus neglected for her sake ?
Venus ! redress the wrongs which she hath done :
        She may in time insnare your Son,
She such an Idol by Mankind is made.
        Your pow'r no more will be obey'd,
        Your Sacred beauty they'l neglect,
Your Deity will have no more respect.
  Aglau. No Incense more will on your Altars smoke,
        No Victims more will burn,
        Each Prince her Worshipper will turn.
Let this your great Divinity provoke ;
        Revenge your self, and take our part.
        Punish her stubborn heart,
And by your utmost fury let her smart   [*A Symphony of soft Musick.*
  Cidip. What Divine Harmony is this we hear !
        Such never yet approach'd my Ear !
            [Venus *descends in her Chariot, drawn with Doves.*
  Aglau. See *Venus's* Chariot hovering in the Air ;
        The Goddess sure has heard our pray'r.

  Venus sings. *With kindness I your pray'rs receive,*
        And to your hopes success will give.
        I have with anger seen Mankind adore
        Your Sister's beauty, and her scorn deplore,
          Which they shall do no more.
        For their Idolatry I'll so resent,
        As shall your wishes to the full content.
        Your Father is with Psyche *now,*
        And to Apollo's Oracle they'll go,
          Her destiny to know.
        I by the God of Wit shall be obey'd,

(293)

For *Wit* to beauty ſtill is ſubjeƈt made.
  He'll so resent your cause and mine,
    That you will not repine,
  But will applaud the Oracle's design.

Cidip.　　　　Great Goddess, we our thanks return,
　　　　　　We after this no more shall mourn.
Aglau. Your sacred Pow'r for ever we'll obey,
And to your Altars our whole Worship pay.
　　　　　　　　　　　　[Venus *ascends with soft Musick.*

　　　Enter Theander *with his Followers, and* Psyche *with two Ladies.*

Thean.　　　　Daughters, no more you shall contend,
　　　　　　This happy day your ſtrife shall end :
The Oracle shall ease you of your care ;
　　　　　We to the Temple will repair,
　　　　　　And *Psyche* will obey,
　　　　Whate're the *Delphick* God shall say.
And——
Whate're *Apollo* shall command, shall be,
I swear by all the Gods, perform'd by me.
　Psyc. And on my Knees I make this solemn vow,
To his Decree I will devoutly bow.
　　　　Let his commands be what they will,
　　　　　I chearfully will them fulfill.
　　Thean. Let's to *Apollo*'s Temple then repair,
And seek the God with Sacrifice and Pray'r.　　　　[*Exeunt omnes.*

ACT II.

The Scene is the Temple of Apollo Delphicus, *with Columns of the* Dorick
　Order, *inrich'd with Gold, in the middle a ſtately Cupolo, on the top of it*
　the Figure of the Sun ; *some diſtance before it an Altar lin'd with Brass ;*
　under it a large Image of Apollo, *before which ſtands the Tripod.*
Enter in a Solemn Procession, the Chief Prieſt Crown'd with Lawrel in a white
　Veſtment, over that a Purple Gown, over that a Cope embroidered with
　Gold, over all a Lambs-skin Hood with the Wool on : He has four Boys at-
　tending, two before, two behind, clad in Surplices, and girt with Girdles
　of Gold ; the firſt carrying a golden Censor with Myrrhe, Frankincense, and
　sweet Gums, &c. The second a Barley Cake, or Barley Meal, with Salt,

upon a golden Service. The third a golden Cruise, full of Honey and Water. The fourth a large gilt Book emboss'd with Gold. After them six Priests, with Books of Hymns, clad in Surplices and embroider'd Copes. Then Men with Wind-Instruments, clad in Surplices, all crown'd with Wreathes of Lawrel. After them Nicander, Cedippe, Polynices, Aglaura, Theander, Psyche. Then a Train of Ladies. All the Women with their faces cover'd with white Veils. After all Theander's Attendants and Guards in their Procession. This following Hymn is sung in Chorus.

Chor.   L*Et's to* Apollo's *Altar now repair,*
       And offer up our Vows and Pray'r;
      Let us enquire fair Psyche's *destiny.*
Repeat.   {*The Gods to her will sure propitious be,*
      {*If Innocence and Beauty may go free.*
Ch. Pr. *Go on, and to the Altar lead.*

Chief Priest turns to the People, and sings on,

This hallow'd ground let no one tread,
Who is defil'd with Whoredom, or with Bloud,
Lest all our Pray'rs should be for them withstood.
   Let none be present at our Sacrifice,
But of an humble uncorrupted mind.
The God for wicked men will all our vows despise,
   And will to all our wishes be unkind.

[By this time they come near the Altar, they all bow, and divide, and stand on each side of the Altar, and the Chief Priest before. The Chief Priest kneels and kisses the Altar. The Priest and Boys kneel with him; they rise, and he, holding the Altar in his hands, sings alone, as follows.

Ch. Pr.   *Son of* Latona *and great* Jove,
In Delos *born, which thou so much dost love:*
Great God of Physick and of Archery,
     Of Wisdom, Wit and Harmony;
     God of all Divinations too,
Chor. of Voices{*To thee our Vows and Pray'rs are due,*
  and Instrum. {*To thee our,* &c.

[Chief Priest kneels, kisses the Altar,
then rises and sings.

Ch. Pr. *Thou gav'st the cruel Serpent* Python *death,*
Depriv'dst the Giant Tyrion *of his breath:*
Thou didst the monstrous Cyclops *too destroy,*
Who form'd the Thunder, which did kill thy Son.

(295)

Chor. *Thou light of all our life, and all our joy,*
　　　Our Offerings with our hearts are all thine own.

　　　　　　　　　　　　　　[Chief Priest kneels, and kisses the
　　　　　　　　　　　　　　　　Altar again.

Ch. Pr. *By sacred* Hyacinth, *thy much lov'd Flower,*
By Daphne*'s memory we thee implore,*
Thou wou'dst be present at our Sacrifice,
And not our humble Offerings despise.

Chorus of ⎫ *And we for ever will thy praise advance,*
Voices and ⎬ *Thou Author of all Light and Heat.*
Instrum. ⎭ *Let Pipes and Timbrels sound, and let them dance.*
　　　　　　Each day our worship we'll repeat.
　　　　　　Each day, &c.

　　　　　　　　　　　[A Dance of Priests entring from each
　　　　　　　　　　　　side of the Stage, with Cymbals, Bells,
　　　　　　　　　　　　and Flambeaux.

After the Dance, they all kneel, and the Chief Priest begins with a loud Voice ;
All answer as follows.

Ch. Pr. *Jupiter, Juno, Minerva, Saturn, Cibele.*
Respons. Be propitious to our Vows and Prayers.
Ch. Pr. *Mars, Bellona, Venus, Cupido, Vulcanus.*
Resp. Be propitious, *&c.*
Ch. Pr. *Bacchus, Pan, Neptunus, Sylvanus, Fawnus, Vertumnus, Palæmon.*
Resp. Be propitious, *&c.*
Ch. Pr. All ye Gods, Goddesses, and all the Powers.
Resp. Be propitious, *&c.*

They rise : The Chief Priest turns to the left hand, and runs, or dances about
the Altar, Priests and Boys following him, all the Instruments sounding.
They sing as follows :

　　　　　　　Chor. To Apollo *our Celestial King,* ⎰ The Dancers mingle
　　　　　　　　　We will Io Pæan *sing;* ⎱ 　with the Singers.
　　　　　　　　　Io Pæan, Io Pæan,
　　　　　　　　　Io Pæan *will we sing :*

The Chief Priest kneels at the Altar. The Boys stands about him. The Priest
takes the Libamina *from the Boys, after a little Pause. One Priest rises and*
waves a Wand. Then all fall on their knees.

1 *Pr.* Favete linguis, favete linguis, favete linguis.
2 *Pr. (rises, waves a wand)* Hoc agite, hoc agite, hoc agite.
　　　　　　　　　　　　　Ch. Pr. rises, and turns to the people.
Ch. Pr. *(with a loud Voice)* Τ ΊΣ ΤΗ ΔΕ.
Response *of all.* ΠΟΛΛΟΊ Κ'ΑΓΑΘΟΙ.

Chief Priest turns and kneels at the Altar again. The Boys run out and fetch, one a Flambeaux, the other little Fagots of Cedar, Juniper, &c. The Priest rises and lays them on the Altar. All but the Chief Priest and Boys are kneeling, intent upon the Altar without speech or motion. As soon as the fire is kindled, which the Priest does himself with the Flambeau.

Ch. Pr. (with a loud voice) Behold the Fire.

All but the Chief Priest fall flat on their faces, then rise again. The Boys reach the Libamina *to the Chief Priest: 1. The Censor, with Gums, which he offers. 2. The Barley Cake, which he strews with salt, then lays it on the Fire. Then sprinkles the Honey and Water on the Fire. Chief Priest waves his Wand to* Theander *and* Psyche, *who draw near, and kneel just behind.*

Ch. Pr. Now ask the God the thing for which you came,
And after that we'll sacrifice a Ram.
Thean. That we may know, we humbly pray,
Who shall *Psyche's* Husband be.
   She will most cheerfully obey
   Her Destiny, and your Decree.

As the Priestess Pythia *is mounting the Tripod, it Thunders and Lightens extreamly.* Apollo's *Image trembles, at which they all rise affrighted.*

Ch. Pr.   O Heaven! what prodigy is this?
   Something is in our holy Rites amiss.

It Thunders and Lightens again, the Image trembling, and in Convulsions, with a very loud and hollow Voice, utters these following Lines.

Apollo. **Y**OU must conduct her to that fatal place,
   Where miserable Lovers that despair,
   With howls and Lamentations fill the air;
  A Husband there your Daughter shall embrace.
   On *Venus* Rock upon the Sea,
   She must by you deserted be:
   A poys'nous Serpent there She'll find,
  By Heav'n he *Psyche's* Husband is design'd.
       [At this they all start, affrighted.

Thean. Gods! that I e'r should live to see this day.
     'Tis for some great offence
Of mine, that thou art to be snatch'd from hence.
   Oh take my life, and let her stay.

But 'tis in vain to ask, we must obey :
For which I'll weep my hated life away.
   Cydip. *Venus* has kept her word, and she shall be
                 Much more ador'd by me,
                 Then any other Deity.
   Aglau. Now my fair Sister must a Serpent have,
              'Stead of a Nuptial Bed, a Grave.
              Now she shall suffer for her Pride ;
Our Love and Hate will now be satisfi'd.
   Psyc. To whatsoe'r the Oracle thinks fit,
               I cheerfully submit :
     I have not liv'd so ill, but I
               With ease can die :
       I with a willing heart
       Can with my Life as with a trifle part :
       As no joy yet could ever fill my mind,
       I from no danger can distraction find.
   Thean.   Lead on ; and with a funeral pace,
       For I in that unhappy place
Must bury all my joy, and leave my life behind.
   Nican.   Stay but a moment, stay ;
You will not sure this Oracle obey.
             Consider and be wise :
If it be good *Psyche* to Sacrifice,
You were oblig'd to't without this command,
And we the action should not then withstand.
   Polyn. If bad, then Heav'n it self can't make it good :
All good and ill's already understood.
Heav'n has forbid the shedding guiltless blood.
If good and ill anew it has design'd,
The Gods are mutable, and change their mind.
   Nican. Be not by this Imposture, Sir, betray'd,
By this dull Idol which the Priests have made :
Too many Cheats are in the Temple found,
Their fraud does more then piety abound :
They make the sensless Image speak with ease
            What e'r themselves shall please.
   Ch. Pr. Do not the sacred Image thus profane,
Which will revenge it self, and all its Rites maintain.
   Polyn. If that be sacred, and you that adore,
Then him that made it you should worship more :
To th' poor Mechanick you give no respect,
Y' adore his Workmanship, but him neglect.

Nican. For Sacred you impose what you decree,
And the deluded Multitude believe,
By boaſting of Infallibility,
Th' unthinking Rabble you with ease deceive.
 Pol. Whatever in Divinity you know,
In all concernments of Mankind below :
    In all the objeſts of the Mind,
And in all humane Science we can find.
In Prieſts more Errors than in all Mankind.
 Nican. In Sacred Things yet you so much excel
All others, in your Sleeps you can foretel ;
When after Surfeits in your holy Feaſts
You sleep in Skins of sacrificed Beaſts,
The troubled Dreams you from those fumes receive,
To the unheedful World for Oracles you give.
 Thean. In holy Myſteries you muſt lay by
    Your Intricate Philosophy.
After the dreadful Cloud with Thunder broke,
It was some loud immortal Voice that spoke.
 Ch. Pr. The holy Rites you saw perform'd,
    By Miracles were now confirm'd.
 Nican. Miracles !
Your holy Cheats t' advance your Myſtery :
The nobleſt Science is Divinity.
But when become a Trade, I see, 'twill be
Like other Trades, maintain'd by Knavery.
 Ch. Pr. By Miracles the pow'r of Heav'n is known.
 Polyn. Heav'ns power is more by setl'd order shown.
The beauty of that order which is found,
To govern the Creation in a round,
The fix'd uninterrupted Chain, whereby
All things on one another muſt depend ;
This method proves a wise Divinity,
As much as should the Gods on earth deſcend.
 Ch. Pr. You speak from Nature, which is ignorance ;
But we to inspiration muſt advance.
 Nican. If, Prieſt, by Means not nat'ral Heav'n declares
Its will, and our obedience so prepares ;
The Gods by this their weakness wou'd confess,
What you call Miracles wou'd make them less.
If somthing without Nature they produce,
Nature is then defeſtive to their use :
And when by that they cannot work their end,

My Miracle their Instrument they mend.

    Polyn. If this be granted, Priest, by this we find,
The Gods foresee not, or else change their mind.
But Heav'n does nothing to our sense produce,
But it does outward Nat'ral Causes use.
Fools trust in Miracles, and Fools ne'r doubt :
'Tis ignorance of Causes, Priest, makes Fools devout.   [*Thunders again.*
    Ch. Pr.   Be gone, profane and wicked men,
           You have provok'd Heav'ns wrath again.
Heav'n does again to you in Thunder speak !
    Nican. 'Twas nothing but a petty cloud did break ;
What, can your Priesthoods grave Philosophy
So much amaz'd at common Thunder be ?
    Psyc. We should obey without these Prodigies ;
I to Heav'ns Will my own will sacrifice.
    Cidip. Must I then with my much lov'd Sister part ?
    Aglau. The dismal loss will break my tender heart.
    Thean. Joy of my Life, let's to the fatal place,
Where thine and all my sorrow is design'd :
When thee the pois'onous Serpent shall embrace,
Assure thy self I'll not stay long behind.
    Polyn. Thus the great *Agamemnon* was betray'd,
And *Iphigenia* thus a Victim made :
Such horrid ills Religion can perswade.   [*Exeunt omnes.*

The Scene changes to a Rocky Desart full of dreadful Caves, Cliffs, and
    Precipices, with a high Rock looking down into the Sea.

Enter two despairing Lovers.

    1 *Lov.* Ah what a dreadful Rocky Desart's this,
The Melancholy Region of despair :
Where e'er I turn me, poisonous Serpents hiss,
And with their venomous breaths infect the Air.
    2 *Lov.* Here pestilential vapours do abound,
And killing Damps the Vaults and Caverns breath ;
From dreadful gapings of the craggy ground,
The fatal Desart seems to yawn forth death.
    1 *Lov.* A gloomy darkness hovers o'r this place ;
Here sure the Sun ne'r shews his joyful face.
Nature this place for horrour did design :
           No beam of comfort here can shine.
    2 *Lov.*   Nothing but howls of sad despair,
And dismal groans of Wretches fill the Air.

Who in Agonies their hated lives resign.

    1 *Lov.* How many various ways to death we have :
Some from that Rock have plung'd into the Deep ;
And in the Sea we saw 'em find a grave.

    2 *Lov.* Some by their Ponyards meet deaths easie sleep :
        Some desp'rate Lovers find out death,
        By wilful stopping their own breath.

    1 *Lov.* Nature this place did for my grief intend.

    2 *Lov.* And here my fatal life and love shall end.

    1 *Lov. Psyche* is hither by *Apollo* sent,
Here to fulfil the Oracles intent.

Two despairing Men, and two despairing Women
sing as follows.

1 Man.   *Break, break distracted heart, there is no cure*
        For Love, my minds too raging Calenture.
1 Wom.   *Sighs which in other passions vent,*
       And give them ease when they lament,
  Are but the bellows to my hot desire.

2 Wom. *And tears in me not quench, but nourish fire.*

2 Man. *Nothing can mollifie my grief,*
    Or give my passion a relief.

1 Man. *Love is not like our earthly fire ;*
    You soon may smother out that flame ;
    Concealing does increase desire,
    No opposition Love can tame.

2 Wom. *Despair in Love transcends all pain,*
    Lost hope will ne'r return again.

1 Wom.   *In Hell there's no such misery,*
      As now oppresses me.
      I this one pang alone
  Wou'd change for Sisyphus *his Stone.*

2 Man.   *I would the torments which I feel*
      Change for Ixion's *Wheel.*

2 Wom. *The Vulture should on me for ever feed,*
  Rather than thus my heart for Love should bleed.

1 Man. *Oh* Tantalus ! *for thy eternal Thirst ;*
  I'm more on Earth then thou in Hell accurst.

1 Wom.   *Was ever grief like mine ?*

2 Wom.   *Like mine ?*

1 Man.   *Like mine ?*

2 Man.   *Like mine ?*

Cho-⎱ rus. ⎰	*Was ever grief like mine?* *Was ever, &c.*
2 Wom.	*Nothing but death can cure our misery.*
1 Wom.	*I'll die.*
1 Man.	*I'll die.*
2 Man.	*I'll die.*
Cho-⎱ rus. ⎰	*Nothing but death can cure our misery.* *Nothing but, &c.*

1 *Man speaks.* How long shall I for this dull Serpent stay,
   Ere I become his prey ?
  Come forth from out thy pois'nous Den :
  Dost thou despise the flesh of men ?
 2 *Man.* The lazy Serpent breakfasted to day ;
I will not for his waking stomach stay :
I'll b' Author of my fate, and make my self away. *[Falls on his sword.*
 1 *Wom.* Your Sex no more in courage shall excel,
   For I can die as well.
I in this Dagger my Relief will find,
And kill my Body thus to ease my mind.   *[Kills her self.*
  1 *Man.* I to the top of all the Rock will climb ;
   And if in little time
  The Serpent there I cannot see,
  I'll find a way to follow thee.
 2 *Wom.* My heart that office will perform for me.
   A death-like pang I feel,
   I have no need of steel.
  A faint cold sweat besmears my face,
  I can make hast and dye apace.
And these are the last words I e're shall speak,
Farewel my cruel Love, for thee my heart does break. *[She dies.*
   Then he on the top of the Rock falls headlong into the Sea.

Enter Theander, Psyche, Cidippe, Aglaura, Psyche's *two* Women, *and other*
  Attendants, *in Funeral habits, weeping ; then the Guards.*

 Psyc. Oh stop those Royal Fountains, tears are things
Which ill become the Majesty of Kings.
 Thean. But they become a Father, who must lose
The only comfort of his fading life ;
Who barbarously must his Child expose,
By Heavens command, to be a Serpents Wife.
 Psyc. That dread command I'm ready to obey,
   I beg you will no longer stay.

Deaths cold embraces I will court ;
I can my fate, but not your tears support.
 Thean.   Ye Gods, why did ye ever bless
Me with this gift, to snatch it back again ?
My burden's greater than I can suftain !
 Psyc. I never could deserve such tenderness ;
Nay, good Sir, dry your eyes, my heart will break ;
   To bear your grief, I am too weak.
 Thean. Oh that I'd never seen thy much-lov'd face,
   And that thou'dft perish'd in the womb :
I had not led thee to this fatal place,
Thy Father had not brought thee living to thy Tomb.
 Psyc.   Your sad complaints so soften me,
   My heart will melt to that degree,
That I shall have none left when death I see.
 Thean. Heav'ns ! what could thus your cruelty provoke ?
Your Altars, by my bounty, daily smoke.
   With Fat, with Incense, and with Gums :
   Nor have you wanted *Hecatombs*.
   And muft I thus rewarded be ?
 Cidip. See how the Dotard weeps, while we
   Rejoyce at this her Deftiny.
   Oh how it wou'd my envy feed,
   Could my glad eyes behold her bleed !
 Aglau. O good dear Serpent, make her sure,
   Her death, our grief can only cure.
   Oh that she were at my command,
And that her heart were throbbing in my hand.
   Some miracle may else relieve
Her from this death, and we afresh may grieve.
 Psyc. Good Sir, be gone, the will of Heav'n obey.
   Besides, if you should longer ftay,
Before the Serpent comes, my life will fteal away.
Weigh not your loss, but what you have remain ;
You have the comfort of my Sifters left,
   Who will your drooping Age suftain,
   When y'are of me bereft.
Sifters, be good, and to my Father give
   All comfort, and his grief relieve ;
He, from you Two, much pleasure may receive.
 Cid. Our grief as much as his relief will need,
   Of that I might with *Psyche* bleed :
   Did not the Gods self-murder hate,

I wou'd accompany your Fate.

Aglau. Oh that the Gods would suffer me
　　　To be exchang'd for thee!

Psyc. Sisters, farewel, pray dry your eyes:　　　　　*[Kisses her Sisters.*
　　　I am for you a Sacrifice.
You may your choice of many Princes have,
When I am cold, forgotten in my Grave.

Thean. Gods! can I yet hear this and live?
Oh take my Life, or me my *Psyche* give.

Psyc.　　　Sir, if you longer stay,
　　　You'll cause my Death, not they.
　　　I on my Knees beseech you quit
This fatal place, and to Heaven's will submit.
　　　Farewel: 'tis time,
I now the Rock my fatal Tomb must climb,
　　　Farewel for ever——

Thean.　　　Say not so,
　　　For I to death will go,
My Soul to morrow shall meet thine below.　　　*[Exeunt all but* Psyche.

Psyche sola. Even now grim death I slightly did esteem;
With the wrong end o' th' Glass I look'd on him;
Then afar off and little did he seem:
　　　Now my Perspective draws him near,
He very big and ugly does appear.
Away——it is the base false Glass of fear.

Enter Nicander *and* Polynices.

Why do you come to see me wretched here?
What can you hope from her whose death's so near?

Polyn. To save your life, our lives we will expose.

Psyc. Can mortal Men the heav'nly pow'rs oppose?

Nican.　　　What Heav'n commands is surely good.
Heav'n has declar'd 'gainst shedding humane bloud.
Bores, Rams and Bulls will serve *Apollo*'s turn,
Whilst Gums and Incense on his Altars burn.
'Tis to the Priests that you are sacrific'd.

Psyc. I must not hear the Oracle despis'd.

Nican. In vain, 'gainst prejudice we still dispute:
Our Swords shall this great Oracle confute.
No Serpent whilst we live shall you embrace,
Nor any other Rival in this place.

Psyc. He carries deadly venom in his breath,
　　　Which certainly will give you death.

Polyn. *Cadmus*, without Love's aid, the Dragon slew ;
Inspir'd by Love, what cannot Princes do ?
  Psyc. Why for my preservation shou'd you strive ?
For neither my affection e'r cou'd move.
Though Heav'n for that wou'd suffer me to live :
No Prince on Earth cou'd ever make me love.
  Nican. 'Tis time we both of us shou'd dye,
Since we from you no pity can deserve.
Yet——
Had we no love for generosity,
Spight of your self we wou'd your Life preserve.
  Polyn.   You have made Rivals thus agree,
Though cou'd you love, but one cou'd happy be.
Each will assist the other, and you'll see,
In spight of Oracles we'll set you free.
  Psyc. Farewel : I must not hear this blasphemy.
  Nican.   We cannot leave you till you dye,
            No Oracle shall that deny.

> [*The Earth opens, infernal Spirits rise and*
> *hurry the Princes away.   Two Zephiri*
> *descend and take* Psyche *by each arm,*
> *and fly into the Clouds with her.*

Cupid *descends a little way, hanging in the Air.*

  Cup. Be gone, you Rivals of an angry Deity :
Shall I by insolent Princes rivall'd be ?
Shall Mortals for my *Psyche* strive with me ?
          Vulcan make hast, prepare
          My costly Palace for my fair ;
          I in that splendid place,
My Love, my Dear, my *Psyche* will embrace.   [*He flies away.*

Enter Nicander *and* Polynices.

  Nican. By what Enchantment were we hurri'd hence ?
Psyche is gone.   Let's use all diligence
          Soon to prevent her fate,
          Or we shall come too late.
  Polyn.   We will our much-lov'd *Psyche* find.
Or we will leave our hated lives behind.   [*Exeunt.*

ACT III.

The Scene is the Palace of Cupid, *Compos'd of wreath'd Columns of the*
Corinthian *Order ; the Wreathing is adorn'd with Roses, and the Columns
have several little* Cupids *flying about 'em, and a single* Cupid *standing
upon every Capital. At a good distance are seen three Arches, which divide
the first Court from the other part of the Building : The middle Arch is noble
and high, beautified with* Cupids *and* Festoons, *and supported with Columns
of the foresaid Order. Through these Arches is seen another Court, that
leads to the main Building, which is at a mighty distance. All the* Cupids,
Capitals and Inrichments of the whole Palace are of Gold. Here the Cyclops
*are at work at a Forge, forging great Vases of Silver. The Musick strikes
up, they dance, hammering the Vases upon Anvils.*

After the Dance, Enter Vulcan.

Vulcan *sings.* YE bold Sons of Earth, that attend upon Fire,
  Make haste with the Palace, lest Cupid *should stay ;*
  You must not be lazy when Love does require,
For Love is impatient, and brooks no delay.
When Cupid *you serve, you must toil and must sweat,*
Redouble your blows, and your labour repeat.

  The vigorous young God's not with laziness serv'd,
  He makes all his Vassals their diligence show,
  And nothing from him but with pains is deserv'd ;
  The brisk Youth that falls on, and still follows his blow,
  Is his favourite still. The considerate Fool,
  He as useless lays by for a pitiful Tool.

1 Cycl. *This Palace is finish'd, and the other shall be*
   Made fit for his small Deity.

2 Cycl. *But fire makes us cholerick, and apt to repine,*
   Unless you will give us some Wine.

 Chor. *With swinging great Bowls,*
    Let's refresh our dry Souls,
 And then we'll to work with a Clink, clink, clink ;
 But first let us drink, but first let us drink.

Vulcan. *Let each take his Bowl then, and hold it to his nose,*
   Then let him redouble his blows.

 Cycl. *Nay, stint us not so, but let each take his two,*
    And twice as much as we can do.

(306)

Chor.   *With swinging great Bowls,*
            Let's refresh, &c.

Vulc. *Ye Slaves, will you never from drunkenness refrain?*
          Remember Ulysses *again.*
Cycl. Ulysses *is a Dog, were he here he shou'd find,*
          We'd scorn him, and drink our selves blind.

Chor.   *With swinging great Bowls,*
            Let's refresh, &c.
                    [They take their Kans in their hands

Pyra. *Here,* Harpes, *to you.*   Harp. *Here,* Brontes, *to you,*
      And so take each Cyclops *his due.*
Bron. *To thee,* Steropes.   Ster. Pyracmon, *to thee.*
Omn. *And thus in our Cups we'll agree.*

Chor.   *With swinging great Bowls,*
            Let's refresh, &c.

Vulc. *Be gone, or great* Jove *will for Thunder-bolts stay,*
          The World grows so wicked each day.
Cycl. *He has less need of Thunder than we have of Wine :*
          We'd drink, though great Jove *should repine.*

Chor.   *With swinging great Bowls,*
            Let's refresh, &c.   [The *Cyclops* dance again.

      Enter Cupid *and* Zephyrus, *at which they all run away.*
    Cup. You are my best of Servants, y'have done well.
Say, *Zephryus,* how do you like my Love ?
    Zeph. Her Beauty does all mortal forms excel,
She should be snatch'd from Earth to reign above.
But why do you a humane shape now wear ?
Why will you not your self a God appear ?
    Cup.   At first, invisible I'll be.
          Then like a Prince I will be seen ;
          Me like a God when she shall see,
          I'll make her my Immortal Queen.
When Love thus slily his approaches makes,
          He takes fast hold, and long will stay ;
But if by storm he once possession takes,
His Empire in the heart will soon decay.
          Here comes my Love, Away,
And to her honour dedicate this day.   [*Exeunt* Cupid *and* Zephyrus.

Enter Psyche.

Psyc. To what enchant'd Palace am I brought,
   Adorn'd beyond all humane thought ?
Here Art and Natures utmost powers conspire,
   To make the Ornament entire.
Where e'r I turn me, here my dazl'd eye
Does nought but Gold, or precious Gems descry :
   This sure is some divine abode,
   The splendid Palace of some God :
And not a Den where Humane bloud is spilt.
This sure was never for a Serpent built.
   I am at this no less amaz'd,
Than at my sudden passage to the place.
   With wonder round about I've gaz'd,
And, which is strange, I've seen no humane face.
'Tis sure some Aery Vision which I see,
And I to this imaginary height
   Was rais'd by Heav'n in cruelty,
That I might suffer a severer Fate.
I on a Precipice of hope was plac'd,
   That so my fall might greater be,
And down with violence I shall be cast
To th' bottom of despair, th' Abyss of misery.
Where is the Serpent ? when will he appear ?
 Cup. The Serpent which you must embrace is near.
 Psyc. What Divine Harmony invades my Ear ?
This is a voice I cou'd for ever hear.
O speak again, and strike my ravish'd sense
   With thy harmonious excellence !
What Pow'r Divine provokes within my bloud,
I know not what, that cannot be withstood ?
 Cup. Whatever can be pleasant but in thought,   *[within.*
   Shall for my Love be sought :
This shall her Palace, here her Empire be ;
She shall have Sovereign command o'r that and me.
 Psyc.   No object of my sense could e'r
   Transport me till this hour ;
I feel a Passion mix'd with Joy and Fear,
That's caus'd by this unknown invisible Power.
   Who are you that does charm me so ?
Such pain and pleasure I ne'r felt before ;
   You are by this some God, I know,
   And I must you adore——   *[she kneels.*

Enter Cupid *and takes her up.*

Oh Heaven! what glorious thing is this I see?
        What unknown Deity?
His shape is humane, but his face divine;
He calls me Love: but ah! would he were mine.
    Cup. I am the Serpent Heav'n for you design'd,
        Which shou'd on you his poison breathe.
    Psyc. This poison ne'r can cause my death,
For such a Serpent I wou'd quit Mankind.
Yours is the pleasant'st Poison e'r was felt;
My eyes drop showers of joy, my heart will melt.
        My mind was never full before,
        But now my swelling Joys run o'r;
        My heart does pant like a seal'd Doves:
        What is it thus my passion moves?
    Cup.   How does my charming fair, my Dove?
        Let me approach, my Dear, my Love:
        Let me but touch thy snowy hand,
        And thou shalt all my heart command.
    Psyc. There's no request of yours I can withstand.
        Oh I am stung! what's this I feel?
            It is no pointed Steel:
        'Tis such a pretty tingling smart,
            Now it invades my heart.
        Oh it encreases on me still,
        And now my blood begins to chill.
        But, Oh the pleasure! Oh the pain!
And, Oh! might both a thousand years remain!
    Cup.   Courage, my Dove, I have thee here,   [*embraces her.*
        Thou need'st no Serpent fear;
For I am all the Serpents thou shalt see,
And Love is all the poison I'll enfuse in thee.
    Psyc. What can it be my senses thus allarms?
What have you done t' your hand that thus it charms?
But, Oh your pow'rful eyes bewitch me more.
I never saw or felt such eyes before.
Nor know I now what 'tis I feel or see.   [*He turns his head aside.*
Turn not away those eyes that poison me.
        Those sweet, those piercing am'rous eyes,
That can so easily a heart surprize.
Oh, may my breast this poison ne'r forsake!
        I'm sure no Antidote I'll take.
Why do you sigh? are you transported too?

(309)

Cup. As you by me, so I am charm'd by you.
      Oh let my wandring heart find rest
      Within thy soft and snowy breast.
      Thou must to me thy heart resign,
      And in exchange I'll give thee mine.
And when my heart within thy breast does sit,
Thou must be kind, and nurse, and cherish it.
   Psyc. Oh! how mine flutters ; yet I hold it fast,
      It beats till it it self will tire ;
'Twill lose it self with violent desire :
Do what I can, it will be gone at last.
Oh give me thine, for mine will fly away ;
Ah give it me ! for if you longer stay,
      Mine will be gone, and I shall die.
Pray let your heart the want of mine supply.
   Cup. Thou through thy Lips, my Love, must mine˗receive,
And the same way thine to my breast convey ;
And when to me that pretty thing thou'lt give,
I'll use't so kindly, 'tshall not fly away.
   Psyc. Then take it, for with me it will not stay.   *[They kiss.*
      What have I done ! I am to blame ;
      I blush and feel a secret shame :
But I feel something which o'rcomes that sense.
      I'm charm'd with so much excellence !
Some Power Divine thus animates my bloud,
And 'twere a sin, if that should be withstood.
      Your sacred form so much does move,
      That I pronounce aloud, I love.
How am I rapt ! what is it thus does force
My Inclination from its proper course ?
I was to love an open enemy ;
      But now the more I look on Thee,
      The more I love. My first surprise
Is heighten'd still by thy bewitching eyes.
   Cup. Love's debt was long deny'd by thee,
But now h'as paid himself with usury.
   Psyc. Should I to one I know not be thus kind,
To one who will, perhaps, unconstant be ;
      Pray let me so much favour find,
To let me know who 'tis has conquer'd me.
   Cup. Do not suspect my constancy,
      Believe my sighs, and then trust me.
      Words may be false and full of Art,

Sighs are the nat'ral language of the heart.
But, pray beware of curiosity,
      Lest it should ruine Thee and Me.
      You must not yet know who I am ;
      I will in time disclose my name.
I in this Region a vast Empire have,
Each Prince y' have seen compar'd to me's a Slave.
To me all Grecian Princes Tribute owe,
      Which they shall pay to you.
A thousand Beauties shall be still at hand,
      Waiting for thy command ;
And without envy, they shall thee adore.
The pomp which here thou shalt enjoy, is more
Than e'r was seen in Earthly Princes Courts :
      And pleasures here shall be
      Beyond all mortal Luxury ;
Our Recreation shall be heav'nly sports.
And to such splendid Joys I thee invite,
As do the Gods on Festivals delight.
But first thy palatte thou shalt satisfie,
Thy ear shall then be ravish'd, then thy eye ;
And all thy other Senses thou shalt feast :
Here thou shalt entertain, and I will be the guest.

      This following Song is sung by invisible Singers.

     ALL Joy to fair Psyche *in this happy place,*
       And to our great Master, who her shall embrace :
       May never his Love nor her Beauty decay,
    But be warm as the Spring, and still fresh as the Day.
Chor.   *No Mortals on Earth ever wretched cou'd prove,*
     If still while they liv'd, they'd be always in love.

    There's none without Love ever happy can be,
    Without it each Brute were as happy as we.
    The knowledge men boast of doth nothing but vex,
    And their wandring Reason their Minds does perplex.
Chor.   *But no Mortals, &c.*

    Loves sighs and his tears are mix'd with delights,
    But were he still pester'd with cares and with frights,
    Shou'd a thousand more troubles a Lover invade,
    By one happy moment they'd fully be paid.
Chor.   *No Mortals, &c.*

Then lose not a moment, but in Pleasure employ it ;
For a moment once lost will always be so ;
Your Youth requires Love, let it fully enjoy it,
And push on your Nature as far as 'twill go.

Chor.   *No Mortals,* &c.

Psyc. How am I rap't ! what pleasures do I find !
My Love, I have but one request to thee ;
        Two Sisters I have left behind,
        I hope my Love will be so kind,
        That they the Witnesses may be
Of all my pomp and my felicity.

Enter Zephyrus.

Cup.   My *Zephyrus* is still at hand
        To wait for thy command.
        Be gone !———
Zeph.   I'll fly as quick as thought,
They suddenly shall to this place be brought.   [*Exit* Zephyrus.
   Cup. My Dear, let them not here much time employ,
        For I must thy whole heart enjoy.
From me, my Love, not one poor thought must stray,
For I have given thee all my heart away.
        But now prepare thy Ears and Eyes,
        For I thy senses will surprise.
        Along with me, and thou shalt see
        What Miracles in Love there be.   [*Exeunt.*

The Scene changes to the principal Street of the City, with vast numbers of People looking down from the tops of Houses, and out of the Windows and Balconies, which are hung with Tapestry. In this Street is a large Triumphal Arch, with Columns of the Dorick *Order, adorned with the Statues of* Fame *and* Honour, *&c. Beautified with Festoons of Flowers ; all the Inrichments of Gold. Through this Arch, at a vast distance, in the middle of a Piazza, is seen a stately Obelisk.*

Enter two Men.

   1 *Man.* What shouts are those that echo from the Plain ?
   2 *Man.* The Stranger-Princes have the Monster slain :
The People the victorious Champions meet,
And them with Shouts and Acclamations greet.
   1 *Man.* Our freedom these brave Conqu'rors have restor'd,
The bloud of Men no more shall be devour'd ;
No more young Ladies shall be snatch'd away
        To be the cruel Serpents prey.

2 *Man.* For this the large Triumphal Arch was built,
For this the Joyful People meet in throngs,
The Princes Triumph for the bloud they spilt,
And celebrate the Conquest with loud Songs.
They in this place a Sacrifice prepare,
To pay their vows and thanks to th' God of War.

                [A Consort of Loud Martial Musick.

Enter the Priests of *Mars*, one carrying the Serpents Head upon the
Spear, all of them having Targets, Breast-plates, and Helmets of Brass.
Then the *Praesul*, having a Trophy of Arms carry'd before him.   Then
Nicander, Polynices, Cydippe, Aglaura, Train and Guards. The Priests
sing this following Song, and dance to't.

        L*ET us loudly rejoyce,*
             With glad heart and with voice ;
        For the Monster is dead,
   And here is his head.
   No more shall our Wives
   Be afraid of their Lives,
Nor our Daughters by Serpents miscarry.
    The Oracle then
    Shall bestow them on Men,
And they not with Monsters shall marry.
    Let us lowdly rejoyce
   With glad heart and with voice ;
   For the Monster is dead,
   And here is his head.

Præsul sings.   *Great God of War to thee*
          We offer up our thanks and pray'r
            For by thy mighty Deity
          Triumphing Conquerours we are.
Chor.   *Thou'rt great among this heavenly race,*
         And onely to the Thunderer giv'st place.

Præsul.   Jove *is thy father, but does not exceed*
          Thy Deity on any score.
     Thou, when thou wilt, canst make the whole world bleed,
     And thou canst heal their breaches by thy power.
Chor.   *'Tis thou that must to Armies give success,*
     That thou must Kingdoms too with safety bless,
     Thou that must bring, and then must guard their peace.

They dance, striking their Swords upon the Targets, showing the postures
of their Swords, Kettle-Drums beating, and Trumpets sounding:
Whilst the *Praesul* and the rest prepare the Altar, and kindle the Fire.
After the Dance————

Præs. sings.   *While we to Mars his praises sing,*
        A Horse, th' appointed Victim, bring.
        [*Mars* and *Venus* meet in the Air in their Chariots,
        his drawn by Horses, and hers by Doves.

Venus sings. *Great God of War, if thou dost not despise*
      The power of my victorious eyes,
        Reject this Sacrifice.
      My Deity they disrespect,
        My Altars they neglect,
      And Psyche *onely they adore,*
        Whom they shall see no more.
      Have I yet left such influence on your heart,
      As to enjoyn you wou'd take my part.
      By some known token punish their offence,
        And let them know their insolence.

Mars.   *So much your influence on me remains,*
        That still I glory in my chains,
      What ever you command, shall be
        A sov'reign Law to me.
      These saucy Mortals soon shall see
      What 'tis to disrespect your Deity.
      To show how much for you I them despise,
        Since they with Venus *dare contend,*
        Ye powers of Hell your Furies send,
        And interrupt their Sacrifice.

                         [*Mars* and *Venus* fly away.

*Furies descend and strike the Altar, and break it, and every one flies away with a
fire-brand in's hand.*

1 *Pr.*   What dreadful prodigies are these!
        Hence from this bloudy rage let's flie,
        And in his Temple let us try
      If we his angry Godhead can appease.
Nican. What Magick Charms do this sad place infest,
And us in all our actions thus molest?
Polyn.   The pow'r of Hell it sure must be
        That thus against us wages war;
        For when fair *Psyche* we wou'd free,

It still does mischiefs against us prepare.
But no Enchantment yet our courage binds,
No accidents can alter valiant minds.
    Nican. In spight of Hell we will go on in quest
Of our lov'd *Psyche,* who is charm'd from hence.
    Aglau. You might from all your fruitless toyls have rest,
If of your present fortune y' had a sense.
    Cid. Our Father, who is now at point of death,
Does in his Will us two to you bequeath.
    Aglau.   Envy it self will sure confess,
Our Beauties and our Vertues are not less,
Then the mean Idol's you so much adore,
And whom ye never can see more ;
The monster you have slain did her devour.
    Polyn. We by his rav'nous Maw did find to day,
The Monster had not yet made her his prey.
    Cid. What if he had, we two are left behind,
And by the Gods you are for us design'd.
    Nican. Heav'n has not yet to me reveal'd that mind,
My Inclinations still are hers I find.
The honour's great we might by you enjoy,
But it would all our vows and all our love destroy.
    Polyn. To *Psyche* I have offer'd my whole heart,
Sh' has for no other left me the least part.
Pardon that I the honour must refuse ;
No Mortals can their own affections chuse ;
Love, Heav'ns high power does into us infuse.
    Nican. When we lost *Psyche,* solemnly we swore,
The search of her we never wou'd give o'r.
    Polyn. Should we not find her, we our lives must spend,
Which in th' unwearied search of her must end.
    Aglau. Think you with safety you shall us despise ?
Though we're too weak to wound you with our eyes,
Our full revenge shall both of you pursue,
And give what to your insolence is due.
    Cid. Your heads shall pay for the affront you give,
And you shall dye, or we will cease to live.
    Nican. If danger cou'd our courages remove,
We were not fit t' aspire to *Psyche's* love.
    Polyn.   Our absence now you must excuse,
We in our search no farther time must lose.   [*Exeunt* Nican. Polyn.
    Aglau. I have a trusty Villain which I'll send,
Who in disguise shall their unwary steps attend ;

(315)

And then an ambush shall for them be laid,
That their base lives may be to us betray'd.
   Cid. The powers of all this Kingdom we'll engage,
To sacrifice their lives to our insatiate rage.
   Aglau.   They dearly shall by their example show,
How soon rejected Love to dangerous Rage can grow.   [*Exeunt ambo.*

ACT IV.

*The Scene is a stately Garden belonging to the Magnificent Palace, seen in the
former Act. The great Walk is bounded on either side with Great Statues of
Gold standing upon Pedestals, with small Figures of Gold sitting at their feet :
And in large Vases of Silver are Orenge, Lemon, Citron, Pomegranate : and
behind Mirtle, Jessemine, and other Trees. Beyond this a noble Arbour,
through which is seen a less Walk, all of Cypress Trees, which leads to another
Arbour at a great distance.*

               Enter Aglaura, Cydippe, Psyche *with her Train.*

Aglau. ENough the Splendor of your Court w' have seen,
        Such ne'r was known by any earthly Queen.
      Cyd. But we your Conqu'ring Lover wou'd behold,
Of whom such charming stories you have told.
   Psyc. Oh ! he's the brightest thing your eyes e'r saw ;
Beauty he has might give the whole World Law.
And then such tender kindness you shall see ;
For he delights in nothing but in me.
        We sport and revel all the day,
In soft delights melting the hours away.
And such resistless ways he has to charm.
        We kiss, embrace, and arm in arm,
        With am'rous sighs, and soft discourse,
Our fainting Passions still we reinforce :
When I would speak, my words he does devour ;
And when he speaks, I kiss him o'r and o'r.
And when from kissing we our lips remove,
He tells a thousand pretty Tales of Love.
And all the while his beauty I survey,
And he so greedily beholds my eyes,
As he'd devour them. But a moment stay,
And he will you, as he did me, surprise.   [*Exit* Psyche.

Aglau. What cursed Fate is this, that did ordain,
That she shou'd have such pleasure, we such pain ?
Oh that I had infection in my breath,
I my own life wou'd lose to give her death.
   Cid. Base Fortune ! that on *Psyche* wou'd bestow
          So vast a share of happiness,
And give her elder Sisters so much less,
That she shou'd be so high, and we so low.
   Aglau. Such glory yet no Monarch ever saw ;
Such humble Vassals, such obedient awe,
Such shining Palaces yet ne'r have been
Such pomp the Sun in all his progress ne'r has seen.
   Cid. A thousand Beauties wait for her command,
As many heavenly Youths are still at hand :
         And to our envious eyes she chose
         These hated objects to expose.
   Aglau. When we to our great joy believ'd,
         That she destroy'd had been,
Oh how the Ridling God has us deceiv'd ;
We see her here like some immortal Queen,
Whom all her subjects serve not, but adore.
   Cid. Oh ! I shall die with envy : say no more,
But of some quick revenge let's meditate,
         To interrupt their happy state :
         Let's by some Art cause fatal Jealousies
         Between these prosperous Lovers to arise.

     Enter Cupid *and* Psyche, *with many Attendants.*

   Aglau. They're here : What divine Object strikes my eyes ?
   Cid. What heavenly thing does my weak heart surprise ?
   Aglau. Her hated sight I can no longer bear.
   Cid. Oh with what Joy I could her heart-strings tear !
   Aglau. This is the goodliest Creature Heav'n e're made ;
And I will summon Hell up to my aid.
         But I will *Psyche's* life destroy ;
And I will then this God-like Youth enjoy.
   Cid. When I am dead, he may be had by thee :
But know, *Aglaura,* I'll ne'r live to see
This goodly thing enjoy'd by any one but me.
   Cup. Ladies——
You such a welcome in this place shall find,
As fits the greatness of your Sisters mind ;
And by your entertainment I will show,

What I to my lov'd *Psyche* owe :
For her shall Quires of *Cupids* sing,
For her the Sphears shall their loud Musick bring.

SONG.

LET old *Age* in its envy and malice take pleasure,
  In business that's sower, and in hoarding up treasure :
By dullness seem wise, be still peevish and nice ;
And what they cannot follow, let them rail at as vice.

Wise Youth will in Wine and in Beauty delight,
Will revel all day, and will sport all the night.
For never to love, wou'd be never to live,
And Love must from Wine its new vigour receive.

How insipid were life without those delights,
In which lusty hot Youth spend their dayes and their nights ;
Of our nauseous dull beings we too soon should be cloy'd,
Without those bless'd joys which Fools onely avoid.

Unhappy grave Wretches who live by false measure,
And for empty vain shadows refuse real pleasure ;
To such Fools while vast joys on the witty are waiting,
Life's a tedious long journey without ever baiting.

Now see what is to *Psyche*'s beauty due,
And what th' Almighty pow'r of Love can show :
These senseless Figures motion shall receive ;
Psyche's bright beams can life to Statues give.
  [*Ten Statues leap from their Pedestals, and dance. Ten* Cupids
  *rise from the Pedestals, strew all the Stage with Flowers, and
  fly all several ways. During the Dance,* Cupid *and* Psyche
  retire.

Cid.   What with divine Magnificence
        They in this place treat every sense ?
Aglau. Excess of Love and Hate disturb my rest,
        Which equally divide my breast.
Cid. You may hate her, and other Princes love ;
But your affection must from him remove,
Or th' utmost rage of a revengeful Rival prove.
  Aglau. Mountains shall sooner leap or fly,
The Sun may prove inconstant, but not I :
All my presumptuous Rivals I'll destroy ;
I cannot live, unless I him enjoy.

Cid. Then suddenly resign you hated breath ;
        You shall not live to cause my death.
        Your fruitless Love shall soon be loſt.
You to your elder Siſter shall give place,
For I will this Celeſtial Youth embrace,
Though it the lives of half the world shou'd coſt.
  Aglau. The pow'r of Hell shall ne'r change my design ;
I wou'd a thousand Lives before one Love resign.
  Cid. But *Psyche's* Life and Love muſt have an end,
        Or we in vain for him contend,
What e'r againſt each other we design,
Againſt the common Enemy let's joyn.
  Aglau. Should we kill her, it would provoke his hate,
And on our selves pull down a certain Fate.
        Let's poison them with jealousie ;
        And Lovers had much better die,
        Then suffer that extremity.

Enter Psyche.

Psyc. Now Siſters ! how do you approve my Dear ?
Cid. You are secure : but give us leave to fear.
Psyc. Fear not : you are in my Proteċtion now.
Aglau. We fear not for our selves, but you.
Psyc. For me ! I am so full of Joy,
That nothing can my happiness deſtroy.
I have my Love, and that's enough for me.
My life is one continued Extasie.
        His love to me is infinite,
        Each moment does transcend
        Ages of common gross delight,
For which dull sensual Men so much contend.
  Cid. Why does he ſtill conceal his name ?
It argues little love, or else much shame.
  Psyc. You cannot doubt his love, he is so kind ;
Envy in him no cause of shame can find :
What need I care who 'tis I love,
Since all that see him muſt my choice approve.
  Aglau. This violent Love may soon decay,
And he for some new Miſtriss may
        Your easie heart betray.
  Cid.   When he shall please to frown,
You from this heighth are suddenly thrown down :
And when he thus shall have abandon'd you,

(319)

On whom will you inflict the vengeance due ?

Psyc. Could I this fatal change survive,
I sure should be the wretched'st thing alive.

Aglau. True Love has no reserve, this is some cheat ;
Your wisdom's small, though your affection's great.

Cid. Th' Impostor does by Magick Art surprise !
And this is all delusion of our eyes.
The Miracles each moment does produce,
   Sufficiently may make this clear ;
Your Lover does no Natural Causes use.
All Natures Order is inverted here.

Aglau. You see that his Attendants are
   The winged Spirits of the Air.
He's sure some *Demon*, which commands the Winds,
   And him the Clouds obey :
How easily may he delude our minds,
Wh' our bodies can by Winds and Clouds convey.
   This must be some inchanted place.

Cid. (*aside.*) Let him be what he will, I'll him embrace.
(*To her.*) How soon may Fate your seeming Heav'n destroy,
Which like a dream reflects imaginary Joy.

Psyc. Oh I am seiz'd with an unusual fright,
A sudden stop is put to my delight.

Aglau. This still may be the Serpent you did fear,
Though with a humane shape he cheats your eyes ;
And Heav'n by this more cruel will appear,
After this Joy to ruine by surprise.

Cid. In wrath the Oracle thy doom declar'd,
Here no effects we of its anger see :
Thou know'st not yet what ruine is prepar'd,
What dreadful Fate Heav'n does reserve for thee.

Psyc. How I'm amazed ! Oh my poor trembling heart .

Enter Zephyrus.

Zeph. My Lord commands your Sisters must depart,
   And none must his commands deny.

Aglau. What is't I hear ! I dye, I dye !

Cid. But if I dye, I will not dye alone ;
She shall not here remain when I am gone.

Aglau. Hold ! take me with thee in thy brave design ;
I'll in the noble execution joyn.

   [*Both offer to stab at* Psyche, *as she looks another way, and
   are snatch'd away by* Zephyri.

(320)

Psyc. Ah! what unwelcome change is this I see?
Must they so suddenly be snatch'd from me?

Enter Cupid.

Cup. Now let's enjoy our selves, the time invites:
True Love alone in privacy delights.
         What is't disturbs my *Psyche's* mind?
         What fatal change is this I find?
Such a black storm me-thinks hangs on thee now,
As I have seen upon the Mornings brow;
Which blushing first had promis'd a fair day,
But strait did nought but dark-swoln Clouds display.
Is it your Sisters absence makes you grieve?
All such relations you shou'd now forget;
Lovers should for each other onely live,
And having one another should have no regret.
  Psyc. So small a thing cannot afflict my mind.
  Cup. 'Tis for some Rival then your griefs design'd.
  Psyc. This mean suspition proves my Lord unkind!
Ah! did your charms but to your self appear,
You'd know that I no other chains cou'd wear.
No Rhetorick can paint my Loves excess,
Ere mine can be describ'd, it must be less.
  Cup.   I love thee too at such a rate,
         No Mortal can approach my height.
         What is it can produce thy grief?
  Psyc. I fear you'll not afford it your relief.
  Cup. If thou by any thing my wrath cou'dst move,
'Twou'd be by thy suspicion of my love.
Thou o'r my heart art grown so absolute,
That no commands of thine I can dispute:
Thou of thy pow'r know'st not the large extent;
To ease thy doubt, make an experiment.
  Psyc. No: I shall find a harsh repulse, I fear.
  Cup.   By thy victorious eyes,
Which govern now the heart they did surprise;
By th' Gods inviolable Oath I swear,
By *Styx*, all thy commands shall be to me
         Sacred, as Heav'ns decree.
  Psyc. I with these am'rous vows am doubly pleas'd,
I am of half my grief already eas'd.
By this all fear of coldness you remove,
And then you'll tell me now, who 'tis I love.

Cup. Heav'n!   [*Starts.*

Psyc. 'Tis fit that I who did great Kings refuse,
Shou'd know who is the charming Youth I chuse.

Cup. What do I hear?

Psyc. 'Tis true I love, and glory in my Chains:
But to compleat my joys, it yet remains,
That thou, my Love, wou'dst thy dear name expose,
And my illustrious choice to me disclose.
Why dost thou frown? thou must my doubts secure,
I by my Love and by this Kiss conjure,
If thou dost love me this assurance give:
'Tis Love, my Dear, makes me inquisitive.
Thou shou'dst all secrets to my breast resign,
Besides, th' hast sworn this is no longer thine.

Cup. I've sworn; and, if you will, I must comply,
But then thy fatal curiosity
Inevitably ruines Thee and Me.

Psyc. Is this my Sov'reign Empire over thee?

Cup. You must what e'rs within my power command;
But your extravagant desires withstand:
Unless you will abandon him you love,
And will for ever from my sight remove.

Psyc. You found a heart too ready to believe,
And wou'd you still that poor weak heart deceive?

Cup. Must I my fatal secret then resign?

Psyc. Can you keep your heart, and yet take mine?

Cup.   Consider yet what 'tis you do.

Psyc. I fear'd I shou'd be thus refus'd by you.

Cup.   Let me not yet my name declare.

Psyc. Oh unkind Youth! thou mak'st me now despair,
That thou'lt reward my Love, or ease my care.

Cup. Consider yet, and let me hold my peace.

Psyc. Will your unkind denials never cease?

Cup. Know then, my self a God I must declare,
Whom all the other Deities obey:
          All things in Earth, Hell, Water, Air,
Must to my Godhead their devotion pay.
I am the God of Love, whom, to thy cost,
Thy foolish curiosity has lost.
By this thou dost my Love to Anger turn,
And must in fatal desolation mourn.
          I from thy once lov'd eyes must flye;
For 'tis ordain'd by cruel destiny,

Which rules o'r all the God's and me,
That for thy folly I shou'd thus abandon thee.

> Cupid *flies away.* *The Garden and Palace vanish, and* Psyche *is left alone in a vast Desert, upon the brink of a River in Marish, full of Willows, Flags, Bullrushes, and Water-flowers ; beyond which, is seen a great open Desart.*

Psyc. Oh ! whither art thou fled, my Dear ?
    Why hast thou left me here ?
Of all my glorious pomp I am bereft,
And in despair am in a Desart left.
   Oh my misfortune ! oh my crime !
I lov'd a God, and was ador'd by him.
My self I banish'd, and am left forlorn,
A fatal subject of injurious scorn ;
A scorn to all the Princes I've refus'd,
But my own folly I my self abus'd.
   Yet sure the God is much unkind,
To fly himself, yet leave his power behind.
My Love remains still to increase my care,
And heighten all the torments of despair.
        [Psyche *retires to the River side.*
    Enter Aglaura, Cidippe, *with a Souldier.*
 Sould. We of your Royal Father are bereft,
Who you the Heirs of this great Kingdom left.
So much he for the loss of *Psyche* griev'd,
That he by death his fatal grief reliev'd.
 Aglau. But are not yet the Rival Princes slain ?
 Sould. We have not follow'd your Commands in vain ;
The Princes are in sight upon the Plain :
In quest of *Psyche* they each path will trace,
And their unwearied search will bring them to this place.
So many of us here in ambush lye,
As soon as they approach us, they shall dye.
 Cid. Begone, we largely will reward your Loyalty.   [*Exit Soldier.*
How luckily did *Zephyrus* convey
   Us to this Desart, where we may,
   To our great pleasure, standing by,
   Behold these insolent Rivals die.
 Aglau. Since of all hopes of Love we are bereft,
Revenge is all the pleasure we have left.
   Oh my bless'd Eyes ! behold yon Face ;
Psyche is thrown upon this Desart place.

Cid. With pleasure I my sufferings embrace,
Since her an equal sufferer I find.
Is all your splendid Pomp to this declin'd?
Fate did your Palace to a Desart turn,
And you for all your arrogance shall mourn.
   Psyc. Am I the object of my Sisters scorn?
Ah, had I there your fatal eyes ne'r seen,
I still had prosp'rous in my Palace been.
        You urg'd that curiosity,
Which brought this dreadful ruine upon me.
   Aglau. How well did our first Artifice succeed,
She like a Prince when he's depos'd should bleed.
   Cid. Under our power you now a Slave remain;
Our Father's dead, and has left us to Reign.
   Psyc. No: a more glorious Fate to me's design'd,
Since he is gone, I'll not stay long behind,
   Aglau.   She shall not if she wou'd;
        We to be safe must shed her bloud.
   Cid. Her with her Lovers Heads we'll first surprize,
Then to our rage her life we'll sacrifice.
               [*Exit* Aglaura *and* Cidippe, *smiling on* Psyche.
   Psyc. No longer these misfortunes I'll endure;
Of all such wounds, death is the sovereign cure.
in this deep Stream that softly by does glide,
All my misfortunes and my faults I'll hide.

She offers to throw her self into the River. The God of the River arises
    upon a seat of Bullrushes and Reeds, leaning upon an Urn. The
    Naiades round him sing.

    The God   **S***Tay, stay, this act will much defile my streams:*
    sings.   *With a short patience suffer these extreams.*
                Heav'n has for thee a milder Fate in store,
      The time shall be when thou shalt weep no more.
                    And yet fair Psyche *ne'r shall dye.*
    1 Nymph.   *She ne'r shall dye.*
    2 Nymph.   *She·ne'r shall dye.*
      Chor.   *She ne'r shall dye.*
      But shall be crown'd with immortality.
      But shall be, &c.

    The God Venus *approaches, from her anger fly;*
    sings again. *More troubles yet your constancy must try,*
        But th' happy minute will e're long arrive,

That will to you eternal freedom give.
    And yet fair Psyche *ne'r shall dye.*

1 Nymph.   *She ne'r shall dye.*

2 Nymph.   *She ne'r shall dye.*

Chor.   *She ne'r shall dye.*

But shall be crown'd with immortality.
But shall be, &c.

Psyc. I need not fly, I have done no offence,
I'm strongly guarded by my Innocence.

Venus *descends in her Chariot.*

Venus. Dares *Psyche* before me appear?
    From my dread wrath you scorn to fly:
    'Tis Impudence, not constancy.
I'll bend your stubborn heart, and make you fear.
  Psyc. Dread Goddess! how have I
Provok'd so your unwonted cruelty?
  Venus. You did usurp my Honours: men to you
Did give that Worship which to me was due:
For you they did my Deity despise,
And wou'd have rais'd up Altars to your Eyes.
  Psyc. Is Beauty then (Heav'ns gift) a fault in me?
It is a fault I cannot help, you see.
  Ven. Your Pride did first all Earthly Kings refuse,
    And then my Son, a God, must chuse.
How durst you thus my Heavenly Race abuse?
  Psyc. Against all Kings he harden'd my poor heart,
And for himself he struck me with his Dart:
His Beauty wou'd make hearts of Stone to melt,
And his almighty power your self have felt.
  Ven. Dare you with me expostulate?
I'll make you feel the worst effects of hate:
    My pow'r you fatally shall know.
And for your insolence to Hell shall go.   [Venus *flies away.*

Enter Nicander *and* Polynices.

Nican. How long shall we our search pursue,
Without all hope that we shall *Psyche* find?
  Polyn. Each day our weary labour we renew,
And all our life must be for that design'd.
  Nican. What happy Vision does salute my eyes!
  Polyn. It must be *Psyche's* face that can so much surprize.
  Nican. At length the joy of both our lives is found;

(325)

Blest Fate ! that brought us to this sacred ground !

Polyn. Oh Divine *Psyche !* you're at length restor'd ;
We will defend you now from future harms.

Nican. Now we have found the Goddess we ador'd,
We will protect her against all Hells charms.

Psyc. Oh come not near, Heav'n does not me restore ;
I have committed an unknown offence,
  For which I must be snatch'd from hence,
And, Princes ! I shall never see you more.
       [*Furies rise, and then descend with* Psyche.

Nican. Oh cruel Fate !
Polyn. Oh my curst Stars !

      Enter Soldier.

Sold. Fall on, fall on ——

Enter Soldiers, who lay in ambush, and fall upon the Princes, who kill four or five of them, the rest fly.

Nican. This from the envious Sisters must proceed.
Polyn. 'T must be their stratagem to make us bleed.
Nican. Why should we thus our lives defend,
  Since *Psyche* we've for ever lost !
Polyn. 'Tis fit our hated lives should end,
But not that Slaves shou'd of the victory boast.
Nican. Why I am resolv'd I'll not this loss survive.
Polyn. Nor shou'd you think I am so tame to live.
Nican. Let's hand in hand go plunge into the deep,
There all our sorrows may for ever sleep.
Polyn. Agreed : and our immortal Souls shall that way go,
And meet our much lov'd *Psyche* down below.
      [*They arm in arm fling themselves into the River.*

    Enter Aglaura *and* Cidippe, *with Soldiers.*

Aglau. Villain, what Cowards did you entertain,
That two weak Men could not by you be slain ?
Cid. Oh Heaven ! the Princes are with *Psyche* fled.
  Base Slave ! thou hast forfeited thy head.   [*Soldier runs out.*
     Cupid *descends.*
Cup. Oh envious Fools, that *Psyche* thus pursue !
You both shall soon a deserv'd vengeance find ;
Hells everlasting pangs to you are due,
Since she is gone you shall not stay behind.
'Gainst *Psyche* you provok'd my Mothers rage,

And your destruction must my wrath asswage.
When from below my *Psyche* shall return,
You with damn'd Spirits shall for ever mourn.
Arise ye Furies, snatch 'em down to Hell.
No place becomes such envious Hags so well.   [Aglaura *and* Cidippe *sink.*

ACT V.

The *Scene* represents Hell, consisting of many burning Ruines of Buildings
on each side : In the foremost Pieces are the Figures of *Prometheus* and
Sisyphus, Ixion and *Tantalus.*   Beyond those are a great number of
Furies and Devils, tormenting the damned.   In the middle arises the
Throne of *Pluto,* consisting of Pillars of Fire ; with him *Proserpina ;* at
their feet sit *Minos, Æacus,* and *Rhadamanthus.*   With the Throne of *Pluto*
arise a great number of Devils and Furies, coming up at every rising
about the House.   Through the Pillars of *Pluto*'s Throne, at a great
distance, is seen the Gate of Hell,   through which a Lake of Fire is
seen ; and at a huge distance, on the farther side of that Lake, are vast
Crowds of the Dead, waiting for *Charon*'s Boat.   The following Song
is sung by Furies and Devils.

> TO *what great distresses proud* Psyche *is brought ?*
>   *Oh the brave mischiefs our malice has wrought !*
>   *Such Actions become the black Subjects of Hell,*
> *Our great Prince of Darkness whoe'r will serve well,*
> Chor.{ *Must to all Mortals, nay Gods shew their spight,*
>   { *And in horrour and torments of others delight.*
>
> *How cool are our Flames, and how light are our Chains,*
> *If our craft or our cruelty Souls enow gains :*
> *In perpetual howlings and groans we take pleasure,*
> *Our joys by the torments of others we measure.*
> Chor.{ *To rob Heav'n of the fair is our greatest delight,*
>   { *To darkness seducing the Subjects of Light.*
>
> *How little did Heav'n of its Empire take care,*
> *To let* Pluto *take the Rich, Witty and Fair :*
> *While it does for it self Fools and Monsters preserve,*
> *The Blind, Ugly and Poor, and the Cripple reserve.*
> Chor.{ *Heav'n all the worst Subjects for it self does prepare,*
>   { *And leaves all the best for the Prince of the Air.*

[A Dance of Furies.

(327)

Cidip. Some ease they find i' th' midst of pain,
    When Hell does a new Subject gain.
Aglau. But in the hottest flames this sight would please,
And *Psyche's* howling will our greatest torments ease.
    Cid. Were mine the hottest Furnace of all Hell,
If she were there, my flames I could bear well.
    Aglau. Were I into some dreadful Cavern tost,
Where the Damn'd are bound in eternal Frost ;
Where gnashing teeth and shuddering they lie,
Cursing their Births, wishing in vain to die :
To see her there would warm my icy chain,
And her extream damnation thaw my pain.
    Cidip.   But oh our Hell is yet to come !
        With horror I expect my doom.
    Aglau.   There our eternal Judges are,
By their stern looks of mercy I despair.
    Psyc. Does my too criminal Love deserve this pain ?
Circl'd with horror must I here remain ?
Through thousand terrors I have been convey'd,
With dismal yellings, shrieks and groans dismay'd :
O'er troubl'd Billows of eternal Fire,
Where tortur'd Ghosts must howl, and ne'r expire :
Where Souls ne'r rest, but feel fresh torments still,
Where furious Fiends their utmost rage fulfil ;
Tossing poor howling Wretches to and fro,
From raging Fires into eternal Snow.
From thence to Flames, from thence to Ice again, ⎫
In these extreams th' encounter equal pain, ⎬
And no refreshing intervals can gain. ⎭
The cursed Fiends still laughing at their moans,
Hugging themselves to hear their shrieks and groans ;
Upbraiding them with all their crimes on earth.
Each miserable Ghost curses, in vain, his birth.
        Encompass'd with these horrors round,
        No beam of comfort have I found.
Oh cruel *Venus !* wilt thou ne'r relent ?
Canst thou of Love such an example make ?
        Can Love deserve such punishment ?
        Oh cruel God, thus to forsake.
Me at the moment when I need him most !
        I fear he is for ever lost.
I could endure the horrors of this place,
Could I again behold his much-lov'd Face.

Pluto sings.

REfrain *your Tears, you shall no Pris'ner be ;*
    Beauty and Innocence in Hell *are free :*
    They're Treasons, Murders, Rapes, and Thefts that bring
Subjects to th' infernal King.
You are no subject of this place.
    A God you must embrace.
From Hell *to* Heaven *you must translated be,*
Where you shall live and love to all eternity.

Proserp.
    Psyche, *draw near : with thee this Present take,*
    Which given to Venus, *soon thy Peace will make :*
    Of Beauty, 'tis a Treasury Divine,
    And you're the Messenger she did design.
        Lost Beauty this will soon restore,
          And all defects repair :
    Mortals will now afresh her Beams adore,
    And ease her mind of jealousie and care.
    No Beauty that has this can e're despair.

Pluto.
    Here are your Sisters, who your life once sought :⎤
    Their malice to this place has Psyche *brought,* ⎬
    And against her all these dire mischiefs wrought. ⎦
      For ever here they shall remain,
    And shall in Hell *suffer eternal pain.*
    But Psyche *shall a Deity embrace.*

Proserp.   *Be gone, fair* Psyche *!*
Pluto.   *Be gone, fair* Psyche *!*
Both.   *Be gone, fair* Psyche *! from this place.*
Chor. of all.   *For* Psyche *must the God of Love embrace.*
           For Psyche *must the God of Love embrace.*

Aglau. O mercy, mercy, Sister, we implore ;
      You'll intercede for a Reprieve.
Cidip. No more our malice can fair *Psyche* grieve ;
You'll be a Goddess, we must you adore.
Minos. No grace for you she shall obtain, ⎤
      For you must here remain.   ⎬
Yet for her sake we'll ease you of some pain.⎦
No raging pangs of sense here you shall know,
But must eternal labours undergo ;
And with the *Belides* for ever live,
      Still shall wish death, but never dye ;

Each of you muſt draw water in a Sieve

To all Eternity.

[*The envious Siſters sink, with all the Devils and*
Furies, and the Throne of Pluto *vanishes.*

Psyc. In vain, poor Siſters, I deplore your Fate !
Though living, you pursu'd me with your hate ?
'Tis a dark Cloud upon my happiness.
But I'll ſtrive to forget what's paſt redress.
Were't not for this, my Joys I could not bear.

Immoderate joy would overthrow,
Were it not ballaſted with care.
My Love ! I shall enjoy thee now,
Together we shall happy be,

And live and love to all Eternity !

Enter the Ghoſts of Polynices *and* Nicander.

[Psyche ſtarts.

This was a dismal Tragedy.
These are the Princes Ghoſts we see :

Oh what sad chance has brought you down to me !
   Nican.   We felt the extreams of love and grief,

Which never cou'd have found relief :

And hand in hand we plung'd into the deep,

To seek repose by deaths laſt sleep.

   Polyn. Since you are loſt, to ease us of our care,
We both obey'd a generous despair :

For since we could not live for you,

Our miserable lives we could not bear.
To all th' insipid World we bad adieu,
Since nothing that remain'd could please us there.
   Nican. Death we enjoy'd, and heavy life remov'd,
For we in death behold your charms again :
Those charms which both in life and death we lov'd,
Which we had sigh'd and wept for there in vain.
   Psyc. Poor Ghoſts ! why should you suffer for my sake ?

In vain too 'twas your death design'd,
Now I no recompence can make ;

And then by force I was ungrateful and unkind :
Could I have lov'd, your merits were so much,
Your equal greatness and your vertues such :
I ne'r had fix'd my choice on one of you,
But muſt eternally have waver'd betwixt two.   [*She weeps.*
   Nican. Who would not willingly resign his breath,

(330)

          Who by a glorious death,
          The honor of your Tears might gain?
Polyn.   I cannot now of Fate complain;
Nor would with tedious fools above remain.
Nor can you pity now or love implore.
          Since you from hence must mount above,
And must embrace th' all pow'rful God of Love,
And at an humble distance we must you adore.
  Nican. Nor can we you of cruelty accuse,
Who for a God all mortal Kings refuse.
  Polyn. Farewel! our Destiny recalls us now,
And we t' immortal happiness should go,
          If without you it could be so.
  Psyc. Stay, Princes! and declare where, and what it is,
          This everlasting place of Bliss?
  Nican. In cool sweet shades, and in immortal Groves,
By Chrystal Rivulets, and eternal Springs;
Where the most beauteous Queens and greatest Kings,
Do celebrate their everlasting Loves.
  Polyn. In ever peaceful, fresh, and fragrant Bowers,
Adorn'd with never-fading Fruits and Flowers;
          Where perfum'd Winds refresh their heat,
And where immortal Quires their Loves repeat.
          There your great Father we have seen,
Where he afresh enjoys his beauteous Queen.
  Nican. Who did for hopeless Loves themselves destroy,
          Are there the greatest Hero's far;
Your God with infinite and endless joy,
Rewards their meritorious despair.
  Polyn. Each moment there does far out-go
The happiest minute earthly Lovers know.
With soft eternal Chains of Love combin'd
There they are ever youthful, ever kind:
Their endless pleasure is all Extasie,
And not like Earthly joys disturb'd with care;
Each fruitful minute does new pleasures bear:
From all unwelcome interruption free;
Each moment there more pleasure is design'd,
Than mortal Lovers can, when first united, find.
  Psyc. 'Tis fit that you those glorious Crowns should wear,
Of Friends and Rivals, the unequall'd pair.
  Nican. The splendid Crowns of Lovers we've receiv'd,
          But are by Heav'n of you bereav'd.

Strangers to Love we are alone ;
Our Love is up to Adoration grown :
Our hours in contemplation we'll employ,
Of the transcendent glory which you share ;
Our am'rous sighs shall turn to Holy Pray'r ;
While we that friendship, which you made, enjoy.
 Polyn. For ever without you we must remain.
   And now we must no longer stay,
   Lest we contribute to your pain,
And your immortal happiness delay.
Farewel for ever, and remember me.
 Nican. Farewel for ever, and remember me. [*Ex.* Nic. *and* Polyn.
 Psyc. Farewel ! such Friends and Rivals ne'r were found.
How much am I by Love and Honour bound ?
               [*Exit* Psyc.

The Scene *changes to the Marish which was in the former Act.*

Enter Psyche.

 Psyc. These Lovers must for ever in my thoughts remain ;
   And would for ever give me pain,
Did not the thoughts of him my mind employ,
Who'll banish all my cares, and will compleat my joy.
But ah ! my sufferings have transform'd me so,
   My decay'd Face, and languid Eyes ;
   My ruin'd Beauty he'll not know,
Or if he does, he will my looks despise.
But I have here a sacred Treasury,
   Which all my ruines may repair ;
Since it can make *Venus* her self more fair,
Is't an offence if it be us'd by me ?   [*She opens the Box.*
Oh ! what dark fumes oppress my clouded brain !
I go, and never shall return again.
Farewel, my Love, for ever fare the well.   [*She swounds.*

Cupid *descends.*

 Cup. Love o're my anger has the Victory gain'd ;
   Thy pardon is at length obtain'd :
Thy dangers and thy sufferings I have known,
   My Love has made them all my own :
With thee I languish'd, with thee did complain,
With thee I sigh'd and wept, and suffer'd all thy pain,
   Why dost thou hide thy conqu'ring Eyes ?
Dost thou a Lover and a God despise ?

Open thy pretty Eies, I am still the same,
　I still retain my unresisted flame ;
And all my vows are still paid to thy sacred name.
　She's dead, she's dead ! O whither art thou gone ?
　O Tyrant death ! what has thy bold hand done ?
　O cruel Mother ! whose insatiate rage
　Could thee against such innocence engage ?
Thou hast, by this, all ties of duty broke ;
　　　　No longer I'll endure thy yoke :
　My filial duty to revenge shall turn,
　You soon shall feel what to my pow'r you owe ;
　With hopeless Love you shall for ever burn,
　Your unregarded pains no ease shall know :
You still shall rage with Love, and to despair shall bow.

　　　　Venus *descends in her Chariot.*

Ven. What insolence is this I hear ?
This from a Son I can no longer bear.
Resume your Duty, and put on your fear.
　Cup. Duty to her, who has made *Psyche* dye ?
　　　　Revenge shall Piety succeed,
Revenge shall make your cruel heart to bleed.
And by your torments you shall find that I
　　　　Am much the greater Deity.
　Ven. Sure the great Thunderer asleep does lye,
　Or does not hear this Blasphemy.
　Cup. My pow'r can make the Thund'rer bow ;
You all the dire effects of it shall know.
For thee, dear *Psyche*, full revenge I'll take,
And of my Mother first I'll the example make.
　What hellish Rage provok'd you to this deed ?
　Whom Monsters would have spar'd, you have made bleed.
　Ven. You suffer'd her my glory to invade ;
　And when I call'd *Apollo* to my aid,
　You did the fraudulent God suborne.
　For you he that ambiguous Riddle made,
　And promis'd Judgement did to mercy turn ;
　And by that Oracle I was betray'd.
　Now to deceive me is beyond his power,
　Not all his Art can make her live one hour ;
　For none but I could *Psyche*'s Life restore.
　Cup. Can you ? Oh do, and punish me ;
　　　　If there were any Crime, 'twas mine.

(333)

For her I'd lose my immortality.
Oh give me her, I'll all my power resign.
      Here take my Quiver, take my Darts;
      You when you please shall rule all hearts:
You shall the power of Love to that of Beauty join.
  Ven. *Psyche* and you have so provok'd my hate,
     Your Pray'rs as soon may alter Fate.
  Cup. Behold the all-commanding Deity,   *[Kneels.*
     An humble suppliant on his knee!
Look on my Love! can you this form deſtroy?
Oh my lov'd *Psyche!* Oh my only Joy!
Oh give me her! my duty I'll retain,
Your Son for ever shall your humbleſt Slave remain!
  Ven. I muſt be gone, you sigh and beg in vain.
  Cup. Oh hear my Pray'rs! do not my Tears despise;
Behold the humble offerings of my Eyes.
     If ever yet true grief y'ave felt,
Your marble heart will at this objeƈt melt.
Ah think what pity to your Son is due!
Think but what wonders he has wrought for you!
How many hearts he's wounded for your sake!
Remember this, and then some pity take.
  Ven. No more for her will I negleƈted be,
Nor will I be affronted more by thee:
I'll be reveng'd on all your insolence,
And with eternal death I'll punish her offence.
  Cup. Oh cruel Murdress! I will take her part,⎫
And will revenge my self upon your heart;   ⎬
Againſt your Breaſt I'll sharpen every Dart.   ⎭
You in despair shall languish and decay:
Those feeble charms y' have left shall fly away.
Languid shall be your looks, and weak your Eyes,
Your former Worshippers shall your faint Beams despise!
       No Lover more you e'r shall gain,⎫
I will be deaf when ever you complain;   ⎬
Without Love's pow'r, all Beauty is but vain.⎭
Its seeming Essence Beauty does derive
  Only from the refleƈtion which Love makes
  Like that ——
Which from refleƈted Light a colour takes.
The Body does no being to it give.
Tremble at my revenge, for well you know,
What I by my resiſtless pow'r can do.

Ven. Farewel you insolent and daring Boy :
A living *Psyche* you shall ne'er enjoy.
       [*She mounts her Chariot and flies away.*
 Cup. Oh cruel Mother ! do not fly ;
Oh think how great must be that misery,
Makes an immortal Being wish to dye.
Spight of my self I must for ever live,
And without her, eternally must grieve :
You I conjure by all the Heavenly Race,
By all the pleasure of each stollen embrace ;
By the most ravishing moment of delight
You ever had free from your Husbands sight,
By all the joys of day, and raptures of the night,
Return, return.
     Venus *being almost lost in the Clouds.* Cupid *flies up and*
      gets into her Chariot, and brings her back.
Do but my *Psyche*'s Life restore,
  And I will never ask you more :
Do it, and all your pleasures I'll renew,
And add a thousand which you never knew.
 Ven. At length your sad complaints have soften'd me ———
Psyche shall live ———
 Cup. Oh Heav'n.
 Ven. But not for thee ;
Nature returns, and I forgive my Boy.
Restor'd you her shall see, but never shall enjoy.
 Cup. What dreadful words are these I hear !

     Jupiter *appears upon his Eagle.*
But lo ! the mighty Thund'rer does appear,
To him your cruelty I will reveal :
To the great *Jupiter* I now appeal.
Soul of the World, I beg you'll do me right,
Against my savage Mothers rage and spight.
 Jup. Goddess of Beauty, you must gentle grow,
  And your severe Decree recal ;
T' almighty Love the Universe must bow,
And without him must to confusion fall :
On Earth no Prince, in Heav'n no Deity,
  Is from his pow'rful Scepter free.
Do not the God of Union provoke,
Lest Heav'n and Earth feel his revenging stroke.
Should he the utmost of his Rage employ,

(335)

He might the frame o' th' Universe destroy.
  Ven. Should he a Mortal for his Wife embrace !
And by this hated Match blemish my heavenly Race !
  Jup. *Psyche* to him shall equal be,
She is no Mortal, she shall never dye ;
For I will give her immortality.
  Ven. This puts a happy end to all our strife.
Psyche, arise : from seeming death return,
And with my Son enjoy immortal Life,
Where you shall ever love, and never mourn.   [Psyche *revives.*
  Psyc. Who is it calls me from deaths silent night,
      And makes me thus revisit Light ?
Oh Gods, am I again blest with thy sight !
  Cup. For ever both your Godheads I'll adore,
Who did my *Psyche* to my arms restore,
Nor Hell nor Heaven shall make me quit thee more.
  Psyc. Do I again view thy Celestial Face !
  Cup. Do I again my Dear, my Love embrace !
  Jup. Come, happy Lovers, you with me shall go,
Where you the utmost Joys of Love shall know :
Amongst the Gods I *Psyche* will translate,
And they shall these blest Nuptials celebrate :
  In honour of them, I will summon all
  The pow'rs of Heaven to keep a Festival.

The S C E N E *changes to a* Heav'n.

In the highest part is the Palace of *Jupiter ;* the Columns and all the Ornaments of it of Gold. The lower part is all fill'd with *Angels* and *Cupids*, with a round open *Temple* in the midst of it. This *Temple* is just before the *Sun*, whose Beams break fiercely through it in divers places : Below the Heav'ns, several Semi-circular Clouds, of the breadth of the whole House, descend. In these Clouds sit the Musicians, richly Habited. On the front-Cloud sits *Apollo* alone. While the Musicians are descending, they play a *Symphony*, till *Apollo* begins, and sings as follows.

Apollo Sings.

Apollo.   *Assemble all the Heavenly Quire,*
        And let the God of Love inspire
        Your Hearts with his Celestial Fire.
    The God of Love's a happy Lover made,
    His ravishing delights shall never fade.

(336)

Chorus of *Apollo's* followers with Fla-gellets and Recor-ders.

{ *With his immortal* Psyche *He*
Now tasts those Joys which ought to be
As lasting as Eternity. }

Apollo. *Come Lovers, from the* Elizian *Groves,*
And celebrate these Heavenly Loves.

[*A Symphony* of *Pipes*, then Enter six
Princes of *Elizium*, with six
Ladies.

Apollo. Bacchus *with all your jolly Crew,*
Come revel at these Nuptials too.

[*A Symphony* of *Hoboys*, then Enter *Bacchus*,
with the *Mænades* and *Ægipanes*.

Apollo. *Come all ye winged Spirits of the Skies,*
And all ye mighty Deities.

[*A Symphony* of *Recorders*. *Cupids* and *Spirits*
descend, hanging in the Skies, *Gods* and
Goddesses in Chariots and Clouds.

Apollo. *You all his humble Vassals are*
And in this Joy should have a share.
Chorus. *With his immortal* Psyche *He*
Now tastes, &c.

1 *Elisian*
Lover sings
a Treble.

{ *On Earth by unkindness are often destroy'd*
The Delights in the Nymphs, who are so much ador'd,
Or Else the poor Lovers by kindness are cloy'd,
So faint are the pleasures their Love does afford. }

2 Treble.   *With Sighs and with Tears,*
          With Jealousies, griefs, and with fears,
          The wretched poor Lover is tost,
     For a few moments Pleasure his Liberty's lost.
3 Treble. *How short are those moments, yet how few they employ'd*
          Ah how short ! ah how short is the joy !
2 Treble.   *Ah how short ! ah how short is the joy !*
1 Treble.   *Ah how short ! ah how short is the joy !*

Chorus of three
Trebles to the Re-corder, Organ, and
Harpsicals.

{ *Thus wretched Mankind does suffer below,*
And in Heav'n each Godhead to Cupid *does bow.*
     But Love, Love was ne'r perfect till now. }

A Symphony of soft Musick of all the Instruments. Then *Jupiter* descends in a Machine, with *Cupid* on one side, and *Psyche* on the other. Then a Dance of six *Elizian* Princes, gloriously habited.

Mars sings to a Warlike Movement.

Behold the God, whose mighty pow'r
We all have felt, and all adore ;
To him I all my Triumphs owe,
To him my Trophies I must yield :
He makes victorious Monarchs bow,
And from the Conqu'ror gains the Field.

Chorus to Trumpets, Kettle-Drums, Flutes, and Warlike Musick.

He turns all the Horrors of War to Delight,
And were there no Love, no Heroes would fight.
[A Returnello by Martial Instruments, &c.

Mars.

Honour to Battel spurs them on,
Honour brings Pow'rs, when War is done :
But who would venture Life for Pow'r,
Only to govern dull Mankind !
'Tis Woman, Woman they adore ;
For Beauty they those Dangers find.

Chorus to Warlike Musick.

No Princes the Toils of Ambition would prove,
Or Dominion would prize if it were not for Love.
[A Returnello again.

Bacchus. *The Delights of the Bottle, and the Charms of good Wine,*
To the power and the pleasures of Love must resign :
Though the Night in the joys of good Drinking be past,
The debauches but till the next Morning will last.

Chorus to Hoboys and Rustick Musick of *Menades* and *Ægipanes.*

But Loves great Debauch is more lasting and strong ;
For that often lasts a Man all his Life long.
A Returnello again.

Bacchus. *Love and Wine are the Bonds which fasten us all ;*
The World but for these to confusion would fall ;
Were it not for the Pleasures of Love and good Wine,
Mankind for each trifle their lives would resign.

Chorus. *They'd not value dull Life, or would live without thinking ;*
Nor would Kings rule the World, but for Love and good drinking.
A Returnello again.

Apollo. *But to Love ! to Love the great Union they owe*
All in Earth and in Heav'n to his Sceptre muſt bow.

A general Cho-
rus of all the Voi-
ces and Inſtru-
ments. The Dan-
cers mingle with
the Singers.

> *All Joy to this Celeſtial Pair,*
> *Who thus, by Heav'n, united are :*
> *'Tis a great thing worth Heav'ns Design,*
> *To make Love's Pow'r with Beauty's join.*

[Six Attendants to the *Elizian* Princes bring in Portico's
of Arbours, adorn'd with Feſtoons and Garlands,
through which the Princes and they dance ; the
Attendants ſtill placing them in several Figures.

Jup. For ever happy in your *Psyche* be,
Who now is crown'd with Immortality ;
On Earth Love never is from Troubles free,
But here 'tis one Eternal Extasie :
'Mongſt all the Joys which Heav'n and Earth can find,
Love's the moſt glorious Objeƈt of the Mind.

EPILOGUE.

WHat e'er the Poet has deserv'd from you,
Would you the Actors for his faults undo,
The Painter, Dancer, and Musician too?
For you those Men of skill have done their best:
But we deserve much more then all the rest.
We have stak'd all we have to treat you here,
And therefore, Sirs, you should not be severe.
We in one Vessel have adventur'd all;
The loss, should we be Shipwrack'd, were not small.
But if it be decreed that we must fall,
We fall with honour: Gallants you can tell,
No foreign Stage can ours in Pomp excel,
And here none e'r shall treat you half so well.
Poor Players have this day that Splendor shown,
Which yet but by Great Monarchs has been done.
Whilst our rich neighbours mock us for't, we know
Already th' utmost they intend to do.
Yet all the Fame you give 'em we allow,
To their best Plays, and their best Actors too.
      But, Sirs——
Good Plays from Censure here you'll not exempt,
Yet can like Farces, there below contempt
Drolls which so course, so dull, so bawdy are,
The dirty Rout would damn 'em in a Fair:
Yet Gentlemen such Stuff will daily see;
Nay, Ladies too, will in the Boxes be:
What is become of former Modesty?
            Yet——
Best Judges will our Ornaments allow,
Though they the wrong-side of the Arras show.
But Oh a long farewell to all this sort
Of Plays, which this vast Town can not support.
If you could be content th' Expence to bear,
We would improve and treat you better ev'ry year.

FINIS.

TEXTUAL NOTES

The Miser

p.	7, l. 13.	*1672.* 1691 has: "A.	Comedy	Called The	Miser:	Acted	At The	Theater Royal	Written by *Thomas Shadwell.*	*London,*	Printed for *H. H.* and *T. C.* and sold by *Francis—Saunders* at the *Anchor* in the *New-Exchange,*	and *James Knapton* at the *Crown* in St. *Paul's*	Church-Yard. 1691.	"
p.	15, l. 3.	*Buckhurst.* 1691 has: "Charles, Earl of *Dorset* and *Middlesex, Lord Chamberlain* of *His Majesties Houshold.*"
p.	18, l. 1.	*Epilogue.* 1691 gives this at the end of the play.
p.	19, l. 1.	*The Actors Names.* So in Sir Edmund Gosse's copy. But many copies of the First Quarto, 1672, of *The Miser,* which I have examined, lack this leaf. The same is the case with the 4to 1691. Some copies of the 12mo 1720 of *The Miser,* which is the first play in Vol. III, may give a list of characters, but this leaf is not found in the many copies I have seen.
p.	21, l. 2.	*Act I. Sce.* 1. 1691: Act I. Scene I.
p.	21, l. 3.	*Hazard, Theodore.* 1691: *Hazard* and *Theodore.*
p.	21, l. 8.	*money.* 1691, save in one instance where 4to 1672 has "Money," reads "Money" throughout. The first 4to also reads "man"; 1691, "Man" throughout. There is an abundant use of initial capitals in 4to 1691, but I have not thought it necessary to mark each several divergence in this particular respect from 4to 1672.
p.	22, l. 8.	*Anchovee.* 1691: Anchovy.
p.	22, l. 28.	*Blew Balcone.* 1691: Blue Balcony.
p.	23, l. 33.	*helpe.* 1691: help.
p.	24, l. 14.	*ont.* 1691: on't.
p.	26, l. 26.	*Cloths.* 1691: Cloaths.
p.	26, l. 27.	*Joyn.* 1691: join.
p.	26, l. 34.	*replyes.* 1691: replies.
p.	27, l. 20.	*scorne.* 1691: scorn.
p.	28, l. 8.	*selfe.* 1691: self.
p.	28, l. 17.	*summes.* 1691: Sums.
p.	28, l. 40.	*Raillerie.* 1691: Raillery.
p.	29, l. 20.	*six and thirty shillings a year.* 1691: 36s. a year.
p.	29, l. 22.	*twenty Pound.* 1691: 20l.
p.	30, l. 14.	*tollerable.* 1691: tolerable.
p.	30, l. 34.	*sixty per Cent.* 1691: 60 per Cent.
p.	31, l. 6.	*choyce.* 1691: choice.
p.	33, l. 7.	*Velvit.* 1691: Velvet.
p.	33, l. 14.	*Whetston.* 1691: *Whetstone.*
p.	33, l. 18.	*Hears.* 1691: Hearse.
p.	34, l. 1.	Act II. Sce. I. So 12mo 1720. 4to 1672: Act II. Sce. II. 4to 1691: Act II. Scene II.
p.	34, l. 6.	*Cheere.* 1691: Cheer.
p.	34, l. 34.	*an I were.* 1691: and I were.
p.	34, l. 38.	*Gemini.* 1691: *Gimini.*
p.	35, l. 20.	*accomplisht.* 1691: accomplish'd.

p. 35, l. 25. *wee'l.* 1691 : we'l.
p. 37, l. 7. *Burr.* 1693 : Bur.
p. 38, l. 2. *Midwives.* 1672 misprints " Wid-wifes."
p. 39, l. 24. *reformation.* 1691 : Reformation.
p. 39, l. 42. *Raysins.* 1691 : Raisins.
p. 40, l. 8. *Playes.* 1691 : plays.
p. 41, l. 17. *ayr.* 1691 : air.
p. 41, l. 35. *haſt.* 1691 : haſte.
p. 42, l. 20. *injoy'd.* 1691 : enjoy'd.
p. 43, l. 1. *Ladies your servant.* 1691 misprints : " Ladies you servant."
p. 44, l. 26. *Countrey-Song.* 1691 : Country-Song.
p. 44, l. 27. *Girles.* 1691 : Girls.
p. 44, l. 27. *Voyces.* 1691 : Voices.
p. 46, l. 28. *termes.* 1691 : Terms.
p. 47, l. 1. *in-layd.* 1691 : in-laid.
p. 47, l. 5. *Trump-Marin.* 1691 : Trump Marin.
p. 48, l. 25. *Act III. Scene* 1. So 1720. 4to 1, 1672 : Act III. Scene. III. (as here) 4to 1691 : Act III. Scene III.
p. 50, l. 4. *deſpaire.* 1691 : despair.
p. 50, l. 41. *Frownes.* 1691 : *Frowns.*
p. 52, l. 38. *Fiddles.* 1691 : Fiddlers.
p. 54, l. 19. *twenty Pound.* 1691 : 20*l.*
p. 56, l. 1. *Cloathe's.* 1691 : Cloaths.
p. 57, l. 26. *Chamelions.* 1691 : *Camelions.*
p. 61, l. 2. *suspition.* 1691 : suspicion.
p. 63. l. 1. *Act IV. Scene* 1. So 1720. 4to 1, 1672 : Act IV. Sce. IV. 4to 1691 : Act IV. Scene IV.
p. 63, l. 22. *Souldier.* 1691 : Soldier.
p. 64, l. 12. *& not.* 1691 : and not.
p. 65, l. 21. *I will wait.* 1691 : I wait.
p. 65, l. 33. *Pritty.* 1691 : Pretty.
p. 66, l. 6. *Coven garden.* 1691 : *Covent Garden.*
p. 68, l. 21. *vi et armis.* 1691 : *vi & armis.*
p. 69, l. 18. *Guinnes.* 1691 : Guinea's.
p. 74, l. 1. *well, & did.* 1691 : well, and did.
p. 74, l. 14. *myſticall.* 1691 : myſtical.
p. 74, l. 38. *dore.]* 1691 : door.]
p. 75, l. 7. *upon these Termes.* 1691 prints *upon these Terms* as though it were a ſtage-direction.
p. 75, l. 26. *sicknesse.* 1691 : sickness.
p. 76, l. 14. *Moneths.* 1691 : months.
p. 77, l. 18. *barre the dores.* 1691 : bar the doors.
p. 77, l. 21. *windowes.* 1691 : Windows.
p. 78, l. 1. *noyse.* 1691 : noise.
p. 81, l. 17. *on my conscience.* 1672 misprints : cnoscience.
p. 82, l. 2. *begon.* 1691 : be gone.
p. 82, l. 26. *Oh Sir, your Servant.* Obviously the continuation of Cheatly's speech, but both 4to 1672 and 1691 give speech-prefix *Gold.* 1720 is correct.
p. 82, l. 39. *Oh Thieves, Thieves.* 1672 : Oh, Theeves, theives.
p. 83, l. 19. *Caine.]* 1691 : *Cain.]*
p. 83, l. 29. *Gallowes.* 1691 : Gallows.
p. 84, l. 5. *Speake.* 1691 : Speak.

p. 84, l. 34.   *puffe.*   1691 : puff.
p. 85, l. 26.   *devill.*   1691 : devil.
p. 85, l. 40.   *stollen.*   1691 : ſtolen.
p. 86, l. 19.   *Villaine.*   1691 : Villain.
p. 87, l. 18.   *peace.*   1691 : Peace.
p. 88, l. 19.   *Capital an offender.*   1691 : Capital and Offender.
p. 88, l. 37.   *Releaſt.*   1691 : Releas'd.
p. 88, l. 41.   *extreamities.*   1691 : extremities.
p. 89, l. 30.   *neerer.*   1691 : nearer.
p. 90, l. 4.   *tye.*   1691 : tie.
p. 90, l. 27.   *Inditement.*   1691 : *Indiſtment.*
p. 92, l. 23.   *Closset.*   1691 : Closet.

Epsom-Wells

p. 95, l. 1.   Epsom-Wells. | A | COMEDY, | Aſted at the | DUKE'S THEATRE. | [rule] | Written By | THO. SHADWELL. | [rule] | Μεγάλως ἀπολιθαίνειν ἁμάρτημα εὐγενες. | [rule] | LICENSED, *Feb.* 17. 167$\frac{2}{3}$ Roger L'Estrange. | [double rule] | *LONDON,* | Printed by *J. M.* for *Henry Herringman* at the Sign of the | *Blew Anchor* in the Lower Walk of the *New Exchange.* | M.DC.LXXVI. |

p. 95, l. 1.   *Epsom-Wells.* 4to, 1693, has title-page : Epsom-Wells. | A | COMEDY, | As it is Aſted | By Their MAJESTIES | SERVANTS. | [rule.] | Written By | *THO. SHADWELL.* | [rule.] | Μεγάλως ἀπολιθαίνειν ἁμάρτημα εὐγενές· | [double rule.] | *LONDON.* | Printed for *H. Herringman,* and Sold by *R. Bentley, J. Tonson,* | *F. Saunders,* and *T. Bennet,* 1693. |

p. 101, l. 1.   *Dramatis Personae.*   In 1693 the liſt follows the Prologue to the King and Queen.
p. 104, l. 15.   *Citts.*   1693 : *Cits.*
p. 104, l. 27.   *Burgers.*   1693 : *Burghers.*
p. 107, l. 15.   *you'l.*   1693 : you'll.
p. 108, l. 14.   *Raines.*   1676 and 1693 vary between ' Raines ' and ' Rains.'
p. 108, l. 25.   *ſpleenatick.*   1693 : splenetick.
p. 109, l. 5.   *fellow.*   1693 : Fellow.
p. 110, l. 13.   *Tearm.*   1693 : Term.
p. 111, l. 8.   *He's in the right.*   1693 omits the remainder of the sentence : The Wits are . . . almoſt undone.
p. 111, l. 14.   *horse.*   1693 : Horse.
p. 111, l. 40.   *Sponge.*   1693 : Spunge.
p. 112, l. 17.   *Ball.*   1693 : baul.
p. 112, l. 26.   *God-by.*   1693 : God-b'w'y'.
p. 112, l. 32.   *extreamly.*   1693 : extremely.
p. 112, l. 38.   *Masques.*   1693 : Masks.
p. 113, l. 21.   *wine.*   1693 : Wine.
p. 113, l. 37.   *wall-fac'd.*   1693 : well-fac'd.

p. 113, l. 38. *Perruques.* 1693 : Peruques.
p. 114, l. 4. *fellows.* 1693 : Fellows.
p. 114, l. 14. *wee'd.* 1693 : we'd.
p. 114, l. 28. *Owne.* 1676, 1693 : Own.
p. 115, l. 27. *infallable.* 1693 : infallible.
p. 115, l. 40. *Tigers.* 1693 : Tygers.
p. 116, l. 25. *ſtayed.* 1693 : ſtaid.
p. 116, l. 35. *Vizor-Masque.* 1693 : Vizor-Mask.
p. 118, l. 42. *Wife Allons.* 1693 : Wife alone.
p. 119, l. 26. *I'll meet you.* 1693 has accidentally omitted " you."
p. 120, l. 24. *joynture.* 1693 : jointure.
p. 121, l. 25. *Pothecaries.* 1693 : Pothecary's.
p. 122, l. 8. *I'le not.* 1693 : I'll not.
p. 122, l. 20. *Guds sooks.* 1693 : Gad-sooks.
p. 123, l. 22. *extreamity.* 1693 : extremity.
p. 124, l. 3. *agen.* 1693 : again.
p. 125, l. 18. *popish.* 1693 : Popish.
p. 126, l. 21. *Caudel.* 1693 : Caudle.
p. 128, l. 24. *Mollie.* 1693 : *Molly.*
p. 128, l. 24. *humours.* 1693 : humors.
p. 130, l. 30. [*Enter Woodly.* The quarto by error read [*Exit.* Woodly.
p. 132, l. 28. *Battaille.* 1693 : Battle.
p. 133, l. 26. *Vizor Masks !* 1676, 1693 : Vizor Mask
p. 137, l. 31. *Love-letters.* 1693 : Love-Letters.
p. 138, l. 9. *Coven-garden.* 1693 : *Covent-Garden.*
p. 138, l. 21. *owne.* 1693 : own.
p. 147, l. 3. *Eccho.* 1693 : Echo.
p. 147, l. 29. *tho'.* 1693 : though.
p. 148, l. 32. *Jigue.* 1693 : Jig.
p. 149, l. 2. *Joynts.* 1693 : Joints.
p. 151, l. 25. *Fy.* 1693 : Fie.
p. 151, l. 32. *fox't.* 1693 : fox'd.
p. 154, l. 30. *Mawses.* 1693 : Mawse's.
p. 161, l. 10. *Bowling-green.* 1693 : Bowling-Green.
p. 162, l. 21. *joyn'd.* 1693 : join'd.
p. 162, l. 33. *I'de.* 1693 : I'd.
p. 166, l. 1. *at 5.* 1693 : at five.
p. 166, l. 37. *Ambush.* 1693 : ambush.
p. 168, l. 31. *unty.* 1693 : untie.
p. 169, l. 11. *Godsbud.* 1693 : Gad'sbud.
p. 169, l. 27. *Errant.* 1693 : Errand.
p. 173, l. 14. *Ladiship.* 1693 : Ladyship.
p. 173, l. 26. *S'death.* 1676, 1693 : s'Death.
p. 175, l. 31. *'Slife.* 1693 : 'sLife.
p. 176, l. 13. *busie.* 1693 : busy.
p. 180, l. 34. *Farewell.* 1693 : Farewel.
p. 181, l. 1. *tearms.* 1693 : terms.

The Tempest, or the Enchanted Island

A. TEXTUAL NOTES

p. 183, l. 1. *THE TEMPEST.* The two quartos of 1676 have: THE TEMPEST ... LONDON, Printed by *J. Macock* for *Henry Herringman* ...:

p. 183, l. 1. *THE TEMPEST.* The title-page of 1690 has: THE | TEMPEST, | OR THE | Enchanted Island. | A | COMEDY. | As it is now Acted | At Their Majesties Theatre | IN | *DORSET-GARDEN.* | [rule.] | Printer's device | [rule.] | LONDON, | Printed by *J. M.* for *H. Herringman;* and sold by *R. Bentley,* | at the Post-House in *Russel-street, Covent-Garden.* | 1690. |

p. 202, l. 28. *pray too.* 1674: pray to. 1676, 1690: pray too.

p. 205, l. 21. *Reeds then Hair.* 1676, 1690: than Hair.

p. 205, l. 33. *the Marriners.* 1690: the Mariners.

p. 206, l. 31. *age and envy.* 1690: Age and Envy.

p. 206, l. 43. *blew-ey'd.* 1690: blue-ey'd.

p. 206, l. 43. *child.* 1690: Child.

p. 207, l. 1. *slave.* 1690: Slave.

p. 207, l. 2. *servant.* 1690: Servant.

p. 207, l. 3. *Spirit.* 1690: spirit.

p. 207, l. 4. *Earthy and abhor'd.* 1690: Earthy and Abhor'd.

p. 207, l. 4. *commands.* 1690: Commands.

p. 207, l. 18. *torment.* 1690: Torment.

p. 207, l. 25. *entrails.* 1690: Entrails.

p. 207, l. 30. *I'l discharge.* 1690: I'll.

p. 207, l. 32. *spirit.* 1690: Spirit.

p. 207, l. 35. *years.* 1690: Years.

p. 207, l. 35. *freedom.* 1690: Freedom.

p. 207, l. 42. *my dear.* 1690: my Dear.

p. 208, l. 2. *diligence.* 1690: Diligence.

p. 208, l. 5. *sadness.* 1690: Sadness.

p. 208, l. 5. *story.* 1690: Story.

p. 208, l. 6. *Shake.* 1690: shake.

p. 208, l. 18. *cramps.* 1690: Cramps.

p. 208, l. 18. *side-stiches.* 1690: Side-stiches.

p. 208, l. 26. *day and night.* 1690: Day and Night.

p. 208, l. 27. *barren places and fertile.* 1690: Barren Places and Fertile.

p. 208, l. 32. *stripes.* 1690: Stripes.

p. 208, l. 32. *kindness.* 1690: Kindness.

p. 208, l. 33. *filth.* 1690: Filth.

p. 208, l. 43. *race.* 1690: Race.

p. 209, l. 3. *language.* 1690: Language.

p. 209, l. 3. *profit.* 1690: Profit.

p. 209, l. 11. *Dinn.* 1690: Din.

p. 209, l. 16. *Prospero and Caliban.* 1690: Prosp. *and* Calib.

p. 209, l. 31. *head.* 1690: Head.

p. 209, l. 36.   *crack his belly.*   1690 : Crack his Belly.
p. 210, l. 16.   *ground.*   1690 : Ground.
p. 211, l. 14.   *eyes.*   1690 : Eyes.
p. 211, l. 25.   *Marinner.*   1690 : Mariner.
p. 211, l. 38.   *I'l.*   1690 : I'll.
p. 213, l. 29.   *Laws of the Countrey.*   1690 : Country.
p. 214, l. 15.   *I'l do.*   1690 : I'll do.
p. 214, l. 30.   *I'l swear.*   1674 : 'l swear ; in some copies.   1676 : I'le swear.
p. 214, l. 37.   *I'l pluck.*   1676 : I'le pluck.   1690 : I'll pluck.
p. 214, l. 38.   *I'll fish.*   1676 : I'le fish.   1690 : I'll fish.
p. 216, l. 16.   *prisoner.*   1690 : Prisoner.
p. 217, l. 35.   *Is the man.*   1690 : Man.
p. 218, l. 10.   *nine moneths.*   1690 : nine months.
p. 218, l. 38.   *then lose.*   1676 ; 1690 : than.
p. 219, l. 7.   *men and spirits.*   1690 : Men and Spirits.
p. 219, l. 16.   *tame man.*   1690 : Man.
p. 221, l. 31.   *lowder.*   1676 ; 1690 : *louder.*
p. 221, l. 37.   *Voyces.*   1676 ; 1690 : *Voices.*
p. 224, l. 25.   *Act ends.*   1690 : The End of the Second Act.
p. 226, l. 5.   *gen'rous soul.*   1690 : gen'rous Soul.
p. 226, l. 16.   *nobler guest.*   1690 : Guest.
p. 228, l. 18.   *promise.*   1690 : Promise.
p. 228, l. 39.   *weather-fends.*   1690 : weather fends.
p. 229, l. 27.   *wrack'd Marriners.*   1690 : Mariners.
p. 230, l. 22.   *stomack.*   1676 ; 1690 : stomach.
p. 231, l. 8.   *then 'em.*   1690 : than 'em.
p. 231, l. 21.   *I'l be.*   1690 : I'll be.
p. 232, l. 38.   *I'l not accept.*   1690 : I'll not.
p. 233, l. 13.   *good tongues.*   1674 : good tungs.
p. 233, l. 40.   *Eccho.*   1690 : Echo.
p. 234, l. 7.   *I'l not.*   1690 : I'll not.
p. 235, l. 18.   *own Countrey.*   1690 : own Country.
p. 236, l. 2.   *Traitor.*   1690 : Traytor.
p. 236, l. 34.   *friends.*   1690 : Friends.
p. 236, l. 36.   *prison.*   1690 : Prison.
p. 237, l. 23.   *woman.*   1690 : Woman.
p. 239, l. 15.   *beauty.*   1690 : Beauty.
p. 239, l. 42.   *of 'em.*   1690 punctuates : of 'em :
p. 240, l. 36.   *friendship.*   1690 : Friendship.
p. 241, l. 4.   *Act IV.*   1676 misprints " Act VI."
p. 241, l. 15.   *souls.*   1690 : Souls.
p. 241, l. 22.   *joyn'd.*   1690 : join'd.
p. 241, l. 28.   *then your.*   1690 : than your.
p. 242, l. 7.   *captivity.*   1690 : Captivity.
p. 242, l. 9.   *fool.*   1690 : Fool.
p. 242, l. 36.   *onely.*   1690 : only.
p. 242, l. 39.   *poison.*   1690 : Poison.
p. 244, l. 23.   *enjoyn'd.*   1690 : enjoin'd.
p. 244, l. 39.   *onely him.*   1690 : only him.
p. 245, l. 6.   *I'l see.*   1690 : I'll see.
p. 246, l. 7.   *your friend.*   1690 : your Friend.
p. 247, l. 8.   *friendship.*   1690 : Friendship.

p. 247, l. 9. *sword.* 1690: Sword.
p. 247, l. 34. *I'l fight.* 1690: I'll fight.
p. 248, l. 10. *fundamental.* 1690: Fundamental.
p. 248, l. 24. *ghess.* 1674; 1690: guess.
p. 248, l. 36. *bellies.* 1690: Bellies.
p. 249, l. 37. *shee's tipling.* 1690: she's tipling.
p. 249, l. 40. *virtuous.* 1690: Virtuous.
p. 250, l. 16. *onely.* 1690: only.
p. 250, l. 19. *eye.* 1690: Eye.
p. 250, l. 28. *Countrey.* 1690: Country.
p. 251, l. 19. *swords.* 1690: *Swords.*
p. 253, l. 8. *Hick-up.* 1690: Hickup.
p. 253, l. 12. *then just.* 1676; 1690: than just.
p. 253, l. 31. *your eyes.* 1690: your Eyes.
p. 254, l. 19. *Millain !* 1690: *Milain !*
p. 254, l. 42. *my Millain.* 1690: my *Milain.*
p. 255, l. 42. *he'l come.* 1690: he'll come.
p. 256, l. 31. *his fortune.* 1690: his Fortune.
p. 257, l. 8. *I'l never.* 1690: I'll never.
p. 257, l. 12. *eccho to each blast.* 1690: echo to each blast.
p. 257, l. 15. *ill spirits.* 1690: Spirits.
p. 257, l. 26. *subjects.* 1690: Subjects.
p. 257, l. 29. *passions.* 1690: Passions.
p. 258, l. 17. *destroy the Son.* 1674 misprints: " thee Son."
p. 258, l. 25. *mischief, Wilt thou be.* 1690 prints in two lines, concluding the first with " mischief " and commencing the second : " Wilt thou be . . ."
p. 258, l. 38. *His onely danger.* 1690: only.
p. 259, l. 33. *small blew thing.* 1690: small blue thing.
p. 260, l. 12. *I'l beg.* 1690: I'll beg.
p. 261, l. 13. *another man.* 1690: another Man.
p. 261, l. 40. *I onely love.* 1690: I only love.
p. 262, l. 7. *Recompense.* 1676: Recompence.
p. 262, l. 41. *Young Prince I render.* 1690: Young Prince, I render.
p. 263, l. 5. *o're.* 1690: o'r.
p. 264, l. 28. *mishapen.* 1690: mis-shapen.
p. 264, l. 31. *command.* 1690: Command.
p. 264, l. 32. *power.* 1690: Power.
p. 264, l. 38. *in the world.* 1690: in the World.
p. 266, l. 12. *Afford 'em onely.* 1690: *Afford 'em only.*
p. 266, l. 17. *Amphitrites.* 1690: Amphitrite's.
p. 267, l. 21. *heavenly power.* 1690: Heavenly Power.
p. 267, l. 31. *O wondrous skill.* 1690: O wonderful skill.
p. 268, l. 30. *onely like.* 1690: *only like.*
p. 268, l. 34. *other men.* 1690: *other Men.*

B. VARIANTS

Variants between the D'Avenant-Dryden Comedy,
4to, 1670, and the Opera, 4to, 1674.

Although considerable attention has been given to the Comedy *The Tempest*, 4to, 1670, and the Opera *The Tempest*, 4to, 1674, and the obvious elaboration of the latter in the matter of stage directions more than once emphasized, the many and important divergences between the two texts have by no means received that notice which is their meed. Their importance, however, must be recognized, since it is clear that the alterations which prevail in the Opera are all planned upon deliberate and definite lines. For the most part they are excisions of dialogue to allow time for the new songs, dances, and spectacular effects without unduly prolonging the performance. For the Opera Act II of the Comedy has been wholly re-arranged. This was necessitated by practical stage work, to allow of the setting and convenient changing of the scenes. It is difficult to suppose that these variations were made by Dryden, and here we have another argument in favour of Shadwell's re-handling of the Comedy. This, and similar points, may be small, but they are accumulative in their evidence. It were perhaps over-subtle to point out that in the Opera lines of rare beauty have often been thrown overboard when others could have been equally well spared, and poetic phrase has on several occasions become commonplace, *e.g.*, " Absolute *Millan* " of the Comedy, 1670 (and Shakespeare), in 1674 is " absolute in *Millan*."

p. 199, l. 3. *The Front of the Stage.* The whole of this preliminary direction occurs for the first time in 4to, 1674. 1670 commences : Act I. *Enter* Mustacho *and* Ventoso.

p. 200, l. 3. *what say you?* 1670 : what cheer ?

p. 200, l. 7. *Boy! Boy!* 1670 : Boy! once only.

p. 200, l. 11. *Trinc. Bring the Cable.* 1670 : *Trinc.* Heigh, my hearts, chearly, chearly, my hearts, yare, yare.

p. 200, l. 33. *let's weigh.* 1670 only once.

p. 201, l. 6. *lubbord.* Not in 1670.

p. 201, l. 26. *Let him alone.* 1670 : Furle him again.

p. 201, l. 30. *veeres forward.* 1670 : grows scant.

p. 202, l. 9. *and be pox't.* 1670 omits.

p. 202, l. 12. *Ease the Fore-brace.* 1670 : Brace off the Fore-yard.

p. 202, l. 22. *a long farewel.* 1670 here has a speech for Ferdinand : Some lucky Plank, when we are lost by Ship-wrack, waft hither, and submit it self beneath you.

Your Blessing, and I dye contented. [*Embrace and Exeunt.*

p. 202, l. 28. *our case is now alike.* Here 1670 has :

Ant. We are meerly cheated of our lives by Drunkards. This wide chopt Rascal : would thou might'st lye drowning The long washing of ten Tides.

        [*Exeunt* Trinculo, Mustacho, *and* Ventoso.

Gonz. He'll be hang'd yet, though every drop of Water swears against it ; now would I give ten thousand Furlongs of Sea for one Acre of barren ground. Long-heath, Broom-furs, or anything. The Wills above be done, but I would fain dye a dry death. [*A confused noise within.*

p. 202, l. 37. *Scene II. In the midst of the Shower.* This stage direction does not occur in 1670.

p. 203, l. 11. *allay 'em quickly.* 1670 adds : Had I been any God of Power, I would have sunk the Sea into the Earth, before it should the Vessel so have swallowed.

Pros. Collect your self, and tell your piteous heart : There's no harm done.

Mir. O woe the day !

Pros. There is no harm. I have done nothing. . . .

p. 203, l. 20.   *inform thee farther.* 1670 adds : wipe thou thine Eyes, have comfort ; the direful Spectacle of the Wrack, which touch'd the very virtue of compassion in thee, I have with such a pity safely order'd, that not one Creature in the Ship is lost.

p. 204, l. 1.   *Both, both my Girl.* 1670 : *Mir.* How my heart bleeds to think what you have suffer'd. But, Sir, I pray proceed.

p. 204, l. 5.   *That false Uncle.* 1670 continues : (do'st thou attend me Child ?) *Mir.* Sir, most heedfully.

p. 204, l. 16.   *Prosp. This false Duke.* 1670 :

> *Prosp.*   To have no screen between the part he plaid,
> And whom he plaid it for : he needs would be
> Absolute *Millan,* and confederates
> (So dry he was for Sway) with *Savoy's* Duke,
> To give him Tribute, and to do him homage.

p. 204, l. 29.   *quit it.* 1670 continues : They hoisted us, to cry to Seas which roar'd to us ; to sigh to Winds, whose pity sighing back again, did seem to do us loving wrong.

p. 205, l. 15.   *flame distinctly.* 1670 ends Ariel's speech here. The shower of fire was only in the Opera.

p. 207, l. 31.   *Thanks my great Master.* Milcha does not appear here in 1670, which runs :

> *Ariel.*   That's my noble Master.
> What shall I do ? say ! what, what shall I do ?
> *Prosp.*   Be subject . . .

p. 208, l. 12.   *Wood enough within.* 1670 continues :

> *Prosp.*   Come forth, I say, there's other business for thee.
> Come thou Tortoise, when ?   [*Enter* Ariel.
> Fine Apparition, my quaint *Ariel,*
> Hark in thy Ear.
> *Ariel.*   My Lord, it shall be done.   [*Exit.*
> *Prosp.*   Thou poisonous Slave . . .

p. 210, l. 26.   *The Scene changes.* This stage direction is not in 1670. In Act II, for the Opera of 1674, there is wholesale rearrangement. The Comedy, 1670, commences with the scene between Alonzo, Antonio, Gonzalo, and Attendants. There are many verbal changes in the songs of the Devils. The scene closes at " Before I know thy fortune ? " It is followed by the Ferdinand-Ariel scene which in the Opera begins Act III. Milcha does not here appear in the Comedy. Then 1670 proceeds to the scene between Stephano, Mustacho, and Ventoso, " The Runlet of Brandy was a loving Runlet, . . ." with which Act II of the Opera opens. Then follow, the stage direction *Scene Cypress Trees and Cave* being omitted, the scenes between Prospero and Hippolito ; Prospero, Miranda, and Dorinda ; Hippolito, Miranda, and Dorinda, where in place of *The Scene continues* we have *The Scene changes and discovers* Hippolito *in a Cave walking : his face from the Audience ;* and the Act concludes with the duologue between Hippolito and Dorinda, which in the Opera closes the second scene only.

p. 224, l. 26.   *Act III.* 1670 opens with *Enter* Prospero *and* Miranda. The stage-direction *The Cypress-Trees and Cave* is omitted.

p. 226, l. 21.   *make thee fortunate.* 1670 adds a speech of eight lines.

p. 227, l. 18.   *O fear not him, Sir.* 1670 here has twelve lines omitted by 1674.

p. 229, l. 22.   *With a twinkle, Ariel.* 1670 adds :

> *Ariel.*   Before you can say come and go,
> And breathe twice, and cry so, so
> Each Spirit tripping on his toe,
> Shall bring 'em Meat with mop and moe.
> Do you love me, Master, I or no ?
> *Prosp.*   Dearly, my dainty *Ariel*, but stay, Spirit : . . .

p. 229, l. 37.   *Scene III. Wild Island.* 1670 omits this stage-direction.

p. 229, l. 39.   *no further, Sir.* 1670 adds :

> My old Bones ake, here's a Maze trod indeed,
> Through Forth-rights and Meanders, by your Patience
> I needs must rest.

p. 230, l. 1.   *Spirits.* 1670 adds : Sit and rest.

p. 230, l. 4.   *to find.* 1670 adds : and the Sea mocks
> Our frustrate Search on Land : Well ! let him go.
> *Ant.*   Do not for one repulse forego the purpose
> Which you resolv'd t' effect.
> *Alonz.*   I'm faint with hunger.

p. 230, l. 6.   *despair of food.* 1670 adds : Heav'n hath incens d
> The Seas and Shores against us for our crimes.
> What Harmony agen ! . . .

p. 230, l. 10.   *unlike the first.* 1670 adds :

> And seems as if 'twere meant t' unbend our cares,
> And calm your troubled thoughts.

p. 230, l. 11.   *Milcha.* 1670 omits Milcha here.

p. 230, l. 25.   *Dance of fantastick Spirits.* 1670 : *Enter eight fat Spirits with* Cornu-Copia *in their hands.* This is laughed at in *The Rehearsal*, III, 5, where Bayes cries to his soldiers : " Udzookers, you dance worse than the Angels in *Harry* the Eight, or the fat Spirits in *The Tempest*, I gad."
    From this point for the rest of the scene (nineteen lines) the Comedy, 1670, differs very much from the Opera. No Table, it will be noted, has been brought in on the stage in 1670, and the business of two Spirits bearing off the table was new to the Opera, as Downes remarks.

p. 231, l. 26.   *young Trincalo.* The Comedy here introduces various comical speeches which the Opera has omitted.

p. 232, l. 17.   *these Devils.* 1670 adds : I never loved 'em from my Childhood. The Devil take 'em. I would . . .

p. 233, l. 12.   *let him, my Lord ?* 1670 adds :

> *Vent.*   Lord ! Quoth he : the Monster's a very natural.
> *Syc.*   Lo ! lo ! agen ; bite him to death I prithee.
> *Trinc.*   Vice-Roys ! . . .

p. 233, l. 14.   *business.* 1670 adds : for I have other affairs to dispatch of more importance betwixt Queen Slobber-Chop, and my self.

p. 233, l. 18.   *Comprehended in the Treaty.*   1670 continues :

> *Muſt.*   Is the Butt safe, Duke *Trinculo ?*
> *Trinc.*   The Butt is partly safe : but to comprehend it in the Treaty,
> or indeed to make any Treaty, I cannot, with my honour, without
> your submission.   These two, and the Spirits under me, ſtand like-
> wise upon their honours.
> *Calib.*   Keep the liquor for us, my Lord, and let them drink Brine ; for
> I will not show 'em the quick freshes of the Island.
> *Steph.*   I underſtand . . .

p. 233, l. 31.   *within.*   1670 adds :

> *Syc.*   May I not Marry that other King and his two Subjeɑs to help you
> a Nights ?
> *Trinc.*   What a careful Spouse have I ?   Well !   If she does Cornute me,
> the care is taken.
>
> > When underneath my Power my Foes have truckl'd,
> > To be a Prince, who would not be a Cuckold ?   [*Exeunt.*

p. 233, l. 32.   *Milcha.*   Not in 1670.

p. 234, l. 39.   *Scene IV.*   1670 has no ſtage-direɑion as to the scene.

p. 241, l. 4.   *Aɑ IV. Cypres Trees and Cave.*   1670 omits scene-direɑion.

p. 241, l. 29.   *griefs are vanish'd.*   1670 here has thirteen lines which the Opera omits.

p. 242, l. 30.   *whom you praise.*   1670 follows with eleven lines omitted by the Opera.

p. 243, l. 29.   *even to Innocence.*   1670 here has thirty-one lines omitted by the Opera.

p. 247, l. 38.   *The Wild Island.*   Not in 1670.

p. 249, l. 10.   *pay nothing for't.*   In the place of the table rising, the dance of spirits and
the vanishing of the table, the Comedy, 1670, continues the dialogue
which until " *Stephano,* give me thy hand," the Opera omits.

p. 249, l. 24.   *Pledge my Grace faithfully.*   1670 here has more dialogue omitted in the
Opera until " *Caliban,* Go to the Butt."

p. 251, l. 18.   *The Cypress-trees and Cave.*   Scene-direɑion omitted in 1670.

p. 254, l. 14.   *nothing else.*   1670 continues with ten lines the Opera omits.

p. 254, l. 26.   *you were Shipwrack'd.*   1670 has : you Shipwrackt.

p. 255, l. 15.   *ſpeak for pity.*   1670 follows with thirteen lines the Opera omits.

p. 258, l. 11.   *resemble them.*   1670 has eleven lines which the Opera omits.   This is a
sensible gap, for in the Comedy Miranda employs an argument to
which Prospero's reply is apt, but in the Opera " The Argument is
weak " seems abrupt to say the leaſt.

p. 258, l. 14.   *Pray for him.*   1670 :

> *Mir.*   O ſtay, Sir, I have yet more Arguments.
> *Proſp.*   But none of any weight.
> *Mir.*   Have you not said you are his Judge ?
> *Proſp.*   'Tis true, I am ; what then ?
> *Mir.*   And can you be his Executioner ?
> If that be so, then all Men may declare
> Their Enemies in fault ; and Pow'r without
> The Sword of Juſtice, will presume to punish
> What e'er it calls a Crime.
> *Proſp.*   I cannot force . . .

p. 258, l. 31.   *Ariel. When I was chidden.*   This speech of Ariel's condenses a dialogue
of some forty lines between Prospero and Ariel in the Comedy.

p. 259, l. 35. *smoaking from my Mouth.* Seven rather absurd lines of 1670 are here well omitted in the Opera.

p. 265, l. 5. *Ariel. I'le do it Master.* In the Comedy Ariel here sings *Where the Bee sucks ;* and, the song done, the play concludes thus :

Syc. I'll to Sea with thee, and keep thee warm in thy Cabin.

Trinc. No my dainty Dy-dapper, you have a tender Constitution, and will be sick a Ship-board. You are partly Fish and may swim after me. I wish you a good Voyage.

> *Prosp.* Now to this Royal Company, my Servant
> Be visible, and entertain them with
> A Dance before they part.

> *Ariel.* I have a gentle Spirit for my Love,
> Who twice seven years hath waited for my Freedom,
> It shall appear and foot it featly with me.
> *Milcha,* my Love, thy *Ariel* calls thee.
>   Enter Milcha.

Milcha. Here !   [*They dance a Saraband.*
Prosp. Henceforth this Isle to the afflicted be . . .
    . . .   [*Exeunt.*

It may be noted that Milcha only appears once, in this place, in the Comedy whilst in the Opera Ariel and Milcha are constantly together when songs have to be rendered.

Psyche

p. 271, l. 3. *Tragedy :* 1690 : "As it is now Acted | At Their Majesties Theatre | In *Dorset-Garden.* | Written by | *Tho.* *Shadwell,* Laur. | London, | Printed by *J. M.* for *H. Herringman,* and sold by *R. Bentley,* | at the Post-House in *Russel-street, Covent-Garden.* | 1690. |

p. 277, l. 1. *most.* 1690 : Most.

p. 277, l. 6. *Grace ?* 1690 : *Grace,*

p. 277, l. 19. *Honour then that.* 1690 : Honour than that.

p. 278, l. 9. *onely free.* 1690 : only free.

p. 278, l. 35. *more then I.* 1690 : more than I.

p. 279, l. 13. *French Psyche.* 1690 misprints : Phyche.

p. 280, l. 31. *to rob my self.* In the first quarto, 1675, the Postscript continues : " The Reader may please to take note of several Errata's," and five errata are there listed and corrected. In Sir Edmund Gosse's copy these have been amended in a contemporary hand, and I have printed them aright in this edition. The Postscript concludes : " Several other errors there are, which the sense will help you to correct."

p. 281, l. 14. *labour wrought.* 1690 : labor wrought.

p. 284, l. 10. *the gross Earth exhales.* 4to, 1675 : " The bright Sun exhales." Noted as an Erratum.

p. 285, l. 10. *o're the Lawns.* 1690 : o'er the Lawns.

p. 285, l. 19. *Eccho.* 1690 : Echo.

p. 286, l. 5. *joyn.* 1690 : join.

TEXTUAL NOTES

p. 286, l. 30. *retirment.* 1690 : retirement.
p. 286, l. 34. *unwelcom.* 1690 : unwelcome.
p. 287, l. 15. *With all the Treasures of the East and West.* 1675 drops this line, and notes the omission as an Erratum.
p. 292, l. 40. *Nicander & Polynices.* 1690 : Nicander *and* Polynices.
p. 294, l. 30. *Image of Apollo before which stands the Tripod.* 1675 : *Image of* Apollo *upon the Tripod,* which is noted as an Erratum.
p. 295, l. 4. *Wreathes.* 1690 : Wreaths.
p. 295, l. 5. *Cedippe.* 1690 : Cidippe.
p. 295, l. 8. *Hymn.* 1690 : Hymen.
p. 296, l. 23. *Fawnus.* 1690 : *Faunus.*
p. 297, l. 20. *As the Priestess Pythia is mounting the Tripod.* 1675 drops this to commence stage-direction with : " *It Thunders.*" The omission is noted as an Erratum.
p. 299, l. 9. *more Errors.* 1690 : more Errours.
p. 301, l. 4. *a grave.* 1690 : a Grave.
p. 302, l. 28. *dye.* 1690 : die.
p. 303, l. 7. *eyes.* 1690 : Eyes.
p. 303, l. 22. *Rejoyce.* 1690 : Rejoice.
p. 304, l. 9. *Psyche give.* 1690 misprints : Physche give.
p. 308, l. 18. *cruelty.* 1690 : Cruelty.
p. 309, l. 7. *poison.* 1690 : poyson.
p. 310, l. 33. *first surprise.* 1690 : first surprize.
p. 311, l. 14. *Earthly Princes.* 1690 : earthly Princes.
p. 311, l. 20. *palatte.* 1690 : Palate.
p. 313, l. 11. *Cydippe.* 1690 : *Cidippe.* There are several variants, it may be noted, of this name.
p. 313, l. 23. *lowdly.* 1690 : *loudly.*
p. 314, l. 17. *enjoyn.* 1690 : enjoin.
p. 315, l. 29. *give o'r.* 1690 : give o'er.
p. 316, l. 8. *Great Statues of Gold . . . at their feet.* 1675 has : " *great Statues, Figures of Gold standing on Pedestals, and small sitting at their feet.*" Attention is drawn to this in the note to the Postscript, where it appears among the Errata.
p. 318, l. 6. *sower.* 1690 : sowre.
p. 319, l. 12. *let's joyn.* 1690 : let's join.
p. 322, l. 19. *what e'rs.* 1690 : what e'ers.
p. 323, l. 32. *lye.* 1690 : lie.
p. 323, l. 33. *dye.* 1690 : die.
p. 323, l. 34. *Exit Soldier.* 1690 : [*Exit Souldier.*
p. 324, l. 33. *ne'r shall dye.* 1690 : *ne'er shall die,* and so in the repetition.
p. 326, l. 13. *Soldier.* 1690 : *Souldier,* throughout.
p. 327, l. 7. *Ruines.* 1690 : Ruins.
p. 330, l. 41. [*She weeps.* 1690 : [*Shee weeps.*
p. 331, l. 2. *honor.* 1690 : honour.
p. 331, l. 4. *fools.* 1690 : Fools.
p. 332, l. 26. *ruines.* 1690 : ruins.
p. 333, l. 1. *Eies.* 1690 : Eyes.
p. 333, l. 34. *suborne.* 1690 : subborn.
p. 337, l. 21. *Now tastes.* 1690 : *Now tasts.*
p. 337, l. 22. *I Elisian.* 1690 : *I Elysian.*
p. 337, l. 27. *griefs, and with fears.* 1690 : *Griefs, and with Fears.*

p. 337, l. 31. *joy!* 1690 : *Joy!*
p. 338, l. 23. *power and the pleasures.* 1690 : *Power and the Pleasures.*
p. 338, l. 25. *debauches.* 1690 : *Debauches.*
p. 339, l. 14. *Extasie.* 1690 : Ecstasie.
p. 340, l. 17. *neighbours.* 1690 : *Neighbours.*
p. 240, l. 35. *improve and treat.* 1690 : *Improve and Treat.*
p. 340, l. 35. *year.* 1690 : *Year.*

EXPLANATORY NOTES

The Miser

p. 15.   CHARLES LORD BUCKHURST, 1638–1707. In the second quarto he is called Charles Earl of Dorset and Middlesex. He was created Earl of Middlesex in 1674, and in 1677 he succeeded his father as sixth Earl of Dorset.

p. 16.   L'AVARE. *L'Avare* was produced on 9 September, 1668.

p. 16.   FATAL FIRE. On 25 January, 1672, the Theatre Royal was burned to the ground by a disastrous fire, which did terrible damage in Russell Street and Vinegar Yard. Richard Bell, a young actor of great merit, unhappily lost his life.

p. 17.   PUDDEN FOOLS. Jack Puddings. It may be noted that "Pudden" is Norfolk, and puddin'-head is Northampton for a fool. Pease, *Mark o'Deil*, 1894, 75 : "Ye damned clumsy-footed puddin-head." There is also West Yorkshire "puddin'-heead," *Leeds Mercury Supplement*, 26 May, 1896.

p. 17.   ENGLISH MONSIEURS. French fashions and French affectations were greatly exaggerated by the English Gallomaniacs, who are so frequently portrayed in contemporary drama. *The English Mounsieur* is actually the title of a play by James Howard, which Pepys, who saw it 8 December, 1666, judged to be "very witty and pleasant." It is indeed an amusing piece. Wycherley satirizes the same foppishness in the person of Monsieur de Paris, *The Gentleman Dancing-Master;* and Dryden's Melantha, *Marriage à-la-Mode*, is a complete portrait.

p. 17.   FASHIONS. In October, 1666, the King adopted a new costume, "a vest," as it was termed. Evelyn and Pepys give full descriptions of the new mode. In *The Character of a Trimmer* ("Miscellanies by the Marquis of Halifax," 1704, p. 164), it is stated "that one of the instructions Madame brought along with her was to laugh us out of those vests ; which she performed so effectually, that in a moment, like so many footmen who had quitted their master's livery, we all took it again, and returned to our old service" the French fashion. Henrietta, Duchess of Orleans, was at Dover in May, 1670.

p. 17.   TU QUOQUE. This comedy, *Tu Quoque ; or, The Citie Gallant*, is often known as *Greene's Tu Quoque*, from the acting of Thomas Greene, a famous low-comedian, in the part of Bubble. The earliest extant edition is dated 1614. The play was revived after the Restoration on Thursday, 12 September, 1667, at the Duke's House. Pepys tells us that some alterations were made by Sir William Davenant. The play seems to have been very successful and to have greatly amused the audiences.

p. 18.   SIEGES. The opening lines of this Epilogue particularly refer to Dryden's heroic plays : *The Indian-Queen*, produced at the Theatre Royal in January, 1663–4 ; *The Indian Emperour, or, The Conquest of Mexico* by the Spaniards, produced at the Theatre Royal in the spring of 1665 ; *Tyrannick Love, or, The Royal Martyr*, produced at the Theatre Royal in the summer of 1669 ; and *The Conquest of Granada by the Spaniards*, Part I, Theatre Royal, December, 1670, Part II, at the same house, January, 1671. There is no doubt also a hit at Davenant's popular *The Siege of Rhodes*. Settle's *The Empress of Morocco* had probably been produced at court in 1671. William Joyner's tragedy *The Roman Empress*, produced at the Theatre Royal in 1670, has the scene on the banks of the Tiber, where Valentius is encamped in the nature of a besieger against Hostilius, who is on the Roman side of the river. The Earl of Orrery's dramas, which were then so much admired, are almost wholly concerned with Love and War.

p. 18. MOGUL. Dryden's last rhymed tragedy, produced at Drury Lane late in 1675, probably November, was *Aureng-Zebe*, and the folio of 1701 gives as title *Aureng-Zebe, or, The Great-Mogul.*

p. 18. PRESTER JOHN. Many are the legends which collected about this mythical Eastern priest and King. The first authentic mention of Prester John is to be found in the *Chronicle* of Otto, Bishop of Freising, in 1145. Already the most extravagant stories had gathered, and these increased apace during the centuries. Even the country ruled over by this Presbyter-King was uncertain. The oldest map, on which America is mentioned 1507, places this realm in Tibet: "This is the land of the good King and Lord, known as Prester John, lord of all Eastern and Southern India, lord of all the kings of India, in whose mountains are found all kinds of precious stones." In later times general opinion had it that Abyssinia was the Presbyter's territory. On the *Carta Marina* (1516) it is placed in Africa: "Regnum Habesch et Habacci Presbiteri Ioh. siue India Maior Ethiopie."

p. 18. AMERICAN PRINCE, *e.g.*, Montezuma in Dryden's *The Indian Emperour*. Some quarter of a century later Southerne's great tragedy *Oroonoko* was produced at Drury Lane, and proved one of the most popular dramas the English stage has ever seen. In imitation of Southerne, William Walker, the son of a wealthy Barbadoes planter, wrote his *Victorious Love*, produced at Drury Lane in 1698, and this is very reminiscent of the heroic plays Shadwell is aiming at here.

p. 21. GROOM PORTERS. The groom porter was an official of the court, who regulated all matters connected with gaming and provided the players with cards, dice and other accessories. He also settled all disputes which might arise. The office lapsed entirely during the reign of George III.

p. 22. WHITE PERIWIG. A flaxen or white periwig was greatly affected by young fops of the day. In the Prologue to the second part of *The Conquest of Granada*, 4to, 1672, Dryden's Gallant in the pit " With his white Wigg sets off his Nut-brown Face." Cf. the Song, *Covent Garden Drollery*, p. 73 :

> The Husband has all the vexation,
> The quarrels and care of the Sheets,
> Fair Perriwigs and Fops, in th' Fashion,
> For nothing enjoy all the sweets.

p. 22. BOW STREET. Bow Street, Covent Garden, was built in 1637, and so called " as running in shape of a bent bow." Styrpe says : " The street is open and large, with very good houses, well inhabited, and resorted unto by gentry for lodgings, as are most of the other streets in this parish." This was about 1720. Among the residents in Bow Street were Wallis, 1654–1656; the Earl of Dorset, 1684 and 1685 ; Michael Mohun, 1671–1676; Grinling Gibbons, 1678–1721, the year of his death.

p. 22. HOPKINS AND STERNHOLD. Authors of the famous metrical version of the Psalms. The first edition appeared early in 1549 : " *Certayne Psalmes* . . . drawen into English meter by Thomas Sternhold." In 1549 appeared a second edition with a supplement of seven Psalms by Hopkins, who requested that his additions should not be " fathered on the dead man," because they were not " in any part to be compared with his most exquisite doinges." The British Museum has more than six hundred editions printed between 1549 and 1828. These verses were said to have been recited extempore at Bodicote Church, in the parish of Adderbury. (Cf. *Adderbury*, by H. Gepp, 1924.) These metrical Psalms were often sung by criminals on the way to, and at, the place of execution.

p. 22. LEAN JUDGE. Cf. *Love for Love*, I, where Jeremy says : " I have dispatc'd some half a Dozen Duns, with as much Dexterity as a hungry Judge do's Causes at Dinner-time." Also *The Rape of the Lock*, II, 21–22 :

> The hungry Judges soon the Sentence sign,
> And Wretches hang that Jury-men may Dine.

p. 22. PARTY PER PALE. Pale is a heraldic term signifying the vertical stripe in the middle of a shield.

p. 22. BEAR AT CHARING CROSS. A small house of indifferent reputation.

p. 22. EX TRADUCE. *Tradux*, from *traduco*, " is led or brought over " ; and so a vine-layer trained for propagation, as in Varro, Columella and other writers on husbandry. Hence the technical theological word Traducianism. This is in general the doctrine that, in the process of generation, the human spiritual soul is transmitted (ex traduce) to the offspring by the parents. Traducianism is opposed to Creationism, the doctrine that every soul is created by God. Although it can hardly be maintained that Creationism is strictly *de fide*, since there is no explicit definition authoritatively laid down by the Church, yet it is theologically certain that corporeal Traducianism is heretical. All the Schoolmen uphold Creationism, and S. Thomas emphatically says : " It is heretical to assert that the intellectual soul is transmitted by process of generation " (I, Q. cxviii. a. 2).

p. 23. CATER-DEUCE-AZES. Cater is four at dice or cards. Deuce is two.

p. 23. SHATOLINS. The famous French ordinary in Covent Garden, much frequented by the wits. There are innumerable allusions. Pepys, 22 April, 1668 : " To Chatelin's, the French house in Covent Garden, and there with musick and good company . . . and mighty merry till ten at night."

p. 24. FILIUS ANTE DIEM. Ovid, *Metamorphoses*, I, 148 : Filius ante diem patrios inquirit in annos.

p. 25. SCOMMATICALLY. A scomm is a Flout or Scoff ; σκώπτειν = to jeer. Macrobius, Saturnalia, VII, 3, has *Scomma*, but notes : " λοιδορία et σκώμμα, quibus nec uocabula Latina reperio." Edward Howard in the epistle preceding *The Usurper*, 4to, 1668, writes : " The other extream . . . is that of Farce or Scommatick Plays." Cf. *Six Lessons* (1656), VI, 55 : " Whatsoever is added of contumely, either directly or scommatically, is want of Charity and uncivil." Scomm and its derivatives were fairly common from *circa* 1600–1720.

p. 27. KILLED SEVEN MEN. Cf. Otway's *The Cheats of Scapin*, Dorset Garden, January, 1676–7, III, where Scapin, speaking of the pretended Bully, says : He " makes no more conscience of killing a Man, than cracking of a Lowse ; he has killed sixteen, four for taking the Wall of him, five for looking too big upon him, two he shot pissing against the Wall."

p. 27. DARNOCK CARPET. Darnock, dornick, or dornex, a worsted or woollen fabric used for curtains, hangings and the like, so called from Tournai, where chiefly manufactured. In Mrs. Behn's *The Luckey Chance ; or, An Alderman's Bargain*, produced at Drury Lane in the winter of 1686, I, 3, Bredwel, describing Gayman's poor bed in his Alsatian lodging, says : "There had been Dornex Curtains to't in the days of Yore ; but they were now annihilated." Also cf. *Wit and Drollery* (1681) : Penelope to Ulysses :—

> The Stools of *Dornix* which that you may know well
> Are certain stuffs Upholsterers use to sell.

p. 28. DIVES. The Parable of Dives and Lazarus was a very common subject for old paintings and tapestries. The word Dives is not used in the Bible as a proper noun ; but in the Middle Ages it came to be employed as the actual name of the rich man mentioned in S. Luke xvi, 19–31. It has often been thought that our Lord was speaking of real persons and actual events. The " House of Dives " is still pointed out in Jerusalem ; but, of course, if such a house ever existed, it must have long since disappeared.

p. 29. RIBBANDS. It was a French fashion to wear quantities of ribbands on one's clothes. So in *The Gentleman Dancing-Master* Don Diego reproaches Monsieur De Parris for wearing " all those gew-gaw Ribbons." The coxcomb was imitating the gallants and ladies at the French Court who covered their dresses with yards and yards of gay ribbon. This is satirized by Madame d'Aulnoy when in *La Bonne Petite Souris* she describes the Princess Joliette, " qui avoit une belle robe de satin blanc, toute en broderie d'or, avec des diamants rouges, et plus de mille aunes de rubans partout."

p. 29. FLAXEN MOP. So old Gripe in *Love in a Wood*, III, speaks of " Prodigals in white Perruques." In *L'Ecole des Maris*, produced 24 June, 1661, I, ix, Sganarelle, who has been declaiming against the luxury of the age, addresses Valère as " Monsieur aux blonds cheveux."

p. 29. FLANDERS LACE. *London Gazette*, No. 2170/4, 1686 : " An open Flanders-lac'd Neckcloth."

p. 30. AQUA VITAE. Harpagon is more in keeping with his character when he says : " Allez vite boire dans la cuisine un verre d'eau claire." *L'Avare*, I, v.

p. 32. NURS-KEEPERS. A nurse-keeper is a sick-nurse. *London Gazette*, No. 6250/11, 1724 : " Mary Easton, . . . Widow and Nursekeeper."

p. 33. WHETSTON. Whetstone Park is a narrow roadway, of which the name still remains, between the north side of Lincoln's Inn Fields and the south side of Holborn. In the reign of Charles II this district was infamous, and the abode of the lowest kind of prostitute. There are innumerable allusions, all of which are injurious and insulting. Thus in *Love in a Wood*, I, Dapperwit, as the greatest rudeness of which he is capable, says to Lady Flippant : " If I had met you in Wheatstone's-Park, with a drunken Foot-Soldier, I should not have been jealous of you." Lee in the Dedication to *The Princess of Cleve*, 4to, 1689, writes : " When they expected the most polish'd Hero in *Nemours*, I gave 'em a Ruffian reeking from *Whetstone's-Park*."

p. 33. MANTOPLICEE. *Manteau plissé*, a pleated cloak.

p. 33. AQUA-VITAE BOTTLE. In Duffett's *The Mock-Tempest ; or, The Enchanted Castle*, 4to, 1675, I, 1, Stephania, the bawd, cries : " Stir about, or I'l beat thy brains out with my Bottle." A goodly sized case-bottle was considered part of the essential equipment of a procuress. An ancient sibyl of this profession, with her rundlet of Nancy, figures prominently in the sixth picture of Hogarth's " The Harlot's Progress," and one may remember Foote's Mrs. Cole (a satire on Mother Douglas), with her modest demand for mint-water —but on occasion quaffing French drams supernaculum—and her parting instructions to Sir George's man : " Richard, you may as well give me the bottle into the chair for fear I should be taken ill on the road."

p. 33. HACKNY. Threadbare; worn out by use. A Hackney Trumpeter is an itinerant musician of the lowest class. W. Boghurst, *Loimographia*, 1666, speaks of "your wild, wanton, hackney fiddlers."

p. 33. BEVER. A chapeau de poil, a mark of some distinction in those days. Hence the title of Rubens' famous picture, a lady in a beaver hat or chapeau de poil, which, being corrupted to chapeau de paille, led to much error. Stubbes, *The Anatomie of Abuses* (1583), has: "These they call bever hats of xx, xxx, or xl shillings price, fetched from beyond the sea." Pepys, 28 January, 1660–61, writes: "At Mr. Holden's, where I bought a hat, cost me 35*s*." But 27 June, 1661: "This day Mr. Holden sent me a bever, which cost me £4 5*s*."

p. 33. AB INFERIS. "O spes inanis, o falsa præsumptio! Non credat frustra errore deceptus, quod aliquo pretio sit redimendus, quoniam in inferno nulla est redemptio." Pope Innocent III (ob. 1216), *De Contemptu Mundi siue De Miseria Hominis*, in Migne's Patrologia, vol. ccxvii, column 741B.

(Acc. to J. A. Fabricius, *Bibliotheca Latina Mediae et Infimae Aetatis*, the first edition of this treatise was printed in 1496 at Cologne. Other edd. at Lyons, 1554 & 1641, Douai, 1633. There were also collected editions of his works.)

But I also find the following in Josephus Langius's *Florilegium Magnum seu Polyanthea*, col. 1359, in the 1659 (Lyons) edit., under the Heading, Infernus:

In inferno nulla est redemptio: quoniam qui illic damnatus et demersus fuerit, ulterius non exibit. In inferno nulla redemptio: quoniam nec pater ibi potest adiuuare filium nec filius patrem. Ibi non inuenitur amicus vel propinquus, qui ualeat et argumentum et diuitias dare, quas nunc congregant auari, uidentes pauperes inopia tabescere, et prae nimia fame et siti nuditatem et mortem incurrere; non poterunt sibi praestare aliquod refugium: unde miseri prae nimia doloris amaritudine amarissime flentes et prae angustia spiritus gementes, dicent in inferno: Quid profuit nobis superbia nostra, diuitiae, honores, dignitates, luxuria, gulositas, et omnes delectationes carnales quid profuerunt nobis? Ecce omnia transierunt quasi somnia, quasi fumus et umbra, et quasi non fuerint, et nos cruciatibus deputati sumus et suppliciis æternis. In inferno nulla est redemptio: quoniam ibi gemitus sunt et suspiria, et non est qui misereatur. Ibi est dolor et planctus, et clamor, et non est qui audiat. *S. Augustinus in sermones ad Eremitas.*

I do not find this passage in any of the *Sermones ad Fratres in Eremo* in the Benedictine edition of S. Augustine. Most of this set of sermons are placed by the Benedictine edd. in the Appendix as not by S. Augustine.

p. 34. CITTERN. Or Cithern, an instrument of the guitar kind, but strung with wire, and played with a plectrum or quill. It was commonly kept in barbers' shops for the use of customers, and often had a grotesquely carved head. The Tyrolese form of the instrument, which is known of recent years in England, is generally called the Zither.

p. 34. GEMINI. Gemini, a mild exclamation or petty oath in use principally by the innocent and vulgar. It generally conveys an idea of childishness, real or assumed. It was often corrupted, and we have Jeminy, Jimini, Leminy, Lemine, etc. Cf. Otway's *The Souldier's Fortune*, produced at Dorset Garden in the spring of 1679–80, where Sir Jolly, bantering, cries out: "Gemini! what would become of me!"

p. 35. STUMME. Stumed wine, or stum, is dead and insipid wine invigorated by mixing new wine with it, and so raising a fresh fermentation. Cf. slang (still in

common use) " stumer," a generic name for anything worthless, especially
a worthless cheque. Cf. also the Epilogue (spoken by Mrs. Barry) to Mrs.
Behn's *The False Count*, produced at Dorset Garden in the autumn of 1682,
when she greets the fops of the pit with :

> You everlasting grievance of the Boxes,
> You wither'd Ruins of stum'd Wine and Poxes.

Absalom and Achitophel, II (1682), has the following line (481) addressed to
Shadwell :

> Eat Opium, mingle Arsenick in thy Drink.

Cf. also the *Verse Letter* from Mr. Shadwell, who was staying at Chatterton
Hall, near Oldham, Lancashire, to Wycherley (first printed in a *Miscellany*
of 1698). He praises the country tipple " Nappy, Clear and Stale,"

> While you of Stum, Alom and Sloes,
> Molossus, Arsnick, Lime, take Dose,
> From Roguy Vinter, and do venture
> Your Life, when you in Tavern enter ;
> In White-wine, Claret, Sack, or Hockum.

In *Love in a Wood*, III, Gripe, bribing Mrs. Joyner, gives her a groat with
which to go to the next cellar, and says : " Come, the Wine has Arsenick
in't."

p. 36. PROTECTIONS. Protections were writs issued by the King, which guaranteed
immunity from arrest to those engaged in his particular service. In *Love in
a Wood*, I, 1, Gripe, abusing Dapperwit, says : " He had the impudence to
hold an Argument against me in the defence of Vests and Protections ; and
therefore I forbid him my house."

p. 36. WHITE WINE. In *Love in a Wood*, II, 1, Lady Flippant cries : " Oh drink,
abominable drink ! instead of inflaming Love, it quenches it. . . . Curse
on all Wine, even Rhenish-Wine and Sugar."

p. 36. POPE'S HEAD. A well-known tavern in Lombard Street. On Monday, 26
March, 1665–6, Pepys went with Lord Bruncker " to the Pope's Head
Taverne in Lumbard Streete to dine by appointment with Captain Taylor."
There were several taverns of this name, one in Chancery Lane, one in
Cornhill, and others, which were very much frequented.

p. 37. PAUCA VERBA. An old Elizabethan catch-phrase. In *Every Man in His Humour*,
IV, 2, Wel-bred says : " O the Benchers phrase *pauca verba, pauca verba*."
[Benchers = the loungers on tavern benches.] In *The Silent Woman*,
III, 1, Otter protests : " Nay, good princess, hear me *pauca verba*." Cf. *Love's
Labour's Lost*, IV, 2, Holofernes' " pauca verba." Also *The Merry Wives of
Windsor*, I, 1, Sir Hugh Evans' " Pauca verba, Sir John ; good worts."
A Spanish form, " Paucos Palabros," occurs in Jonson's *Masque of Augurs*,
and in *The Taming of the Shrew*, Induction, 1, Sly hiccups out : " Paucas
Pallabris." " Sed paucis uerbis te uolo," Plautus, *Miles Gloriosus*, II, iv,
22.

p. 37. COVENT GARDEN CHURCH. S. Paul's, Covent Garden, the design of which is
attributed to Inigo Jones, was commenced in 1631, and having been built
at the charge of the Earl of Bedford, was consecrated by Dr. Juxon, Bishop
of London, 27 September, 1638. The Rev. William Bray, Vicar of S.
Martin's-in-the-Field, claimed it as a chapel of ease, but in 1645 it was
constituted a separate parish. In *Love in a Wood*, produced at the Theatre

Royal, Bridges Street, in the autumn of 1671, I, My Lady Flippant says: "Have I not conſtantly kept Covent Garden Church, St. Martin's, the Play-Houses, Hide-Park, Mulbery-Garden, and all other the Publick Marts where Widows and Mayds are expos'd?" In Otway's *The Atheiſt*, produced at Dorset Garden in the autumn of 1683, I, among the daily businesses of London are mentioned "Assignations at Covent Garden Church."

p. 37. FECK. I feck, which signifies in earneſt. As an asseveration Ifeck is a form of i' faith. This mild expression, which was even used by Puritans, is laughed at by Jonson, *The Alchemiſt* (1610), I, 2: "I-fac's no oath." Cf. also in *The Old Batchelour* Fondlewife's conſtant exclamation "Ifeck," IV, 1.

p. 37. SHROVE TUESDAY. On Shrove Tuesday in each year, as also during Eaſtertide, it was cuſtomary for the apprentices of the metropolis to avail themselves of their holidays by assembling in large numbers and making organized assaults upon notorious houses of ill fame, which they sacked and even demolished. In Middleton's *Inner Temple Masque* (4to, 1649), we have:

"Stand forth, Shrove Tuesday, one a' the silenc'ſt bricklayers;
'Tis in your charge to pull down bawdy-houses."

And in Marmion's *Holland's Leaguer*, acted at Salisbury Court, December, 1631, Act IV, 3, which scene is the exterior of the Leaguer:

"Good sir, let's think on some revenge! call up
The gentlemen 'prentices and make a Shrove Tuesday."

Holland's Leaguer was a celebrated brothel, which ſtood where is now Holland Street, Blackfriars.

p. 37. DEUS. Deuce.

p. 38. VIPER WINE. Wine medicated by some extract or decoction obtained from vipers, and formerly much drunk on account of its supposed reſtorative and vitalizing properties. In Tom Brown's *Letters from the Dead to the Living*, Mother Cresswell to Moll Quarles says: "I was never without *Viper-wine* for a fumbler, to give a spur to old age and assiſt impotency." Cf. Massinger, *Believe as You Liſt*, 1631, IV, 1:

Your viper wine
So much in practise with gray bearded gallants,
[is] But vappa to the nectar of her lippe.

Also, Quarles, *Hiſt. Samson*, 1631, *Works*, ed. Grosart, II, 149/2:

Their Viper-wines to make old age presume
To feele new luſt, and youthfull flames agin.

p. 40. HARPSICAL-MASTERS. A harpsichord is an inſtrument larger than a spinet with two or three ſtrings to a note. On Sunday, 31 March, 1661, Pepys notes: "To Mrs. Turner's, where I could not woo The. to give me a lesson upon the harpsicon and was angry at it." There are many variants and corruptions of the word "Harpsichord." In *She Stoops to Conquer*, produced at Covent Garden 15 March, 1773, IV, Tony Lumpkin says: "I always loved cousin Con's hazle eyes, and her pretty long fingers, that she twiſts this way and that, over the haspicholls, like a parcel of bobbins."
This popular malapropism, haspicholls, is also found in a letter written by Gray to Chute in 1746.

p. 41. JOHN OF THE TIMES. Both these patriarchs are mentioned by Oldham in his *Character* as typical of venerable antiquity. "*His Age is out of* Knowledge. . . . *Every Limb about him is* Chronicle : Parr *and* John *of the* Times *were short-Livers to him. They say, he can remember when* Pauls *was founded, and* London-Bridge *built*." The exact age of John of the Times, as he was generally dubbed, seems uncertain, but there can be no doubt that he had lived many decades beyond the ordinary span of human kind.

    Thomas Parr is an even more famous example of antediluvian age, of whom there is an ample account in the *Dictionary of National Biography*. He is said to have been born in 1483, and he died in 1635. He was buried in the south transept of Westminster Abbey, where is an inscription (recut in 1870) which runs : "Tho : Parr of yᵉ county of Sallop. Borne in Aº 1483. He lived in yᵉ reignes of Ten Princes, viz., K. Edw. 4. K. Ed. V. K. Rich. 3. K. Hen. 7. K. Hen. 8. K. Edw. 6. Q. Ma. Q. Eliz. K. Ja. and K. Charles, aged 152 yeares, and was buried here Nov. 15 1635." Rubens painted his portrait from memory, and engravings are not uncommon.

p. 43. BEER-GLASSES. A beer-glass is a glass to hold half a pint. "A Silver cup . . . the Form of a Beer Glass." *London Gazette*, 1707, 4391–3.

p. 45. WEAR THE WILLOW. Cf. *Much Ado About Nothing*, II, 1, where Benedick says : "I offered him my company to a willow tree, either to make him a garland, as being forsaken, or to bind him up a rod, as worthy to be whipped."

p. 45. INNOCENT SHEET. Cf. *Love for Love*, III, Ben's ballad :

> For now the Time was ended,
> When she no more intended,
> To lick her Lips at Men, Sir,
> And gnaw the Sheets in vain, Sir,
> And lie o' Nights alone.

p. 45. CHALK, LIME, OR OATMEAL. Cf. *Love in a Wood*, I, 1, where Lady Flippant says : "Wou'd you have us as tractable as the Wenches that eat Oatmeal, and fool'd like them too." Cf. *Gallantry A-la-Mode, A Satyrical Poem*, 12mo, 1674, II :

> We *Matrons* it *Green-sickness* call,
> Or *Fits* of th' *Mother*, that befall
> Young *Virgins*, 'cause they *Charcoale* eate,
> Or *Chalk*, and *nauceate* wholesome *meat*.

p. 45. LIVERY-MAN. A freeman of the City of London, who is entitled to wear the "livery" of the Company to which he belongs, and to exercise other privileges.

p. 47. ARCH LUTE. Chambers, *Cyclopædia* (1727–51), explains : "*Arcileuto, Archi-lute*, a long and large lute, having its bass strings lengthened after the manner of a theorbo, and each row doubled either with a little octave or a unison. It is used by the Italians for playing a thorough bass."

p. 47. A PAIR OF TABLES. Tables is the old name for backgammon. Pepys, Monday, 11 September, 1665, notes : "I by water to Woolwich, where with my wife to a game of tables, and to bed." Various other obsolete games were played with Tables ; Irish, Tick-tack, Dubblets, Sice-Ace, and Ketch-Dott.

p. 47. CORNUES. A cornue is a retort, a limbeck of glass. Cotgrave gives French *cornue*, "a kind of bending Limbecke of glasse." Latin, *cornuta*. In the parallel passage of *L'Avare*, II, 1, we have : "Un fourneau de brique, avec deux cornues et trois récipients."

p. 49. SHOVEL-BOARD. Shovel-board was a game in which a coin, a counter, or some other disk was driven by a smart blow with the hand along a highly polished board, or table, marked with transverse lines. Among the Herbert documents is a Licence for the "Use of one Shovelboard," *Dramatic Records*, edited by T. Q. Adams, 1917, p. 131.

p. 49. BROAD-PIECES. After the introduction of the guinea in 1663 the name Broad-piece was applied to the "Unite" or twenty-shilling piece ("Jacobus" or "Carolus") of the preceding reigns, which was much thinner and broader than the new-milled coinage. The term is common. In Crowne's *Sir Courtly Nice*, 1685, I, Lord Bellguard says : "A rambling Woman, let her be never so good a manager, will be apt to bring her Virtue as a Traveller does his Money, from a Broad-Piece to a Brass-Farthing."

p. 50. SINK-CATER. Cinq quatre.

p. 51. WEAR THE SURPLICE. Cf. *Love in a Wood*, I, 1, where Lady Flippant speaks of "This counter fashion Brother of mine (who hates a Vest as much as a Surplice)." There are many allusions to the inordinate and irrational hatred of the Puritans for the surplice, an abhorrence which amongst the ignorant and vulgar persists even to the present day. Cf. *All's Well that Ends Well*, I, 3, where the Clown says : "Though honesty be no Puritan, yet it will do no hurt : it will wear the surplice of humility over the black gown of a big heart." In *A Match at Midnight* (4to, 1633), I, Sim cries : "H' has turned his stomach, for all the world like a Puritan's at the sight of a surplice."

p. 52. COG. To cog is quoted in 1532 among "Ruffian's terms" of dice-play. It seems that "cogging" generally meant some sleight of hand, made use of to control the falling of a die ; occasionally it may signify the substitution of a false die for the true one. To cog a die is a very common phrase, meaning fraudulently to direct the fall of the dice.

p. 52. SWEAR NOT. James Howell, *Paroimiologia*, folio, 1659, has : "Who sweareth when he playeth at dice, may challenge his damnation by way of purchase."

p. 53. MUSICIANERS. Hide Park. Pepys, Saturday, 4 July, 1663, notes that there was "a general muster of the King's Guards, Horse and Foot, in Hide Park." He was present at similar musters in the Park on Wednesday, 16 September, 1668, and on Wednesday, 19 May, 1669. These musters were attended by very fashionable crowds, and probably Timothy is only boasting when he says that the city Militia, to which he must have belonged, were reviewed here.

p. 53. SINK, *i.e.*, keep back any of the money, and cheat me of my share.

p. 53. A BOAT, A BOAT. The popular tune otherwise known as *Haste to the Ferry*. In the extraordinary Epilogue, burlesquing *Macbeth*, to Duffett's skit *The Empress of Morocco*, Drury Lane, 1674, the witches sing their ballad *A Health, a Health*, to the tune of *A Boat, a Boat*. *Here's a health unto His Majesty* is a loyal old favourite. The words as found in *Catch that catch can ; or, The Musical Companion, containing Catches and Rounds for three and four voices*, 4to, 1667, are as follows :

> Here's a health unto his Majesty, with a fa, la, la,
> Confusion to his enemies, with a fa, la, la.
> And he that will not pledge his health,
> I wish him neither wit nor wealth,
> Nor yet a rope to hang himself.
> > With a fa, la, la, la,
> > With a fa, la, la, la.

The music is sometimes ascribed to Jeremy Savile.

p. 53. SIMKIN. "The Humours of Simpkin, A continued Farce," Droll nineteen in Kirkman's collection *The Wits, or, Sport upon Sport*. "Drols and Farces, Presented and Shewn For the Merriment and Delight of Wise Men, and the Ignorant: As they have been sundry times Acted In Publique and Private, In London at Bartholomew, In the Countrey at other, Faires. In Halls and Taverns. On several Mountebancks Stages, At *Charing Cross, Lincoln-Inn-Fields*, and other places. By Several Strolling Players, Fools, and Fidlers, And the Mountebancks Zanies With loud Laughter and great Applause."

I have used the edition with date 1673. Simpkin is a Clown, and the actors in the little interlude are Simpkin; Bluster, a Roarer; an old Man; his Wife, a Servant: The wife is entertaining Simpkin, when they are disturbed by Bluster. Simpkin is hidden in a chest; the husband next appears, and the wife feigns that Bluster has pursued his enemy into the house, whereupon she conceal'd him. Bluster departs, and Simpkin is let free. But the Old Man and the servant when supposed to be gone to the Tavern overhear Simpkin and the Wife in very familiar discourse. A general scuffle ensues which, we may well suppose, gave boundless amusement to rustic audiences.

p. 54. AS GREAT AS A KING. There is an interesting anecdote of Charles II, who very apty and wittily quoted this line of the old Bacchanalian Song upon an occasion thus related in *The Spectator*, Wednesday, 20 August, 1712 (No. 462; Steele). King Charles "more than once dined with his good Citizens of *London* on their Lord-Mayor's Day, and did so the Year that Sir *Robert Viner* was Mayor. Sir *Robert* was a very Loyal Man, and if you will allow the Expression, very fond of his Sovereign; but what with the Joy he felt at Heart for the Honour done him by his Prince, and thro' the Warmth he was in with continual toasting Healths to the Royal Family, his Lordship grew a little fond of his Majesty, and entered into a Familiarity not altogether so graceful in so publick a Place. The King understood very well how to extricate himself on all kinds of Difficulties, and with an Hint to the Company to avoid Ceremony, stole off, and made towards his Coach, which stood ready for him in *Guildhall* Yard: But the Mayor liked his Company so well, and was grown so intimate, that he pursued him hastily, and catching him fast by the Hand, cried out with a vehement Oath and Accent, *Sir, you shall stay and take t'other Bottle*. The airy Monarch looked kindly at him over his Shoulder, and with a Smile and graceful Air, (for I saw him at the Time, and do now) repeated this Line of the old Song:

He that's drunk is as great as a King.

and immediately returned back and complied with his Landlord."

p. 54. BACON DID HIS BRAZEN HEAD. In allusion to the famous old story of Roger Bacon. This is told in a prose tract, *The famous history of Friar Bacon*. One chapter relates "How Fryer Bacon made a Brasen Head to speake, by the which hee would have walled England about with brasse." It will be remembered that it was necessary to watch the magic head until it spoke words of wisdom. Unfortunately after three weeks of vigil the weary friar fell asleep, his stupid servant neglected to awake him, the head spoke thrice, and then was silent for ever, and all their labour was lost.

p. 56. PALATES. Ox tongues. Mrs. Haywood, *A New Present for a Servant-Maid*, (1743), 1771, gives directions "To fricassy Ox Palates."

p. 57. DOTRIL. Dotterel. A kind of plover.

p. 57. RUFFS. The ruff is the male of a bird of the sandpiper family, his female being the reeve. Ruffs were accounted a great delicacy. Cf. *The Wild Gallant* (4to, 1669), I, where old Justice Trice boasts : " I have a delicate Dish of Ruffs to Dinner." So in *The Gentleman Dancing-Master*, I, 2, when Mrs. Flirt is ordering an extravagant supper at the expense of her gallant, she insists upon " Some Ruffes " being included.

p. 57. GNATS, GODWITS. The gnat or knot is the red-breasted sandpiper. The god-wit is a marsh bird. Both were considered most epicurean dishes. Cf. *The Alchemist*, acted in 1610, II, 2, where Sir Mammon, in his dreams of feasts that shall outvie Lucullus, exclaims in gorgeous fanfaronade :

> My foot-boy shall eate phesants, calverd salmons,
> Knots, godwits, lampreys.

p. 57. HEATH POUTS. Heath-poults ; heath-birds, especially the female or young. A heath-bird is a bird which lives on heaths, particularly the Black Grouse. Cf. Ray, Willughby's *Ornithology*, 1678 : The Merlin . . . They fly also Heath-pouts with it."

p. 57. RAILS. *Rallus*, represented in Europe by the Water-Rail. The bird is a partial migrant in Britain, a shy creature, slow to take wing. The nest is made in sedge and grasses near water.

p. 57. PICKTHANKS. A pickthank is one who curries favour ; a tell-tale. Cooper, *Thesaurus*, 1565–73 : " *Delator*, . . . a secrete accusour or complaynor ; a tell-tale ; a picke-thanke."

p. 58. PUTNEY. Pepys notes excursions to Putney by water. Tuesday, 11 May, 1669 : " In the evening my wife and I all alone, with the boy, by water up as high as Putney almost, with the tide, and back again, neither staying going nor coming ; . . . and then home to bed."

p. 58. BARRETER. A barrator is a malicious quarreller or fighter, and especially one who deals fraudulently in his business or office. Italian *barattatore* = a cheat, a trickster. Legally a barrator is one who for his own profit vexa-tiously foments and incites to litigation.

p. 59. AS SOME HAVE TO CATS. Cf. *The Merchant of Venice*, IV :

> Some men there are love not a gaping pig ;
> Some, that are mad if they behold a cat.

In Otway's *The Souldiers Fortune*, produced at Dorset Garden early in 1680, I, Sylvia speaks of " some that always sweat when a Cat's in the Room."

p. 61. CHINA ORANGES. *Citrus Aurantium*, originally from China, a favourite sweet orange. Pepys, Tuesday, 5 March, 1665–6, entertaining Lord Brouncker and his mistress, " made them welcome with wine and China oranges (now a great rarity since the war, none to be had)."

p. 61. LIMONADES. Lemonade occurs, probably for the first time, in Thomas Killi-grew's comedy *The Parson's Wedding*, folio, 1663 (in the collected folio Killigrew with general title 1664). IV, 5, Wild says : " Captain, make some *Lemonade*, and send it by the Boy to my Chamber." The obsolete lemonado is found in the Duke of Newcastle's *The Country Captain*, 12mo, 1649 ; and in St. Serfe's *Tarugo's Wiles*, 4to, 1668. See my edition of Killigrew's *The Parson's Wedding, Restoration Comedies*, 1921.

p. 61. SHERBETS. The forms *Zerbet* and *Cerbet* occur in Knolles' *Historie of the Turkes*, 1603. Sandys, *Travels*, 1615, has *Shurbets* and *Sherbets*. It was a fairly common drink in England among the quality in the seventeenth century. Captain Smith, *Travels*, 1630, describes the Turks' *Sherbecke* as being " only honey and water." There were, of course, many imitations and syrups in use which assumed an Oriental nomenclature.

p. 65. GRAY'S INN WALKS. One of the most fashionable promenades of the day. On Sunday, 23 June, 1661, Pepys notes : " So I and the young company to walk first to Graye's Inn Walks, where great store of gallants, but above all the ladies that I there saw, or ever did see, Mrs. Frances Butler (Monsieur L'Impertinent's sister) is the greatest beauty."

p. 66. MULBERRY-GARDEN. The Mulberry-Garden, on the site of the present Buckingham Palace and gardens, was largely frequented. Pepys, however, thought it " a very silly place . . . and but little company, and those a rascally, whoring, roguing sort of people, only a wilderness here, that is somewhat pretty, but rude." See Sir Charles Sedley's famous comedy *The Mulberry-Garden*, Theatre Royal, 18 May, 1668 (4to, 1668).

p. 66. HACKNEY PARSON. A hireling cleric. Cf. Wood, *Life* (Oxford Historical Society), I, 361 : " There were some hackney preachers in the University at this time."

p. 66. CANONICAL HOUR. Cf. *The Way of the World*, I, *Mirabell* : " *Betty*, what says your clock ? " *Betty* : " Turn'd of the last Canonical Hour, Sir." *Mirabell* : " How pertinently the Jade answers me ! Ha ! almost one a clock. (*Looking on his watch*.) " In *The Country-Wife*, IV, 1, Sparkish says to Alithea on their wedding morning, " Come my dearest, pray let us go to Church before the Canonical Hour is past." And a few minutes later he urges her again : " Come Madam, 'tis e'ne twelve a Clock and my Mother charg'd me never to be married out of the Canonical Hours."

p. 67. CAMPAIGNE. Butler, *Hudibras*, 1664, has *Campaign*. Etherege, *The Man of Mode*, 4to, 1676, IV, 1 : *Champaigne*. In *A Satyr* by Buckingham and Rochester, *circa* 1675–6, we find *Champoon*. Champagne, when first introduced into England in 1662, was a greyish or yellowish effervescent wine, creaming, if not actually sparkling. It was the favourite beverage of St. Evremond, gourmet and connoisseur.

p. 67. RANT, AND ROAR. The usual contemporary phrases for behaving noisily and tipsily. To rant is to be boisterously merry, *e.g.*, Mrs. Behn's *The City Heiress*, produced at Dorset Garden in the spring of 1682, II, 2, where Wilding says to Diana : " Before the old Gentleman, you must behave yourself very soberly, simple, and demure, and look as prew as at a Conventicle ; and take heed you drink not off your glass at Table, nor rant, nor swear." Roar has the same signification as rant, *e.g.*, Crowne's *The English Frier ; or, The Town Sparks*, produced at Drury Lane in the spring of 1690, I, where young Ranter and his drunken companions seize on Lord Stately's coach, " and away they drive, kicking and whipping, and singing and fiddling, and bawling and roaring, all to the devil." To tear was to rush swaggering along, elbowing and knocking all other persons out of the way. So the word Tearer came to mean a ruffian or a whore. Cf. *The Old Batchelour*, IV, where Sir Joseph and Bluffe, meeting Araminta and Belinda in S. James's Park mistake the ladies for prostitutes, and Sir Joseph calls out, " Hist, hist, Bully, dost thou see those Tearers ? " He then attempts to be grossly familiar.

p. 67. DRUNK AS A DRUM. This is a fairly common expression. It seems somewhat meaningless, and was probably used just because of the jingling alliteration. In Farquhar's *Sir Harry Wildair*, produced at Drury Lane in 1701, probably April, IV, 2, Sir Harry says of Clincher, " You must know that the Fool got presently as drunk as a Drum."

The expression " As drunk as David's sow " was vulgar and usual enough. It occurs in Gay's *New Songs*.

p. 67. POISE. Or, more usually, Pize. Pize, which was vulgarly used in various imprecatory expressions, is a word of uncertain origin. It has been well suggested that it may be an arbitrary substitute for Pest or Pox, which latter came into common speech *circa* 1600. Pize is a favourite word with old Bellair in Etherege's *The Man of Mode*, 4to, 1676. Cf. also Duffett's *The Mock-Tempest*, 4to, 1675, II, 2 : " Fortune has cheated me of all, pize on her." " A pize take 'em," says Sir Sampson, " meer Outsides," when the modern young man was mentioned. *Love for Love*, V, 1.

p. 67. DISGUIS'D. A very common expression for drunk. So in Dryden's *The Wild Gallant*, 4to, 1669, I, 1, we have the following dialogue : *Bibber :* My Business is to drink my Morning's-draught in Sack with you. *Failer :* Will not Ale serve thy turn, *Will? Bibber :* I had too much of that last Night ; I was a little disguis'd, as they say. *Failer :* Why disguis'd ? Hadst thou put on a clean Band, or Wash'd thy Face lately ? Those are thy Disguises, *Bibber. Bibber :* Well, in short, I was drunk ; damnably drunk with Ale. Cf. also Mrs. Behn's *The Rover*, Part I, 4to, 1677, III, 3 : *Enter* Willmore *drunk.* And presently he says : " I'm as honest a Fellow as breathes, tho I am a little disguis'd at present."

p. 69. PHANATICK. Cf. Fuller, *Mixt Contemplations*, 1660 : " A new word coined within these few months called fanatic . . . seemeth well . . . proportioned to signify . . . the sectaries of our age."

p. 72. THE ROSE. The Rose Tavern was on the west side of Bow Street, Covent Garden, and at the corner of Russell Street. It was one of the most famous houses in Town, and there are innumerable references to it. It was even better known as Will's Coffee House, the name being taken from Will Unwin, who was the Landlord. The Rose was demolished in 1776, when a new front was being built to Drury Lane Theatre.

p. 74. MYSTICALL. With the meaning of " mysterious," and hence implying " nonsensical." So Otway in *The Poet's Complaint of His Muse*, 4to, 1680, speaks of a " Leader in a factious Crew," Shaftesbury's adherents, becoming notorious for " wearing of a Mysticall green Ribband in his Hat."

p. 74. I'LE WATCH YOUR WATERS. To watch one's waters is to keep a sharp eye on any one's actions. Grose's *Classical Dictionary of the Vulgar Tongue*, . . . Revised and corrected by Pierce Egan, 1823. The phrase is not infrequent. Cf. *The Plain-Dealer*, where Jerry cries to Freeman, who is making advances to Widow Blackacre, " I'll watch your waters, Bully, i' fac. Come away, Mother."

p. 76. WHERE IS YOUR LADYSHIP ? Mrs. Cheatly. The title " Lady " was derisively given to bawds. So Mother Bennett, a notorious procuress, was known as " Lady Bennett." Pepys, Saturday, 22 September, 1660, mentions her as " the Lady Bennett (a famous strumpet)," and again, Saturday, 30 May, 1668, he speaks of " my Lady Bennet and her ladies " as taking part in an Adam and Eve ball. Wycherley, with inimitable satire, dedicated *The Plain-Dealer* to the same daughter of Pandarus, commencing " To my Lady B——," and concluding " Your Ladyship's most obedient, faithful, humble Servant."

p. 78. WINDOW. The permanent balcony over one of the proscenium doors. As Squeeze is discovered to have been in bed with Lettice, through putting on her red silk stockings in mistake for his own, so in Mrs. Behn's *The City Heiress* when the mock burglars rob Sir Timothy's house Mrs. Sensure is found to have been sleeping with the old Knight, since in bolting out of his room, half undressed, she wrapped his velvet coat about her in mistake for her gown.

p. 79.   SCOURING. Rampaging violently and rioting in the streets.

p. 80.   STARS, MOONS, SUNS. In *The Extravagant Shepherd, the anti-romance, or The History of the shepherd Lysis*, London, 1653, and another edition, 1660, we have an illustration of a Poet's dream realized. The conventional description of a heroine in epic and romance has been taken literally by the engraver. Two suns have taken the place of the lady's eyes, her teeth are actual pearls, there are lilies and roses in full bloom on her cheeks, Cupid is seated on her forehead, etc.

p. 80.   CRESWELL OR GIFFORD. *Mother Cresswell.* There are very many references to this most notorious procuress. Before the Restoration she was keeping house in Moorfields. *The Proceedings, Votes, Resolves, and Acts of the late Half-quarter Parliament Called The Rump: As it was taken out of their own Journal-Books and Printed for the general Satisfaction of the Nation*, folio 1660 (a MS. note upon the British Museum copy has 6 March, 1659), a pleasant satire upon the Rump Parliament, notes: "*Ordered*, That the Earl of *Pembroke* does very well in going to Mistress *Creswels* in Moor-fields, to mortifie his pamper'd flesh, and that it is no sin for a Quaker to go a whoring after strange women, provided he did not go a whoring after strange gods." In Duffett's extraordinary Epilogue to *The Empress of Morocco*, a farce produced at Drury Lane in 1674, Heccate and the three Witches sing:

> *To the Tune of, A Boat, a Boat, &c.*
>
> *A health, a health to Mother C——*
> *From* Moor-fields *fled to* Mill-bank *Castle*
> *She puts off rotten new-rig'd Vessel.*

Perhaps the most famous mention of all is that in the Prologue to Otway's *Venice Preserv'd*, produced at Dorset Garden 9 February, 1681-2, when, alluding to the character of Antonio, the old senator, a portrait of Shaftesbury, he says:

> *Next is a Senatour that keeps a Whore;*
> *In* Venice *none a higher office bore;*
> *To lewdness every night the Letcher ran:*
> *Shew me all* London, *such another Man,*
> *Match him at Mother* Creswold's *if you can.*

Gallantry A-la-mode, A Satyrical Poem, 1674, which bears the motto from Mantuan, *Semel insaniuimus omnes*, has (p. 8):

> *At* Giffords, Creswels, *and elsewhere*
> *Where precise Damsel does appear,*
> *Perhaps you've bin, no greater* Cheat
> *Is shewn than* Lady spruce *and* neat.

A New Ballad of Londons Loyalty, 1681:

> *Player*, now grows dull for want of Common-whore,
> Poor *Creswell*, she can take his word no more,
> Three Hundred pounds is such a heavy yoak,
> Which not being pay'd the worn-out Bawd is broak.

War Horns, Make Room for the Bucks with Green Bowes, 1682 :

> *Non est Inuentus* yet ?   Then, Do&or ! go
> To *Cresswels*, he's there may be, who does know ?

Radcliffe's *The Ramble*, 1682, *The Poor Whore's Song* (p. 26) :

> From thence I march'd to *Creswels* House,
> Under the name of a Merchants Spouse ;
> And there I play'd the secret Lover,
> Le& jealous Husband shou'd discover.

In Duke's Epilogue to *The Atheist*, Dorset Garden, autumn of 1683, we have :

> Shou'd the Wise City now, *to ease your Fears,*
> Ere& an Office *to Insure your Ears ;*
> Thither such num'rous Shoals of Witnesses,
> *And* Juries, *conscious of their Guilt wou'd press*
> That to the Chamber *hence might more be gain'd*
> *Than ever* Mother Creswell *from it drain'd.*

Oldham's *A Satyr . . . Dissuading the Author from the Study of Poetry,* 1684 :

> Should mighty *Sappho* in these days revive,
> And hope upon her &ick of Wit to live ;
> She mu& to *Creswel's* trudg to mend her Gains,
> And let her Tail to him, as well as Brains.

John Phillips' *Don Quixote*, folio, 1687 (p. 195) : He " carry'd her to much such another House as Mother *Creswel's*, and left her in the cu&ody of an Aunt of his, not so mean as *Mrs. Buly*, and yet a little below the Degree of *Madam Bennet.*"

Robert Gould's *A Satyr Against Woman*, Writ in the Year 1680, *Poems,* 1689 (p. 145) :

> *Creswel* and *Stratford* the same foot&eps tread ;
> In Sin's black Volume so profoundly read,
> That, whensoere they dy, we well may fear,
> The very tin&ure of the Crimes they bare,
> With &range Infusion will inspire the du&,
> And in the Grave commit true a&s of Lu&.

A Choice Colle&ion of 180 *Loyal Songs : Fanatick Zeal* (p. 38) :

> Example, we do own
>   Then Precept better is ;
> For *Creswel* she was safe,
>   When she liv'd a *Private Miss.*

It would seem that Mother Cresswell was celebrated for the same Erotic specialities as in later days won no small renown for a whole Bevy of lu&y ladies, Mrs. Collet, Mrs. James, Emma Lee, Mrs. Shepherd, Mrs. Chalmers, Mrs. Price, and, above all, the famous Mrs. Teresa Berkeley.

A Song at the Loyal Feaſt at Weſtminſter Hall (p. 344):

No more can *Sedition* and *Church-Reformation*
Come from flogging at *Creswels* to saving the Nation.

The Hunting of the Fox (p. 364):

Scour the Globe to the Axles,
From Pole to Pole; then retire
And center at Mother *Creswels*
The *Fox* us'd to harbour there.

A Collection of 80 *Loyal Poems*, 1685 (p. 86):

That's worse than Mother *Creswel's* flogging is.

The Charter (p. 154):

Shall *double Drink* place *to feeling* so give?
Shall't be Madam *Creswel* and not Mis *Keeling*?

Mrs. Cresswell's hospitality was greatly enjoyed by the Whigs, whose party she affected, and so became especially notorious as being very active in miniſtering to the private pleasures of Shaftesbury. Her Puritan piety is admirably satirized by Tom Brown in his *Letters from the Dead to the Living*: "*From Madam* Creswel *of* pious Memory *to her Siſter in Iniquity* Moll Quarles *of* known Integrity." The answer from Moll Quarles has much humour.

In Tempeſt's *Cries of London* may be found an engraving said to represent Mrs. Cresswell, concerning whom some particulars, which are, perhaps, not very authentic, have been collected in Grainger's *Hiſtory of England*, Vol. VI.

The Observator, No. 78, Wednesday, 7 December, 1681: "*Whig.* Yes, yes, *Madam Creswell* is Convicted. *Tory.* So says *Dick Janeway* (No. 64) [*after above Thirty Years Practice of Bawdry.*] Well! 'Tis an unknown deal of mony that Good Woman has got by the way of *True-Proteſtant Concupiscence;* But *Moor-Fields* ſtands in so Pleasant an Air; and then there's the Fineſt Walk there, for *Meditation*, from a *Wench* to a *Sacrament.*" Presumably Mother Cresswell died about 1683, as *The Observator*, Monday, 2 June, 1684, has: "What an *Encouragement* and matter of *Edification*, would it be to *Youth*, to see a *Grave Senator*, doing his *Gamboles* in *Moor-Fields* at the *Vaulting-School* of *Mother Cresswell* of *Famous Memory*."

In *The Female Fire-Ships, A Satyr againſt Whoring*, 4to, 1691, we have:

Then would no *Bewly, Stratford, Temple, Whipple,*
Cresswell nor *Cozens*, who so lov'd the Nipple;
Nor other Female Fachesses unknown,
Want that disgrace is due to *Vice* alone.

As will be noted, Mother Gifford is mentioned (with Cresswell) in *Gallantry A-la-mode*, 1674, cited above. In Dryden's *Sir Martin Mar-All*, produced at the Duke's House Thursday, 15 Auguſt, 1667, IV, 1, Lord Dartmouth says: "Every Night I fin'd out for a new Maiden-Head, and she has sold it to me as often as ever Mother *Temple, Bennet*, or *Gifford*, have put off boil'd Capons for Quails and Partridges." Of Mother Gifford too the burlesque epilogue to Duffett's *The Empress of Morocco*, 1674, tells us :

> *She needs must be in spight of fate Rich*
> *Who sells tough Hen for Quail and Partridg.*

In Wycherley's *Love in a Wood*, Drury Lane, autumn of 1671, Vincent says to Ranger : " I was going to look you out, between the Scenes at the Play-House, the Coffee-house, Tennis-Court, or *Gifford's*." " Do you want a pretence to go to a Bawdy-house ? " laughs his friend.

p. 81. OVERTAKEN. Still in use in dialect for drunk. Cf. *Hamlet*, II, 1, where Polonius says : " There was a' gaming ; there o'ertook in's rouse." Also, *The Spectator*, No. 450, Wednesday, 6 August, 1712 (Steele) : " Since my coming into the World I do not remember I was ever overtaken in Drink, save nine times, once at the Christening of my first Child, thrice at our City Feasts, and five times at driving of Bargains."

p. 81. WHAT A DICKENS. Cf. *The Merry Wives of Windsor*, III, 2, where Mrs. Page says : " I cannot tell what the dickens his name is." Dickens = devilkins.

p. 81. CAWDLE. Latin *caldellum*, a hot drink. Especially an invigorating drink of warm wine with sugar and spices.

p. 83. MITTIMUS. A warrant of commitment to prison. Cf. Dryden's *The Wild Gallant*, 4to, 1669, IV, 1, where Justice Trice says : " Hang him, rogue ; make his mittimus immediately."

p. 87. WITHOUT BAIL OR MAINPRIZE. That is to say, with no permission to obtain release by finding sureties. Mainprize is a legal term for suretyship. Cf. Barham's *The House-Warming, Ingoldsby Legends* :

> —That as to Prince Hal's being taken to jail,
> By the London Police, without mainprize or bail,
>   For cuffing a judge, it's a regular fudge ;
> And that Chief-Justice Gascoigne, it's very well known,
> Was kick'd out the moment he came to the throne.

p. 87. MORTMAIN. The condition of lands or tenements held inalienably by ecclesiastical and other corporations.

p. 89. SPIRIT OF CONTENTION. One may compare the dark Italian charm, when to rouse bitter strife between persons on their wedding-day, and to cause impotency in a husband whilst inflaming the wife's desires, the witch takes an orange flower pounded with salt, pepper, cummin, and the herb *sconcordia* (literally *variance*), and this she scatters secretly over the bride's dress, muttering meanwhile : " Tu sia maladetta, Tu non possa avere un giorno di pace, E quando vai, Inginnochiarti, Avanti l'altare, Tu possa essere gia peniti, Del passa che tu fai."

p. 92. SHE'S MY WIFE. So in Wycherley's *Love in a Wood*, produced at the Theatre Royal in the autumn of 1671, possibly October, old Alderman Gripe deems it convenient to marry Miss Lucy, with whom he has been found in a very compromising situation.

Epsom-Wells

p. 95. *ΜΕΓΑΛΩΣ.* Professor Bensly has obliged me with the following interesting note :

The original author of this Greek quotation is unknown. It occurs as an anonymous quotation in section 3 of the 3d chapter of the treatise which used to be known and is still, for convenience, described as " Longinus on the Sublime," though, as W. Rhys Roberts says in the preface to his 2d edition of it (1907), " the modern editor must . . . challenge the ascription and explain the description. He must point out that the author is probably *not* the historical Longinus, while the subject is *not* ' the Sublime ' in the ordinary acceptation of that term."

The text of the quotation is given thus in modern editions (J. Vahlen, 1905, W. Rhys Roberts, 1907) :

' μεγάλων ἀπολισθαίνειν ὅμως εὐγενὲς ἁμάρτημα,' transl. by Roberts "failure in a great attempt is at least a noble error."

As regards the *text* of the quotation, in the edition by Paulus Manutius (Venice, 1555), it is printed as μεγάλως ἀπολισθαίνειν ἁμάρτημ' εὐγενές, thus forming an unsatisfactory iambic trimeter.

For the *thought* compare the epitaph on Phæthon, Ovid Metamorphoses, ii., 327–328.

> Hic situs est Phæthon, currus auriga paterni :
> Quem si 'non tenuit, *magnis tamen excidit ausis.*

(& Browning, *passim*).

The context in which the author of the περί ὕψους introduces the quotation is this :—

Writers find it hard to avoid tumidity and fearing to be feeble they fall into the opposite extreme πειθόμενοι τῷ 'μεγάλων ἀπολισθαίνειν ὅμως εὐγενὲς ἁμάρτημα'.

The way in which the quotation is introduced by " trusting in the saying " looks as though it was once well known. I do not find it in the collections of old Greek proverbs.

The forms ὀλισθαίνω & ὀλισθάνω are both found, but ὀλισθαίνω is later.

p. 101. CLODPATE. This old nickname was given to Oliver Cromwell, and in ballads *circa* 1678 to Scroggs. Underhill excelled in this rôle. Chattering about the theatre, Sir Quibble Queere in D'Urfey's *The Richmond Heiress,* produced at Drury Lane in the spring of 1692–3, cries : " And jolly *Cave Underhill* in *Epsom Wells ?* How does my comical justice do, hah ? "

p. 101. CAROLINA. This part was originally played by Mrs. Johnson, an actress famous for her beauty. Etherege, writing from Ratisbon to Lord Middleton in November, 1686, mentions that a company from Nuremberg has visited the local theatre. He adds : " There is a Comedian in the Troop as handsom at least as the faire made of the West, wch you have seen at Newmarket, and makes as much noise in this little Town, & gives as much jealousies to ye Ladys as ever Mrs. Wright, or Mrs. Johnson did in London."

p. 104. SIR C. S. Sir Charles Sedley.

p. 104.   THEY DID SO TO BEN.   *The New Inn*; *or, The Light Heart*, was produced 19
January, 1629, but was received so unfavourably as not to be even heard
to the end.   It was published by the author two years afterwards, with an
angry title-page declaring it to be here offered " As it was never Acted, but
most negligently Played by some, the *King's Servants*; and more
squeamishly beheld and censured by others, the *King's Subjects*, 1629. Now
at last set at Liberty to the Readers, his *Majesty's* Servants and Subjects,
1631."   *A Tale of a Tub*, acted in 1633, the last dramatic work Jonson
brought on the stage, seems to have fared little better.

p. 104.   HALF CROWN.   The price of admittance to the Pit.   Pepys, Wednesday, 1
January, 1667-8, notes : " after dinner to the Duke of York's playhouse,
and there saw ' Sir Martin Mar-all ' . . . Here a mighty company of
citizens, 'prentices, and others ; and it makes me observe, that when I
begun first to be able to bestow a play on myself, I do not remember that
I saw so many by half of the ordinary 'prentices and mean people in the pit
at 2*s*. 6*d*. a-piece as now ; I going for several years no higher than the 12*d*.
and then the 18*d*. places, though I strained hard to go in then when I did :
so much the vanity and prodigality of the age is to be observed in this
particular."
       In the Epilogue to *The Generous Enemies*, a comedy by John Corye, pro-
duced at Drury Lane in 1671, Mrs. Boutell spoke the lines :

> Though there I see—Propitious Angels sit, (*Points at the boxes.*
> Still there's a Nest of Devils in the Pit,
> By whom our Plays, like Children, just alive,
> Pinch'd by the Fairies, never after thrive :
> 'Tis but your Half-crown, Sirs ; that wont undo.

       In a snarling *Satire* on Otway, printed in *Poems on State-Affairs*, Vol. III.
(The Second Edition, 1716, p. 110. Also MS. Harl. 7317, folio 6b), the
following couplet occurs :

> Was't not enough, that at his tedious Play
> I lavish'd half a Crown, and half a Day.

p. 104.   MASKS.   Cf. Dryden's Prologue to *Marriage-A-la-Mode*, produced at Lincoln's
Inn Fields about Easter, 1672 :

> Poor pensive Punk now peeps ere Plays begin,
> Sees the bare Bench, and dares not venture in ;
> But manages her last Half-crown with care,
> And trudges to the Mall, on foot, for Air.

p. 105.   WHITEHALL.   *Epsom Wells* was acted at Whitehall on the 27 December, 1672.

p. 105.   HAD BEEN BY OTHERS DONE.   It was commonly rumoured that Sir Charles
Sedley had revised Shadwell's comedy.   So in *Mac Flecknoe* Dryden suggests
this :

> But let no alien *S–dl–y* interpose
> To lard with wit thy hungry *Epsom* prose.

p. 105.   YOUR ROYAL LORD FORGAVE.   Charles II, had seen *Epsom Wells* at the Theatre
on 2 December, 1672, probably the day of the first production.   He also
was present on the 4 December following, so pleased was he with Shadwell's
scenes.

p. 107.   SOVERAIGNLY. A modish expression. Cf. *Marriage-A-la-Mode*, III, 1, where Melantha asks Philotis : "How does that Laugh become my Face ? " " Sovereignly well, Madam," answers the Abigail. " *Sovereignly ?* " cries the lady, all agog, " Let me die that's not amiss. That Word shall not be yours ; I'll invent it, and bring it up my self. My new point Gorget shall be yours upon't. Not a word of the Word, I charge you."

p. 107.   THE HEY. It has been suggested that the name of this dance (hey or hay) is derived from the French, haie = a hedge, the dancers, who stood in two rows, being compared to hedges. It seems to have been a kind of reel, and Thornot Arbeau describes one of the passages-at-arms in the Buffons or Matassins as the " Passage de la Haye." This was solely danced by men who imitated a combat. In Playford's *Musick's Handmaid* (1678), an air is found entitled " The Canaries, or the Hay." The Canaries was greatly in vogue in France temp. Louis XIV. Two partners danced, and it appears a variant of the jig.

p. 107.   LYONS IN THE TOWER. Until the reign of William IV, when the few animals that remained were removed in November, 1834, to the Zoological Gardens, Regent's Park, the Town Menagerie was one of the sights of London. Stow says that in 1235 the Emperor Frederick sent Henry III three leopards, " since the which time these lions and others have been kept in a part of this bulwark [the Tower] called the Lion Tower, and their keepers there lodged. . . . In the 16th of Edward III, one lion, one lioness, and one leopard, and two cat lions in the said Tower, were committed to the custody of Robert, the son of John Bown." For an account of a visit to the Lions see Addison, *The Freeholder*, No. 47.

p. 108.   RAP AND REND. A common alliteration in the sixteenth and seventeenth centuries signifying to snatch and seize. Chaucer, *The Chanowns Yemannes Tale*, G. 1422, Skeat :

> Ye shul nat winne a myte on that chaffare,
> But wasten al that ye may rape and renne.

" Rape and renne " is corrupted from an older phrase *repen* and *rinen*. Anglo-Saxon ; *hrepian and hrinan, i.e.*, handle and touch.

Fuller, *Church History*, 1655, IV, 1, 12 : " She . . . snatched all she could rape and rend, unto herselfe."

p. 108.   GALENISTS. Those who followed, or were presumed to follow, the rules and prescriptions of the famous Galen, A.D. 130—*circa* 200. It may be remarked that Galen refused absolutely to attach himself to any one medical school of thought, and dubbed the exclusive followers of Hippocrates, Praxagoras, or any other master, mere slaves. He himself chose from the tenets of each what he believed to be good, practical, and true. The Third Book of William Salmon's *Synopsis Medecinal*, 8vo, 1671, shows " the way of curing, according to the precepts of *Galen* and *Paracelsus*." Gideon Harvey in 1675 published " The disease of *London*, or A new discovery of the Scurvey . . . and several methods of curing the said Disease, by Remedies both Galenical and Chymical." 8vo.

p. 109.   AT BOTH ENDS. Cotgrave has : " Brusler la chandelle par les deux bouts."

p. 110.   LOCK OF HAY. A lock is a quantity, usually a small one, especially of hay or straw. *Prom. Paru., circa* 1440 : Lok of hey . . . *uola.* The phrase is still in dialect use.

p. 110. AS FAT, AND AS FOGGY. Foggy is "bloated," "pursy," or as we often say "puffy." Cf. Etherege *The Man of Mode*, 4to, 1676, I, 1, where the "overgrown Jade with the Flasket of Guts before her" is dubbed "Foggy Nan."

p. 110. FRENCHMAN. Pepys, Friday, 7 September, 1666, notes that Sir William Coventry "hopes we shall have no publique distractions upon this fire, which is what every body fears, because of the talke of the French having a hand in it."

p. 110. THE SECOND OF SEPTEMBER. Under which date Evelyn has : "This fatal night, about ten, began the deplorable fire, near Fish-Street, in London." The fire actually began at the house of a baker named Farryner, in Pudding Lane, leading from Eastcheap to Lower Thames Street.

p. 110. SODOM. Evelyn speaking of the Great Fire, 3 September, 1666, writes : Thus, I left it this afternoon burning, a resemblance of Sodom, or the last day. . . . London was, but it is no more ! "

p. 111. SEA-COAL. Coal brought to London by sea, and as sea-coal distinguished from charcoal the common coal of the period. Cf. *Venice Preserv'd*, produced at Dorset Garden, 9 February, 1681–2, II, 3, where Renault says :

> Give but an Englishman his Whore and ease,
> Beef and a Sea-coal fire, he's yours for ever.

p. 111. GAD-OOKS. Godsookers, Godsokers. A combination of God's and a second element which is meaningless or hopelessly corrupt. These petty oaths were common. Cf. *The Rehearsal*, produced at the Theatre Royal, December, 1671, III, 2, where Bayes cries : "Nay, pray, Sir, have a little patience : Godsookers you'l spoil all my Play."

p. 112. PILLING TREES. To pill = to peel, to decorticate, to strip off the bark. Cf. *The Merchant of Venice*, I, 3, of Jacob : "The skilful shepherd pill'd me certain wands."

p. 112. BURY IN FLANNEL. The Woollen Act, 18 & 19 Charles II, c. 4, made it obligatory for shrouds to be of flannel. Cf. Oldham, *circa* 1683, *Satire in Imitation of the Third of Juvenal*, 1682 :

> To speak the truth great part of *England* now
> In their own Cloth will scarce vouchsafe to go :
> Only, the Statutes Penalty to save
> Some few perhaps wear Wollen in the Grave.

Shadwell himself in his will, for which see Introduction, directed that he should be buried in flannel.

When the executors of Sir Charles Sedley, who was buried 26 August, 1701, in the family vault at Southfleet Church, were unable to certify that the body had been clothed in cerements of wool according to the statute they were mulcted in a fine of fifty shillings for the poor of the Parish.

p. 112. FRENCH KICK-SHAWS. Kickshaw is a corruption of the French quelque chose. The word meaning a trifle, something quite unimportant, is common in contemporary literature. Cf. *Timon A Satyr*, by Buckingham and Rochester, where the very English host says :

> As for *French* Kickshaws, Cellery, and Champoon,
> Ragous *and* Fricasses, in troth we'ave none.

p. 112. STAND OF ALE. To dust a stand is to toss off liquor ; to tipple merrily. Shadwell's own liking for ale was notorious, and this is a favourite phrase with him. Cf. the concluding couplet of his *Letter* in Verse to Wycherley :

> To Morrow he's to dust a Stand,
> That is your Servant to Command.

p. 112. WINOWISKY. 19 June, 1669, Michael Korybut Wisniowiecki, a Lithuanian Piast, was elected by the Diet King of Poland. Accepting the honour with tears, he proved indeed a timid sovereign, and on 18 October, 1672, became a suppliant for peace against his Turkish foe. This was only granted on the most degrading terms. Despised by his subjects, King Michael died in shame and sorrow, 10 November, 1673.

p. 113. NINEPINS. Mrs. Pinchwife in *The Country-Wife* envying the London ladies, cries : that they are " drest every day in their best Gowns ; and I warrant you, play at nine Pins every day of the week, so they do."

p. 113. STUM'D WINE. To stum is to raise a new fermentation in wine by the trickish addition of stum or must.

p. 113. WALL-FAC'D. Stupid ; expressionless as a blank wall.

p. 113. PANTALOONS. The fashionable French canons or wide breeches. In *The Gentleman Dancing-Master*, III, 1, the Spanish Don in mockery calls Monsieur " Monsieur de Pantalloons."

p. 116. BLUNTS AND SHARPS. Foils for fencing. Sir W. Hope, *Swordsman's Vade Mecum*, 1694, speaks of " The only Safe and Secure Play, with either Blunts or Sharpes."

p. 118. COD-SNIGGS. A mincing meaningless oath. Cod is a corruption of God, and nigs, not being found in any other context, is probably a fabrication. Simpkin the Clown in the little interlude *Simpkin, Cox's Drolls*, 1672, swears " Uds niggers noggers."

p. 118. CRIBACH. A rare form of Cribbage, not recorded by the *N. E. D.* Cribbage was introduced into England early in the seventeenth century, and is fully described by Cotton, *Compleat Gamester*, 1672.

p. 119. THE CHURCH. S. Martin's. The old church was pulled down in 1824, when the present nave and aisles were built, and the only old part of the present edifice is the tower, which dates from the fifteenth century, but has been recased and grossly modernized. From a print *circa* 1800 it would seem that the chancel was of the thirteenth century. The first book of the registers has baptisms and marriages from 1695 to 1740.

p. 119. BUFF BELTS. In *The Souldier's Fortune*, I, Sylvia describes Courtine as dressing " Filthily enough of all Conscience, with a thred-bare Red-Coat, which his Taylor duns him for to this Day, over which a great broad greasie buff Belt, enough to turn any one's Stomach but a disbanded Souldier." In Mrs. Behn's *The Luckey Chance*, II, 1, Gammer Grime, Gayman's Landlady in Alsatia, taunts her guest with wearing an " old Campaign—with tan'd coloured Lining—once red—but now all the Colours of the Rain-bow, a Cloke to sculk in a Nights, and a pair of piss-burn'd shammy Breeches."

p. 121. PLAIN-DEALING. " Plain dealing is best " is quoted as a proverb in the rough old *Tragical Comedy of Apius and Virginia*, which was probably acted as early as 1563, although not printed until 1575. There was a game of cards called " Plain Dealing," which is described by Cotton in his *Compleat Gamester*, 1680.

p. 121. POTHECARIES SHOP. In Killigrew's *The Parson's Wedding*, I, 3, Jolly describes a visit to his Cousin in the country ; " I never visited such an hospital," he cries, " it stunk like *Bedlam*. . . . She is my Cozen ; but he made such a complaint to me, I thought he had married the Company of Surgeons-hall ; for his directions to me for several things for his Wife's use, were fitter for a pothecaries-shop than a Ladies Closet."

p. 121.　GREEN-SALVE.　Or Green Butter.　This unguent is fully described in *A Chymical Dispensatory*, 1669, Book II, c. 87, p. 146. " Written in Latine by Dr. Joannes Schroeder . . . and Englished by W. Rowland."

p. 121.　SORE LEGS.　In *The Beaux Strategem*, produced at the Haymarket in March, 1706–7, Lady Bountiful is described as " An old, civil country gentlewoman, that cures all her neighbours of all distempers," and at the beginning of Act IV a rustic goody makes application to her, saying, " I come seventeen long mail to have a cure for my husband's sore leg."

p. 121.　TONGS AND KEY.　Cf. *A Midsummer Night's Dream* (4to, 1600), IV : " Clown : I have a reasonable good ease in musicke. Let us have the tongs and the bones." Musicke Tongs, Rurall Musicke. Inigo Jones has a sketch representing this " rural music." Tongs were struck by a key, and they belong to the domain of " kitchen music," for an account of which see *The Spectator*, 570, Wednesday, 21 July, 1714, where Daintry's concert is described. " Finding our Landlord so great a Proficient in Kitchen-Musick, I asked him if he was Master of the Tongs and Key. He told me that he had laid it down some years since, as a little unfashionable ; but that if I pleased he would give me a lesson upon the Gridiron."

p. 121.　JOHN HOPKINS OR ROBERT WISDOM.　Hopkins, died 1570, part-translator with Thomas Sternhold and others of the famous metrical version of the *Psalms*. In 1549 Sternhold's *Certayne Psalmes*, actually nineteen, was printed, and in December of the same year, the author being dead, the book was re-issued with additions, some of the new versions being by Hopkins. The British Museum contains more than 600 editions of this doggerel, between 1549 and 1828. Robert Wisdom, died 1568, Archdeacon of Ely, was a sour fanatic, " Archbotcher of a psalm or prayer." His metrical translation of Psalm cxxv, was in use as late as 1695. Cf. Dr. Speed's *Batt upon Batt*, written in 1679 :

> Could I with equal Metre *Hopkins* fit,
> Out-*Sternhold Sternhold, Wisdom* eke out wit.

p. 123.　CROSS I WIN, PILE YOU LOSE.　Croix ou pile.　As we cry : Heads I win, Tails you lose.　In Killigrew's *The Parson's Wedding*, I, 3, Mrs. Pleasant says : " Cross or Pile, will you have him yet or no ? "

p. 123.　TICK.　The phrase " on tick " was then coming into general use.　Cf. Dryden's *An Evening's Love*, Theatre Royal, June, 1668, where Wildblood says to Jacintha, who wishes to gamble : " Play on tick, and lose the *Indies*."

p. 123.　42.　*I.e.*, 1642.　In allusion to the more ceremonious gallantry of the Court of Charles I, and perhaps particularly to the fashion of the so-called Platonic Love, which James Howell in a letter, 3 June, 1634, describes as consisting " in contemplations, and ideas of the mind, not in any carnal fruition." He adds : " This Love sets the Wits of the Town on work."

p. 123.　COMBS HIS PERUQUE.　In *The Parson's Wedding*, folio 1663, I, 3, we have : " Enter *Jack Constant, Will Sadd, Jolly*, and a Footman, they comb their heads, and talk." In *Les Precieuses Ridicules*, first acted at Paris 18 November, 1659, Mascarille, " Apres s'etre peigné et avoir ajusté ses canons," seriously commences his conversation.

p. 123.   MOTHER OF THE MAIDS.   The Maids of Honour had a Mother at least as early as the reign of Elizabeth.   The office is supposed to have been abolished about the period of the Revolution in 1688.   The Mother of the Maids in the Court of Queen Katherine was Bridget, Lady Sanderson, daughter of Sir Edward Tyrrell, Knt., and wife of Sir William Sanderson, Gentleman of the Privy Chamber.   On Saturday, 17 May, 1662, Pepys and Mr. Moore "to the Wardrobe to dinner where dined Mrs. Sanderson, the mother of the maids."   19 July, 1676, Evelyn notes : " Went to the funeral of Sir William Sanderson, husband to the Mother of the Maids. . . . He was buried at Westminster."   But the Portuguese ladies attending on the Queen had their own Guarda-damas.   Evelyn, 2 June, 1662 : " Now saw I (the Queen's) Portuguese ladies, and the Guarda-damas, or Mother of the Maids."

p. 125.   LAY BY YOUR PLEADING.   In *The Loyal Garland*, 5th edition, 1686, is given " The Dominion of the Sword.   A Song made in the Rebellion," which commences :—

> Lay by your pleading, Law lies a-bleeding
> Burn all your studies, and throw away your reading, . . .

It is also in *Loyal Songs*, 1731, I, p. 223, as " The *Power* of the Sword " ; in *Merry Drollery Complete*, 1661 and 1670 ; in *Pills to Purge Melancholy*, VI, 190 ; and in other collections.   *Love lies a-bleeding ;* in imitation of *Law lies a-bleeding*, is given in *Merry Drollery Complete*, 1661 and 1670.   There are also copies in ballad form, in which the tune is entitled *The Cyclops ;* it begins :

> Lay by your pleading, Love lies a-bleeding,
> Burn all your poetry, and throw away your reading, . . .

p. 125.   FIRE-SHIP.   A vessel freighted with combustibles and explosives, which is sent adrift among the enemy's ships to destroy 'em.   Steele, *Tatler*, XXI, 1709 : " Sir Edward Whitaker with five Men of War, four Transports, and two Fire-ships was arrived at that Port."

p. 126.   AQUA MIRABILIS.   A well-known invigorating cordial.   Cf. Dryden's *Marriage-a-la-Mode*, 4to, 1672, III, 1 : " The Country Gentlewoman . . . who treats her with Furmity and Custard, and opens her dear Bottle of *Mirabilis* beside, for a Jill-glass of it at parting."   Also Mrs. Behn's *Sir Patient Fancy*, produced at Dorset Garden January, 1677–8, IV, 4, where Sir Patient exclaims : " Oh, I'm sick at Heart, *Maundy* fetch me the Bottle of *Mirabilis* in the Closet."

p. 127.   IF SHE WOULD EAT GOLD.   Cf. Dryden's *The Kind Keeper ; or, Mr. Limberham*, Dorset Garden, March, 1677–8, II, 1, where Aldo says of Mrs. Tricksy, " Would I were worthy to be a young Man, for her sake : She should eat Pearl, if she would have 'em."   And Limberham replies : " She can digest 'em, and Gold too.   Let me tell you, Father *Aldo*, she has the Stomach of an Estrich."

p. 128.   TORY RORY.   In a rowdy, boisterous way.   Cf. Cotton's *Scarronides*, *Virgil Travestie*, IV :

> She found him set among his Mates,
> The rest o' th' *Trojan* Runagates,
> Puff'd like a Foot-ball with Vain-glory,
> Roaring and drinking tory-rory.

The phrase is of somewhat obscure origin ; probably a rhyming expansion of "rory." It has no connexion with Tory, although after 1680 it is often linked up for the sake of the obvious jingle and application.

p. 128. MUM. A kind of beer, originally brewed Brunswick. Cf. the Epilogue to Duffett's skit *The Empress of Morocco*, produced at Drury Lane in the spring of 1674:

> Brumsick Mum's meer puddle,
> And Rhenish Wine bare fuddle,
> But Brandy is the Liquor
> Makes all your veins flow quicker.

p. 128. LOLPOOP. *The Dictionary of the Canting Crew* has: "*Lolpoop*, a Lazy, Idle Drone."

p. 129. GLEEK. An early French game at cards supposed to be derived in title from the German word Gluck, hazard or chance. It is played by three persons who hold twelve cards each and draw from the remainder, which is called the Stock. The players bid successively for the Stock, and the successful bidder pays for his cards in accordance with the value of the cards held by his opponents. Cotton, *The Compleat Gamester*, 1680, pp. 64, *sqq.*

p. 134. FALSTAFF. "Beware instinct; the lion will not touch the true prince. Instinct is a great matter, I was a coward on instinct. I shall think the better of myself and thee during my life; I for a valiant lion, and thou for a true prince." I *King Henry IV*, ii, 4.

p. 134. SCOWER. To scower was to rampage the streets at night noisily and drunkenly. The dangerous rowdies who infested London with their nocturnal blackguardism for well-nigh two hundred and fifty years were known in the reign of Charles II as Scourers, which name seems to have come into use after the Restoration. The Scourers were succeeded by the Rake-hells; and afterward by the Mohocks.

p. 134. OMBRE. It is said that this excellent and long fashionable card-game was introduced into England by Queen Catherine of Braganza, and that the name is from the Spanish Hombre, a man. It can be played by three or by two persons. Quadrille is a variety of hombre played by four. There is an elaborate treatise on this interesting game by Lord Aldenham, Third Edition, 1902, Privately Printed for the Roxburghe Club.

p. 134. LANGTRILOO. Or Lanterloo, an old form of the game now called Loo. It was exceedingly fashionable, and there are many references. Cf. Crowne, *Sir Courtly Nice*, produced at Drury Lane in the spring of 1685, III, Surly's raillery of Sir Courtly: "thou art the only Court-Card Women love to play with? the very Pam at Lanterleoo, the Knave that picks up all." Pam is the Knave of clubs, especially in the game of Five-card Loo, in which this card is the highest trump. Cf. Pope, *The Rape of the Lock* (1712–14), III, 61–2:

> Ev'n mighty *Pam*, that Kings and Queens o'er threw
> And mow'd down Armies in the Fights of *Lu*.

p. 137. YOU HAD REASON. Avoir Raison = to be in the right. The phrase is very frequent. Cf. *The Gentleman Dancing-Master*, Dorset Garden, March, 1672; 4to, 1672, IV, 1: "The Fool has reason, I find, and I am the Coxcomb while I thought him so."

p. 137. HOCKAMORE. Hock, the Anglicized form of Hockheimer from Hockheim on the Main, where this wine is chiefly vintaged. Cf. Sedley's *Bellamira; or, The Mistress*, produced at Drury Lane, May, 1687 (4to, 1687), II, 1, when

Lionel is rapturously talking of Isabella, and Merryman asks " Her Age ? " " Seventeen," replies Lionel. " I have drunk excellent *Hockamore* of that Age," reflects Merryman, to be violently interrupted by Lionel's " Damn thy dull *Hockamore !* "

p. 138. THAT'S ONCE. A vulgar phrase expressing determination. Cf. *The Country-Wife*, III, 1, where Mrs. Pinchwife, longing to see London sights, declares : " Nay, I will go abroad, that's once."

p. 138. I AM THE DUKE OF NORFOLK. Or Paul's Steeple. This very old tune is frequently mentioned under both names. In Playford's *Dancing Master* from 1650 to 1695, it is called " Paul's Steeple." In his *Division Violin*, 1685, at p. 2, it is called " The Duke of Norfolk, or, Paul's Steeple " ; and at p. 18 " Paul's Steeple, or, the Duke of Norfolk." The steeple of the old Cathedral of S. Paul which was proverbial for height was set on fire by lightning and burned down 4 June, 1561. The original ballad does not appear to be known, but there is a reference to it in Fletcher's *Monsieur Thomas*, III, 3, where the fiddler when asked by Thomas which ballads he best knows commences his list thus :

> Under your mastership's correction, I can sing
> The Duke of Norfolk.

Within recent memory there prevailed in Suffolk at the harvest suppers a curious custom of trolling out an old song which began :

> I am the Duke of Norfolk,
> Newly come to Suffolk,
> Say shall I be attended, or no, no, no ?
> Good Duke be not offended,
> And you shall be attended,
> And you shall be attended, now, now, now.

p. 138. GREEN SLEEVES. Or *Which nobody can deny*, has been a favourite tune from the days of Elizabeth until the present time. The earliest mention seems to be the ballad of *Green Sleeves*, licensed September, 1580, " A new Northern Dittye of the *Lady Greene Sleeves*." But it was popular even earlier. In *The Dancing Master*, 1686, the tune appears as *Green Sleeves and Pudding Pies*.

p. 138. VIRGINALS. All instruments of the harpsichord and spinet kind were termed virginals, it is said because maidens were wont to play upon 'em.

p. 139. THE SUBURB DEBAUCHES. In the days of Queen Elizabeth and for more than a century and a half after her reign the London suburbs were notorious for houses of ill-fame, so that a " suburbian " meant a whore. In Heywood's *The Rape of Lucrece*, 4to, 1608, the merry lord Valerius sings " a song of all the pretty suburbians," II, 3. Dekker, *Lanthorne and Candle-Light*, 1608, IX, writes of " The Infection of the Suburbs," and cries " How happy therefore were Cities if they had no Suburbes ! " He describes at length the brothels and dens of the London suburbs, " the dores of notorious *Carted Bawdes*, like Hell-gates."

p. 142. NEW INN. The New Inn dates from about 1660. It stood in the High Street, and is now called Waterloo House, being occupied by shops. At present it is mainly an eighteenth century two-story building of red brick with plastered quoins, and a low gable in the middle of the front ; in the roof are attics lighted by good dormer windows. There is a fine gable end over the original entrance, which leads into a narrow central courtyard, whence there is an exit at the opposite end. On the first floor, approached by a wide staircase with carved baluster, was the Assembly Room, now cut up by partitions.

p. 143.   SIR POL. Sir Politick Would-Bee in *Volpone*.

p. 143.   RUB, RUB. *Dictionary Canting Crew, circa* 1700 : " *Rub-rub*, us'd on Greens when the Bowl flees too fast, to have it forbear, if Words wou'd do it."

p. 144.   THE WINDOW. Supposed to be the window of the inn overlooking the bowling-green. Actually the actresses would use one of the balconies over the permanent proscenium doors.

p. 145.   CACARACAMOUCHI. Edward Ravenscroft's *The Citizen Turn'd Gentleman* was produced at Dorset Garden in the summer of 1672, probably on 4 July. This comedy was printed 4to, 1672, and re-issued as *Mamamouchi*, 4to, 1675. It is largely borrowed from *Le Bourgeois Gentilhomme*, which was produced at Chambord 14 October, 1670, and at Paris on the following 29 November. It will readily be remembered that in *Le Bourgeois Gentilhomme*, IV, 1, we have :
Coveille. Savez-vous bien ce que veut dire *cacaracamouchen ?*
Monsieur Jourdain. Cacaracamouchen ? Non.
Coveille. C'est à dire : Ma chère âme.
Monsieur Jourdain. Cacaracamouchen veut dire : Ma chère âme.
Coveille. Oui.
Monsieur Jourdain. Voilà qui est merveilleux ! *Cacaracamouchen :* Ma chère âme.

p. 145.   PIGS NYE. Pet, darling. The word is from baby talk. Cf. Massinger's *The Picture*, licensed 8 June, 1629, 4to, 1630, II, 1 :

" If thou art,
As I believe, the pigzney of his heart."

In *The Tempest,* as altered by Davenant and Dryden, IV, 4, Trinculo addresses Sycorax with " how does my Pigs-nye ? "

p. 148.   CHARM THE AIR. *Macbeth*, IV, 1, the First Witch, " I'll charm the air to give a sound." In D'Avenant's version this line is given to " Heccate." *Macbeth* was one of the most popular of Shakespeare's plays upon the Restoration stage, and it was frequently seen by Pepys. D'Avenant considerably expanded the witch scenes with much theatrical effect, so that Downes considered the tragedy as " being in the nature of an Opera " and remarks " it proves still a lasting play."

p. 149.   FEED THEIR DOGS. Cf. in D'Urfey's *The Marriage-Hater Match'd*, produced at Drury Lane in January, 1691–2, the character of La Pupsey, acted by Charlotte Butler, " An Impertinent Creature, always stuffing her Discourse with hard words, and perpetually kissing and talking to her Lapdog."

p. 149.   SHOP-LIFTS. An abbreviated form of Shop-lifter.

p. 150.   RECULLISENCE. A corruption of Recognizance. Cf. Middleton's *Michaelmas Term*, 1607, III, 4 : " Come then, and be a witness to a Recullisence."

p. 150.   STINGO. Humming ale. *Ingoldsby Legends :*

Thys Franklyn, Syrs, he brewed goode ayle,
And he called it Rare goode Styngo !
S, T, Y, N, G, O !
He call'd it Rare goode Styngo.

p. 150.   PUTHER. Or, pother. The old and correct form of bother.

p. 151. SOBIESKI. Prince Lubomirsky was a great Polish magnate, whose ambition, just when the Peace of Darovicha was being concluded in 1664, nearly wrecked his country by involving her in a bloody Civil War. Michael Wisniowiecki was elected King of Poland, 19 June, 1669. Upon his death in 1674 he was succeeded by John Sobieski (1624–1696), the heroic deliverer of Vienna and defender of Poland against the Ottomans. Wenceslaus Potocki was, in his epic poems, at the end of the seventeenth century a worthy representative of the true national spirit.

p. 151. LATTIN WARE. Latten, a mixed yellow metal like (or the same as) brass.

p. 151. THE BISHOP OF MUNSTER. Christoph Bernhard Von Galen, Bishop of Munster 1650–78, a most notable secular as well as ecclesiastical ruler. He compelled the rebellious city of Munster, after a long siege, to acknowledge his sovran rights. He succeeded in clearing his territory of foreign troops. On 13 June, 1665, he made a private treaty with Charles II, and in August of that year invaded Holland. In 1674–5, during the war with Sweden, he overran Pomerania, and gained parts of the Archdiocese of Bremen and the Diocese of Verdun. At home he restored Church discipline and established an excellent school system throughout his domain.

p. 151. FOX'T. A common old word for drunk. It is a favourite with Pepys. *E.g.*, Tuesday, 14 July, 1663 : " I made him almost foxed, the poor man having but a bad head, and not used I believe now-a-days to drink much wine."

p. 152. BELLARMINE. A large glazed drinking-jug with capacious belly and narrow neck, originally designed by the Protestants of the Low Countries as a grotesque likeness of their great opponent the Blessed Robert Bellarmine, S.J. (1542–1621). Ainsworth's *Latin Dictionary*, 1783, has : *Amphithetum*, a great cup or jug . . . a rummer ; a bellarmine. See also Chambers's *Book of Days*, I, 371.

p. 152. BON NOUSCIUS. Rather "bonus noscius." The Spanish *buenas noches* passed into general parlance, just as since certain French tags have especially become popular. One may compare the use of this phrase in Porter's *The Carnival* (although here the scene is laid in Seville), 4to, 1664, V, 2, where Felices says :

> Come if you will,
> If you won't, chuse, *bonus Nochios*.

p. 154. CLAY HILL. In Henry Pownall's *History of Epsom*, 1825, Toland (1711) is quoted : " Two or three pleasant lanes branch out, being the extremity of the roads which lead to the town from the slow declivities of the neighbouring hills. These are preferred to the principal streets, by such as are lovers of silence and retirement and are known of the names of Clay Hill, New Inn Lane, and Woodcote Green."

p. 157. AT THE DOOR. One of the permanent proscenium doors.

p. 158. TO SHOW YOUR BREEDING. A frequent quotation from *The Rehearsal*, II, 2 : 1. *King*. You must begin *Mon foy*. 2. *King*. Sweet Sir, *Pardonnes moy*. *Bayes*. Mark that : I makes 'em both speak *French*, to shew their breeding. In her address " To The Reader " prefixed to *Sir Patient Fancy*, 4to, 1678, Mrs. Behn disclaiming plagiarism, writes : " Others to show their breeding (as *Bays* sayes) cryed it was made out of at least four *French* Plays."

p. 160. RAW-HEAD. Bugbears and bugaboos. Cf. Beaumont and Fletcher, *The Prophetess*, 1622, IV, 5, Geta's cry :

> My face was bad enough : But now I look
> Like Bloody-Bone and Raw-head to frighten children.

p. 160. PRACTICE OF PIETY. *The Practice of Piety* was a popular little religious manual which with some slight alterations ran through many editions. We have : *Of the Daily Practice of Piety, also Devotions and Praiers in time of Captivity.* London. Printed by J. F., for R[ichard] Royston, at the Angel in *Ivy-Lane*, 1660. Also : *The Practise of Piety; directing a Christian how to walk* . . . printed in Twelves ; and in a small Volume for the Pocket in Twenty-Fours, 1684. There are cheap editions of these as late as 1709. Cf. *The Old Batchelour*, IV, where Bellmour's book, Scarron's *Novels*, is examined, and he cries : "If I had gone a-whoring with the *Practice of Piety* in my Pocket, I had never been discover'd." In Tom Brown's *Letters from the Dead to the Living*, Mother Cresswell, writing to Moll Quarles, and describing her old bagnio, says : "had every room in my house furnish'd with the *Practice of Piety*, and other good books, for the edification of my family."

p. 161. BLOODILY. A very early use of this expletive. The phrase here means "swearing like a lord." The adjective is generally used to qualify the word drunk, and it was not until towards the end of the seventeenth century that its use became extended. As employed to-day it is vulgar and offensive enough, but not swearing, as the word is not connected either with Our Lady or with the Precious Blood of Christ.

p. 161. BED-STAFF. Bed-staves were of various sizes and had several uses. One kind was that used for beating up the bed when it was made. In the series of nineteen plates depicting home life, designed by the French artist Abraham Bosse, and engraved by le Blond and Tavernier, the bedroom scene "La Nourrice," engraved by Tavernier, shows a servant who is busied in making the bed ; she smoothes the clothes with a short stick. Cf. Brome's *The City Wit, or, The Woman wears the Breeches*, 8vo, 1653, IV, 3, where Josina says : "If I do not make him an Example to all the bawdy Quacks in the Kingdome ; say there is no virtue in Cudgels, and Bedstaves."

p. 162. DUE CORRECTION. The law technically allowed a man to chastise his wife, who after all is his property and a chattel, with a rod, provided that it was no thicker than a thumb.

p. 162. MAN AND WIFE. Cf. Molière, *Le Médecin Malgré Lui*, I, 2, where M. Robert intervenes betwixt Sganarelle and Martine.

p. 162. CASTIGO TE. This old flogging line is continually quoted with point and propriety. Congreve in his *Amendments of Mr. Collier*, 1698, has a very apt reference. In *Tom Jones*, III, 6, we are told that Mr. Thwackum loved to repeat this adage : "and this, indeed, he often had in his mouth, or rather, according to the old phrase, never more properly applied, at his fingers' ends." S. Paul to the *Hebrews*, XII, 6, says : "Quem enim diligit Dominus, castigat ; flagellat autem omnem filium, quem recipit."

p. 163. TRY A PLUCK. Have a "set to" ; a turn or bout. Cf. Bunyan's *Pilgrim's Progress*, 1684, II, 158, *margin :* "They being come to By-path Stile, have a mind to have a pluck with Gyant Despair."

p. 165. NIMMEGEN. The Peace Conference at Nimwegen began in the summer of 1677, and was protracted until August, 1678.

p. 166. HEY FOR CAVALIERS. The words of this excellent old song have been attributed to Butler, and are printed in his posthumous works. They also appear in various collections such as *Westminster Drollery* (1672), II, p. 48 ; *Loyal Songs written against the Rump ; Pills to Purge Melancholy ;* and others.

The title is sometimes given as *The Clear Cavalier*. The lines here quoted run :

> We'll conquer and come again, beat up the drum again,
> Hey for Cavaliers, ho for Cavaliers, drink for Cavaliers, fight for
> Cavaliers.
> Dub-a-dub, dub-a-dub, have at old Beelzebub, Oliver quakes for fear.

It may be remembered that in *Peveril of the Peak*, chapter I, at news of the Restoration Sir Geoffrey Peveril thunders forth " this elegant effusion of loyal enthusiasm " : " Hey for Cavaliers. . . . Oliver shakes in his bier."

p. 167. DAPPER'S GAG. *The Alchemist*, III, 5, where Face and Subtle thrust a gag of gingerbread into Dapper's mouth. In Act V, 4, Subtle enters leading Dapper, and cries : " How ! ha' you eaten your gag ? " Dapper replies : " Yes, faith, it crumbled Away i' my mouth."

p. 168. WHISTLING. For fear. Cf. Blair *The Grave* :

> The school-boy, with his satchel in his hand,
> Whistling aloud to keep his courage up.

So in Dryden's *Amphitryon*, produced at Drury Lane early in October, 1690, II, Sosia in the night mutters to himself : " I am devilishly afraid, that's certain . . . I'll sing that I may seem valiant."

p. 169. BOB. A bitter jest ; a sharp hit. The word is very common. Cf. *The Rehearsal*, III, 1, where Tom Thimble says : " I'm sure, Sir, I made your Cloaths, in the Court-fashion, for you never paid me yet," and Bayes interrupts with " There's a bob for the Court ! "

p. 170. ALMOND MILK. This wash for the face was very popular in the seventeenth century. Thomas Goulard, who was a famous physician of Montpellier and greatly esteemed by King Charles II, has left three recipes for this cosmetic. *Goulard's Lotion or Milk of Almonds*. " Blanched Jordan almonds 1 oz. Bitter almonds 2 to 3 drachms. Distilled water 2 pints. Form into an emulsion, strain, and add very gradually 15 grains of bichloride of mercury in coarse powder, previously dissolved in half a pint of distilled water, after which add enough distilled water to make the whole measure 1 pint." *A Stronger Lotion of the same Nature*. " Valencia almonds blanched 1 oz. Bitter almonds $\frac{1}{2}$ oz. Water 1 pint. Add to the strained emulsion 25 grains of bichloride of mercury previously dissolved in $2\frac{1}{2}$ fluid drachms of rectified spirit, with water to make the whole measure 1 pint. *Goulard's Lotion*. Bitter almonds 3 oz. Distilled water 16 oz. Corrosive sublimate $1\frac{1}{2}$ grains. Sal ammoniac 2 drachms. Alcohol 4 drachms. Cherry laurel water 4 drachms. Grind the almonds with the water and strain through a cloth. Dissolve the salts in the cherry laurel water and alcohol, and mix the two solutions." All these lotions were to be applied to the face with lint or wool.

p. 173. WINDOW. One of the balconies over a permanent proscenium door. It is certainly curious that when the scene is a field, Rains and Mrs. Woodly should appear at a window, but Shadwell was very indifferent about these details, he had his window as a part of the structure of the theatre, and he made use of it. One may suppose it to be the window of a house overlooking the field.

p. 176. PLATONICK LOVE. An affected gallantry fashionable at the court of Charles I. James Howell in a letter 3 June, 1634, giving news of the court and its fashion, says " there is a Love called Platonick Love which much sways there of late." Davenant has a play *The Platonick Lovers*, 4to, 1636. Mrs. Centlivre's *The Platonick Lady*, produced at the Haymarket, 25 November, 1707, only lasted three or four nights. It is an amusing enough comedy, but the name is not particularly apt, for the character of Lucinda, created by Mrs. Bracegirdle, is not sufficiently well drawn.

p. 177. MALL. CUTPURSE. The common name of Mary Frith, the virago daughter of a shoemaker. She was born in 1584, or rather later, in Aldersgate Street, and from her earliest years she showed a most rampant masculinity. Probably to-day she would pass unnoticed in the crowd, but a more decent age was justly scandalized at her exploits. After being sent to service, which she abandoned, this " lusty and sturdy wench " assumed male attire, and " to her dying day she would not leave it off." Middleton and Dekker have a comedy *The Roaring Girl ; or, Mol Cutpurse*, 4to, 1611. She is supposed to have been a hermaphrodite, and in any case she was notorious as a prostitute, a procuress, and a pickpocket. She died of a dropsy in 1659 at her house in Fleet Street. She is said to have been the first woman to indulge in smoking, and certainly the woodcut on the title-page of the original edition of the play represents her puffing from a great pipe.

p. 177. DOLL COMMON. A boisterous and riotous punk, the colleague of Subtle and Face in *The Alchemist*. In Restoration days the part was inimitably acted by Mrs. Corey, whom Pepys so highly praises, and in our own time, when Jonson's comedy was revived under my direction, for two special performances at the Regent Theatre, in March, 1923, the genius of Miss Margaret Yarde never shone more brilliantly than in this rôle.

p. 178. CUT YOUR NOSE. Probably in allusion to the assault upon Sir John Coventry, a Member of Parliament, on the night of 21 December, 1670. Coventry had moved that a tax should be imposed upon the playhouses. This was strongly opposed by the Court party, and Sir John Birkenhead argued that the actors were the King's servants and a part of his pleasure. Whereupon Coventry bitterly asked if the royal pleasure lay among the men or women players. For this idle speech he was waylaid as he returned to his own house from supping abroad, and seized by some five-and-twenty Guards of the Duke of Monmouth's troop, who disarmed him and cut his nose to the bone, almost severing the end. The House of Commons passed a bill of banishment against the offenders, and inserted a clause to prevent the King pardoning them, thus depriving His Majesty of a part of his prerogative. The affair made a tremendous noise and is more than once very openly referred to by Marvell. There is also a ballad " *call'd the* Hay-market *Hectors*," *Poems on Affairs of State*, III (1704), pp. 68–70, which was writ upon that occasion. Stanza VIII runs :—

> Beware all ye Parliamenteers,
> How each of his Voice disposes ;
> *Bab May* in the Commons, *C. Rex* in the Peers,
> Sit telling your Fates on your Noses ;
> And decree, at the mention of every Slut,
> Whose Nose shall continue, and whose shall be cut.

p. 179. CANONICAL. The canonical hours are those during which marriages may be legally solemnized.

p. 180. PULLS HIS BEARD OFF. So at the end of *The Silent Woman* Dauphine unmasks " Doctor Cutbeard and Parson Otter," and pulls off their false beards and gowns. A mock-marriage, at which a trumpeter, dressed as a clergyman, is said actually to have officiated, is mentioned by Grammont when Aubrey De Vere, Earl of Oxford, thus deceived Roxolana, the actress of Davenant's company.

p. 180.   WITNESSES TO OUR AGREEMENT. This scene possibly suggested to Farquhar the separation of Sullen and his wife at the conclusion of *The Beaux Strategem*, produced at the Haymarket, 8 March, 1707. It is said that Mrs. Oldfield during a rehearsal objected to the very casual way in which husband and wife are separated at the end of the play. When this was reported to him, Farquhar, who was incurably ill, replied : " Tell the lady I will marry her myself, and leave her a widow in less than six weeks."

p. 182.   EPILOGUE. Spoken by Bisket.

p. 182.   BLACK-FRYARS. The First Blackfriars was a roofed theatre constructed by Robert Farrant early in 1577, and abandoned about May, 1584. The Second Blackfriars was a far more important and popular house, and it is to this that reference is here intended. It was a small roofed theatre, built in 1596 by Burbage on the first floor of the south section of Blackfriars Priory ; it was pulled down 6 August, 1655. It must be held to take its place as the first organized private theatre, and is here mentioned as the typical Pre-Restoration playhouse.

The Tempest

p. 193.   AN IMPOSITION. A task imposed on us.

p. 193.   SEA-VOYAGE. *The Sea-voyage*, acted at the Globe, was licensed by Sir Henry Herbert, 22 June, 1622. It was first printed in the folio of 1647. After the Restoration it was revived 25 September, 1667, at the Theatre Royal, when Mrs. Knepp acted Aminta. It seems to have been frequently played at this time as a counter-attraction to *The Tempest* at the rival theatre.

In July-August, 1685, there was produced at the Theatre Royal *A Commonwealth of Women*, an alteration of Fletcher's play by Thomas D'Urfey. This proved very successful, and was seen at intervals for more than half a century. At Drury Lane, 21st April, 1746, Macklin, Peg Woffington, and Kitty Clive appeared in D'Urfey's romantic drama.

p. 193.   GOBLINS. *The Goblins*, acted at Blackfriars, was printed 8vo, 1646. It was revived at the Theatre Royal, 24 January, 1667. " The Goblins are Tamoren and his friends, who, having been defeated in a battle, retreat to a wood, turn thieves, and disguise themselves as Devils " (Genest). The character of Reginella (not Regmella, as Dryden calls her) has considerable charm, but the course of action of the play on the whole is utterly bewildering and confused.

p. 194.   OLD LATINE PROVERB. Cicero, *Philippic*, XII. 2, 5, " Cuiusuis hominis est errare, nullius nisi insipientis in errore perseuerare. Posteriores enim cogitationes, ut aiunt, sapientiores solent esse." The " ut aiunt " shows that the sentiment was proverbial. There is an earlier instance in Euripides, *Hippolytus*, 434, 435.

$$\text{'Εν βροτοῖς}$$
$$\text{Αἱ δεύτεραί πως φροντίδες σοφώτεραι.}$$

(in a speech of the Nurse to Phaedra)

Cicero, *Epist. ad Quintum Fratrem*, III, i, 5, 18, says, " Ego uero nullas δευτέρας φροντίδας habere possum in Caesaris rebus."

The Greek proverbial saying Δευτέρων ἀμεινόνων is a little different in meaning, referring originally to the performance of a sacrifice a second time when the first had been under unfavourable auspices. Hence of making a second attempt in the hope of better fortune.

p. 195. ONE OF OUR WOMEN TO PRESENT A BOY. The rôle was that of Hippolito, which was probably taken in 1667 by Moll Davis.

p. 196. ACTED WOOMEN STILL. Cf. The new epilogue to the revival of *The Parson's Wedding*, as printed in *Covent Garden Drollery*, 1672 :

> When boys play'd women's parts, you'd think the Stage,
> Was innocent in that untempting Age.
> No : for your amorous Fathers then, like you,
> Amongst those Boys had Play-house Misses too :
> They set those bearded Beauties on their laps,
> Men gave 'em Kisses, and the Ladies Claps.
> But they, poor hearts, could not supply our room ;
> They went but Females to the Tyring-room :
> While we, in kindness to our selves, and you,
> Can hold out Women to our Lodgings too.

p. 196. THE BEST POET'S HEADS. Cf. Tom D'Urfey's *Collin's Walk Through London* (1690), Canto IV, where the peripatetic, on visiting Dorset Garden :

> saw each box with beauty crown'd
> And pictures deck the structure round,
> *Ben, Shakespear*, and the learned Rout,
> With noses some and some without.

Mr. W. J. Lawrence tells us : " These portraits remained in situ until the demolition of the theatre in 1709." Cf. also the smart reference to Dorset Garden in Dryden's Epilogue *Spoken at the opening of the New House* (Theatre Royal, Drury-Lane), 26 March, 1674 :

> Though in their House the Poets Heads appear,
> We hope we may presume their Wits are here.

p. 199. 24 VIOLINS. Pepys, Friday, 8 May, 1663, visited the Theatre Royal, " being the second day of its being opened." He remarks : " The house is made with extraordinary good contrivance, and yet hath some faults, as the narrowness of the passages in and out of the pitt, and the distance from the stage to the boxes, which I am confident cannot hear ; but for all other things it is well, only, above all, the musique being below, and most of it sounding under the very stage, there is no hearing of the bases at all, nor very well of the trebles, which sure must be mended." Upon the occasion of an important production the musicians of the King were frequently employed in the theatres. On 20 March, 1664-5, a grant of £40 was made for habits to clothe 24 " violins," and on 18 March an order was issued " to make vp Habitts of seurall coloured rich Taffataes for fower and twenty violins." The orchestra had no doubt been specially augmented for this occasion. So Chappuzeau, *L'Europe Vivante*, Geneva, 1667, mentions that six musicians were increased to twelve for a particular performance at Paris. It should be noticed too that a large chorus consisting of the Chapel

Royal boys had been specially introduced into the operatic *Tempest*. The following Order was issued on 16 May, 1674 : " It is his Maties pleasure that Mr. Turner & Mr. Hart or any other Men or Boyes belonging to His Maties Chappell Royall that sing in ye Tempest at His Royall Highnesse Theatre doe remain in Towne all the Weeke (dureing his Maties absence from Whitehall) to perform that service, only Saterdayes to repaire to Windsor & to returne to London on Mundayes if there be occacon for them And that (they) also performe ye like Service in ye Opera in ye said Theatre or any other thing in ye like Nature where their help may be desired."

p. 199. COMPASS-PEDIMENT. A circular, or curving pediment. Cf. Entick, *London*, 1766, IV, 100: " The north front . . . has a triangular instead of two compass-pediments."

p. 199. A HOAMING SEA. Hoaming, a very rare word for " tempestuous."

> When a strong sudden Flow and Hoaming Seas
> Our trembling Fleet with uncouth Furies seize.

The First Book of Virgil's Aeneid, " Made English " by Luke Milbourne, 4to, 1688. " Hoaming " also occurs in Echard's translation of the *Rudens* (1694) : " Now 'tis such a hoaming Sea, we've little hopes o' Sport."

p. 199. SCUD. The light feathery portions of cloud blown off the main clouds are technically known as " scud." The sentence is obscure.

p. 200. YAW, YAW. A corruption of " Yare, yare." Yare signifies eager ; ready ; prepared, from the Anglo-Saxon " geáro." Cf. *Measure for Measure*, IV, 2 : " You shall find me yare." Ray gives it as a Suffolk word, and the " Hear, hear " of Lowestoft boatmen of to-day is probably a disguised " Yare, yare."

p. 200. CAPSTORM. A rare form of capstan.

p. 200. REEF BOTH TOPSAILS. This is to reduce the area of the sail by taking a sort of tuck in them (like the tuck in a shirt-sleeve) by means of reef points.

p. 200. SEERE CAPSTORM. The stern or aftermost capstan. The order directs that more men should be put on to work it round and round.

p. 201. NIPPERS. A piece of braided cordage used to prevent a cable from slipping.

p. 201. LUBBORD. Larboard. This older term, in order to save confusion with starboard, is now replaced by port.

p. 201. VIAL-BLOCK. Vial or Vial-block, " a large single-sheaved block through which the messenger passed when the anchor was weighed by the fore or jeer capstan." Admiral Smyth, *Sailor's Word-Book*, 1867.

p. 201. A PEEK. " The anchor is apeek when the cable has been sufficiently hove in to bring the ship over it." Smyth, *Sailor's Word-Book*, 1867.

p. 201. CUT THE ANCHOR. A misprint for " Cat the anchor."

p. 201. HAUL CATT. " Cat is . . . a . . . strong tackle, or complication of pulleys, to hook and draw the anchor . . . up to the cat head." Falconer, *Marine Dictionary*, 1789.

p. 201. HAUL AFT MISEN-SHEET. The sheet is the rope at the bottom corner of a sail to haul it round in a different direction.

p. 201. MACKREL-GALE. A strong breeze such as when mackerel are caught. Cf. Dryden, *The Hind and the Panther*, III, 456 :

> The wind was fair, but blew a *mackrel* gale.

p. 201. FLAT IN THE FORE-SHEET. The fore-sheet is the rope by which the lee corner of the foresail is kept in place. To flat in a sail is to draw in the aftermost lower corner or clue of a sail towards the middle of a ship in order to give the sail greater power to turn the vessel.

p. 202.   OVERHAUL YOUR FORE BOLING. A "fore bowline" is a rope on a sail, and to "overhaul" it you let it go loose and slack on the sail.

p. 202.   BRACE IN THE LAR-BOARD. To brace in is to lay the yards less obliquely athwartships.

p. 202.   BLASPHEMOUS, UNCHARITABLE DOG. This is Shakespearean. But why is Trincalo, or in Shakespeare, the Boatswain, blasphemous? Trincalo has certainly said nothing profane, but in Shakespeare, to Gonzalo's remonstrances the Boatswain replies: "What care these roarers for the name of King?" And when he is told to remember whom he has aboard, he answers: "None that I more love than myself." Perhaps this was regarded as blasphemy against the divinity of the monarch who was in the ship.

> There's such divinity doth hedge a king
> That treason can but peep to what it would.

p. 202.   LUFF. When a ship is sailing sideways in a slanting direction, the wind being in the wrong quarter, and it is needful to use the wind as much as possible, the ship goes to one side and is in more or less danger. When getting too much over it is necessary to luff, that is the ship must be brought round with the rudder to catch the wind full behind her, to drive her along evenly although she will not be going in the exact direction required.

p. 204.   LOP, FOR OVER-TOPPING. Shakespeare has "Trash for over-topping." To trash has been explained as to cut down or lop trees and hedges which are overgrown. Also as a hunting term, to keep in check hounds which outdistance the pack.
From this present passage it would appear that the first explanation of "To trash" is the more exact.

p. 205.   BORESPRIT. Bowsprit, a spar running out from the ship's stem, to which forestays are fastened.

p. 205.   BERMOOTHES. The Bermudas. In 1610 Sylvester Jourdain published his *Discovery of the Bermudas, otherwise called the Isle of Divels.* There is mention of "the dreadful coast of the Bermudas" in Howe's supplement to Stowe's *Annals.*

p. 206.   BLEW-EY'D. Sycorax is termed blue-eyed, because her eyes were dark and sunken, a sign of pregnancy. So in *The Dutchesse of Malfy*, 4to, 1623, II, 1, Bosola says that he suspects that the Duchess is with child because:

> The fins of her eie-lids look most teeming blew,
> She waines i' th' cheeke, and waxes fat i' th' flanke;
> And (contrary to our Italian fashion)
> Weares a loose-bodied gowne.

And in Otway's *Friendship and Fashion*, Dorset Garden, April, 1678, II, Mrs. Goodvile and Lettice rally Victoria. "*Mrs. Goodvile.* Lord, you are paler than you use to be. *Lettice.* Ay, and then that blewness under the eyes. *Mrs. Goodvile.* Besides, you are not so lively as I have known you: pardon me, Cousin. *Lettice.* Well, if there be a fault, Marriage will cure all."

p. 208.   ABHOR'D SLAVE. It may be noticed that in the First Folio Shakespeare, 1623, this speech, which Dryden assigns to Prospero, is given (improperly, as I am convinced) to Miranda. Theobald well says: "I am persuaded the author never designed the speech for Miranda," and Capell supports him. Several modern authors justly follow Theobald.

p. 209.   RED BOTCH. An inflamed ulcer.

p. 209.   SETEBOS. This name is evidently formed from that of *Settaboth*, " A divinity of the Patagonians, described by Master Francis Fletcher in an account of Drake's great voyage."

p. 211.   SALVAGES. This obsolete form of savage is found in Gower, and persisted for several centuries. Thus in Tate and Brady's version (1696) of the *Psalms*, vii, 2, we have :

> Lest, like a salvage Lion, he
> My helpless Soul devour.

p. 212.   OLD SIMON THE KING. Simon Wadloe, landlord of the Old Devil Tavern, Temple Bar, which was frequented and made famous by Ben Jonson. Wadloe was the original of the popular old song *Old Simon the King*, which was, it may be remembered, the favourite air of Squire Western in *Tom Jones*, IV, 5.

p. 214.   MOON-CALF. An abortion, a monstrosity. Moon-calf, *partus lunaris*, was an old name for a false conception—*mola carnea*, or fœtus imperfectly formed, being supposed to be occasioned by the influence of the moon.

p. 214.   OUT OF THE MOON. There is a French legend that the Man in the Moon is Judas Iscariot. Others say Cain. An English superstition prefers that he should be the man who gathered sticks upon the Sabbath Day, *Numbers*, xv, 32–36. A more graceful classical mythology fables that he was Endymion, a shepherd boy of Mount Latmus in Caria, who was beloved by Selene, the goddess of the moon. Cicero, *Tusculanae Disputationes*, I, 38, 92.

p. 214.   PIG-NUTS. The tuber of *Bunium flexuosum* ; earth-nuts.

p. 221.   BLOOD PURSU'D MY HAND. Cf. Vergil, *Aeneid*, III, 24–33 :

> Accessi, uiridemque ab humo conuellere siluam
> conatus, ramis tegerem ut frondentibus aras,
> horrendum et dictu uideo mirabile monstrum.
> Nam quae prima solo ruptis radicibus arbos
> uellitur, huic atro liquuntur sanguine guttae
> et terram tabo maculant. Mihi frigidus horror
> membra quatit, gelidusque coit formidine sanguis.
> Rursus et alterius lentum conuellere uimen
> insequor et causas penitus temptare latentes :
> alter et alterius sequitur de cortice sanguis.

p. 223.   TRILLS DOWN. To trill is to flow in a slender stream, but more constantly and continuously than to trickle.

p. 2   BOSENS WHISTLE. " A silver whistle, suspended from the neck by a lanyard, is the modern Boatswain's badge of office, and it is familiarly termed his ' call.' " Shakespeare a Seaman, *St. James' Magazine*, July, 1862.

p. 231.   FUSS. A misprint for " Fubs." Fubs is a term of endearment, usually applied to a small chubby person. Cf. *Sir Courtly Nice*, 4to, 1685, V, where Crack talks of " my *Indian* Fubs of a Sister." Fubs was a nickname given by Charles II to the Duchess of Portsmouth.

p. 233.   BLOUZE. A vulgar term for a common slatternly woman. In D'Urfey's *Famous History of the Rise and Fall of Massaniello*, Two Parts, acted at Drury Lane in 1699, the name of Massaniello's wife is rather absurdly given as Blowzabella.

p. 237. DIVIDE THE WATERS. Cf. the song of Arbaces in Arne's opera *Artaxerxes*, 1762 :

> Water parted from the sea
>   May increase the river's tide ;
> To the bubbling fount may flee,
>   Or thro' fertile vallies glide :
> Yet in search of lost repose,
>   Doom'd like me, forlorn to roam,
> Still it murmurs as it flows,
>   Till it reach its native home.

p. 248. SKINK ABOUT. Serve drink round ; pour out liquor. Cf. Shirley's *The Lady of Pleasure*, licensed 15 October, 1635 ; 4to, 1637 ; IV, 2 : " A drawer is my Ganymede, he shall skink brisk nectar to us."

p. 248. ROWSE. A full bumper ; a draught of liquor. Cf. *Othello*, II, 3, the drinking scene where Cassio enters half tippled, exclaiming " 'Fore God, they have given me a rouse already."

p. 248. HAUNSE IN KELDER. Literally Jack-in-the-Cellar, *i.e.*, the unborn babe in the womb. This is a favourite expression with Dryden. Cf. *Amboyna*, acted in 1673, IV, 1, where Harman senior remarks at Towerson and Ysabinda's wedding : " You *Englishmen* . . . cannot stay for Ceremonies ; a good honest *Dutchman* would have been plying the glass all this while, and drunk to the hopes of *Hans in Kelder* till 'twas Bedtime."

p. 249. THE WITCHES ARE OF GREAT FAMILY IN LAPLAND. In mediæval times it was often believed that supernatural powers were the heritage of certain families and even races, descending from one generation to another, and that all Lap women in particular were born witches. There are many allusions to this traditional superstition. Cf. Fletcher's *The Chances*, folio 1647, V, where Don John says :

>   Sure his devil
> Comes out of Lapland.

Also Mrs. Behn's *The Dutch Lover*, produced at Dorset Garden in 1673, V, where Haunce says : " Do you think I creep in like a *Lapland* Witch through the Keyholes ? "

p. 250. WILDINGS. Wild apples, or any wild fruit. Cf. *The Faerie Queen*, III, vii, 17 :

> Oft from the forrest wildings he did bring,
> Whose sides empurpled were with smyling red.

p. 250. HACKNEY DEVIL. A parody on " hackney coach." Hackney means plying for common hire.

p. 250. PIGS-NYE. Pet ; darling. The word is from baby talk. Cf. Massinger's *The Picture* (licensed 8 June, 1629), 4to, 1630, II, 1 :

>   " If thou art,
> As I believe, the pigzney of his heart."

p. 253. HEILA. A misprint for Hecla. Hecla is given correctly in *The Tempest*, 4to, 1670.

p. 258. VULNERARY. Healing ; curative. Latin, *Uulnerarius*. Cf. Pliny *Historia Naturalis*, XXIII, 4, 40 : Oleum oenanthinum " uulnerariis emplastris utile " est.

p. 260. HIPPOLITO'S SWORD. There is an error here. Miranda should have brought Ferdinand's sword. Ariel had said:

> " Anoint the Sword which pierc'd him with this Weapon-Salve,
> And wrap it close from Air till I have time
> To visit him again."

Weapon-salve was supposed to cure a wounded person by being applied to the sword by which the hurt had been inflicted. It was first discovered by Paracelsus. Cf. Davenant's *The Unfortunate Lovers*, 4to, 1649, II, 1 :

> " Our medecine we apply,
> Like the weapon-salve, not to ourselves but him
> Who was the sword that made the wound."

Also Mrs. Behn's *The Young King*, 4to, 1683, V, 5 :

> " That Balm it was, that like the Weapon-salve
> Heals at a Distance——"

Lord Bacon, *Sylva Sylvarum*, sixth edition (1651), p. 217, writes : " It is constantly Received, and Avouched, that the *Anointing* of the *Weapon*, that maketh the *Wound*, wil heale the *Wound* it selfe. . . . And thus much hath been tried, that the *Ointment* (for *Experiments* sake) hath been wiped off the *Weapon*, without the knowledge of the *Party Hurt*, and presently the *Party Hurt*, hath been in great *Rage* of *Paine*, till the *Weapon* was *Reannointed*."
One may compare in Scott's *Lay of the Last Minstrel* the magical cure of William of Deloraine's wound by " The Ladye of Branksome." See also *Bygone Beliefs*, by H. S. Redgrove, chapter V, " The Powder of Sympathy : a Curious Medical Superstition."

p. 264. SHE WOULD CONTROUL THE MOON. Cf. *Paradise Lost*, II, 662–666 :

> Nor uglier follow the Night-Hag, when call'd
> In secret, riding through the Air she comes
> Lur'd with the smell of infant blood, to dance
> With *Lapland* Witches, while the labouring Moon
> Eclipses at thir charms.

p. 267. THE RISING SUN. In Settle's opera *The World in the Moon*, produced at Dorset Garden in May, 1697, in the first Act, there is an elaborate scene where " *a Circular part of the back Clouds rolls softly away, and gradually discovers a Silver Moon, near Fourteen Foot Diameter : After which, the Silver Moon wanes off by degrees, and discovers the World within, consisting of Four grand Circles of Clouds, illustrated with* Cupids, etc." D'Urfey's opera *Wonders in the Sun*, produced at the Haymarket in April, 1706, has " *The Scene a Luminous Country, adorn'd with Gorgeous Rays of the Sun.*"

p. 268. THE RHYMING MONSIUR, AND THE SPANISH PLOT. It must be remembered that this is the Epilogue to *The Tempest* as produced at the Duke's Theatre on Thursday, 7 November, 1667. In the winter of 1667 the vogue of the heroic drama written in couplets was already very great, and in spite of parodies and criticism rhyme long continued to hold its own on the stage. Howard and Dryden's *The Indian-Queen*, produced at the Theatre Royal in January, 1663–4, and Dryden's Sequel *The Indian Emperour*, produced at the same house in the spring of 1665, both had an unprecedented success.

In the Prologue to *Aureng-Zebe* (Theatre Royal, 1675), Dryden confesses that he

> Grows weary of his long-lived Miſtris Rhyme.

None the less *Aureng-Zebe* drew thronging audiences, as also did Crowne's *The Deſtruction of Jerusalem*, a rhyming tragedy in two parts, produced at the Theatre Royal in the spring of 1677. In the Prologue to *Secret Love* (Theatre Royal, 2 March, 1667) Dryden insiſts that he has observed in this play

> "The Unities of Action, Place, and Time;
> The scenes unbroken; and a mingled chime
> Of *Johnsons* Humour with *Corneilles* rhyme."

Spanish influence had been very ſtrong in the English drama before the closing of the theatres in 1642. Fletcher in particular is indebted to Spanish literature. But immediately after the Reſtoration, and for at least half a century following, the Spanish playwrights were even more largely drawn upon by English authors. In some cases, it is true, Spanish comedies filtered into England by way of France. But Charles II himself suggeſted *Los Empeños de Seis Horas* to Sir Samuel Tuke as "an excellent design" for an English play, and he also handed Moreto's *No Puede Ser* to Crowne. Tuke's *The Adventures of Five Hours*, produced at the Duke's House, 8 January, 1663, won an inſtant triumph, "and the house by its frequent plaudits did show their sufficient approbation." "It took successively 13 days altogether, no other Play intervening," and was conſtantly in the bills.

In the original Prologue to *The Wild Gallant*, as produced at the Vere Street Theatre, 5 February, 1662–3, Dryden introduces two aſtrologers to foretell the fate of the new play, and after some prognoſtication the second Aſtrologer says:

> "But yet the greateſt Mischief does remain,
> The twelfth Apartment bears the Lord of Spain;
> Whence I conclude, it is your Author's Lot,
> To be Indanger'd by a Spanish Plot."

The reference is probably to Tuke's *The Adventures of Five Hours* at the rival house. It is probable that in spite of his assertion later in the Prologue, "This Play is *English*, and the growth your own," Dryden drew something for *The Wild Gallant* from the Spanish theatre.

p. 268. VISIONS BLOUDIER THAN KING RICHARD'S. This allusion would almoſt seem to point to a fairly recent revival of *Richard III*, which was one of the plays assigned as a monopoly to Killigrew's company. In *Covent Garden Drollery*, 1672, p. 13, is a "*Prologue to* Richard *the Third*," but this gives no indication of the theatre or actors. Contemporary allusions, however, indicate that the tragedy enjoyed some popularity. In Henry Higden's *A Modern Essay On the Thirteenth Satyr of Juvenal*, 4to, 1686, we have:

> Bath'd in cold Sweats he frighted Shrieks
> At visions bloodier than King *Dicks*.

Upon this the author gives a note: "*Vision Dicks*. In the Tragedy of *Richard* the 3rd." In D'Urfey's *A Fool's Preferment*, produced at Dorset Garden in the spring of 1688, Act III, 2, Lyonel the diſtracted gentleman, cries out: "A Horse; a Horse; my Kingdom for a Horse."

(397)

The famous alteration of *Richard III* by Colley Cibber, which was produced at Drury Lane in February, 1699–1700, with Cibber himself as crookback'd Dick, has kept the stage until the present time.

p. 269. AT DOUBLE CHARGES SHINE. Mr. W. J. Lawrence, *The Elizabethan Playhouse*, First Series, p. 201, says : " Prices of admission were advanced during the run of new operas, owing to the expense of mounting. Duffett girds at the practice in the prologue to his *Psyche Debauch'd*," produced at Drury-Lane in 1675, 4to, 1678.

p. 269. FLYING WITCHES. There had been a revival of the Davenant *Macbeth* at Dorset Garden early in 1673. A special feature was made of machines for the witches, who were thus carried through the air. Cf. the anonymous Epilogue to *The Ordinary*. " A Collection of Poems written upon several Occasions By several Persons." London, 8vo, 1673, p. 167 :

> Now empty shows must want of sense supply
> Angels shall dance and *Macbeth's* Witches fly.

p. 269. FFRANCE. Betterton had visited Paris by the special command of the King, in order to observe how the English theatre might be improved in the matter of scenery and decorations.

p. 269. 30 WARBLING VOYCES. The men and boys of the Chapel Royal. In the Lord Chamberlain's Accounts there is an Order, 16 May, 1674 : " It is his Maties pleasure that Mr. Turner & Mr. Hart or any other Men or Boyes belonging to His Maties Chappell Royall that sing in ye Tempest at His Royall Highnesse Theatre doe remaine in Towne all the Weeke (dureing his Maties absence from Whitehall).

Psyche

p. 278. MASTRICK. In January, 1670, Monmouth succeeded Albemarle (Monck) as captain-general of the King's forces. In 1672 he commanded the English auxiliary force against the Dutch under the eyes of Turenne and of Louis XIV himself, and on his return, in the company of the Earl of Feversham, to the seat of war in 1673, he took an active part in the siege of Maestricht, which capitulated on 2 July. In England he was fêted and pensioned, and generally, says Burnet, " much considered " on account of these services.

p. 280. LOCK. Matthew Locke, the famous composer, was born at Exeter in 1629, and died in August, 1677. He was buried in the Savoy, where he had resided during his last years.

p. 280. DRAGHI. Giovanni Baptista Draghi. This celebrated musician was organist to Queen Catharine, and is said by Wanley to have taught the lute to the Princess (afterwards Queen) Anne before her marriage to Prince George of Denmark in 1683. He is mentioned by Pepys, and in 1687 he set Dryden's S. Cecilia's song *From Harmony, from heav'nly Harmony*. He was living in 1706, when he composed some part of the music of D'Urfey's opera *Wonders in the Sun ; or, The Kingdom of the Birds*, which was produced at the Haymarket, 5 April of that year. His setting of the song sung in the first act by Hospitality in the character of a Dame of Honour was much admired. The opera, however, was not a success, for Downes tells us : " It lasted only Six Days, not answering half the expences of it."

p. 280.   St. Andree.   There are many contemporary allusions to this famous dancer, and his name heads the list of a dozen dancers who appeared when Crowne's elaborate masque *Calisto ; or, The Chaste Nimph*, was given at Court early in 1675. Sir Fopling in *The Man of Mode*, acted in 1676, IV, says : " I am fit for nothing but low dancing now, a Corant, a Borée, or a Minnuét : but St. *André* tells me, if I will but be Regular in one Month I shall rise agen." Oldham, *An Imitation of Horace, Book I, Satyr IX, Written in June*, 1681, has :

> Next for the Dancing part I all surpass,
> St. *Andrew* never mov'd with such a grace.

Dryden, *Mac Flecknoe*, 1682, writes :

> St. *André's* feet ne'er kept more equal time,
> Not ev'n the feet of thy own *Psyche's* rhime.

The author of *A Comparison between the Two Stages*, 1702, has an anecdote regarding St. André, which I cannot but consider suspicious, or at least exaggerated, as the French dancer certainly achieved a great success, although I make no doubt that Hart and Mohun could not be for a moment displaced, however attractive and highly patronized the novelty : " The late *Duke of Monmouth* was a good judge of dancing, and a good Dancer himself ; when he returned from *France*, he brought with him *St. André*, then the best Master in *France* : the *Duke* presented him to the Stage, the Stage to gratifie the *Duke* admitted him ; and the *Duke* himself thought he wou'd prove a mighty advantage to 'em, tho' he had no body else of his Opinion : A Day was publish'd in the Bills for him to dance, but not one more besides the *Duke* and his Friends came to see him ; the reason was, the Plays were then so good, and *Hart* and *Mohun* acted 'em so well, that the Audience wou'd not be interrupted for so short a time tho' 'twas to see the best Master in *Europe*."

p. 280.   Stephenson.   The other work of this scene-painter cannot certainly be identified.   He was one of the best-known theatrical artists of the day, the compeer of John Webb ; Robert Aggas ; Robert Streeter, " Serjeant Painter to the King," whose " glorious scenes and perspectives " for *The Conquest of Granada* were much admired by Evelyn ; Samuel Towers ; Isaac Fuller ; and Robert Robinson.

p. 281.   As a young wanton.   Cf. Sir Car Scroope's Prologue to *The Man of Mode*, 1676 :

> *With modest Fears a Muse does first begin,*
> *Like a young Wench newly entic'd to Sin :*
> *But tickl'd once with praise, by her good Will,*
> *The Wanton Fool wou'd never more lie still.*

p. 284.   Recorders.   The Recorder is an instrument of the flute family, now obsolete. It is described at length in *The Genteel Companion, being exact directions for the Recorder, . . . Carefully composed and gathered by Humphrey Salter, London, . . .* 1683."

p. 286.   Flajolets.   The Flageolet is the modern form of the old *Flute à bec* or straight flute.   Burney ascribes the invention of the Flageolet to the Sieur Juvigny, who played it in the famous *Ballet comique de la Royne*, 1581.   In 1682 was published the *Pleasant companion, or new lessons and instructions for the Flagelet by Thomas Greeting, Gent.*   The instrument seems to have superseded the more ancient Recorder, much as the Violin did the Viol.

p. 286. SACKBUTS. The name is here used for the Trombone, or Bass-Trumpet. In Dr. Burney's *Account of the musical performances in Westminster Abbey and the Pantheon on May* 26, 27, 29, *and June* 3 *and* 5, 1784, it is stated that " the Sacbut or Double Trumpet was sought ; but so many years had elapsed since it had been used in this kingdom, that neither the instrument nor a performer upon it could easily be found. It was however discovered . . . that in his Majesty's private military band there were six musicians who played the three several species of sacbut, tenor, bass, and double bass." Mr. Karst, Mr. Kneller, Mr. Moeller, Mr. Neibour, Mr. Pick, Mr. Zink, were the performers.

p. 286. HOA-BOYS. Hautboy ; French *Haut-bois, i.e.,* a wooden instrument with a high tone. In Handel's time it was phoneticized into Hoboy. The Italians spell it " Oboe," under which name it is generally known.

p. 294. APOLLO DELPHICUS. Especially regarded under this title as the god of prophecy and oracular wisdom. Pliny, *Historia Naturalis,* XXXIV, 8, speaks of Apollo Delphicus and distinguishes the god under this aspect from Apollo Palatinus, who was so called because he had a temple built on the Palatine Hill, founded by Augustus Cæsar. Apollo was venerated under a vast number of names, *e.g.,* Pæan, the Healer ; Apollo Smintheus, the Mouse-killer.

p. 294. DORICK. The earliest temples seem to have been built in the Doric style, and the impression made was that of massiveness.

p. 295. SERVICE. Now almost always with a defining word : *dinner, dessert, breakfast, tea service.* Luttrell, *Brief Relation* (ed. 1857), VI, 597, speaks of " A magnificent service of plate, consisting of many large silver dishes, stands, plates, etc."

p. 295. TYRION. Probably a mistake for Typhon, who in Hesiod is a terrible monster ; the youngest son of Tartarus and Gæa, only subdued by Zeus after a terrific contest.

p. 295. CYCLOPS. An old tradition, which is partially related by Hesiod, says that the Cyclops were Titans, three in number, and that they were killed by Apollo for having furnished Zeus with the thunderbolts to destroy Aesculapius.

p. 296. HYACINTH. The legend of Apollo and Hyacinth is very ancient. It has been most beautifully told by Ovid, *Metamorphoses,* X, 162, *sqq.*

p. 296. PALÆMON. A Greek marine deity, formerly called Melicertes, the son of Athamas and Ino. " O Palæmon, sancte Neptuni comes." Plautus, *Rudens,* I, ii, 70.

p. 296. LIBAMINA. That which is poured out in offerings to the gods, a drink-offering, a libation. Libamen is poetical for libamentum. Ovid, *Fasti,* III, 733–4 :

> Nomine ab auctoris ducunt Libamina nomen,
> Libaque ; quod sacris pars datur inde focis.

p. 296. FAVETE LINGUIS. The phrase is best known from Horace, *Carminum,* III, i, 2. As the utterance of ill-omened words vitiated any sacred rite, it was customary for the priest before commencing to ask the people " to be favourable with their lips " (*ore* or *linguis fauere*), *i.e.,* to utter none but favourable words, and as the safest way of doing so was to be silent, the phrase often practically means " be silent." The Greek is εὐφημεῖτε. Cf. Propertius, IV, vi, 1 : " sacra facit uates, sint ora fauentia sacris " ; and Vergil, *Aeneid,* V, 71 : " ore fauete omnes."

p. 297. A FLAMBEAUX. So Mrs. Behn, *The Emperor of the Moon,* 4to, 1687, II, 2, has *Enter Page with a Flambeaux.* Sir T. Herbert, *Travels* (1638), uses a plural,

"Flambeauxes," and Mrs. Manley, *Atalantis*, I, p. 88 (2nd edition, 1709), mentions " white Flambeaux's."

p. 297. SALT. The Latin *mola* means grits or grains of spelt coarsely ground and mixed with salt, hence called *mola salsa*, which it was customary to strew upon the victims at a sacrifice. Festus the grammarian (150 ? A.D.) has : " mola etiam uocatur far tostum, et sale sparsum, quod eo molito hostiae aspergantur." Plautus, *Amphitruo*, II, ii, 100, uses the phrase " aut mola salsa aut ture comprecari." Pliny, XVIII, 2, has : " mola salsa supplicare."

p. 298. HIS WORKMANSHIP. Cf. Horace, *Sermonum*, I, viii, 1–3 :

Olim truncus eram ficulnus, inutile lignum,
cum faber, incertus scamnum faceretne Priapum,
maluit esse deum.

p. 300. RELIGION. " Tantum religio potuit suadere malorum," Lucretius, *De Natura Rerum*, I, 101.

p. 301. SOME FROM THAT ROCK. One may compare the story of the love of Sappho for Phaon, and her leap from the Leucadian rock in consequence of his disdain. Although so long implicitly believed, this legend has no historical basis. Servius, who wrote about 400 A.D., says that a woman who was in love with Phaon when rejected threw herself in despair from the cliff of Leucas. But he does not mention her name. Strabo in his *Geography* writes : " There is a white rock which stretches out from Leucas to the sea and towards Cephallenia, that takes its name from its whiteness. The rock of Leucas has upon it a temple of Apollo, and the leap from it was believed to stop love. From this it is said that Sappho first, as Menander somewhere remarks, ' in pursuit of the haughty Phaon, urged on by maddening desire, threw herself from its far-seen rocks, imploring thee [Apollo] lord and king.' " Ovid repeats the story of Sappho's leap, but his witness is merely poetical. Ptolemy Hephæstion, about 100 A.D. who, in the extant summary of his works published in the *Myriobiblion* of Photius, gives a list of many men and women who by the Leucadian leap were either cured of the madness of love or else perished, does not so much as mention the name of Sappho. Probably the modern literary idea in England of Sappho's leap is founded upon Addison's imaginative description in the *Spectator*, No. 233, 27 November, 1711. Athenæus quotes from a poem by Stesichorus concerning a maiden named Calyca, who was in love with a youth called Euathius, and when he would not consent to marry her she threw herself from a precipice, and this is supposed to have happened near Leucas. Mrs. Browning has written :

And Sappho, with that gloriole
Of ebon hair on calmed brows—
O poet-woman, none foregoes
The leap, attaining the repose !

It is worth noting in this connexion that the part of the cliff of Santa Maura or Leukadi, known to this day as " Sappho's Leap," was used, even in historical times, as a place whence criminals condemned to death were thrown into the sea.

p. 305. CUPID DESCENDS. One may compare that fine tragedy of Beaumont and Fletcher's *Cupid's Revenge*, written about 1611, 4to, 1615, which was one of the plays after the Restoration especially allotted to Davenant, and revived on Monday, 17 August, 1668, under the name of *Love Despised*. In

Aft I we have the ftage direftion "Cornets. *Cupid* descends," and the same is repeated during the course of the drama.

p. 306.   CORINTHIAN.   The lighteft and moft ornate of the three Grecian orders, having a bell-shaped capital adorned with rows of acanthus leaves, giving rise to graceful volutes and helices.

p. 306.   VULCAN.   In Act V of Sir Robert Stapylton's *The Slighted Maid*, produced at Lincoln's Inn Fields in February, 1662–3, we have : " The Scene : Vulcan's court, over it is writ, 'Foro del Volcano.' Soft music." There is an excellent song by the Cyclops, who are rated by Vulcan for idleness.

p. 307.   ULYSSES.   Who blinded Polyphemus when that Cyclops was drunk with the ftrong tipple the crafty Greek had brewed for him.

p. 307.   HARPES.   According to Hesiod, *Theogony*, there were three Cyclops : Brontes, Steropes, and Arges.   In later authors, Strabo, Callimachus, Apollonius Rhodius, and Vergil (*Aeneid*, VIII, 416), there were many more Cyclops, and we have the names of Pyracmon and Acamas.   Shadwell's Harpes seems to be founded upon an erroneous reading in Callimachus, *Hymn to Artemis*, where Hermes is mentioned as coming from the forge of the Cyclops, all smutted with black ashes.   But this cannot be the heavenly Mercury.   So one reading is Harpes.   Spanheim retains Hermes, but says that this is the son of Cyllenius, who is mentioned by Servius in his note at Vergil, *Aeneid*, IV, 577.   Ruhnken rejefts Hermes and has a clever emendation.

p. 310.   THEN TAKE IT.   There is a very beautiful pifture by the great French painter Jacques Louis David, 1748–1825, representing the kiss given by Cupid to Psyche.

p. 312.   THE PRINCIPAL STREET.   The persons looking out of the windows were perhaps aftually painted upon the scene, as seems to have been the case in the revival of *Henry VIII* at the Duke's Theatre in December, 1663.

p. 318.   TEN STATUES.   So in *Prunella*, by Laurence Houseman and Granville Barker, the ftatue of Cupid in the garden comes to life.

p. 323.   MARISH.   A not uncommon form of " Marsh."

p. 324.   THE GOD OF THE RIVER.   In Fletcher's *The Faithful Shepherdess*, 4to, *circa* 1609–10, when Amoret is flung into the river the god of the river rises from his ftream with the maiden in his arms.   *The Faithful Shepherdess* was revived 24 and 25 June, 1923, under the direftion of Sir Thomas Beecham, for the Phœnix.   " The God of the River " was sung by Frederick Ranalow.   The speech of Fletcher's river-god was used as a model by William Browne for the episode in his *Britannia's Paftorals*, II, i, ii, where Marina, having thrown herself into the river, is rescued by the god of the ftream.

p. 327.   THE SCENE REPRESENTS HELL.   A "dismal Hell " was shown, IV, 1, in *The Descent of Orpheus into Hell*, " Presented by the French Comedians at the Cock-Pit in Drury Lane " in 1661.   Aft II of Dryden's opera *Albion and Albanius*, produced at Dorset Garden, 6 June, 1685, begins : " *The Scene is a Poetical Hell.   The Change is Total.   The Upper Part of the House, as well as the Side-Scenes.   There is the Figure of Prometheus chain'd to a Rock, the Vulture gnawing his Liver.   Sisiphus rowling the Stone ; the Belides, &c. Beyond, Abundance of Figures in various Torments.   Then a great Arch of Fire. Behind this, three Pyramids of Flames in perpetual Agitation.   Beyond this, glowing Fire, which terminates the Profpeft.   Pluto, the Furies ; with* Alefto." Hell also appears in Powell's opera *Brutus of Alba ; or, Augusta's Triumph*, I, 1 and 2, produced at Dorset Garden in 1696.

p. 327. PLUTO. In Settle's *The Empress of Morocco*, Dorset Garden, November, 1673, Act IV, there is presented a mask : " the Scene open'd ; is presented a Hell, in which Pluto ; Proserpine, and other Women-Spirits appear seated, attended by Furies."

p. 328. ETERNAL FROST. Cf. Dante, *Inferno*, XXXII, the frozen depths of hell.

> E sotto i piedi un lago che per gelo
> Avea di vetro e non d'acqua sembiante
> Non fece al corso suo si grosso velo
> Di verno la Danoia in Ostericch,
> Nì Tanai là sotto il freddo cielo
> Com'era quivi.

p. 329. BELIDES. The granddaughters of Belus, father of Danaus, and therefore the Danaides. Upon their marriage night the fifty sons of Aegyptus were murdered by the fifty daughters of Danaus. There was one exception, the life of Lynceus was spared by his wife Hypermnestra. According to the poets the Danaides were punished in Hades by being compelled everlastingly to pour water into a sieve, " inane lymphae dolium fundo pereuntis imo," Horace, *Odes*, III, xi, 26. Ovid, *Metamorphoses*, IV, 463 :

> Assiduae repetunt, quas perdant, Belides undas.

p. 335. JUPITER. Cf. Dryden's *Amphitryon*, produced at Drury Lane early in October, 1690, Act V, where amid peals of thunder " Jupiter appears in a Machine."

p. 336. HEAV'N. In Dryden's *Tyrannick Love ; or, The Royal Martyr*, produced at the Theatre Royal about June, 1669, IV, the magician transports S. Catherine in her sleep to his " Indian Cave." " A Scene of a Paradise is discovered," and a dance of Spirits follows. For a discussion of the scenery and stage-effects in *Psyche* see the Introduction.

p. 336. CLOUDS. Clouds were greatly used for effect in Restoration operas. In his preface to *The World in the Moon*, produced at Dorset Garden in the spring of 1697 ; 4to, 1697 ; Settle triumphantly boasts that he has " thrown away all our old *French* Lumber, our Clouds of Clouts, and set Theatrical Paintings at a much fairer light." In Steele's famous inventory of the " Moveables of *Ch . . . r R . . . ch* Esq, " *Tatler*, XLII, we find : " A Dozen and a half of Clouds, trimm'd with Black, and well conditioned ; . . . A Set of Clouds after the *French* Mode, streaked with Lightning, and furbelow'd."

p. 336. APOLLO. In *Albion and Albanius*, II : " *The further Part of the Heaven opens, and discovers a Machine ; as it moves forwards, the Clouds which are before it divide, and shew the Person of* Apollo, *holding the Reins in his Hand. As they fall lower, the Horses appear with the Rays, and a great Glory about* Apollo."

p. 337. AEGIPANES. Goat-Pans, *i.e.*, goat-shaped Pans, well-known sylvan deities with goats' feet and a rough body ; Panisci, or attendants on the great god Pan. See C. Julius Hyginus, *Astronomia*, II, 28.

p. 338. RETURNELLO. Alessandro Scarlatti, 1659–1725, was the first to introduce into an opera score the ritornello—the instrumental introduction, interlude, or postlude to a composition for the voice.

p. 338. THE DELIGHTS OF THE BOTTLE. The words of this bacchanal are printed in Playford's *Choice Ayres*, 1681 ; and also in *The Antidote to Melancholy*, 1682. In the *Roxburghe Ballads*, II, 106, they are given as *The Delights of the Bottle*, " a most admirable new tune, everywhere much in Request." Since the original song was too short for a ballad, some laymonger has added ten stanzas.

MRS·
BETTER-
TON·
as
MRS·
JILT·

in

THO·
SHADWELL'S

"EPSOM·
·WELLS"

PAUL
RODA.

MR.
BETTERTON
as
DON.
JOHN

in

THO.
SHAD-
WELL'S

"THE
LIBER-
TINE."

PAUL
ROTHA

My L^d

I wrott a complaint to y^r L^p against y^e players
& governes and again I renew it and humbly
beg if y^u ever had any favour for mee y^u right
mee in it by commanding that y^e Innocent
Imposters bee the next new play to bee
acted. I would have had it acted in Roman
habits and then wth a Mantle to have coverd
her hips, Mrs Barry would have acted y^e
part but Tho Davenant has wth a great slight
turnd mee of and sayes hee will trouble
himself noe more about ye play. I beseech
y^u any L^d bee pleasd to favour the Author
and once. they have putt Surreys play
before ours. and this day a play of Drydens
is read to them and that is to bee acted before
ours too. I never was soe much conceernd in
any thing in my life, or soe much surprizd
at ill usage where I deserve none but good
y^r L^p pardon mee that I putt y^r L^p in mind
of this once more for this is ye onely time
to right.

Chelsea Jan 19   My L^d
        91
                        y^r L^{ps} most obligd
                        humble serv^t
                        Tho: Shadwell

Mr Cooling knows this to
have been practisd by y^r L^{ps} predeccssours and I
have twice his hand against mee in a contest
between Mr Croon and mee twice.